HIMALAYAN PASSAGE

SEVEN MONTHS IN THE HIGH COUNTRY OF TIBET, NEPAL, CHINA, INDIA & PAKISTAN

HIMALAYAN PASSAGE

SEVEN MONTHS IN THE HIGH COUNTRY OF TIBET, NEPAL, CHINA, INDIA, & PAKISTAN

By Jeremy Schmidt
Photographs by Patrick Morrow

The Mountaineers/Seattle

© 1991 by Jeremy Schmidt, photographs by Patrick Morrow

Published by The Mountaineers
1011 S.W. Klickitat Way, Seattle, Washington 98134

Published simultaneously in Canada by Douglas & McIntyre, Ltd., 1615 Venables Street, Vancouver, B.C. V5L 2H1

Published simultaneously in Great Britain by Cordee, 3a DeMontfort Street, Leicester, England, LE1 7HD
Manufactured in the United States of America

Edited by Linda Gunnarson
Maps by Wendy Baylor
Map borders by Jocelyn Slack
All photographs by Patrick Morrow except as noted
Cover design by Elizabeth Watson

Cover photo: View of Mount Kailas from Chiu Monastery; inset: Baiba with Uighurs going to market on the road to Kashgar.

The poem "On the Mountain Question and Answer" by Li Po was taken from *Why I Live on the Mountain: Thirty Chinese Poems from the Great Dynasties: A New Translation* (San Francisco: Golden Mountain Press, 1958), C.H. Kwock and Vincent McHugh, translators.

Library of Congress Cataloging-in-Publication Data to come.

ISBN 0-89886-343-0

Contents

LIST OF MAPS

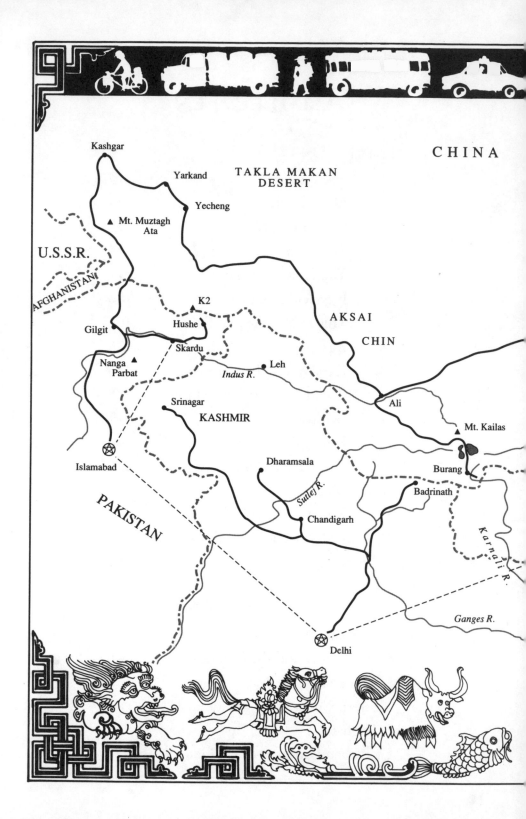

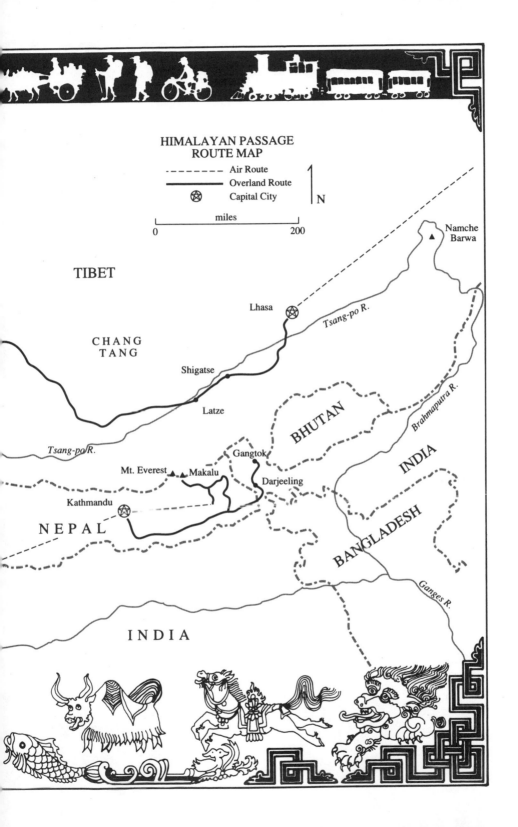

HIMALAYAN PASSAGE
ROUTE MAP

- - - - - Air Route
────── Overland Route
⊛ Capital City

N

miles
0   200

TIBET

CHANG
TANG

Namche
Barwa

Lhasa

Tsang-po R.

Shigatse

Latze

Tsang-po R.

BHUTAN

Brahmaputra R.

INDIA

Gangtok

Mt. Everest Makalu

Darjeeling

Kathmandu

NEPAL

BANGLADESH

Ganges R.

INDIA

To Wendy and Baiba

ON THE MOUNTAIN:
QUESTION AND ANSWER

You ask me
>> *why do I live*
On this green mountain?
> *I smile,*
>> *no answer*
>>> *my heart serene.*

On flowing water
>> *peachblow*
>> *quietly going*
>> *far away.*

>> *another earth*
This is
>> *another sky*
No likeness
>>> *to that human world below.*

>>>> ——*Li Po*, A.D. *701–762*
>>>> *(Translated by C.H. Kwock and*
>>>> *Vincent McHugh)*

Travel seems to me a splendid lesson in disillusion.
>>>>> ——*D. H. Lawrence (letter to a friend)*

Preface

If there are no famous hills, then nothing need be said, but since there are, they must be visited.

——Chang Ch'ao

Travel might not be what you have in mind.

——Travelers' saying

MOUNTAINS HAVE ALWAYS made me restless.
I grew up in the Midwest, but as soon as I was old enough, whenever I could get away from school, I headed out across the plains into the craggiest and wildest places I could find. To me the Rocky Mountains were paradise. Every sight and smell, every stream and ridge and meadow went straight to my heart and filled it.

I live now in Wyoming, in the Teton mountains south of Yellowstone National Park. For seven years the park was my home, and like a newly hatched gosling, I became imprinted to its contours and smells and seasonal motions. Although I've tried living elsewhere, this place—Yellowstone country—is the only place that feels right.

But I can't stay. Not forever. Not continuously. Every so often I get restless, caught up by a gypsy urge, and it doesn't matter which direction I go, as long as I go somewhere. Preferably somewhere wild and mountainous.

So it was natural when my friend Pat Morrow suggested a trip around the Himalaya that I would be eager to join him. We went there with our wives, Wendy and Baiba, for seven months during 1987.

About Baiba and Wendy I should say a little more, in case it seems they came along like good troopers, tolerating their husbands' whim to wander strange places. Far from it. Both women are sturdy, even-tempered, skilled travelers. Had it been their desire to do so, they could have gone without us. Pat and I are both fortunate that they wanted us along.

The idea for this trip arose from a new opportunity. China had recently opened two roads to independent travelers—the only road crossings in the entire length of the Himalaya. The Friendship Highway was opened in 1985, connecting Kathmandu, Nepal, with Lhasa in Tibet. At the other end of the range, the Karakoram Highway stretches between far western China and northern Pakistan. Built largely by the Chinese, and perhaps the world's most spectacular road, it opened to general travel in the summer of 1986. Suddenly, for the first time ever, it was possible for ordinary travelers to make a circle around the bulk of the Himalaya.

This is the story of that not entirely smooth journey—in one sense, an impossible journey, because it was made during the brief time when most of Tibet lay open to independent travelers. Had we waited four months, until after the Lhasa riots of October 1987 and the subsequent Chinese crackdown, we could not have done it.

From the beginning, we knew better than to nail ourselves to an itinerary. Asia has a way of destroying plans and defying schedules. With that in mind, we left everything to chance. We went prepared to take things as they came, traveling by whatever method seemed appropriate at the time, be it mountain bike, foot, truck, bus, taxi, or donkey cart. The mountains themselves would provide continuity. They would define our journey in the same broad sense that rails do for a train or that a river does for a boat. We would be carried along, as it were, by the slope of the world's greatest range.

We did have a rough plan. Starting from Tibet we would travel west along the north slope of the mountains, returning eastward on the south side. From Lhasa back to Lhasa, staying as close to the crest of the mountains as we could manage.

On the north side, we hoped to follow the Tsang-po River—which becomes the Brahmaputra where it flows into India—to Mount Kailas, the holiest mountain on Earth, and from Kailas through the Kun Lun Range to western China, to the world's greatest confluence of high peaks and sensitive borders. There, five countries converge on six tremendous ranges—the Himalaya, Karakoram, Tien Shan, Hindu Kush, Kun Lun, and Pamirs.

From the desert oasis city of Kashgar, we would follow the ancient Silk Road past two huge ice peaks, Muztagh Ata and Kungur, then head across the divide to Pakistan and down through the storied Hunza Valley, a place Eric Shipton called "the ultimate manifestation of mountain grandeur."

South of Hunza, 26,660-foot Nanga Parbat, a stupendous blockhouse of a peak, anchors the western end of the Himalaya. It would mark for us the turning point. From there, we would head eastward, into the granite needles of the Karakoram Range, then on to Ladakh, or Little Tibet, from whose ancient capital, Leh, we could walk through Zanskar to the Himalayan foothills.

Kailas? Zanskar? Ladakh? All these names were magic to my ear.

Then to the Ganges River—Holy Ganga—where we could follow a time-worn Hindu pilgrimage route to its headwaters, among icy giants such as Dunagiri, Kamet, and what many consider to be the most perfectly formed mountain on earth, Nanda Devi. After that would come Nepal, where we planned a long walk before returning to Lhasa via the Friendship Highway, thus completing the circle.

What we had in mind was a journey that any adventurous person willing to put up with the attendant discomforts could have done. By saying this, I don't mean to imply that travel in the Himalaya has become lacking in challenge. It certainly has not. These are still the most rugged mountains on earth, danger-ous mountains armed with serious hazards, everything from avalanches to altitude sickness to meningitis to out-of-control buses on winding roads. Trav-elers die there—even well-equipped, seasoned travelers who set off with no in-tention of doing risky things.

On the other hand, the death of a traveler is rare; the more likely risk involves plans and expectations. In the Himalaya, you can never be sure of getting where you want to be, either in body or spirit. The mountains are full of surprises and politics and changes of plan, but then, that's the essence of travel. If you knew everything about a place before getting there, why would you go?

1
Snowland

But is not everything a fairy tale in this extraordinary country, even to the name it gives itself, that of Khang Yul, "the land of snows"?
——Alexandra David-Neel,
My Journey to Lhasa

A COOL TIBETAN WIND blew across the Tsang-po River. Three hours earlier we had been dripping with sweat in the muggy summer atmosphere of southern China. Now, the fresh mountain air felt good, even as it brought storms of dust through the broken windows of the old bus that carried us from the airport to Lhasa, a distance of sixty miles.

Perched on the edge of the seat ahead of us, a young Chinese man was speaking Mandarin with the bus driver, yelling to be heard over the whining engine and loose windows rattling in their frames. He wore an expensive black suit and held a small travel bag on his lap, up off the dusty metal floor. Every time a gust of wind disturbed his hair, he combed it back in place.

Across the aisle sat a Tibetan family, two teen-age daughters and their parents. They wore Western clothes. The girls, in jeans and sweaters and running shoes, rode with their faces to the window and spoke English. "Look, there's a yak!" one of them shouted. In a field, a man dressed in felt boots, a black bowler hat, and a *chuba* (the traditional black Tibetan robe) walked beside a loaded yak. The Chinese tourist looked up and shouted to the driver. The bus stopped. The tourist jumped out with his camera.

I took advantage of the momentary quiet to ask the Tibetan family where they were from.

The mother smiled broadly. "Canada," she said. "Toronto."

They were the Rabgey family. The mother, Tashi, had grown up in Tingri, near the Nepal border. Tenzing had been a monk at Sera monastery just outside Lhasa. In 1959, when the Chinese army occupied Tibet, both Tenzing and Tashi had joined the flood of refugees who followed the Dalai Lama into exile in India. Eventually, the two of them made their way to Canada, where they met each other and married. Now, under the new, less stringent Chinese policy, they were coming back for the first time in twenty-eight years. Their daughters, Tashi and Lobsang, had never seen Tibet. "Next week," said Tenzing, "we are visiting my family home near Batang," in eastern Tibet.

"You can get permission for that?"

"To visit family, yes."

"Are you seeing family in Lhasa?"

"No. But we have names of people to see." That was to be expected. Several thousand Tibetan refugees live in or near Toronto, and the Rabgeys had numerous contacts.

The Chinese tourist climbed back onto the bus and sat in front of me. "This is great," he said. "I've never seen a yak before. Have you?"

I took a closer look. "You're American?"

"Yeah. Portland, Oregon. My parents left Taiwan after World War II. I grew up speaking Chinese."

We introduced ourselves. His name was David Lee. "Do you come to China often?" I asked.

"First trip. You too?"

"I was here last year."

"Yeah? You like it? I mean Lhasa?"

"I've wanted to come back ever since."

"Good. I don't know anything about it. I'm here to meet my girlfriend."

David had spent the first ten days of a three-week vacation chasing after his girlfriend. "First she wasn't going to come to China. Then she did, after I left, but we never set up a rendezvous."

He had left messages and sent telegrams wherever he thought she might be. A day earlier, in Urumqi, police pounded on his door in the middle of the night. They took him to their headquarters to answer a phone call. He thought it was trouble, but it was his girlfriend. She had shouted down the hissing wire, "I'm in Lhasa!" He had put on his suit, combed his hair, and caught the first available flight to Tibet.

"Pretty dusty," he said, pulling from his bag a little cylinder mounted, like a wheel, on a stick. It had a sticky surface. He rolled the cylinder over his clothing to remove dust.

"That's your prayer wheel?" I asked.

He grinned. "Yeah!" Unlike the ones carried by Tibetan worshipers, his wheel had no prayers written on it; but his journey had become a pilgrimage, and he clearly hoped to gain merit through its use.

As the bus came around the end of a mountain ridge, the Potala Palace, former home of the Dalai Lama, was suddenly visible, its legendary golden roofs gleaming above Lhasa. The Rabgey daughters announced it excitedly and then fell silent. A few miles later, Tenzing pointed to a great pile of buildings perched in a side valley at the base of high mountains.

"Drepung," he said, naming what was once the largest monastery in Tibet, the home of some seven thousand monks, and one of three important Gelug sect monasteries near Lhasa. The others were Tenzing's former home, Sera, a few miles east, and Ganden, thirty miles from the city.

When the Chinese army first invaded Tibet in 1950, not much changed in Drepung and the other monasteries. The Dalai Lama, having fled to India, was coaxed back to Lhasa by Chinese promises of noninterference, and for a time life went on more or less as it had before. Yet gradually the Chinese exerted increasing control. In 1956, the Khampa people of eastern Tibet began a rebellion that climaxed in March 1959 with a massive demonstration around the Dalai Lama's summer residence. The Chinese army responded with force. The Dalai Lama, along with thousands of his followers, fled once again and this time stayed gone. In succeeding years, China set about to destroy Tibetan society and reform it in the image of Mao—a bloody, violent process. Monasteries were emptied and the monks imprisoned, executed, or assigned to labor camps. Religious expression was outlawed. Tibetans were forced into communes. Much of the food they raised was confiscated and sent to China. People starved and were punished for complaining. Perhaps a million people died between 1959 and 1976. The worst came with the Cultural Revolution, a time of mob violence throughout China. In Tibet, it resulted in the physical destruction of almost every monastery and temple, of almost every vestige of Tibet's ancient culture.

Of the three important Gelug monasteries, Ganden was leveled and only Sera's central buildings survived. Drepung, for unexplained reasons, suffered little damage. Although looted, defaced, and largely emptied, its buildings still stood beneath the looming mountains.

"You were at Drepung before 1959?" I asked Tenzing, but I don't think he heard me. He was staring fixedly at the great empty monastery, and I could only imagine his thoughts.

We rode through the outskirts of Lhasa, through the new Chinese part of the city. When Tenzing had last seen the city, it had a population of twenty-five thousand, clustered mostly around the Jokhang Temple, an ancient structure and the holiest temple in Tibet. Now, with eighty thousand, Lhasa was still a small city, divided between two cultures occupying different districts.

The Chinese district formed the periphery, with buildings sprawling outward from the city center, surrounding and enveloping the old Tibetan quarters. Lined up along straight, wide streets, the new buildings were stacked cubicles of whitewashed, dirt-spattered concrete.

In the old quarter, as they had for centuries, Tibetan buildings crowded narrow winding alleys around the Jokhang Temple. Built of stone, tapered toward their flat, walled roofs, and decked with bundles of prayer flags and pleated banners that rippled in the wind, they had an air of solidity and aliveness, like a natural feature of the landscape. Organic architecture, human geology: these buildings had grown out of the rocky Tibetan plateau the way mushrooms grow from the forest floor.

Our bus came to rattling halt in a walled compound at the base of the Potala, followed a few minutes later by the luggage truck. We claimed our bags, but our bicycles were not with them. This was an ominous sign. We had brought mountain bikes, light, fat-tired, and rugged, expecting to use them in western Tibet. However, since arriving in China we had learned that the ownership of bicycles by foreigners was illegal. Apparently we had gotten ours across the border only through the inconsistency of customs officials, but we worried continually that they would be spotted and impounded, which had happened to other travelers. For that reason, we had carried them around China wrapped in bright, checkered tablecloths with their wheels and handlebars off—disguised, we joked, as picnic tables. But clearly, to anyone interested—and the Chinese, among the world's most devoted bicyclists, were always interested—these were not only bikes but very specialized ones. Now what? Had an airport official recognized them and confiscated them without our knowing it?

"*Mingtian,*" said the luggage clerk. Tomorrow. "*Mingtian, mingtian,*" he repeated and shooed us out of the office.

Having claimed his luggage and straightened his black suit, David was headed through the compound gate. "Where are you staying?" I asked him.

"She's at the Lhasa Hotel," he said, meaning his girlfriend. "I hope. I really hope."

I wished him luck in his pursuit of love and turned toward the Rabgeys, thinking how different were the expectations of all us travelers. I wanted to tell the Rabgeys that we would look for them later, but they were at the center of a tight knot of Tibetans. Their arrival had created a small sensation. Word had spread fast. A crowd had gathered. People were in tears, and I felt that even saying good-bye at that moment would be an intrusion.

Different travelers, different expectations. For Pat and Baiba, this trip represented a change of pace in their lives. Over the past five years they had run a rat race—a highly unusual one, but stressful nonetheless. In 1982, Pat had climbed Mount Everest with the first successful Canadian expedition. He remembered that climb with pride although, with typical modesty, he would never boast about it. If you asked him direct questions, he was likely to tell a joke on himself or to change the subject entirely. When changing the subject, he would often talk about Nepal, saying that the best part of climbing Everest had been seeing the country in which it was located. He had enjoyed the Nepali people, the ancient trails, and the rich landscape. He had liked being in the foothills, where you could get far enough back from the highest mountains to see them towering white and noble above the green ridges.

Pat's only regret was that on the trail to Everest—a three-week walk—it had rained much of the time and the mountains had frequently been obscured. On the way out, having spent some two months in the sterile zone of rock and ice, he was exhausted, his brain numb. It had taken more than a month for him to start feeling some euphoria at having succeeded on the mountain. That was followed by a desire to see more of the inhabited parts of Nepal.

Instead, he and Baiba had set out to fulfill a major ambition: the difficult task of getting him to the top of the highest peak on each of the seven continents. Before Everest, he had climbed Denali in Alaska and Aconcagua in Argentina, leaving him four others yet to climb. Two of them—the Carstenz Pyramid in Irian Jaya (New Guinea) and the Vinson Massif in Antarctica— were among the most remote, unapproachable peaks anywhere. Beyond the mountains' natural defenses, Pat and Baiba had to surmount intimidating diplomatic and logistical obstacles. It took a lot of money and a lot of talking. They had spent far more time chained to an office raising funds and drumming up support than being out in the mountains. Once the climbing was over, they still had work to do: debts to pay, lectures to give, and a book to write—*Beyond Everest: Quest for the Seven Summits*.

Finally, in early 1987, claiming that their nerves were fried, they were eager for an extended, rambling mountain journey. They saw this trip as a reward for their hard office work. They anticipated an emotionally restful time, wandering amidst the finest mountains anywhere, far removed from telephones and hassles, following no schedule, sleeping late when they wanted to, and in general quietly absorbing the balm of wild open places.

As an example of the perfect mountain excursion, Pat would describe his 1981 expedition to a peak called Muztagh Ata in China's far western Xinjiang province. He had gone there on a training climb in preparation for Everest. Hard against the Chinese border with Soviet Turkestan, Pakistan, and Afghanistan, the mountain was about as remote a place as a Westerner could go

17

in the world, a far corner in a wildly exotic setting. Pat and his three climbing partners were only the second expedition admitted to the area in forty years. Being there gave him a great sense of privilege, not only for the chance to climb the mountain but also for contacts with the Kirghiz people who lived on the pamirs, the grassy valleys at its base. The Muztagh Ata expedition had provided a pleasing balance of vertical and horizontal travel, of physical challenge and adventurous tourism.

During fifteen years of friendship, Pat and I had made various trips together, often collaborating on magazine articles and other projects. I had joined him on two of his Seven Summit climbs (the easiest ones), and together we had spent many happy days in wilderness settings around the world. We had also spent some not-so-happy days, stormbound in tiny tents, banging shoulders on gut-wrenching Third World bus trips, or sweating out long desert slogs in soft sand. In more recent years, Wendy and Baiba had joined us, bringing their own abilities and enthusiasm, and as luck would have it, we had remained fast friends. Wendy and I agreed that of all the people we knew, Pat and Baiba Morrow—flexible, self-motivated, easygoing, skilled travelers—were the only ones with whom we would contemplate spending eight months on the road. We knew that trips like these test marriages, let alone friendships.

As for Wendy, I've never known a person of such stalwart good humor. It has something to do with her being a nurse, I think, stripped of nonsense and blessed with the attitude that life is a gift, not a trial. She could be terribly tired, but I've almost never seen it affect her temper.

Wendy and I had been to the Himalaya several times before. In our view, there was no better place to walk than in the mountains of Nepal, where ancient trails and neat little villages and timeless days stretched to the horizon. Like so many before us, we had fallen in love with that tiny country and needed only a tiny excuse to go back.

But Tibet had grabbed our hearts and would not let go.

We had gone there from Nepal at the end of winter, first to Lhasa across high passes, then eastward down the valley of the Tsang-po River. The whole time, my eyes were like saucers. I couldn't stop staring at the place, at the wild landscape and the weathered faces of people living in black tents in high golden valleys.

On the Tibetan Plateau, at 16,000 feet, the landscape was all dried grass, dark rock, snowy mountains, and enormous distances under a piercing blue sky. It was a land without moderation, where nights were black and days were brilliant; where the sun felt hot but ice stayed hard in the shade; where calm mornings turned into furious afternoons, battered by winds that knocked people flat and drove sand to the tops of mountains. Tibet, I thought, had the sharp purity of a razor's edge.

On that first trip, we had covered nearly two thousand miles of unpaved road and trail. We had hitchhiked in the backs of trucks, hopped buses, hired jeeps, and walked, and although we had seen only a thin slice of that enormous region, it was enough to make me think of Tibet's landscape as the most compelling I had ever experienced. On the night we returned to Nepal, I wrote this in my diary:

Yak trains, horsemen, ancient ruins, mountains abrupt and naked; the enormous spaces between them utterly flat. Shadows run for miles, sharp and black across gold grass stubble. A man walking at dawn, black figure surrounded by gold, his black shadow stretched out ahead of him. Where was he going? Nothing out there but flatness and light for fifty miles. Images burned in my mind. Tibet has forever changed the way I see.

That was what we wanted to find on this trip with Pat and Baiba: the Himalaya of high mountains and wind-sharpened romance. And beyond that, we were after something that existed on no map: an inner landscape, a landscape of the heart and mind, that region of peace that exists within all of us, and which, for me, is most easily attained in the company of wild mountains, surrounded by what Eunice Tietjens called "the white windy presence of eternity.". The Himalaya possess power, beauty, and magic. I was eager to see more.

ALTHOUGH THE TRUE HIMALAYA lie well to the south, Lhasa is clearly a Himalayan city, situated 12,000 feet above sea level and surrounded by big brown desert mountains.

We carried our packs into the heart of the old quarter, to the Snowland Hotel. Wendy and I had stayed there the year before, and it felt a bit like coming home. The Snowland had been the first Tibetan-run lodging in Lhasa to open for foreign visitors, and after three years it was still as primitive as ever. Its total lack of plumbing discouraged most tourists. We might have felt the same way, but we had a sort of nostalgic loyalty to the place. The manager, Tenzing, was a congenial friend from our previous visit, and his staff included a cheerful gaggle of young women. When they weren't wrestling and shrieking with their boyfriends, or having water fights in the courtyards, they were singing.

They had sweet voices, as clear as the Tibetan air. I was in love with them all. To Wendy's delight, several of them recognized her and gave her a warm greeting.

The staff's cheerful presence almost compensated for the infamous two-story toilet, a sort of elevator shaft with openings on both floors. It occupied one corner of the hotel but made its fragrant presence felt in every room when the wind was wrong. We managed to get beds generally upwind of it and philosophically thought of the toilet as a means of acclimating to the wilder aspects of Tibet that lay ahead.

While registering, I had a pleasant surprise. On the bulletin board was a handwritten notice: "Wanted—Riders to Kailas. We need six to eight people to share a truck to Kailas." It was signed by Jeff and Naomi, room twelve.

Jeff Alford and Naomi Duguid. Naomi had been a lawyer in Toronto before she met Jeff, in Lhasa, in 1985. Jeff, an American, had spent most of seven years roaming the backroads of Asia, professionally footloose, making his living by trading gemstones or doing odd jobs. When Naomi met him he was leaving on a bicycle trip to Kathmandu over the newly opened Friendship Highway. She was hitchhiking the same route and met up with him again part way along the road. A few nights under the stars somewhere north of Mount Everest and that was the end of Naomi's lawyering. They had gotten married that winter and launched a joint career writing about and photographing Asian places.

The last time I had seen them was in that same hotel, the Snowland, one year before. They had been preparing for a bicycle trip on the Karakoram Highway in far western China. I knew they had made the trip, and I had tried getting in touch with them at their home in Canada before leaving to ask how things had gone. But I had failed in that, and now I knew why. What a surprise it was to find them here!

I ran up rickety stairs, along a courtyard balcony, and banged on their door. Naomi opened it, performed a classic double take, and gave me a hearty hug punctuated by yelps of surprise. Jeff got up from the bed, where he was sitting in a midden of maps, and did the same. Their room looked just like it had a year earlier—gear strewn from one end to the other, bicycles stacked against the wall, tape player turned up loud.

"What, have you been here all year?" I asked.

No, they had been home to Canada twice. They had bicycled from Kashgar over the Kunjerab Pass to Pakistan. They had been in Thailand for a while. And they had gone—without permits—to Mount Kailas. Now they were back with a friend, Antony Southam, a twenty-two-year-old bicycle racer vibrating with energy. "I'm the mechanic. They invited me along to change flat tires."

"Actually, Ant's the strong man," said Naomi. "We brought him to carry the tools for us old folks."

We talked about our respective plans. Naomi was surprised that we had gotten our bicycles through customs without trouble. Their bikes had been impounded for two days in Chengdu. "They wouldn't let us have them," she said, "until we proved we were flying to Lhasa. Out of their jurisdiction, you know, not their problem. Lee came up—do you remember Lee from New York?"

"Vaguely. He was here last year?"

"That's right. He came up from Nepal on a bus two weeks ago. At the border they tied string around his back wheel and sealed it with wax. He cut it off when he got here, and so far no one's bothered him. I hope they didn't impound yours."

So did we. I asked about Mount Kailas. Kailas was the first big step on our itinerary. Rising over one of the world's more remote wild areas, this one mountain represents, for millions of Buddhists and Hindus, the spiritual center of the earth, the geographical focus of their devotion. It exists in splendid, sacred isolation, standing alone in a vast empty region north of the Himalayan main chain. Four of Asia's most important rivers begin in the immediate area—the Brahmaputra (Tsang-po), Sutlej, Indus, and Karnali. Hindus view Kailas as the spiritual, if not physical, source of the Ganges, Mother of India.

Our hope was to go there and join pilgrims on the sacred trail that encircles the mountain, a trail that has been in use for more than a thousand years. Pilgrims walk around Kailas chanting, fingering their prayer beads, visiting sacred sites, and leaving offerings along the way. Some prostrate themselves, measuring the entire distance on their bellies, a process that takes about twenty days. But even that seems a short time compared to the months and sometimes years it takes a pilgrim to walk across Tibet's windswept miles to reach Kailas. Now, of course, there are roads, but some people, as a matter of faith, still choose to walk.

The last we had heard, the only legal way to get there was on an escorted tour organized by the China International Travel Service, known to travelers as CITS. Which is not to say that official policy meant much. For about a year, foreign travelers had been getting there without permission, hitchhiking in the backs of trucks just like the natives. It was the Tibetan transit system: pay your share and away you go, jammed in with a happy mob of yak-robed fellow travelers. You might not get to Kailas for a month or more, but with patience, some luck, and enough food, you could probably do it. The only real worry was being picked up by the authorities and sent back to Lhasa for illegally riding in a truck in a closed area. Then you might have to pay a fine or write a self-criticism, a statement of contrition and admission of fault. The Chinese see this punishment as a serious loss of face. Western travelers view it as a joke.

Jeff and Naomi themselves had gone there the year before, without an official permit, in a hired jeep. It was a hurried, often uncomfortable trip with a driver they didn't like, and they had run into trouble with the police near Kailas. Not serious trouble, but enough to taint their memories of the place.

"This year, we have permits," said Naomi.

"You mean it's open?"

Naomi handed me a little blue folder, an Alien Travel Permit, with lots of Chinese writing and, in block letters, the word "Kangrinpoche"—the Tibetan name for Kailas. "You can get these at the PSB," she said, meaning the Public Security Bureau, or police station.

"Do you have to go with CITS?" I asked.

"That's the catch. We've been talking to some truckers from Ali. They'd like to take us, if they can get a permit. Apparently the government has clamped down on trucks. They can't carry foreigners without a permit or they get fined. These guys won't do it without a permit. But if they can, the price is good—four thousand yuan."

"How much does CITS want?"

"How much does CITS want?" The three of them were giggling. Antony put a pillow over his head in mock despair.

"For one truck and one Beijing jeep and four passengers—ninety thousand yuan!" I did a quick calculation. "That's twenty-five thousand dollars."

"See why we're laughing?"

———

Later in the day, having moved into our rooms, I was on my way downstairs past the infamous toilet when a middle-aged European with grizzled beard accosted me. He was clearly upset. He said, "I dropped by dife dowdere!"

"What did you say?" I asked. Many foreign languages were spoken at the Snowland, but I didn't recognize this one.

"By dife, by dife, it wed dowduh ho!"

I still didn't get it. He motioned me into the toilet. It was a tiny, plastered room with nothing but a slit in the floor. "Look! See!" he said, pointing down the grim opening.

I had seen it other times. I thought I'd seen it enough. But he insisted. "Cub, cub, der it is, you cad see it!"

Reluctantly, I looked. Two stories down, an access doorway used for clean-out purposes illuminated the bottom of the shaft. I could see the man's bright red Swiss army knife. "Outtub by pocket, dowduh ho," he said.

"I'd say dat's de ehd of it." Now I was talking like him.

"Ahh," he said. "But I deed by dife. I cad't get adudder wud id Tibet."

"Let's get out," I said. We moved to the balcony overlooking the hotel's inner courtyard. The hotel girls were doing laundry—and singing—around the hand pump that served as the Snowland's water supply. One of the cooks hacked with an axe at a pile of firewood brought up from the eastern mountains. We began breathing through our noses again.

"I am from Switzerland," said my unhappy companion. His name was Karl. "I come overland through Turkey, Iran, Pakistan, Kashgar. In all that time I never drop my knife. Now, in there—what a place."

"I think you could get to it from the alley," I said. "If you wanted it badly enough."

"No," he said. "I will pay you to get it. How much?"

I grinned. I knew he was kidding. He looked hurt. Maybe he wasn't kidding. He told me he wanted to buy a horse and ride off across Tibet. He looked capable of doing that, and more, but he could not face an expedition to recover his knife. I asked, "How did you come from Pakistan?"

"By bus. The Karakoram Highway. That's some trip, I tell you."

"Was it good? We're going that way ourselves."

"Yes, yes. It's beautiful. But be careful. The Pakis. They arc crazy. They are mad for sex." He described a brawl on the bus. A drunk Pakistani man had made lewd comments to an English woman. Her friends had told the drunk to shut up, and he had started swinging his fists. At that point, Karl stood up and punched the Pakistani in the face, which excited the drunk's friends. "They all jumped on me and started grabbing me, and yelling, yelling! And the bus driver, he just went faster."

"What happened?"

"Ah. They stop. The drunk, he sits down and is quiet like a mouse. I tell you, I was mad. I never before have hit anyone. Never."

Lhasa was filled with people, like him, going places. People with ambitious plans. People eager to talk. Bulletin boards at the budget hotels held numerous requests for traveling partners and people to share the costs of hired vehicles.

Before long, we were caught up in the social whirl of Lhasa's community of travelers—collecting news, hearing tales, swapping rumors. Lhasa may have been isolated from world events—you couldn't buy a newspaper there—but it was a crossroads for very specialized and accurate information that was available virtually nowhere else on the planet: how to go places in Tibet, what it cost, where to stay, which officials were impossible to deal with, which ones were more likely to give out special permits, where to buy food in remote areas, what supplies were available, and so on.

These conversations usually happened over meals in local restaurants. In the part of town near the four budget hotels (they charged about three dollars per night) a covey of little eateries had sprung up. Most were run by Chinese immigrants, several of them independent proprietors. They had adapted quickly to the desires of foreigners: beer, chips, vegetables, rock music on the cassette player, good food cooked fast at all hours. Whatever else the Chinese had done with Tibet, they had at least brought good food.

Travel stories: Two German boys wanted to walk to Nepal from Lhasa and to cross illegally somewhere north of Kathmandu. They had tried it earlier with a yak, but the yak ran off after a few days and they were back in Lhasa to regroup.

A Canadian, bicycling in northeastern Tibet, had been chased by a dog, lost control of his bike, and had broken his thumb. The dog had run away, frightened by the crash, but two months later the thumb had still not healed properly. An American, bitten on the arm by a dog, was taking rabies shots at the Lhasa hospital. Doctors there had tried to dissuade him, saying that there was no rabies in Tibet, but word had it that all Tibetans got annual rabies vaccinations. A British woman who had cycled alone from Chengdu, the capital of Sichuan province, was also getting shots. Dressed in Chinese clothing, she had ridden through populated areas at night; then a dog jumped her from behind. She was staying in Lhasa for a month of treatment.

Yet another British woman, also traveling alone, had taken a four-day walk over the mountains south of Lhasa. It was a wild place to be, and after encountering a few swaggering male nomads, she got to feeling nervous about being alone. So when the old white-haired pilgrim came by, she was happy to see him.

They walked together. He spun his prayer wheel, chanted "*Om mani padme hum,*" and smiled a lot. She felt safe with him. "He was very picturesque," she said.

They camped together by the trail. He wrapped himself in a homespun blanket. She pulled the drawstring on her sleeping bag tight until only her face showed. Sometime in the night, she turned in the bag so that her ear was at the opening, and it was her ear that the old man chose as a target. "I woke up with him poking his john thomas in my ear! Can you imagine? A holy man!"

"What did you do?" I asked.

"Well, I shouted. I sat up. And he had the gall to ask me to. . . to do something with it. I'm not sure what he had in mind. I said, 'Not on your Nelly! Put that thing away!'"

"Did you stay with him?"

"Oh, yes. Once that was established, it was all smiles again."

2
Lhasa Nights

Wherever I live, I shall feel homesick for Tibet. I often think I can still hear the wild cries of geese and cranes and the beating of their wings as they fly over Lhasa in the clear cold moonlight.

——Heinrich Harrer, *Seven Years in Tibet*

F OR MORE THAN A WEEK, Naomi, Jeff, and Antony had been trying to find a truck to hire. They had found a pair of drivers willing to take them at least as far as Ali, a town on the Indus River west of Mount Kailas. But the permit was a problem. Without a permit, the drivers risked a fine worth several months' salary. Matters dragged on for a week with no permit, until the truckers reluctantly gave it up.

Since we wanted to go in the same direction, we joined forces and went looking, chasing every lead. First we tried to hire a tourist bus at a place called the Taxi Company. A bus wouldn't take us all the way, but it would get us officially past the Latze checkpoint—a difficult one, we'd heard. Beyond there, our bicycles might not be challenged. It was still a long way from Latze to Kailas, but we might be able to hitchhike part of it—and after all, this was the reason we had brought bikes, wasn't it? (Our cycles *had* shown up, after an unexplained two-day delay.)

The people at the Taxi Company were agreeable to the plan and even went so far as to negotiate a price before announcing that their bus was broken and all their jeeps were engaged, which made us wonder what the real reason was. Then someone told us that a new hotel being built west of the city had vehicles for hire. We went to ask, but no one there would admit to it. Other rumors told of pilgrimage buses to Kailas that left from a compound behind the Jokhang Temple. After much searching we found the compound, where an offi-

25

cious Chinese woman brushed us off, so we never learned whether they had buses or not.

The outlook was uncertain, but I didn't mind. We all needed time to acclimatize. It would have been foolish to set out too quickly across a remote region where the elevation averaged 17,000 feet. We would be crossing passes that were higher than 18,000 feet, and we all knew that even a week at Lhasa's 12,000-foot elevation was not enough time. Besides, I was enjoying the city.

Despite its lack of plumbing, the Snowland Hotel occupies the best location in Lhasa—right around the corner from the Jokhang Temple and the Barkhor, the circular street that runs around it. For some twelve hundred years, this place has been the heart of Tibetan Lhasa and the main goal for generations of pilgrims. Stand for an hour in the Barkhor and you will see people from every corner of Tibet. They come to make offerings, say their prayers, and walk around the Barkhor in devotional exercise, around and around, always clockwise. Some pilgrims have stayed for months, living on alms, sleeping wherever they can find shelter. Some have walked across Tibet to get there, a journey that takes a year or more. Others have prostrated themselves across the country—that can take a lifetime.

The Barkhor serves also as a market center for pilgrims, residents of Lhasa, and tourists. Here, and in the many side streets, we did all our shopping for supplies, buying everything from Chinese noodles to canned peaches and dried apples. This was the best place to watch the colorful bazaar that was Lhasa—pilgrims, merchants, traders, tourists, and scruffy, street-smart dogs. Armies of dogs. So many dogs that I remember them not as individuals but collectively, as a sort of natural phenomenon like the Tibetan wind.

During the day, lying groggy in the sun, they seemed like nice enough animals. But at night! You would think there was nothing out there except murderous dogs, dogs in agony, dogs dying. They ran in marauding packs down narrow streets between stone houses. Their wild cries, distorted by echoes, rose above the flat roofs. To sleep, I wore ear plugs.

In the morning there would be evidence of canine warfare—dead dogs and cats, or what was left of them. In front of the Jokhang Temple one morning, beside a brick incense burner, I saw a snarling, black cur standing guard over an animal spine stripped of flesh. All around the dog, Tibetan pilgrims performed devotions. They gave the animal wide berth but scant attention. In a nearby alley, a black cat, its body torn but not eaten, lay dead against a stone wall as if thrown there.

Antony Southam, Jeff and Naomi's friend, was wakened one night by a racket just outside his window. Sitting up in bed, he looked out to see two cats scuffling on top of a stone wall. A pack of dogs, attracted by the sound, gathered below, howling their approval until one cat lost its footing and fell. The dogs finished it off.

Antony had an eye for the doings of street animals. After a day of gomping (his term for visiting the *gompas*, or Buddhist temples of Lhasa), he reported having seen a mortally wounded dog—"Its guts were dragging!"—still alive, still somehow moving along the filthy street. Late one evening I saw one with its back broken—an old injury from which it refused to die. It was hauling its crumpled hind legs along the pavement, headed toward a gang of other dogs, barking furiously. A white-haired German couple stood watching. "Why don't they kill it?" the woman said to me.

It's been tried. A few years ago the Chinese authorities, viewing street dogs as a nuisance, sent patrols out at night armed with shotguns. You could hear the guns shooting the dogs. This was stopped, perhaps in deference to tourist feelings (wounded survivors sometimes showed up in the daytime). But I heard a different reason: that Tibetans had objected to such an un-Buddhist treatment of fellow creatures, and the Chinese had listened.

Tibetans love their dogs—all their dogs. In the countryside, dogs are essential allies: sentinels, shepherds, protectors, and friends. In Lhasa, many are kept as pets and cared for lovingly. Others are homeless, the wild mongrels of the city. If they can make a living, however hard it may be, Tibetans apparently reckon they are welcome to try.

I wondered if the tolerance Tibetans showed to other animals had anything to do with the difficulty of their own lives. Even in the best of times, Tibet would be a demanding place to live. These years of foreign occupation were not the best of times; yet Tibetans managed to laugh, easily and heartily. They were enormously attractive people. After a few days among them, I found my feelings changing toward the Chinese who lived in Lhasa. I didn't much like them, a sentiment complicated by the fondness I had felt for the Chinese people we had met outside Tibet.

Before getting to Lhasa, we had spent several weeks in southern China, doing magazine work to help pay for our trip. There, amid ugly industrial cities reeking of coal smoke, the people, in my eyes, blossomed like bright flowers. Not speaking their language, and having to hassle with our disguised bikes, we had had some difficult times. Too often, China seemed rife with apparently capricious and obstructive regulations. More than once I had found myself seething and speechless, or just unhappy over some trivial event. Yet almost always, before things got really impossible, some voluntary stranger would kindly intervene and redeem the situation.

Sometimes it could seem the deliberate result of a hotel clerk's bad attitude, or a waiter's dislike of foreigners. "Yes, there are rooms; no, you cannot have a registration form" when other people are busily signing in and taking their keys. "No, you can't eat here" when the restaurant was filled with diners devouring mounds of food. But once explained, there was usually a reason. The reason might not make sense. It might be caused by clumsy, arbitrary bureaucratic regulations, but the clerk or the waiter would be frustrated by it too, and even embarrassed by it. These things happened daily, but time after time, some stranger would approach and, through an act of unsolicited kindness, make things right. Or right enough.

By and large, I thought it was the Chinese people who made China worth visiting. They had treated us well, and I had liked them very much.

In Tibet, the Chinese were different.

Lhasa, I should interject, is a bright, pleasant place decorated with colored flags and banners and painted windows and flowers, where traffic is light and the air is always clear—except during summer dust storms, which are a different matter altogether. Few cities in the world shine as brightly and pleasantly as Lhasa, particularly at dawn, when gentle summits catch the first light and, glowing, bathe the valley in reflected warmth.

But instead of being happy there, many of the Chinese people I met were dull—unhelpful, unfriendly, dour. Whether civilians or military, they acted like the occupiers and exiles that they were.

For example, Chinese girls sported light straw hats and frilly dresses just as they had in the warm cities of southern China, where I had been charmed by their delicate beauty. Here the girls wore the same dainties over blue Mao suits and (besides looking ridiculous) appeared unaware of what strange symbols they made—military conformity beneath a decorative veneer. Meanwhile, uniformed army soldiers strutted the wrong way around the Barkhor, pushing disdainfully against the flow of worshipers in what could only be seen as an intentionally aggressive act. One day, during a border crisis with India, Chinese fighter jets made several low passes over the city. They flew well out of their way to make that gesture, and their meaning was clear: We are in charge.

In charge but not happy. Chinese residents occasionally expressed to me their frustration. Government policies, not personal choice, had sent them to this high, foreign land, far from their homes and families, to live among people they viewed as primitive, people who resented their presence and wished them gone.

Tibetans, of course, loved Lhasa, and it showed. In my eyes, they were among the handsomest of people—bronze skin, ruddy cheeks, strong features, bright eyes, jet black hair, and a proud demeanor.

The women could be downright stunning, with turquoise and coral in their braided hair, felt bowlers, and dazzling smiles. The best tricked out were young peddlers wearing their merchandise—turquoise, coral, and silver jewelry, the colors of which, against copper skin, were irresistible. I thought so, and they knew it. We played a delicious little game. If I showed interest, several of these decorated ladies would press around me, creating a small island of intimacy and a spell I was loath to break. Several times, if I said no to every proffered stone and locket and snuff bottle and reliquary, one of these sweet peddlers would beckon me into an alley, through a gate, and into a house. She would sit close beside me on a carpeted window seat—a bed, really—in a low-ceilinged room fragrant with incense, and there, with a dazzling smile and mysterious eyes, pull more jewels from her bodice.

Irresistible, to be sure, but not so haunting as the wild ones, the ones from the country. They wore leather, silver, turquoise, and coral, often with long hair done in many tiny braids hanging far down their backs, each braid ending in a silver bead. In hot weather they went naked beneath their oily sheepskins. I knew this because in the heat of midday they would slip out of the sleeves and drop the top half of their *chubas*. And because they would pee standing up, having made no adjustment except to plant their feet as wide as a *chuba* would allow. These women did no beckoning whatsoever, no flirting at all, and pissing in the street was hardly designed to get my blood going—but they would look, in passing, and their eyes were unforgettable.

In their own way, the men were equally impressive, especially the Khampas, men from the region of Kham in eastern Tibet. They wore a uniform of sorts, a proud identifier that men from other parts of Tibet, not Khampas, had recently adopted. Actually, the uniform sounds a bit comic—a dark, knee-length *chuba* worn over filthy white polyester shirts, Mao pants, and high-heeled plastic shoes sporting fake buttons or patches of bright corduroy. Under the *chuba,* around his waist, each Khampa wore a portable commissary, an elaborate belt of red and black leather, the sort of thing that would appeal to motorcycle gangs or punk rockers. Each belt had a dozen or so pockets with flaps and zippers and snaps and luggage locks and polished chrome studs and little chains. From the pockets came an incredible variety of things—money, jewelry, old coins, cartridge casings, dried meat, sunflower seeds, and more. One time, I asked a Khampa if I could take his picture. He said yes, but first he withdrew from his supply belt a comb and a round dime-store mirror with a pink plastic handle and spent several minutes arranging his long, black hair.

A Khampa's hair, I learned, was important to him. Tibetan men who lived in the city as members of various work units wore Mao suits and close-cropped Chinese-style haircuts. A Khampa, on the other hand, a real Khampa, a man of the open spaces, would never cut his hair. Instead, he would wind it on top of his head, securing it with a long, flamboyant, red tassel, a tassel often matched in color by the woven sash at the waist, which held a long knife in a silver sheath.

29

They might have looked ludicrous, but they didn't—maybe because they were all so much bigger than I, and strong as hell. They reeked strength (among other things) and used their fragrant auras to advantage in market negotiations. One would approach with a conspiratorial manner, remove some trinket from the folds of his *chuba,* followed by another and another, displaying each item in his grimy rock of a hand.

While he did this, his friends would gather around as if on prearranged signal, and then you wanted to watch your backside. They could start pushing against you, closing in, waiting for a reaction. One day I saw a young European handled that way until he erupted in anger and they broke into laughter.

Khampas had a rough edge to them—an intense, challenging masculinity. I was reminded that before the Chinese invasion these were the warriors and bandits of Tibet, proud horsemen of the plains. They were testing, I think, wondering: Who are these smiling, easily charmed foreigners? Are they really so soft and amiable and immune to insult as they appear?

None more so than Lee Day, the rangy New Yorker, the one who'd had his bicycle sealed at the border and who later became our traveling companion. Lee spent a lot of time watching the action in a side street off the Barkhor where Khampas gathered to trade. He called it Khampa Corner. Items being traded were usually small and valuable: turquoise, silver, antiques, FECs (Foreign Exchange Certificates, the alternate money that is supposedly reserved for foreign visitors but that has created a currency black market throughout China), and God's eyes (glass beads with protective powers; very old ones are said to have occurred naturally).

Lee had told me, "There's a lot of money in those belts! I saw a God's eye go for seven thousand yuan." One bead, almost two thousand dollars!

Lee was as tall as any of the Khampas and often joined in the joking and pushing. He liked the jostle. He used his elbows freely. Then one day he got more than he expected out of a handshake. A Khampa extended his right hand, Lee took it, and the Khampa grabbed Lee's crotch with his left: "Hey, happy rich man from New York, you got balls or not?" We all made mileage on that one, at Lee's expense, but we knew it hadn't been done entirely in fun.

A T NIGHT IN LHASA, the years seemed to roll back with the sun. Except for dogs barking, the streets were quiet, with shops closed and boarded. Upstairs windows glowed dimly. A few zealots prostrated themselves along the stone pavement of the Barkhor. Here and there, sleeping pilgrims lay bundled in doorways.

Main thoroughfares were empty and bright, except when the electricity failed, which happened often. But in the Tibetan district there were few bright lights at any time. Electricity had not been universally installed. It was as if the Chinese government were trying to illustrate its oft-repeated claim that communism had dispelled the darkness of Tibet's feudalism. Mercury arc lamps, symbols of the new order, illuminated only the broad, Chinese-built streets.

But one culture's darkness is another culture's peace, and I suspect that the Tibetans felt comfortable with the light of candles and kerosene. I certainly did. I liked walking the dim streets and back alleys. Night gave me a feeling that ancient rhythms remained intact. As if, like stars, they were always there and you just couldn't see them when the sun shone.

I went often to a small temple I called the night *gompa,* located behind the Jokhang in a maze of narrow passages. On the way, I would pass a tiny chapel, just one room simply decorated. Two old monks lived upstairs. I often heard them up there, chanting behind dusty, candle-lit windows; sometimes no voices, just a slow, steady, deep drumbeat. A few times I went in. They would offer me a cup of salt tea. I would sit cross-legged by the doorway, sip my tea, and listen.

Beyond that little chapel, the alley opened into a sheltered courtyard and the unimposing entrance to Mura Nyingma *gompa.* I thought that was its name, but I could not be certain. The first time I went, I tried to ask a young monk. He was about twenty years old, with a shaven head, wearing purple robes and blue army tennis shoes. I stood looking at statues, completely ignorant of their meaning. He began naming them for me—incomprehensible names that I tried to write down phonetically. But when I looked them up in my guidebook, I found that I was hearing them completely wrong. So I had no confidence that I was getting it right when I asked, *"Gompa ming ray?"*

"Mura Nyingma," he said, with a circular gesture of his hand.

"Mura Nyingma *gompa?*" I said, repeating his gesture and then pointing to the floor.

"Mura Nyingma," he answered, nodding. He took my notebook and wrote the words in Tibetan. A beautiful script. I know how to pronounce what he wrote, but I'm not certain what it means.

We could have been saying the equivalent of "Very Holy *gompa*"? Very Holy. Or "Wonderful *gompa*"? or "I've seen better *gompa*"? My guidebook called it the Nechung Branch Monastery. *Nyingma,* I read, means old. It also refers to one of the four main Buddhist orders. Whether correct or not, I liked the sound of the words, and I will always think fondly of that temple as Mura Nyingma.

One time Wendy and I went later than usual, near midnight. The courtyard was deserted and silent. The only light came from the main hall, shining out across polished stone steps, illuminating two huge prayer wheels mounted like gateposts at the doorway. A woman in sheepskin and black braids stood by one, lazily turning it. The wheel creaked and, with each revolution, rang a small bell.

Walking in, we found the hall empty except for smoky air and a Tibetan boy, about twelve years old, who sat in the center of the room writing in a notebook. He looked up, gestured for us to sit down, and came over to sit with us. He showed me his notebook, bound in red plastic decorated with a sickle and hammer. The first few pages were filled with Tibetan script.

He asked where we came from, the opening line of nearly every conversation in Lhasa and one of the first bits of Tibetan we had learned to speak. *"Meiguo,"* we answered, America, speaking in Chinese because the Tibetan language lacks a word for our country. From there we proceeded to a numbers lesson, with him pointing to the Tibetan script in my guidebook. Counting from one to seven sounded like a child's nursery rhyme: *"Chik, nyi, soom, shi, nga, drook, doon."* He took the book from me and paged through the pictures. Some he recognized—*gompas* and horses, yaks, Khampas. "You have been there?" he asked by gesture.

In this way we made slow conversation. The room was quiet, very peaceful, dimly lit. A few other Tibetans, old men and not monks, moved around attending to small chores. I could easily have lain back on the floor mats and fallen asleep.

Time to go. Wendy, unseen by the boy, slipped a photo of the Dalai Lama into his red notebook. We stood and made a circuit of the room in the prescribed manner, pausing before the statue of Padmasambhava, the patron saint of Tibet. As we went out the door, I glanced back in time to see our young friend find the picture. He had asked repeatedly for one. We had shaken our heads, not willing to attract the attention of the others in the room, until he had finally stopped asking. Now, turning it over in his hand, he made no sign of surprise. *"Kalishu,"* we said. Good-bye. *"Kalipe,"* he waved.

Another evening I found Mura Nyingma packed. A crowd of pilgrims filled the courtyard; they were camped there, mats spread on the paving stones, sitting or sleeping, some cooking over a central wood fire. A vigil was being conducted in the prayer hall by hundreds of people who had come in from the countryside for this event. Pushing up the front steps, I entered the hall. There was hardly room to stand. I breathed warm air, redolent with the smoky smell of country people and the oily odor of butter lamps. Groping forward, I stumbled but, instead of falling, was caught by strong hands that pulled me into a seated crowd and held me there, gripping my shoulders, my jacket, my hand. Faces smiled welcome.

Everyone was chanting the same words, led by several very old monks seated on prayer mats near the front of the hall. The monks beat on large painted drums, blew cacophonous horns, and clanged cymbals. *"Dorje Drak-den,"* said one man, when I looked questioningly. I could make nothing of it, except that the devotion of these people was as tangible and forceful as their knees and shoulders against my back.

Supplication, not celebration. An expression of urgent, joyless need. I saw it other times. Once, at midday, I went into the Jokhang Temple, wending my way through pilgrims prostrating themselves at the entrance, under a big cotton awning, past the huge, barrel-shaped prayer wheels to the inner courtyard and down a dark passage toward the ancient twilight of the inner chambers.

In the passage the air was warm, the floor slippery with butter. Tibetans smelling of campfires stood in line, tightly against each other, waiting to get in or pushing to get out. I was happy to wait with them, in their jam of smoky raw wool, but people, when they saw me, wrestled me forward, shoving me against the traffic coming out, as if to say, "Go on, you don't have to wait!" So in I went, carried on a tide of strong fingers and woolen robes, feeling out of control like a man treading water in a flood. In! In! Hands pushed. Butter lamps spilled against my clothing. My feet slid on the smooth, buttered stones, and finally I surfaced in the main hall. It was like surfacing in a dream. The place was a confusion of deep shadows, flickering lamps, dimly visible statues and the oceanic sound of many voices chanting and praying, punctuated by the crystal ting of tiny bells. I walked slowly through a maze of dim chambers. I had no choice but to go slowly. The place was packed.

Before seeing Tibetan temples, I had thought of Buddhism as a contemplative faith emphasizing meditation and spiritual calm. Yet here, the only things that didn't move were the statues. Three in particular, dominating the main hall, sat like islands of peace in a throbbing sea of religious zeal. A thousand butter lamps flickered. Shadows moved. Heat from the lamps turned umbrella-shaped pinwheels. Pilgrims bowed, prostrated themselves, swayed, worked their strings of prayer beads, spun hand-held prayer wheels, and lifted offerings to altars. Smoke plumes from incense burners curled upward.

Everywhere, people—dark figures with unfocused eyes, people jammed into every corner, every corridor, every stairway and anteroom. There was nothing serene about their worship, and nothing like it to be seen in the Western world. Trembling intensity, fists closed tight, eyes moist with emotion. Painful desire, urgent craving.

An old man and two women confronted me from out of the gloom. One of the women clutched my arm with buttery fingers, gazing at me through dark eyes and a face like deeply worn leather. I smiled at her—the normal nervous reaction of an American abroad—and felt inexplicably inadequate. What could she be looking for in me? She tightened her fingers on my arm with one hand and, with the other, touched her forehead. Then her eyes dropped, and she left me alone. I made my way to a wooden pillar, craving the feel of something solid, and stood there for a long time.

Was this the way Tibetans normally worshiped? Or was it a sign of the times? Any religion is a mix of praise and longing, but this seemed terribly heavy on the latter. I thought of the ghost dance of 1888, performed with such terrible intensity by Native Americans on the Dakota plains—a dance that if performed long enough, they believed, and with true hearts, would banish the white invaders, restore the slaughtered bison herds, and return the indigenous peoples to their old way of life.

Only later did I learn how much was wrong. The riots that have occurred in the past two years in Lhasa—along with such events as Tiananmen Square—have made things more evident to the world in general, but during the summer of 1987, it was easy to not see the unhappiness of Tibetans.

On the contrary, people seemed better off than they had been the year before, during our first visit to Lhasa. Since then, much rebuilding had gone on at monasteries and temples destroyed during the Cultural Revolution. The Tibetan-run hotels were expanding. There was a look of physical prosperity. But more than that, these good-natured people displayed a sort of emotional prosperity that I took to be a hopeful sign and, only later, when I got to know some of them better, came to regard as a national characteristic—an inherent strength that survives and even flowers in the face of adversity.

The capacity for joy, after all, is carved—and countered—by the knives of pain, and once we learned to see it, pain lurked everywhere.

One year earlier, the only anti-Chinese comment I had heard from a Tibetan was deep inside the Potala Palace, where, beside the tomb of the sixth Dalai Lama, an elderly monk described his twenty years in chains. Was he happy to be out? I asked. "To be a guard in this room all day? No, but better than prison." He said these things in whispers, with forceful bitter gestures, all the time watching down the corridor to be sure we were alone.

On that first trip, Wendy and I had been given a parcel from a Tibetan friend in Kathmandu, in hopes that we could deliver it to her Lhasa relatives. Our friend had drawn a rough map and had written the family name on an envelope. By showing the envelope to people in the neighborhood, we had located the apartment block where they lived. It was a big, faceless concrete structure surrounded by a concrete wall. Entering through a gate, we climbed rickety wooden stairs on the outside of the building to the family's two-room quarters. I knocked on the door. A young woman opened it and smiled. Behind her, I could see that the front room was packed with people. It looked like a party in full swing.

Even before I presented the parcel, they had seemed delighted to see us. The woman who opened the door was joined by another, and together they hugged us, pulled us inside, and sat us down on a carpeted bench facing a low table. A huge tray of food was brought. When the family opened the parcel, they knew who had sent us. We were embraced all over again, by the whole group, tearfully this time. There were photos in the parcel, and these caused quite a stir.

An interpreter was called. It took him an hour to get there. During that time we nodded and smiled and showed them pictures of our family and our home in the Rocky Mountains. We also drank a lot of *chang,* beer made from rice or barley. Everyone drank a lot of *chang.* Lobsang, a young woman with bright red cheeks and a maroon sweater, took it upon herself to fill our glasses and be sure we drank. I tried to nurse mine along by sipping, but she would grip my glass and not let me take it down until it was empty, whereupon someone else would instantly refill it.

The interpreter was a Tibetan man in his thirties. When he arrived, he made a speech. These people were all members of one family, he said. Many of them worked in a machine-parts factory. This apartment belonged to their work unit and came with the job. They were pleased to welcome foreign visitors into their home. Until recently, it would have been dangerous for them to have us there. Two years earlier, Tibetans were being watched and questioned by Chinese security men merely for talking to other Tibetans on the street. There had been many improvements recently. Many foreigners coming. The world was learning about Tibet. This was good. And by the way, had we, in our travels, seen the Dalai Lama?

"No," said Wendy, "but we want to go to Dharamsala some day. Maybe we will see him there."

When her answer was translated, everyone got excited.

Before long, we all were laughing and hugging and spilling *chang.* Lobsang kept pushing a full cup on me until I emptied it. If I left the cup on the table, she would clutch my arm anyway. I began to feel like a long-lost cousin whom they had not seen for years, but who was leaving again forever. All afternoon, an old woman sat in an armchair in the corner. When she could catch my eye, she would say, "Dalai Lama, Dalai Lama," and with her hands indicate that he was gone. She would wring her eyes, pull a sad face, and mime tears falling down her cheeks. Before we left, the tears were real.

Later, from our friend in Kathmandu, we had learned that the old woman's son had died in prison one year before—like them all, an exile in his own country. What we had taken to be a festive occasion was a remembrance, the anniversary of a death. They did not tell us that. Nor did they tell us about the two children who were not there. They weren't in Lhasa at all. They had been assigned, against their parents' wishes, to school in China. The family had no hope of seeing them for years.

They had told us none of that. We had left in high spirits, late in the evening, weaving from too much *chang.* Walking between us, Lobsang gripped us as in a vise. We were out the gate and a block away before she released her hold.

That had happened in 1986. Now, more than a year later, we were back, and I believe that Lobsang and her family, had we gone to visit them, would have told us more, and told us bitterly. In 1987, people had become more vocal.

For example, we visited a small *gompa* at the base of Medical College Hill, across from the Potala. A twelve-year-old student monk met us at the gate and told us the name of the place. I wrote the way it sounded: Daklha Lhubug Temple. My guidebook spelled it Palhalupuk, which seemed, as usual, remotely connected to the word as I heard it.

"My name is Sonam Wangyal," he said, and I spelled it as well as I could. "You've done a lot of work since last year," I said. "These two buildings are new, I think." Or rather, rebuilt after having been destroyed.

"Thank you," said Sonam, with an air of gravity. "Please come in."

"Where did you learn English?" I asked as we walked up a steep flight of stairs.

"From my teacher."

"You sound like you learned in India."

"No. My teacher went to school in India. He learned there. In Kalimpong."

"Did he just come from there?" I was confused. How could a Tibetan have studied in India during recent years? I had heard so much about increased tolerance on the part of the Chinese that I was prepared to hear that a teacher— an exile—had been allowed to return to Lhasa as an English instructor. I was wrong.

"No. My teacher went to school in Kalimpong as a boy. Now he is old. Until two years ago, he was in prison."

Sonam was joined by Tashi, another apprentice monk. Palhalupuk was crowded with students their age, and as they showed us around the heavily decorated rooms, they taught us a sort of mantra: "English good, Tibeti good, Chinese bad." They sang this in chorus and roared with laughter.

The boys said this in the presence of a Chinese tourist who had entered the *gompa.* In theory, there was an admission charge. They would accept no money from us, but they collected it from the Chinese man. He paid politely and behaved with respect. The monks were polite to him too, but cast sly glances our way.

As we were leaving, Sangay Gyatso, the abbot of Palhalupuk, asked us in for tea. In his sixties, dressed in maroon and saffron, he perched on a carpeted bench beside a large window made of many unwashed panes. We talked about the reconstruction work. He accepted our congratulations and told us we were welcome at the *gompa*.

"It is good that you come here. Americans are generous," translated Sonam Wangyal, "and they respect Tibetan things. He thanks you. The Chinese do not respect." Sangay said this forcefully, then repeated himself: "They do not respect."

Another day I accepted the invitation of a young student of English, Miwang, to visit the hospital of traditional Tibetan medicine. After watching doctors at work, we climbed stairs to a small chapel on the fourth floor. Miwang explained the three seated statues behind glass, but I'd never have gotten the names without the help of a card that read: "Desi Sanggye Gyatso (1653–1706), Prince Regent of the fifth Dalai Lama. He wrote Be Sngon (Bengon) and Be Dkar (Begar) both of which are important medical texts... " and so on, through a litany of strange-sounding, impossible-to-remember names. I suppose Miwang would have the same difficulty with names such as George Washington, John Adams, and Henry Clay.

Walking across the hall to another room, he showed me a library of *thankas*—paintings on canvas. Most were of medical subjects—anatomy diagrams, herb charts, and so forth. But one, quite large, was a scenic view of a building on top of a hill.

"This is Chakpuri, the medical college," Miwang said.

"Yes, I've been to the *gompa* at the bottom of this hill. It's called Pal-halupuk?"

He hesitated over my pronunciation. Then he smiled. "Daklha Lhubug. Yes."

"But the college is not there now. There's just a steel radio tower."

Miwang hesitated before saying, "It was destroyed."

"When?"

"During the Cultural Revolution."

I prodded him for more information. He looked around the room before speaking. "All culture was destroyed," he told me. "Many things taken to Beijing. It is very sad. But we are not allowed to tell this. The Chinese say we must not talk about this to foreigners. But I am telling you."

Among the transient tourist community, this sort of thing was the occasion of much talk. That Tibetans would speak so freely, we thought, was a good sign of increasing freedom and tolerance. I reminded myself that Tibet has had a long history of maintaining a proud if isolated independence. I have never known people who seemed more resilient, more capable of making good things come from difficult situations, than Tibetans. Just look at the landscape from which they have sprung and you know they are survivors.

Nonetheless, hearing since then of riots, torture, and executions, of violence in the night, of old monks back in prison, of foreigners ordered out of Lhasa, and of Tibetan communities in India once again swelling with refugees, I change the names in my notebook and hope that the Tibetans with whom I spoke were not misled and given false hope by what they took to be substantial support from people like me.

I wonder in particular about one elderly monk.

He was at Drepung monastery. We had bicycled there, out of town and up a dusty hill. Once the largest monastery in the world, Drepung had been reduced to an echoing hive of mostly empty buildings. Now it was starting to come back to life. Since 1982, several hundred monks had joined the monastery. And not just monks, but children too. From one building came the sound of young voices, repeating lessons. It was a gentle, happy sound, one that had been absent from this center of Buddhist learning for many years. I sat where I could hear it, on the wall of a courtyard in front of the biggest assembly hall. Far below, scattered across the Lhasa Valley, the steel roofs of Chinese buildings glinted in the sunlight. I was feeling good about the future of Drepung when an elderly monk, passing, stopped.

"Where do you come from?"

"*Meiguo.*"

"Ahh." He took my hand between his palms, pressed it, and touched his forehead to my fingers. Then turning his head, he spat at the ground and said, "China!"

3
Crossing to Kailas

This—this is really living. Now I am really alive.
——Francis Younghusband, entering the
mountains after months of desert
travel, *The Heart of a Continent*

WE TRAVELED LIKE A BUNCH OF DOGS in a Wyoming pickup, heads out the sides, faces to the wind. Sometimes we acted like dogs. Passing a village, the local barkers streamed out to chase our truck, and we snapped to attention, yelling and barking back with exuberant fury.

It was a beautiful day to be on the move. Thunderstorms rode dark mountains streaked with purple and grey and shades of ocher. Sunlight dappled the broad valleys, spotlighting irrigated fields of green barley and yellow flowering rapeseed.

We were riding in a liberation truck, the all-purpose vehicle of China, rough road machines little changed since Mao's revolution. There were eight of us: Wendy and I, Pat and Baiba, Jeff and Naomi, their friend Antony, and Lee, the lanky New Yorker who liked rubbing shoulders with the Khampas. The front half of the truckbed, covered with a canvas canopy, was piled with our gear: two drums of gasoline, eight bikes, tents, pots, cookstoves, bulging duffels of warm clothing, camera equipment, and food for two months.

Events had moved quickly. After spending two weeks in Lhasa, we had decided it was time to leave, to get on around the Himalaya—if only we could find transport in a westward direction, and the chances of that had begun to seem pretty slim. Truck drivers, although personally willing to carry us, feared stiff fines if they were caught. We talked about trying to bicycle out of the city,

39

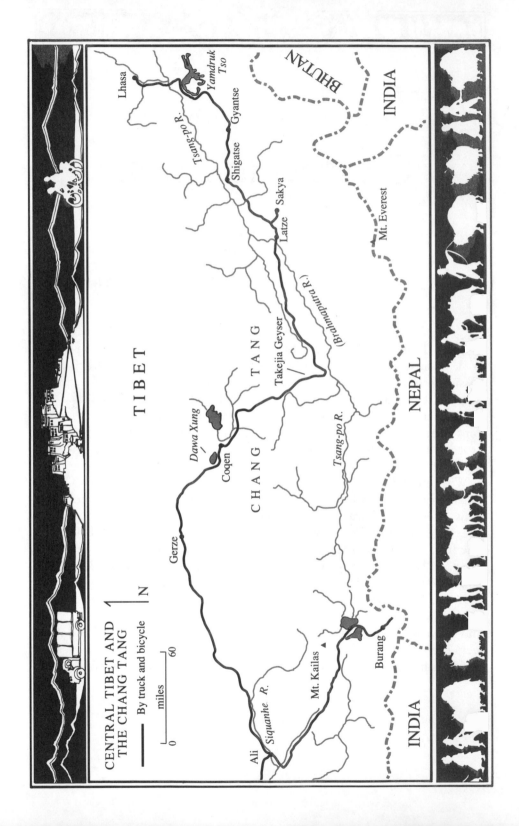

CENTRAL TIBET AND
THE CHANG TANG

—— By truck and bicycle

N

miles
0   60

TIBET

Lhasa

Tsang-po R.

Yamdruk
Tso

Gyantse

Shigatse

Sakya

Latze

(Brahmaputra R.)

Takejia Geyser

C H A N G   T A N G

Coqen

Dawa Xung

Tsang-po R.

Gerze

Siquanhe R.

Ali

Mt. Kailas

Burang

Mt. Everest

BHUTAN

INDIA

NEPAL

INDIA

INDIA

but the travelers' grapevine warned against that. People who had tried, even on the well-traveled route to Nepal, were being turned back.

Finally I had remembered a business card given to me in Chengdu (the capital of Sichuan province) by a travel agent. It was the card of his friend, Mr. Chophel, who, he assured me, would be happy to help us with any difficulty we might have. I hadn't put much stock in it but mentioned Mr. Chopel to Tenzing, the Snowland's manager.

"Oh, yes," he said. "I have heard of him."

"Do you think he could help?"

"Maybe. He is a very big man." Tenzing meant important.

"Do you know where his office is located?"

"I will call." He shouted into his phone for a few minutes while I leaned in the doorway. "Yes. Now I know. Sunlight Hotel. Maybe he can help. He is a big man."

Pat went to see Mr. Chophel that morning and came back with an amazing tale: "He's a Tibetan. He has a truck he'll rent to us for six thousand."

"Yuan? Impossible."

Four of us, including Naomi, who spoke Mandarin, returned that afternoon with a fistful of money, hoping to nail Mr. Chophel to his price before he had a chance to reconsider.

Mr. Chophel was, in fact, a big man sitting behind a big desk. His office was like a scene from a fifties movie about some political boss. Three phones kept ringing. Lackeys ran in and out with messages. We wanted to close the door, afraid we were doing something illegal. Chophel wanted it open. That way he could shout orders to people he saw walking past in the corridor. We sank into deep chintz armchairs with doilies. Chophel offered, of all things, canned Coke. Between interruptions, we discussed arrangements. He said there was no problem.

What about bikes?

"No problem," he said.

We wanted to travel slowly and avoid staying in roadhouses, which were nearly always unpleasant hovels.

"Fine. You camp out, you see the sights."

We said we would not be returning from Kailas, expecting this to cause consternation: foreign tourists out of control? But Chophel was unfazed.

"But you must pay for the truck to return," was his only comment.

That was reasonable. Could we have a letter of agreement before paying?

"Of course." The phones kept ringing. At one time he had a receiver in each hand, a cigar in his mouth, and an assistant standing in front of his desk with some sort of emergency.

Could we pay half now, half at Kailas?

"For fuel, we need more than half now."

How much?

"Four thousand."

At this point, I think he recognized our incredulity. He smiled. "I know some people. Otherwise, this is impossible."

We paid. Chophel and an assistant filled out forty 100-yuan receipts. The date was set for Monday.

"Something's not right," said Naomi as we left. "It's too good to be true." But Naomi was wrong.

On the morning we left, Tenzing, the Snowland's manager, had given us a string of brightly colored prayer flags as we loaded the truck in front of the hotel. "Pilgrims must have prayer flags," he had said. "Pilgrims to Kangrinpoche." We had tied them across the tailgate, where they would catch the wind. Then he distributed packets of Lhasa postcards to each of us, a personal gift representing considerable expense on his part.

"We wish you were coming," said Jeff. Tenzing smiled wanly and raised his shoulders. We had invited him to join us. He had wanted to come. Although for us this was primarily an adventure, for him it would have been an important religious opportunity. But Tenzing was considered crucial to the operation of his hotel; he had failed to get permission from his work unit to be away for so long.

We were nervous about our own permission to go—none of us had seen anything in writing—and, in fact, we thought the trip might be over when Chinese guards at a checkpost pulled us off the road on the outskirts of Lhasa. Tashi, our Tibetan driver, talked with the guards briefly, then sat waiting behind the wheel. He was a slight, wiry man in his thirties, wearing a vinyl imitation-leather jacket, polyester pants, and a continual smile. He spoke no English but shared with Naomi a smattering of Mandarin. She had met with him the day before leaving and had given us an enthusiastic report. "We're really lucky, you guys," she had said. "He's a Tibetan, and he's really happy to be going to Kailas. He doesn't mind camping out. He says he has eighteen days to make the trip and he's in no hurry. We can go as slowly as we want."

That was great news. Most of us, at one time or another, had experienced uncooperative, pushy drivers who stuck grimly to their personal itineraries, grumbling about photo stops and completely unwilling to travel in a spontaneous fashion. A bad driver could ruin a trip. Not Tashi. We soon realized that, for him, this outing was a lark. He was playing tourist, just like us. And we were pleased to see that he had invited his brother-in-law along for company. The two of them shared the truck cab and innumerable cigarettes the whole trip.

But first, the checkpost: after an hour, we still hadn't moved. Guards would occasionally look our way. Tashi would walk over to them and come back with his hands in his pockets. We sat nervously on the wooden truckbed, expecting any moment to be ordered out to face some English-speaking official. "Probably that's what we're waiting for," said Naomi. "Some supervisor's having a siesta, and they're trying to roust him out so he can come and tell us we can't go any farther."

But instead, after nearly two hours, to our great relief, Tashi must have gotten a signal because he banged his door shut, started his engine, and we were off, prayer flags snapping in the breeze.

From Lhasa, the road led south through the relatively fertile Lhasa Valley, crossed the Tsang-po River, and began the long climb to Kamba Pass.

"Kamba La," said Baiba. She was learning Tibetan words. *La* is pass; *tso* means lake; *chuu* is river. The pass was marked by a celebration of mani stones, prayer flags, yak skulls, and other offerings, and by a superb view of the famous turquoise lake, Yamdruk Tso, lying sinuously among treeless hills.

In the distance, snow peaks rose on the border of Bhutan, marking the Himalayan crest, our first glimpse of the great range.

By general definition, the Himalaya constitute a great mountainous crescent 1800 miles in length, stretching between the Indus River on the west and the Brahmaputra River on the east. Most authorities include the Karakoram Range in northern Pakistan, and some include the Hindu Kush Mountains, which reach all the way into central Afghanistan. Others dispute this, either cutting the range into smaller pieces or enlarging the concept to include even the Altai Mountains of Russian Turkestan. If you look on a large-scale map, it appears that all the mountains in central Asia are in the Himalaya. On the other hand, if you ask local people in Tibet or Nepal, you find that their concept of the range rarely extends much beyond their home valleys.

The word *Himalaya,* derived from Sanskrit, means "Abode of Snow" and is used in speaking about the entire range and all its various mountains. As such, it is both a singular and plural expression. In the Rocky Mountain West we use the term "high country" in the same way, referring collectively to any or all of the many peaks and mountain chains that make up the Rockies. And, just as there are separate ranges in Montana—the Bitterroots, the Bridgers, the Crazies, the Beartooths—there are also many ranges in the Abode of Snow. In Nepal alone there are the Annapurna Himal, the Ganesh Himal, the Manaslu Himal, the Langtang, Lamjang, Rolwaling, Jaljale, and Khumbakarna ranges, and numerous others.

Taken together, they are simply the highest, biggest, most spectacular, most beautiful, most sacred, most dangerous, most difficult, and most interesting mountains on earth. All of the world's peaks over 8000 meters (14 of them) are in the Himalaya, and except for a few in neighboring ranges, all of the world's 7000-meter peaks as well (more than 250). The range includes some of the largest alpine glaciers outside Antarctica; the world's highest habitations; the most powerful flash floods, avalanches, and landslides; the deepest river gorges (at least two of which measure more than 20,000 vertical feet); and an astonishing variety of cultures, climates, plants, and animals.

There are still snow leopards here, and ibex, wild yak, Marco Polo sheep, wolves, takin, goral, serow, tahr, argali, lammergeier, and griffons—strange names that by themselves evoke images of the wild places where these animals live. In Nepal's Arun River Valley (which has its origin in Tibet on the north side of Everest) you can find more bird species than in all of North America.

This enormous rampart is collision damage—the result of a slow crash of tectonic plates that started forty million to sixty million years ago, the Indian plate meeting the Asian plate. Since motion began, India, which was once an island, has moved 1200 miles into the belly of Asia, causing ground to buckle and rise and the earth's crust to thicken. The movement continues. The Himalaya are still rising at an average rate of about two inches a year—sometimes much faster. Less than two million years ago, a dramatic surge heaved the range 10,000 feet further above the sea than it had been—nearly two additional miles of elevation in the wink of a geologic eye.

Cut off from monsoon moisture by this fast-rising wall, Tibet gets drier all the time. It was once the floor of an ocean, the Sea of Tethys. Now it is called the Roof of the World. There are sea fossils in the limestone on top of Mount Everest.

The mountains divide cultures as well as climates. On one side throbs the energetic Hindu world of India; on the other, the almost empty Buddhist lands of Tibet; to the west, Muslim countries; and, in isolated pockets, cultural remnants as yet tantalizingly unknown in the world at large. Kham, Lahul, Spiti, Zanskar, Bhutan, Bongbo, Trans-Himalaya, Ladakh, Mustang, Wakhan, Sikkim, and others.

Our ignorance about the Himalaya can be astonishing. In 1986, satellite measurements indicated that K2, generally accepted as the second-highest mountain in the world, might in fact be higher than Everest, a recalculation involving some 900 vertical feet of error. A small battalion of scientists leaped into action, made new measurements in 1987, and declared that K2 was indeed higher than previously thought but still not higher than Everest.

The interesting thing about all this was that both these mountains are extremely well known. More than two hundred people have climbed them. Thousands have walked to their bases just to look up at them. A small mountain of books has been written about them. Dozens of climbers have died on them. Yet it seemed entirely plausible that our knowledge of their heights could be so far wrong as to have them in reverse order.

Which is nothing new for the Himalaya. Travel there has always been arduous. Answers remain equivocal. Fiction and fact change places like beads in a kaleidoscope. There, more than any other place on earth, myths come easily and ancient mysteries survive like the creature of Loch Ness.

Do mountain gurus really live in the snowy waste wearing little more than underwear, staying warm by mental energy that causes them to glow faintly in the dark? Can they survive by eating pebbles? What of *lung-gompas,* the trance walkers of Tibet, who could cover three hundred miles in three days of nonstop walking? Did Christ study Buddhism in Ladakh as a young man? Did he die not in Palestine but in Kashmir at age 115, to be buried by his once doubting apostle Thomas? Are there yeti, and if so, are there really two types of them? Do their females attempt to seduce Chinese soldiers? Does the Ganges River have the spiritual power to purify itself of India's awful bacterial pollution? Can Tibetan lamas really fly? Can they see the future? Do they meditate unto transparency so that all you see of them is their hair? Can they cut their bellies open and close them with the pass of a hand?

The answer to that last question is yes, according to Évariste Regis Huc, a French Lazarist priest who traveled through China, Tibet, and Mongolia from 1844 to 1846. He described various wonders in his *Travels in Tartary,* including reversible self-evisceration by a character called a *Bokté:*

> At length the *Bokté* appears. He advances gravely, amid the acclamations of the crowd, seats himself upon the altar, and takes from his girdle a large knife, which he places upon his knees. At his feet numerous lamas, ranged in a circle, commence the terrible invocations of this frightful ceremony. As the recitation of the prayers proceeds, you see the *Bokté* trembling in every limb and gradually working himself up into phrenetic convulsions. The lamas themselves become excited; their voices are raised; their song observes no order and at last becomes a mere confusion of yelling and outcry. Then the *Bokté* suddenly throws aside the scarf which envelops him, unfastens his girdle, and, seizing the sacred knife, slits open his stomach in one long cut. While the blood flows in every direction, the multitude prostrate themselves before the terrible spectacle, and the enthusiast is interrogated about all sorts of hidden things, as to future events, as to the destiny of certain personages. The replies of the *Bokté* to all these questions are regarded by everybody as oracles.
>
> When the devout curiosity of the numerous pilgrims is satisfied, the lamas resume, but now calmly and gravely, the recitation of their prayers. The

Bokté takes, in his right hand, blood from his wound, raises it to his mouth, breathes thrice upon it, and then throws it into the air, with loud cries. He next passes his hand rapidly over his wound, closes it, and everything after a while resumes its pristine condition. . . .

These horrible ceremonies are of frequent occurrence in the great lamaseries of Tartary and Thibet.

Huc was quick to add that the real spiritualists of Tibet saw this skill as an abuse of learning done generally by "lay lamas of indifferent character, and little esteemed by their comrades. Good lamas, they say, are incapable of performing such acts, and should not even desire to attain the impious talents."

Yeah, impious maybe. But they do it! Or did it. Or said they did. And because it was the Himalaya, the most mysterious and awesome landscape on earth, it seemed to Huc to be not just possible but observable. A guy with a mystic zipper in his belly! Mind you, Huc was a Catholic missionary. He should have denied that such unholy things could happen at all. He didn't even see the *Bokté*'s performance; yet there he was in the grip of Himalayan romance, reinforcing, like so many other writers, the mountains' ancient reputation for unlimited mystical possibility.

The road tumbled down from the pass to the lake. I think that since the morning of time, there was never lovelier water than that of Yamdruk Tso, clear and cold, set among the burnished hills. Gulls and grebes floated on the turquoise waves. The wind drew white lines of froth near the shore. Our truck rumbled on the rough road, sending yaks leaping across green meadows—yaks with red prayer flags braided into their black shoulder hair.

Along the shoreline, herds of miniature sheep and goats grazed, tended by Tibetans loafing in the sun. As we went by, people waved and shouted. Two women reclined together on the grass. One of them, displaying the usual unself-consciousness of Tibetan women, waved with her leg, as though doing calisthenics. Scattered homes and villages stood above the road. The buildings possessed whitewashed adobe walls, black windows, and red moon-and-sun designs on the doors. Firewood and bricks of dried yak dung, piled on rooftops, were exhibits of wealth.

Away from the lake we went, over Karo La pass, where glaciers approached the road and black clouds spit wet snow on us, then down a long valley past irrigated fields to the town of Gyantse, where the first thing you notice is a craggy fortress flung high on a rock the size of Gibraltar.

It was here that the British, during their invasion of 1904, fought a decisive

■ *Above:* View of the religious and geographical center of Lhasa, Jokhang Temple, from the roof of the Snowland Hotel. The October 1987 demonstrations and rioting against Chinese rule took place in the square in front of the temple. ■ *Right:* Pilgrims, such as this *chuba*-clad *drogpa* (nomad) and his children, come to Lhasa from all parts of Tibet, their prayer books in hand. (Photo: Jeremy Schmidt)

■ *Opposite:* The Kumbum, or Temple of 100,000 Buddhas, was built more than 500 years ago in Gyantse, when this Tibetan town was capital of an independent kingdom. The surrounding monastery was ransacked during the Cultural Revolution, but the Kumbum survived with minor damage. (Photo: Jeremy Schmidt) ■ *Above:* Mustard fields near Gyantse provide a nice contrast to the mostly dull brown desertscape of Tibet. ■ *Below:* In the broad valley leading to Mount Kailas, a woman milks her flock of goats and sheep.

■ A Buddhist devotee says her prayers on the shores of holy Lake Manasarowar. The cluster of prayer flags marks a shrine where the waters of the neighboring lake Rakshas Tal and Manasarowar periodically flow together via a shallow watercourse. When the water flows, it is said to augur well for the Tibetan people. After some thirty-five dry years, water began flowing again in the mid-1980s.

■ *Right:* We dubbed ourselves "Mountain Truckers," vying for space with some aggressive Khampas on the rough road from Burang to Ali. (Photo: Jeremy Schmidt)

■ *Below:* A short-lived fire, fueled with bits of scrub, warms our camp at night on the plain beneath Mount Kailas.

■ *Above, left:* Tsede Ang Marde, a *drogpa* (nomad) whose camp was set up beside Takejia hot springs on the road to Ali, spends his entire life at or above 15,000 feet elevation. ■ *Above, right:* A Hindu holy man from Simi-kot in Nepal, equipped with a trident and bells, passes through Burang on a pilgrimage to Lake Manasarowar and Mount Kailas. ■ *Below:* Traditional Tibetan clothing and colorful coral and turquoise jewelry comes out of the closet on August 1 for the People's Liberation Army celebrations in Burang. This photo was taken after the Chinese officials went home, prompting spontaneous dancing and singing, with lots of *chang* (rice beer) to lubricate the dancers' movements.

■ An elderly pilgrim makes her way along the path that circles the impos-
ing central structure of Sakya monastery, central Tibet.

battle, all for the purpose of getting to Lhasa and forcing a trade agreement on the aloof Tibetan government. They had shot their way up from India during winter, and despite the difficulties of high altitude, bitter cold, and stretched supply lines, the British suffered almost no casualties. It was the ill-equipped, archaic Tibetan army that lost at least a thousand men.

Even then, at the height of Victorian self-importance, there was controversy about that British invasion. Its ostensible objective was to enforce the terms of a border treaty on the unapproachable Tibetan government. But the larger concern, the overriding concern of the Indian government at that time, lay in rumors of Russian influence—and even Russian soldiers—in Lhasa. The Tsar, some feared, had his eyes on India, and Britain had better do something to stop him before the Cossacks came pouring over the passes. For that matter, the British didn't even know where the passes were. The world's most devoted travelers, they had been frustrated in all attempts to visit and study this most unknown of blank spots on their military maps. They wanted in, and finally, in 1904, they beat down the door to have a look. As things turned out, there never were Russian armies in Lhasa, and the trade agreement proved to be of almost no consequence. The whole action, according to critics, was nothing more than the imperial bully throwing his weight around.

Whether that was true or not, the awful disparity between the power of British India and the weakness of Tibet was not lost on the British commander, Colonel Francis Younghusband. More an explorer than a military man, and deeply religious as well, Younghusband had little stomach for military conquest. He spent the entire summer camped near Gyantse Dzong (*dzong* means fortress) trying unsuccessfully to negotiate his way to Lhasa while a Tibetan army hurled taunts from the precipitous heights of the fort. Finally, after having exercised what they considered to be unwarranted patience, the British turned their field guns on the *dzong* and stormed it through the breached walls.

There followed a brief but spirited battle on the stormy heights of Karo La before the last defenders fled and the forbidden road to Lhasa lay open for the first time ever.

When we arrived in Gyantse and saw the old Tibetan fort, still standing, half ruined (by the Chinese, not the British), I was thinking about gunpowder; but I smelled the sweet fragrance of flowers. The fields were full of rapeseed in bloom. Gyantse itself was a tiny place the size of an Iowa farm village, comprising two or three streets on level ground between the empty fort at one end and a half-ruined *gompa* at the other. In the warm light of late afternoon, it was a pretty sight. I went walking and, in an alley, came upon a dog gnawing on the jawbone of another dog. Teeth on teeth, just in case I had forgotten that life has never been easy in Tibet.

We stayed that night in what amounted to a truckstop—a small, two-story building in a big, walled compound. The sleeping rooms were on the second floor, accessible from an outdoor balcony that overlooked the compound. An attendant showed us to a room equipped with standard-issue furnishings found in any lodging anywhere in China: cots, cotton quilts, straw pillows, and thermoses of hot water standing beside porcelain basins. I claimed a bed and went outside to join Antony where he stood leaning on the balcony railing. A warm sunset was lighting up the semiruins of the old fort, towering above us on its great rock. Empty, it was a fierce and stirring scene. It must have been something to see, in 1904, with a thousand wild-haired Tibetans manning the walls.

"Do you hear that?" asked Ant. I did—bongo drums and a guitar, played poorly in a room next to ours, hacking out "House of the Rising Sun." A thin, female, French-accented voice: ". . . the ruin of many a poor girl, and me, oh Lord, for one." Bongo, bongo. I was reminded that this was, after all, the road to Kathmandu, where the youth culture of the sixties retained a feeble hold on life.

Ant's grip also seemed a bit weak that evening. His face opaque with orange road dust, his eyes bloodshot, he sought support from the balcony railing like an old drunk. "Ant, you all right?" I asked.

"Fine, I'm fine." He sounded terrible.

"How about dinner?"

He rolled his sunset eyes at me, so I went down without him. It was a self-serve kitchen, a sort of buffet set up for foreigners who couldn't speak the language. Choosing ingredients from an array of chipped enamel bowls, I took them on a plate to the cook. He fried them in a smoking wok and shouted the price to a girl with the cash box. She held up fingers to indicate the price. I paid five yuan—potatoes and eggs cooked with chili peppers, and a quart of beer—and returned to the balcony.

Now it was "Michael, Row the Boat Ashore" sung in French. Someone had also turned on the Gyantse loudspeakers, which made no sense because the system was broken. Nothing came out but white static. Nonetheless, some functionary had mindlessly flipped the switch. Loudspeakers were a daily routine in towns all over China. Every evening, every morning, in every place that had electricity, Orwellian speakers mounted on poles shrieked political speeches from Beijing, martial music, and Chinese comedy routines. I wanted to throw rocks at the damned things.

Jeff came up the stairs behind me with a plate of plain boiled potatoes for Naomi. She looked no better than Antony.

"Not feeling well?" I asked her.

"Motion sickness. I'll be fine."

Wendy also had plain potatoes. She said, "I was okay until the last hour." She had had a fever of 102 degrees Fahrenheit the night before leaving. Flu. There had been an epidemic of it among travelers in Lhasa, and all of us had suffered from it. I still ached in the joints. I felt stripped of energy and knew it was a combination of fever and altitude. We shouldn't have left Lhasa so soon.

Pat wasn't much better. He struggled up the stairs and sat down heavily. "Feels like 22,000 feet," he said.

"Feels like dogshit," I agreed. But we each had a huge plate of food and a full quart of beer. One thing about Pat and me; we could always eat.

The guitar noise quit. A blond boy in bare feet and Rastafarian dreadlocks came out on the balcony with his girlfriend. They stood and looked down at our truck for several minutes.

"You are riding in this truck?" asked the boy. His accent sounded German.

"Yes," said Jeff.

"You are paying the driver?"

"We hired the truck."

"Where are you going?"

"To Kailas."

"All the way to Kailas! I believe you will go through Shigatse on the way?"

"Yes."

"We could ride along that far?"

"We're full." Jeff was pretending to be a hard guy. Back in Lhasa, we had made the decision that we would take no riders. Our permit was for only eight persons, and we were nervous about its validity even for ourselves. Besides that—this was the main reason for our policy—we didn't know each other very well yet. We would be together for a long time, and any addition of strangers could result in the sort of frictions that tear a group apart. Twenty people would have ridden with us had we let them, so we had made the flat decision to take no one except in an emergency.

"Full?" said the blond boy, with a dubious expression. "With eight people only?"

"Yes, eight."

"But a whole truck . . . I think—"

Pat spoke up. "It's full."

They went back into their room mumbling. From their perspective we weren't abiding with the code of the road—namely, that those who have, should give to those who have not, or not be thought of as bosom buddies. The hotel was full of bosom buddies, all headed for Kathmandu, all wanting to ride with us. We told each of them no, and felt a little bad about it, having done plenty of hitchhiking ourselves. We knew what it meant to be without a ride, especially in a place like Tibet.

"Funny how we've managed to make enemies just by having a truck," said Antony.

"They don't know what they're missing," said Pat. "We'd give them something contagious."

We really had no business heading out across Tibet feeling the way we did. Among us, only Baiba and Jeff were halfway healthy.

By morning, Ant had lost his voice, and with it, the strength to stuff his sleeping bag into its carrying sack. In fairness to him, it was quite a job. His sleeping bag was very thick and about as compressible as spring steel. Getting it into a stuffsack was a ten-minute struggle even for a well person. Jeff and Naomi had the same bags, made by a company called Wiggy. Each morning the three of them performed what they called their Wiggy workouts. The morning we left Gyantse, Ant flunked the workout and needed help.

But the road made up for any concerns about health. In the lovely light of morning, we drove past great expanses of rapeseed in which field workers, as they bent down or stood up, winked like diving ducks in a yellow sea. The road, running straight through a corridor of tall poplars, was busy with people on foot or riding bicycles or donkeys. Road workers pedaled past, carrying shovels and picks over their shoulders. The houses made me think of old Italian villas, substantial places surrounded by poplars and green fields and workers hauling things on handcarts.

Outside Shigatse, soldiers at the fourth checkpoint since Lhasa waved Tashi to a stop. Uniformed faces peered over the side of the truck, saw us sitting there, and registered surprise. Lee lit up and waved as if recognizing friends.

"Hi there, good to see you guys," he said.

"Don't pimp them," said Naomi. "We don't want them doing a baggage check." She was thinking of the bicycles, the eight illegal bicycles. We had wrapped them in quilts and buried them beneath other gear, hoping they would not be discovered.

The faces scowled and disappeared. Angry voices shouted. Tashi was out of the truck standing on the ground. More soldiers climbed up to have a look at us. It felt like trouble. But ten minutes later we were bouncing along into Shigatse. Naomi said it for all of us: "Good old Mr. Chophel. We must really have a permit." Later in the day, leaving yet another checkpoint, she said, "I'm gaining confidence. The guy must really have some influence." Nonetheless, each time we were stopped, we would scrunch down on the bed of the truck trying to look inoffensive and obliging.

Shigatse is a town of drab buildings and shadeless streets swept by dust storms, overlooked by the near-total ruin of its ancient *dzong* and by the Tashi Lunpo, an elaborate fantasy among monasteries, maintained for tourists on the Kathmandu-to-Lhasa road. Wendy and I had stopped to see it the year before. There is a large Buddha statue you can photograph for forty dollars—a marvelous thing to see—but the monastery itself, lacking all but a few caretaker monks, lacks the vitality of its original purpose. Imagine St. Peter's Basilica being operated for profit by a group of K mart shoe salesmen, and you get a sense of how the Tashi Lunpo feels these days.

I was happy to pass it by. Continuing westward, the road climbed a rough track through a broad valley. Gusts of wind roared through the wooden truck sides, bringing thick clouds of yellow powder, forcing us to tie scarves over our faces and cinch our goggles tight. As the elevation increased, the land became drier and less fruitful. Although the crops near Gyantse were nearly ready for harvest, people in this region were still sowing seeds. The ground looked impossible. Yak teams plowed dust.

We had entered the classic landscape of central Tibet—dry, water-color hills and burnt mountains under a hard, blue sky—a skeletal landscape, stripped to its bright, thirsty bones. It was like living in a Georgia O'Keeffe painting, I thought, where the land has the beauty and authority of a polished skull. Almost nothing grew beyond occasional patches of irrigated land, where a little water, trailing green like spilled paint, ran down from the mountains.

Late in the afternoon, Tashi turned from the main road and drove south twenty miles to Sakya, once the ruling center of Tibet, now a small Tibetan community gathered around a magnificent monastery and temple. The *gompa* rose from flat country at the base of a steep hill. A massive wall surrounding the windowless central block gave it the appearance of a fortress painted in desert colors: dark grey with a rust-purple top and striking horizontal midlines. The Tibetan houses clustered around the *gompa* were also grey with vertical stripes of purple and white. These were the colors of Sakya, distinctive throughout the surrounding countryside, marking buildings for miles around as being under the sway of this *gompa*. I thought it was wonderfully picturesque. It reminded me of Hopi villages in northern Arizona—the same dry land, flat tiered roofs, and views of distant, sacred mountains.

Behind the village, on the dun-colored hill, lay strewn the ruins of dozens of buildings. I went up there in the late-afternoon light and walked among scattered yellow stones, trying to rebuild the structures in my mind. Some had been quite large, judging from the foundations and the few remaining walls. At one point I came across hundreds of conical clay sculptures, simple forms two inches in diameter with Buddha figures pressed into their surfaces. Picking up several of them, I realized that underneath the jumbled top layer were more layers, carefully arranged, packed tightly. These were *tse-tse,* or clay reliquaries. The ashes of a cremated body would be mixed with clay and formed into these shapes, which would then become the core of a *chorten,* a religious monument. What I had found was an elaborate, half-ruined memorial.

51

Nearby, I noticed a stone inscribed with very fine writing. When I picked it up, however, I realized it was too light for a stone. In fact it was paper—a book fragment two inches thick and ten inches in diameter, tan in color, its edges burned. It was coming apart. Inside, I found cobalt blue paper and gold writing. It was a beautiful thing to discover, like opening a geode to reveal crystals sparkling in the sun.

Having been handwritten in gold ink, this scripture must have been quite valuable at one time, part of a library that now, along with everything else on that hillside, had been reduced to rubble. I took a loose scrap for my notebook—a delicate, ragged leaf—to remind me that even stones have stories.

But not all was ruined. Strolling into the *gompa,* Wendy and I found a group of Tibetans busy with reconstruction work. Spread out around them on the floor of a large room were the shards of broken masks, costumes for religious dances—gargoyle heads, weird birds, and monsters. Using the old pieces as models, the Tibetans were fashioning new clay molds.

One of the workers was a young woman.

"Hello," I said.

"Hello." She laughed as if she had made a joke and jiggled the little boy on her lap.

I thought she understood English, so I said, "What do you do with these masks?"

"What do you do with these masks?" she said, her smile widening.

It took me a moment to realize she wasn't speaking English; she was simply a gifted mimic. I said, "These are terrific masks."

She answered, "These are terrific masks."

"*Pero no hablo Español!*"

She even nailed the Spanish. I photographed her with her son. Then she took my camera and made several pictures of me with one of the young male workers, who afterward pulled the two of us together and suggested that she kiss me. And more. I laughed, shook my head, and gestured toward Wendy. I did that mostly from a sense of propriety. But the laughing woman made it clear by the look on her face that bawdy jokes were part of life at Sakya, as they are all across Tibet.

The pictures she took turned out quite well, although the camera was tilted from her laughing.

That night, Lee lit fireworks. It was American Independence Day. But for us, Sakya marked a more important turn, the true start of our journey. We were in Tibet at last, the wide-open Tibet of our imaginings. No loudspeakers played warped recordings of Chinese music that evening. There were no Mao suits in sight, no latter-day hippies pounding guitars.

For supper we ate yak-filled dumplings beside a smoky hearth—Tibetan food in a Tibetan setting. Once again, our room overlooked a courtyard, but this one was filled with pilgrims. A group from a nearby commune had arrived just before dark riding a flat-bed trailer behind a red farm tractor. They cooked on the ground over yak-dung fires blown to life with goatskin bellows. A ragged musician approached with his *dranyen,* a six-stringed Tibetan lute. He played Tibetan folk tunes and danced a sort of jig, taking food as payment. When it was dark, the whole crowd went to sleep on the ground, together, under big yak-skin robes, while the full moon rose into thin banners of cloud and poured liquid silver over the soft, rounded hills.

4
The Chang Tang

On paper, the journey to Kailas appears easy. In practice it is difficult and attended by great discomfort. The pilgrim must take his own food with him; the climate is bleak; the wind is a blizzard; there is the fear of dacoits; the road is very bad, and the country eerie and almost uninhabited.
———W. S. Cassels, British official, 1907

THE FOLLOWING MORNING, at a road junction called Latze, we turned north, leaving the well-traveled road to Kathmandu. I had been to Kathmandu on that road twice before. It was a magnificent route past Mount Everest and Cho Oyu and other Himalayan giants, and we expected to end our journey by returning to Lhasa that way, thus completing the circle. I mentally took in the low, dusty buildings of Latze and wondered if it would look any different in seven months. That seemed unlikely; there wasn't much in this treeless place that could change with the seasons.

And then, crossing the Tsang-po River on a cable-guided barge, we headed into new country—the great central plateau of Tibet, the Chang Tang. Although the name means high plateau, the land is anything but flat. I thought of Nevada but on a much bigger scale, much drier, the mountains more widely spaced.

Until midafternoon, the truck labored steeply through a series of small valleys dotted with tiny, white-painted settlements and patches of irrigated green. Up side valleys, I caught glimpses of mysterious hermitages, painted white and perched on the most unlikely heights. Crossing passes from one valley to another, each pass successively higher, we rose to 16,100 feet among rolling slopes naked but for bright pink flowers growing singly and bravely.

Climbing down from the truck on the highest pass, Pat and I stood in the cold wind, breathing hard, feeling rubbery from the altitude. The view was enormous, a great expanse of dry ridges and distant snowy mountains.

"So that's the Chang Tang," I said. "Where it starts anyway." The high, wild heart of Tibet, averaging 17,000 feet in elevation, scoured by winds so strong you can't believe the atmosphere is only half the density of sea level. Austrian mountaineer Heinrich Harrer called this "the loneliest landscape I had ever seen," and he knew whereof he spoke. He had been on a climbing expedition in the Karakoram Range, then part of British India, when World War II broke out. Emerging from the mountains, he was arrested and interned in a British prisoner-of-war camp. He hated that, so he and his climbing partner, Peter Aufschneiter, made off one night. Security wasn't tight because the British knew there was nowhere to run, except Tibet, and no one could get far there without being sent back across the border. Of course Harrer and Aufschneiter made straight for Tibet and, in the course of one of the best adventures of their time, took two years getting to Lhasa. During the winter of 1945–46, they struggled across a large part of the Chang Tang, in terrible conditions, wearing clothes that even the Tibetans considered to be rags. The passes were high; temperatures were minus forty degrees or lower. Often they slept in the open. When they finally reached Lhasa, and political sanctuary, they knew they were lucky to have survived. Even Tibetans died out there. They still do.

Half a century before Harrer, Sven Hedin, the Swedish explorer for whom Tibet became an obsession, knew well enough about such conditions. For him the Chang Tang, sixty-five thousand square miles in extent, was one of three "white areas," blank spots on the map of central Asia. It called to him, and he could not resist. More than once he attempted winter journeys across those vast spaces. Despite all his best preparations, they became terrible journeys during which he lost hundreds of animals and several companions. In his book *A Conquest of Tibet,* Hedin wrote of one such expedition:

Quietly we moved through the drifts. The storm swept around us. Two horses dropped. Two men threw themselves into a drift, complained of pains in their hearts and declared themselves unable to continue. They limped to the camp at twilight. Deeply distressed, Abdul Kerim explained that if we did not find Nomads within ten days our situation would be hopeless. . . .

We had strength only to travel three miles to a slope, where four wild yaks plunged through the drifts like snowplows. The animals were given tsamba and rice. Everything was cast off that could be spared, the remaining articles were packed in rice sacks. The framework of the chests was used for fuel and the leather for footwear. All passes were snowed under. We must go forward.

Even in summer, as we stood beside a flag-decked liberation truck, the Chang Tang was a tremendous and beautiful and punishing landscape.

Pat said, "Serious stuff."

"Just being here, you mean?"

"Yeah, get sick or something. Nowhere to go."

You could head for Nepal, but it would take several days to reach a significantly lower elevation. From the Mount Kailas area, where we were going, it would take longer than that. Maybe too long. In Lhasa we had heard the story of a young German who had arrived from Kathmandu on a bus. During the three-day trip, fellow passengers had noticed he was ill. By the time he had reached Lhasa, he was comatose. Thinking it could be either meningitis or altitude sickness, doctors had worried about the risks of moving him even as far as the airport. While they worried, he died, and the rumor mill had predictably blamed the Chinese doctors.

But the real villains had been altitude and imprudence. Just that morning, as we had waited to cross the Tsang-po River, Tashi had heard a chilling story from an eastbound truck driver. A young British trekker, he said, had died at Mount Kailas of exposure and altitude sickness a few days earlier. There were no other details, but we could imagine.

It is wrong to think that travel in our motorized world has become easy and safe. One glance at Antony, curled up red-eyed and wheezing on our baggage, was enough to remind us of potential dangers. "We really have to keep an eye on him," said Pat.

From the pass, Tashi edged down into a broad valley bounded by snow mountains to the east and south. Occasionally, we passed black nomad tents pitched in grassless fields, surrounded by herds of yak and sheep that derived sustenance, apparently, from stones. The yaks looked healthy and well fed, but I couldn't imagine what they ate. A gentle midwestern Holstein, dropped into that brown landscape, would suffer heart failure just from looking at the place.

Actually, we weren't seeing many real yaks. The word *yak* refers only to a castrated male. A bull of the species is a *boa;* a female is a *dri;* crossed with a domestic cow it becomes a *dzo.* Which means that yak milk and yak butter are as rare as yeti butter. Even so, yak is a convenient word to use when speaking of these shaggy animals in general, and we called them all yaks.

Near evening, we turned north at another road junction. Had we kept going west at that point, we'd have rejoined the Tsang-po Valley. Originally that had been our desire—to go up the river to Kailas—but we had been warned against it. It was too late in the season, people said. We should have left a month ago, before the snow started melting. In July there were many river crossings too deep for the truck and soft, marshy areas where we would sink into the mud. No way, they said. Better go through the Chang Tang, where the roads are dry.

Dry, perhaps, but hardly what you'd call roads. After turning north, the track soon disappeared into a huge field of river cobbles the size of softballs. Tashi crept along in first gear, but even at such a slow pace, we had to hold on tight or be knocked silly. The way angled toward a dark brown line of mountains called the Gangdise Range, at the base of which, among pastel hills, after another hour, we came to a patch of boggy ground where the Takejia Geyser spouted continuously among bubbling hot springs.

Beside it stood a single black nomad tent. A man and a boy came out when they heard the truck. Tashi waved a cheery hello to the man and told us his name was Tsede Ang Marde, but I didn't learn much else that night. I was incapable of expending energy.

That was no fault of our surroundings. The view seemed to stretch beyond any horizon. I could see the tops of mountains that seemed far enough away to have been on a different planet. I should have felt exhilarated, but I was too tired, too battered by the truck ride, and too dizzy from the altitude. Even Baiba had a fever now. Pat wrapped her in a sleeping bag and tucked her into a tent.

Antony was a complete wreck. His pulse was 120. His face was red, his eyes bloodshot. He admitted to having a rough throat and chest congestion. He had slept most of the day, despite the truck's wild pitching. And of course he said, "I'm fine. I've just got a cold."

Partly with those concerns in mind, we decided to rest one day at the geyser. I slept late the next morning and then lolled in the sun, telling myself I was busy building red blood cells. Tashi took the opportunity to buy a sheep for thirty yuan from Tsede, who killed the animal in a way I'd never seen before. Putting an arm under its chest, he lifted its front legs off the ground, extracted a five-inch needle from a leather holder on his belt, and pushed the needle between two ribs. The sheep hardly struggled and made no sound. Its eyes turned dull and it was dead—as simple as that. The needle, I saw when the sheep was cut open, had sliced a neat one-inch gash in the sheep's aorta, causing it to bleed to death into its lung cavity.

Before cutting, Tsede placed a Tibetan religious book on the dead sheep, said what sounded like a well-known prayer, and proceeded with the job of butchering. He did it as easily as some of us would prepare a salad.

First he cut the throat, then tied the esophagus to prevent stomach contents from escaping. Next he deftly skinned the sheep and laid the gleaming carcass on the skin as though on a table. Opening the chest, he ladled blood into a pot held by his son.

"What does he do with the blood?" I asked Tashi.

"He mixes it with *tsampa* and makes sausage in the intestine," he said. *Tsampa* is flour made from roasted barley. We both spoke in gestures and single words, but the meaning was clear.

The butchering was done neatly, and all parts were saved except the stomach and bowel, which were put out for the ravens. Last of all, Tsede cut behind the rear leg tendons, stuffed the fore hooves through the slits, and hung the tidy, bloodless package on the sunny side of the truck.

Later, Jeff made a stew from our half of the sheep. Tashi wanted his share dried. He tossed it, unwrapped, into a wicker basket in the back of the truck, where over the next week it grew a protective layer of road dust.

That evening, Tsede's son came to our tent and sat by the entrance. Wendy had named him Roger Munchkin for his elfin appearance—less than four feet tall, with an intense, earnest expression, dressed in a rough wool tunic, home-spun pants, and blue Chinese tennis shoes. He watched for a while as I wrote in my diary. When I put it away, he reached into his tunic and pulled out a handful of little treasures, the sort of things all boys carry around in their pockets—bright pebbles, an imitation coral bead, an old coin with a square hole in the center, a yak molar, and a tiny leather folder that contained two sewing needles.

He told us the Tibetan names for these things as we passed them back and forth. When we had finished, he put them back in his tunic and turned his attention to the curiosities in our tent—everything from the nylon tent fabric to the pen with which I had been writing. Handling each item carefully in case it was fragile, and reverently in case it was a religious object, he investigated my pocketknife, compass, sun goggles, flashlight, propane lighter, telephoto lens, film cans, tripod, cable release, and toothbrush. That was all good stuff, but what caught his lasting interest was a stack of postcards of Tibetan scenes. He was entranced by the pictures. He went through them very slowly, naming everything he saw, particularly the yaks and horses and tents, but also—and this surprised me—he put names to several of the monasteries. He recognized Drepung and Sakya and Ramoche, the last one being a small, rather obscure *gompa* on a Lhasa back street.

"You've been to Ramoche?" I asked, using my pidgin Tibetan. He shook his head. "You've been to Lhasa?" I asked. Again he said no. But he knew those places as I had known St. Peter's Basilica before I ever went to Rome, or the Lincoln Memorial before I went to Washington. To Roger Munchkin, Ramoche was a national monument.

I told him he could have a postcard, whichever one he wanted. He went through them all again and chose a picture of a summer nomad encampment, a picture of bright cotton tents and herds of animals on a broad, green plain.

We said good night and closed the tent, but fifteen minutes later Wendy went out for a moment and Roger was still there, standing back away from the tent. Seeing her, he came over again, dug into his tunic, and presented us with a handful of dried yak cheese, hard little chunks like white stones mixed with wooly lint from his pocket. I chewed on a piece, made appreciative noises, put the rest aside, and said good night. I think he would have stayed for hours had we let him.

That day of rest did us good. Even Antony looked better the next morning, although once again he flunked the Wiggy workout. After watching him struggle for a few minutes I offered to help, and despite the efforts of us both, Wiggy nearly won. Wiggy and the altitude. We finished and lay beside the bulging stuffsack trying to catch our breath.

"Ready, Ant?" I wheezed.

"Let's go," he croaked.

Then onward past the two lakes, Pun Tso and Mum Tso. The second one was big, pewter-grey, with a backdrop of snow mountains that would be a major feature in Montana, but here it was only another of many anonymous ranges. Creeping like an insect track across that gigantic place, the road just got rougher. In fact, it wasn't a road; it was a faint trail made by trucks going wherever their drivers thought best. Sometimes there would be five or six tracks running roughly parallel, and none better than the others. The truck rattled and pitched as Tashi tried first one way, then another, climbing steadily into a landscape of rolling hills above 18,000 feet.

"I know we're high," I told Pat. "I get this burning sensation behind my eyes."

He pointed out that in Canada, pilots of small planes were required to breathe oxygen when flying above 12,000 feet. "We're 6000 feet higher than that, and Tashi has a frigging cigarette in his mouth!"

Altitude, hot sun, cold air, a rough road, and maybe, like the rest of us, Tashi was a bit dizzy. One time, sighting a small herd of gazelles across a flat plain, he turned suddenly, punched the accelerator, and tried to run them down with his truck. The animals dodged and spun. Tashi lurched and careened. We held on tight.

"How many wheels were on the ground that time, Ant?" asked Lee. They were both hanging over the side trying to watch.

"About four. Two on this side were off. Four out of six isn't bad."

Tashi gave up the chase and settled back into the dusty grind.

It was indeed meager country. All day, we passed only three or four nomad camps, a sure sign of thin pickings. Where there was no grass, there was colored stone, rainbow mountains of tinted sediments—red and black and yellow with streaks of olive, swirled together in twisted strata. Glaciers brooded above. Boulders and cobbles covered the valley bottoms, through which diminutive streams supported ribbons of pale green grass. If you don't like this sort of landscape, if your eye craves lush greenery and shade trees, Tibet can seem to be a terrible wasteland. But if you like open spaces, the Chang Tang is a continual wonder.

As days went by, riding the truck developed into an effective training regimen. We were constantly flexed, braced, hanging on, with our thighs, calves, arms, back, and stomach all getting a workout—at 16,000 feet, no less.

Each of us adopted a different style of travel. Jeff would hitch in close to the canvas wall, face thrust out into the full brunt of the wind. Pat and I did the same, on one side or the other, taking the bumps with our legs. Somehow Lee managed to sit cross-legged on a pack on the truckbed, bolt upright to minimize the shock on his long back. Even so, the bumps jiggled him from one side of the floor to the other, and I wondered how he could stand it. Wendy clung to the wooden tailgate and Baiba was always in motion, dancing back and forth, shaking with the rhythm. Ant generally spent his time half conscious on the luggage.

Actually, we took turns lying on the load, a slightly less violent place to ride and a good place from which to watch the dance: figures standing on a platform holding on to steel bars, jerking and jumping, leaving the ground in unison, blasts of dust blown in periodically, the dancers dressed in bright clothes covered with clay, dark goggles over their eyes, scarves wound tightly over their faces, hats pulled down to cover their ears. One dancer lets go of the metal bar, throws himself to the floor, bounces there a few times, and staggers to his feet.

Lee drops a lens cap. He, Baiba, and Jeff scramble around trying to catch it. We hit a bump and all of them are thrown to the floor. They stand up and down they go again. The lens cap leaps around like a terrified mouse.

"My kidneys are fluttering like prayer flags," said Pat one day. I tried to answer him and nearly bit my tongue off as we hit a bump.

Of us all, Baiba was the sturdiest. I suppose it had something to do with her Latvian genes, some quality of endurance from her ancestors that belied her diminutive figure. Whatever the cause, she could keep going when the bigger, apparently more robust physiques had packed it in for the day. Many times, I lay prostrate on the bouncing baggage as she weathered the journey upright, eyes determinedly to the front.

Strange skills of Tibetan travelers: We soon became adept at staying up-right on the wildly jolting surface and at wrapping scarves around our faces so they would keep out dust but wouldn't slip off in the wind. We put up our tents quickly in the evening and had them down again early in the morning. Sleeping well required finding smooth ground each night; Wendy could sleep on anything, but gradually I was getting better at bending myself around im-movable rocks and tussocks.

Most of all, I was impressed by how quickly we had formed a cohesive group, keeping an eye out for each other's welfare. Everyone pitched in on whatever needed doing, and things got done. If one of us was too tired or too sick to move, someone else would take up the slack. Being the acknowledged magician with our limited commissary, Jeff often took over cooking. But if he delayed, someone else would take that as a sign that Jeff wanted a break, and pretty soon a meal would be ready.

Each day we stopped for lunch somewhere. Not that we had anything good to eat. It was just an excuse to lie on solid ground while our heads spun in cir-cles. We never tried cooking anything.

Mostly we had dry food. That meant a lot of *tsampa,* a staple I had learned to appreciate in the Sherpa villages of Nepal. There, people mix it with sweet, milky tea, making it into a pleasant breakfast porridge. I could eat huge quan-tities of it, especially after throwing a few raisins into the bowl.

In Tibet, however, sugar is hard to come by, and Tibetans eat *tsampa,* in their ancient manner, mixed with salt tea or yak butter or both. Often, they add yak jerky, which they grind to a powder so it mixes thoroughly with the flour. They keep it in skin bags with chunks of butter embedded like plums in a pudding, and the routine is to put your hand in the bag, knead the *tsampa* into one of the butter chunks, and pull out a doughy greaseball. The butter tastes the way a yak smells. It takes some getting used to.

The first time a Tibetan offered me *tsampa* from a skin bag was in eastern Tibet, where Wendy and I had gone hitchhiking in 1986. Walking along a dirt road, we had come across a group of Lhasa-bound pilgrims, twenty-three of them traveling in the back of a liberation truck. They were breaking camp and had a fire going. They offered us breakfast, which we happily accepted.

At that time, I hadn't learned about kneading the *tsampa* into the butter. I watched my host and his friends reach into a goatskin bag and pull out wads of dough, which they rolled into carrot shapes and took bites from while they drank their tea: a bite of *tsampa,* a drink of tea. It looked easy, and I was hun-gry. Reaching into the bag and feeling a soft wad, I pulled it out, rolled it be-tween my palms, and took a bite. Pure butter! The size of a Snickers bar. The

Tibetans widened their eyes. I must have looked sick. "Hah!" said one of them, his open mouth twisting into a toothy smile. Everyone turned my way. There was giggling. The laughing man became a man rolling on the ground shrieking with glee.

I had to eat it. It would have been wrong to put a bitten chunk of butter back in the bag, wouldn't it? I was trying to be polite, but before long, after they had offered us a ride in the back of the truck, and I was crammed into a tiny space surrounded by the smoky fragrance of nomads, I was worried that I might commit a much worse faux pas—throwing it back up all over my hosts. It was with great effort that I had kept my stomach down for the next hour.

Despite that experience, I had eaten *tsampa* the right way on occasion, made from recently roasted flour mixed with fresh butter and powdered jerky. Taken that way, it was delicious stuff. A wad or two, washed down with salt tea, made a powerful meal. I had developed a strong faith in *tsampa*'s food value and on this trip insisted that we carry plenty of it. ("Plenty?" Pat had said in Lhasa. "A mouthful is plenty.")

We also carried a supply of dried noodles and the unforgettable Chinese army rations called 761 bars—cookie crumbs and milk powder mixed with lard and pounded into rock-hard bricks. The idea is much like *tsampa*. If you can eat one, it will keep you going for hours.

While chewing on those lunch treats, we would pore over our maps—a set of American military aeronautical charts drawn to a scale of eight miles to the inch, taken from satellite data. The contours were fairly reliable, but with intervals of 1000 vertical feet, there were many features even in a place as big as Tibet that escaped being shown on the maps. Sometimes we couldn't tell where we were. Adding to our confusion, the roads were usually marked wrong and categorized according to an American highway engineer's fantasy: dual lane (divided) highways, primary roads, and secondary roads! The route we followed had no marking whatsoever. I noticed roads drawn in where I am certain not even trails exist.

That was all right with me. I liked the puzzle presented by the maps. I enjoyed thinking that I was pitting my brain, on location as it were, with the digital, computerized perfection of an invisible satellite.

One evening, we arrived at a horrible place called Coqen, a clutter of mud hovels on a dusty plain. Mountains hunkered low on the horizon, their backs to us. The wind sent clouds of dust going this way and that. It was a terrible place to put a town. It would have been sensible to abandon it in favor of a more protected location. Instead, they were making it more permanent. New buildings were going up, concrete buildings to replace old mud ones. Crews of

Tibetans and Chinese in green uniforms were making concrete blocks and digging foundations in the loose dust.

Tashi pulled into the yard of a hotel. We knew it was a hotel by its long, sagging front, its numbered green doors, and its mud-covered windows. Odd, I thought, that the raw landscape should seem so beautiful and visually rich; but here, where people lived in as much comfort as they could manage to provide for themselves, everything was ugly.

Well, almost everything. Through spinning clouds of dust we could make out a line of Tibetan tents owned by scruffy traders with various wares spread out before them—metal chests, dime-store mirrors, orange and pink yarn, that sort of thing. Among the trinkets, Lee spied objects of beauty—a truckload of cartons clearly labeled: Lanzhou Pijiu. Beer made in Lanzhou. The way I felt just then, I couldn't have looked at a beer if it had sprouted horns and attacked me. But Lee knew better. Lee might run out of food some day, we joked, but he'd never run low on beer if it killed him. He bought a case, and later I was grateful he had.

Beer or not, Coqen was no place to spend the night, and good-natured Tashi, once he heard our objections, was happy to drive on. Within a few miles the country became beautiful again—rolling grasslands dotted with nomad camps beside little streams. It was a gentle place. There were wildflowers. Why had those responsible for Coqen not located here in these soft hills? Or better yet, on the other side of a low ridge, where we came to a big lake called Dawa Xung, shining in the evening sun. We camped there very happily ourselves, on thick grass between the lake shore and a winding creek that in Wyoming would have had trout hanging in the shade of its overhung banks.

The only reason I could think of for not putting Coqen here was that grass-covered meadows were perhaps too valuable for buildings. In the Chang Tang, pasture was the key to survival. *Drogpa,* the nomad people, knew where all the pastures were, and at what time of year the grass would be good. I wished I could have seen the land through their eyes. I'd like to see how they would draw maps. Instead of roads, I suspect that the main features would be pastures and sources of water.

These thoughts came to me as we pitched our tents on the greenest, softest patch of grass in the area. Two nomad families were camped nearby, and they had put their tents on gravel. But no one showed resentment at our choice of tent site. Instead, when Wendy and I went up to have a look at the lake shore, we were given a warm welcome by a young woman who had just collected her sheep for milking in a stone-walled corral. We leaned on the wall and watched as she deftly caught the sheep, one after the other, and tied them in a line—or rather strung them. It was like stringing beads. Using a thick, hand-spun wool rope, she took a twist around each head until she had two rows of sheep facing each other, their heads intertwined like you do with your fingers if you push your palms together.

It was an arrangement the sheep seemed to enjoy. They had been running around agitated until tied together in this manner. Now they settled down and stood quietly while the woman went down the row doing her milking. As she finished with each animal, she would thump it in the belly with the back of her hand. Wendy noticed that and wondered why. Did lambs thump the mothers with their heads? Or was this woman just saying thanks?

We were fascinated. The woman was amused at the way we paid such close attention to this routine job. She kept looking up from behind the furry rumps, and seeing us still watching, she would laugh in that lovely silver voice common among Tibetan women when they are happy.

Watching her, I was suddenly struck by an amazing thought—amazing for me, anyway—that here we were, way out in the middle of this tremendous landscape, feeling very remote indeed, really *Out There;* yet despite that feeling of remoteness, I knew that if we had met, on the shores of Dawa Xung, another party of foreigners traveling in a motor vehicle, we might have been surprised to see them, but we'd have understood their presence as if it were entirely natural for people like us to visit the center of Tibet. Hello, we'd have said—in English—and then we'd have gotten down to a conversation about distance and cost and probably some politics, and wasn't this just an amazing landscape to be motoring through?

But here I stood watching a Tibetan woman who *lived* in the Chang Tang, one of nearly 500,000 such nomads who thought of this land as home. For all I knew, she had never been to a city. Obviously she regarded her life here as a natural thing. And yet I thought *her* presence was stupendous! Living Out There, in a handmade tent woven from the skins of her yaks on the shore of an enormous, brilliant, icy lake ringed by huge mountains? Going about her daily chores the way I would pull weeds in my garden, and then having us show up?

I mentally reversed the image and thought about having a bunch of Tibetan nomads walk up to my house in Wyoming, tie their yaks to a tree, and with no introduction beyond an acknowledging smile, take a keen interest in the way I was yanking dandelions.

Our being there, hauled in like space creatures by jets and trucks to gawk at sheep being milked, was in my mind not the least bit remarkable. "Well, yes, ma'am," I might have said, had she asked. "It was simple. We flew here from America. Well, actually only to Lhasa . . . " The conversation would have gone nowhere. She knew as much about jets as I knew about milking sheep; as much about America as I knew about the valley over the next ridge.

Anyone reading this book could go to Dawa Xung. Although independent travel has been cut off by the Chinese, you can still book a custom tour through CITS or any number of adventure travel operators and go straight to that lake.

Of course, the woman, being a nomad, would be gone.

The next morning: clear, warm, the sun bright, the road rough. Jolting along the shoreline with a tail wind. Dust and lake flies in clouds.

Beyond the lake we entered a huge valley with glacier-topped mountains radiating in several directions. The highest ones were well over 22,000 feet, but I had to look at the map to know that. The scale of the landscape was difficult to gauge. Without the map, I would have believed the valley was anywhere from five to twenty-five miles across. Central Tibet: on and on it went, an awesome, enormously huge place.

We crossed big valleys and dry lakebeds, climbed from them over ancient shoreline terraces to windy passes, then dropped to other lakebeds. Always there were mountains, great massifs smeared with snow, their colored rock layers twisted and eroded in bizarre shapes. Occasionally we came to streams, full of fury and powdered rock, crashing down from the glaciers. They were dead-end torrents, all of them. Water flows in the Chang Tang; it forms streams and gathers in lakes, but there is no outlet to any ocean.

I tried to trace our progress by mentally marking the passes, noting the watersheds, paying attention to rock formations, colors, and types. I tried to correlate all this with the maps and to engrave the sequence of geographic features in my mind each night. But as the days wore on, my knees lost their strength, the bumps went straight to my spine, and all that grand scenery began to blur.

There was a lake, Zhaxi Tso, too big to judge its size, white salt flats in the foreground, turquoise water reaching into the far distance. Tail winds drove salty filth back on top of us. It came in choking billows. The grit penetrated my scarf and coated my teeth. I couldn't keep my eyes open. Terrible beauty indeed.

There was Gerze, another dusty outpost of mud walls, mud roads, and dried mud swirling in the air, ringed with broken shards of beer bottles—so much glass the green shimmer was visible from a mile away. We stopped there for a few minutes one evening. The wind sobbed around mud corners and set tin cans to rolling. They tinktonked across the gravel, and now when I think of those settlements in the middle of open nomadic spaces, I hear that sound above all.

But there were also places of memorable beauty. One evening I climbed a rocky promontory above our camp and looked out over a dry seabed. It must have been a headland once, where I stood. It felt that way, even without water.

I could imagine waves beating against the rocks. Several hundred feet above camp, I came across a cluster of *mani* stones, dozens of them, placed by pilgrims. What were they doing here so far from anywhere? Even in this wild place of enormous skies (or maybe especially in this place) people had recognized and honored an important point in the landscape.

So did we, in our own way. On the seventh day, the truck rattled into yet another treeless valley, but this one had a river. It was the Siquanhe (pronounced approximately "sish-wan-huh"), headwaters of the Indus, clear and brilliant, flowing down from just north of Mount Kailas. Seeing that brought us to our feet, cheering through dust-caked scarves. We stopped there for the night, washed our heads, and lay on green sun-warmed grass. Lee was so excited by it that he flung himself into the icy water, clothes and all.

"JUST ANOTHER dogbark town," said Wendy as we rolled into Ali the next morning.

It was an unimpressive place, but it had a hotel, newly built and, according to Chinese architectural fashion, already half ruined. Already there were doors ajar, holes punched in their panels, paint spattered on the floor, windows broken, spittoons standing empty beside the dark stains of gob that missed, and the lobby floor covered with a millimeter of dust.

"Nice place," said Naomi. "I wonder where everyone is."

In a back room, several of us found the office staff. They were unhappy to see us. They were hiding. Little wonder; we were a gang of dusty clods in goggles and scarves, an invading horde from the desert. Naomi spoke with the manager while the rest of us stood in ruffianish support.

"He says there aren't any rooms."

"That's no surprise," said Jeff.

We knew there were rooms. The manager's statement was just the opening gambit of every Chinese hotel negotiation. There are never any rooms until you've had a chance to talk price and look determined. Naomi was our negotiator, and having once been a lawyer, she could be a hard one.

"One hundred yuan?" she was saying in Chinese, and then to me, in English, "Thirty dollars a bed!" That was my cue. I shook my head and walked out, demonstrating that we didn't need to stay there. One by one the others followed me until all of us except Naomi were out on the crumbling concrete steps at the hotel entrance.

She walked out a few minutes later grinning as if she had just won a lawsuit. "Eight yuan sound okay?"

We were shown to rooms with beds whose sheets still bore the dusty imprints of previous bodies. They looked like Shrouds of Turin; you could make out heads, shoulders, feet. Not that it mattered. We were as dirty as anyone else, and because the hotel lacked plumbing, there was no chance for a bath. I sat on the bed. A dust cloud rose. I sneezed uncontrollably and had to move. Wendy picked up a teacup. It was half filled with a dark liquid. She took it to a hotel girl and asked for a clean one. Instead, the girl gave her a dirty look, threw the contents across the lobby floor, and handed back the dirty cup.

"China!" Wendy fumed. "Three thousand years of civilization." It had become a favorite refrain of ours when confronting such modern examples of that ancient heritage as the Hotel Ali.

The building was a two-story maze with hundreds of rooms, all but empty and designed like a blockhouse. At night, when the lights came on, we were mocked by brightly lit lavatories complete with showers, washstands, flush toilets, wet floors (there actually was water in the pipes?), all visible through windows in the locked doors. The baths hadn't worked since the hotel was opened, the manager confessed, but no one had turned out the lights or fixed the leaky pipes. The functioning pit toilet, in the yard, was horrific even by local standards.

Wendy came back from a visit to that facility, saying, "It's not safe to go out there in the dark without a flashlight, there's so much shit on the ground."

Pat: "That's okay, just go barefoot."

Morrow's contrarian humor.

Later, Tashi consulted with Naomi. She translated. "Tashi's worried about the truck. He says Ali is notorious for thieves. Someone should sleep in the back."

Wendy volunteered us. I was willing, but it occurred to me that two extremely nearsighted, exhausted travelers might not make the best guards.

"What do we do if someone comes?" I asked. "A couple of huge Khampas?" I could imagine them standing over us, hands on those long knives, while we groped for our glasses.

"Take a dog stick with you and bang the truck sides," offered Naomi.

"Yell like hell," wheezed Ant, clearly eliminating himself from the task. Ant still looked pretty bad.

Lee, ever the New Yorker, had the only practical solution. He handed me a can of Mace. Lying in the truck, I looked up at the gap in the canvas canopy where a head, if it came, would appear. I tried the Mace for range. It sprayed the canopy with a stream of liquid that drifted back down in our faces. Wendy didn't like that. "At least the stuff works," I croaked. But no thieves came.

We had an easier night of it than Pat and Baiba did in their room. Chinese guys—truck drivers and PLA soldiers—kept barging in. They would enter, stand blinking drunkenly, and walk out, leaving the door open. Pat finally barred the door with a chair and table. The next visitor hit it full force. "Sounded like he broke his wrists," said Baiba the next morning. She said that hopefully.

At breakfast we talked about plans for the next month. Jeff said, "When you think about it, we don't have much choice," and went on to summarize our situation. We would have no authorized transport after Tashi dropped us at the base of Kailas. It was illegal for us to ride on trucks without a permit. It was also illegal for us to ride bikes. Supposedly the road to Kashgar was entirely closed to foreigners. The road to Lhasa was open, but we weren't allowed to go in a truck. And there were no buses in any direction at all.

"Yep," said Pat. "We're sittin' purty."

We all agreed to take things as they came, whether that meant staying together or splitting into smaller groups, riding our bikes or walking or whatever. The only thing we knew for certain was that we would somehow have to get back to Ali in order to continue westward to Kashgar and Chinese Turkestan.

Ali was an administrative and transport center. It had no agriculture and no distinguishing features beyond the hotel and a three-story concrete Friendship Store, where we bought an ultimate luxury: canned tomatoes. The best part of the town was its open market, a spirited clutter of hovels and lean-tos filled with stuff from China, Tibet, Nepal, India, Hong Kong, and Japan. There were Spring Thunder radios, T-shirts reading "CHINA TOURISM," dried apricots, TDK cassette tapes, TV sets, piles of brilliant synthetic clothing in bright purple, hot pink, flaming orange, and lime green. Merchants standing behind stacks of polyester pants whacked at them to remove dust. There were wooden saddles, cases of Lanzhou Pijiu, rolls of synthetic pile (as if supplies of sheepskin were low), and huge blocks of yak butter looking like old cheeses wrapped in leather or burlap.

Red-braided Khampas stood in clusters, revealing treasures from their fantastic belts. A noisy gang of workers hammered stoves, chests, pots, and buckets from sheets of galvanized steel. There were Tibetans, Chinese, and Uighurs from Xinjiang. Some of the Uighurs looked Irish, their foreheads white and their cheeks ruddy beneath black hair. One wore a sweater and a black wool coat and would have fit right in on a Belfast wharf. There were melons, cabbages, tomatoes, onions, cucumbers, and apples from Kashgar. Soup kitchens and slop shops cooked a variety of food. One cafe was a blue tin box with hammered patterns and welded filigree, creating a playhouse imitation of Persian architecture. Inside, a man baked Kashgar-style flatbread, one loaf at a time, in a pressure cooker on a kerosene burner.

I was trying to find a melon when I saw Lee surrounded by Khampas—Lee, in his Aussie bush hat, making a deal. As I approached, a happy Khampa slapped my shoulder and held out his hand. "Nah, I know that trick," I said, and whacked his shoulder back.

"Change money?" he said.

Lee turned to me. "Remember this guy?"

"No."

"He was in Lhasa. Wanted to change money there. Real traveler."

"Hash?" said the Khampa, digging deep in his *chuba.*

That's what Lee was buying. Hash from Nepal. The arm came out of the *chuba* holding a greasy bead of imitation coral. Lee looked at it. "That's the same one you had in Lhasa. I didn't want it then!"

We bought a few supplies—canned food, more noodles, no *tsampa*—and ate lunch in a slop shop where the proprietress dumped greasy soup on Wendy's shirt. Wendy made her wash it, a demand that brought astonishment, then compliance, but poor results. The woman did not use soap. She returned a wet shirt with grease spread around on it. For her part, Wendy felt she had at least made a point.

Then we were off on the last leg to Kailas. After thirty miles, we crossed the Gar Zangbo River just above its confluence with the Siquanhe. Together they formed the Indus River—the great Indus, flowing eighteen hundred miles from western Tibet through India and Pakistan, around Nanga Parbat, and through the sweltering Punjab to the Arabian Sea. India was fifty miles downstream from where we crossed. You could so easily float there in a few hours, but it was a good way to get shot. India and China were serious about that border. My map showed a road paralleling the river all the way to Pakistan. It might have existed once, or it might have been a mapmaker's fantasy. Certainly it is now impassable to anyone.

We looked down that valley as we went past and felt bad that such a natural route through the mountains was closed. Sven Hedin had similar feelings. Entranced by the interior of Tibet, but having been repeatedly turned away by various authorities, he complained that "If one can storm the opposing bulwark of Nature, one should be able to overcome the obstinacy of man." Pat put it differently: "Politics in mountains is like shit on an altar."

Even so, he was happy. We were driving at the base of a great line of white peaks on the other side of which was India. The sight of those mountains lifted Pat's spirits, which had been flattened somewhat by the bleak Chang Tang. When a smooth, razor-edged tower came into view, like something from the Karakoram Range, he became positively enthused. "Look at that! Now that's fine." He was a mountain guy, after all, and these were the mountains we had come to see.

In all the many places I had gone with Pat, his pleasure (or lack of it) could most easily be measured by his comments about mountains and the rock comprising them. Pat loved rock—the way it looked, the way it felt, the way it sounded when he tossed a pebble into a boulder field.

He paid attention to rock not as a geologist but as a climber, concerned less with its origins than with the feel of it under his boots, the texture against his hand, the line drawn by a clean rock face against the sky. He thought of it in aesthetic terms, but it was an odd aesthetic standard. Beauty might reflect the climb, not necessarily the shape of the rock. A massive, soaring mountain face might be gorgeous and enticing to the eye, but loose rubble, avalanche hazard, and exposure to weather would make it unattractive. That could change with the season. A mountain that was beautiful in summer weather could become nasty in winter. "I wouldn't want to be there when it's bad," he might say. Or "It's going to be horrible up there this winter." So while Pat could appreciate a mountain as a photographer, he could dislike and even fear it as a mountaineer.

It took two more days to reach Mount Kailas. Two days of gorgeous country and roads so rough we could hardly appreciate the surroundings.

By now, even Tashi had had enough. He complained to Naomi, "Chinese trucks! Chinese roads! Terrible! In America the roads are straight and wide and smooth, right?"

We traveled in spurts, no one willing to suffer the motion for more than an hour at a time. At each stop everyone piled out, Tashi too, and collapsed on the ground—in the road, in the dust, on the rocks. It felt very much like we were near the end of a journey.

Finally, topping a gentle rise, we came around the end of a black ridge, and there, alone against the hard blue sky, rose the gleaming, snow-covered summit of Mount Kailas.

5
The Holy Mountain

Our wanderings round Kang-rinpoche, the "holy ice mountain" or the "ice jewel," is one of my most memorable recollections of Tibet, and I quite understand how the Tibetans can regard as a divine sanctuary this wonderful mountain.
——Sven Hedin, *Transhimalaya*

This part of Western Tibet and the British Borderland is a country most sacred to the Hindus and Buddhists, and appealing as it does with its awful solemnity and weird grandeur of landscape to all that is romantic in the human soul, it is . . . the fit abode of the great gods of Hinduism and Buddhism.
——C. A. Sherring, *Western Tibet and the British Borderlands*

THERE WAS NEVER A MORE BEAUTIFUL CAMP than ours on the plain at the base of Kailas. The entire southern horizon was a sea of snowy mountains—the Himalaya of western Nepal and India. Mount Gurla Mandhata, 25,390 feet high, shrouded in glaciers, glowed like a science-fiction scene over the blue waters of Rakshas Tal. When the weather was clear, as it was much of the time, I could see the graceful summit Nanda Devi, near the headwaters of the Ganges River, and know that in four months we would be there ourselves.

It was monsoon season. In the evening, ragged clouds moved up from the south and, without dropping rain, became fiery as the sun went down. I had a sense of being raised up as if on a dome, so that everything around us was below us.

Except for Kailas. And Kailas was something to see.

It rose to the north of our camp, alone and elegant, a nearly perfect pyramid

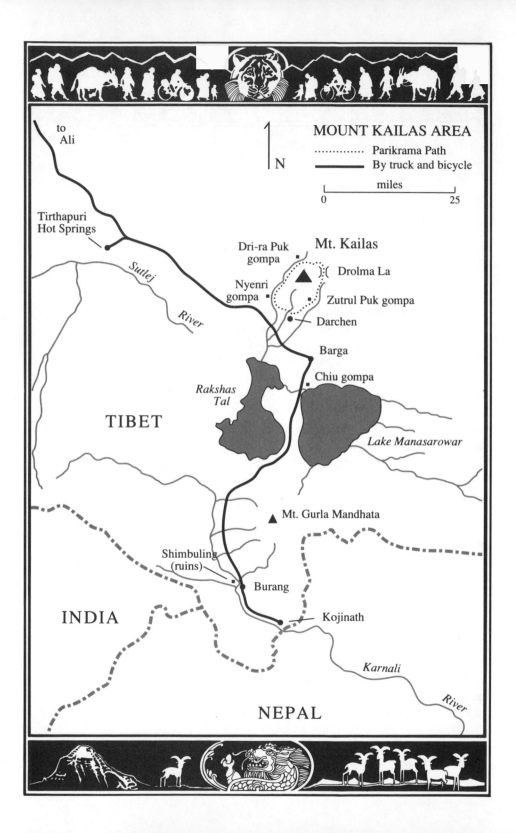

to
Ali

MOUNT KAILAS AREA

N

.... Parikrama Path
———— By truck and bicycle

miles

0   25

Tirthapuri
Hot Springs

Dri-ra Puk
gompa

Mt. Kailas

Drolma La

Nyenri
gompa

Zutrul Puk gompa

Darchen

Barga

Chiu gompa

Rakshas
Tal

TIBET

Lake Manasarowar

Mt. Gurla Mandhata

Shimbuling
(ruins)

Burang

Kojinath

INDIA

Karnali

River

NEPAL

of snow and ice and black rock, several thousand feet higher than any of the lesser summits around it, a peak almost unknown in the West but arguably the world's most famous and revered mountain.

Pilgrims—Hindu and Buddhist along with followers of more obscure creeds such as Bon and Jain—have been coming to Kailas for centuries. According to Hindus, Kailas is the abode of Shiva and his consort, Devi. The waters of heaven fall upon Shiva's head, disappear into his matted hair, and by various channels reappear as the sacred Ganges River on the other side of the Himalaya. For Buddhists, Kailas (Kangrinpoche in Tibetan) marks the spiritual center of the earth and the lowest level of heaven. Members of both faiths gain merit by making a pilgrimage to the area and walking around the mountain, or Lake Manasarowar, or both.

Over time, the circular route has become a thoroughly ritualized walk until almost every rock, every turn of the path, every aspect of the mountain has its own significance. Of its four symmetrical sides, the south face is sapphire, the west is ruby, the north is gold, and the east is silver or crystal.

Even without religious prominence, Kailas would be a significant mountain. Four major rivers rise within a few miles of its shining unclimbed summit: the Tsang-po (Brahmaputra), Indus, Sutlej, and Karnali. Of these, the Indus and the Tsang-po perform amazing journeys to opposite ends of the Himalaya, where each river falls through a spectacular gorge to the plains of the Indian subcontinent. In effect, these two rivers embrace the mountains, delineating the range from its spiritual high point, Kailas, all the way to the sea.

Sven Hedin also camped here, in 1907. Having entered Tibet, as always without permission, he had been caught and was being booted out of the country in the normal Tibetan style—polite and unhurried. In his own customary manner, Hedin was making the best of the situation, stalling and dragging his heels and dashing off to explore some new valley when no one was looking, then making amends later. It seems that he rarely offended anyone. He truly loved Tibet, and it must have showed, because officials, however firm they had to be, so often became his friends. At least that's the way he told it.

So when he arrived at the base of Kailas with his Tibetan escort and saw the sacred mountain shining above him, it was only natural that he made secret plans to follow the pilgrimage trail. Pretending he was going off on a short ride just for the day, he left his escort behind and sneaked in a three-day trip around the mountain—by his reckoning, the first Christian ever to do so. Although he hoped for accolades back home, in *Transhimalaya* he acknowledged his tiny place as just another of legions of devotees:

Thousands of pilgrims come hither annually, to pace slowly and in deep meditation the 28 miles round the navel of the earth, the mountain of salvation. I saw the silent procession. . . youths and maidens, strong men with wife and child, grey old men who would before their death follow in the footsteps of countless pilgrims to win a happier existence, ragged fellows who lived like parasites on the charity of the other pilgrims, scoundrels who had to do penance for a crime, robbers who had plundered peaceful travellers, chiefs, officials, herdsmen, and nomads, a varied train of shady humanity on the thorny road, which after interminable ages ends in the deep peace of Nirvana.

Now we were at Kailas on our own pilgrimage—around the holy mountain, around the Himalaya, in search of spiritual rewards and answers to our own personal cravings.

Tashi had left us with a scandalous quantity of gear. Mount Equipment, we called it: eight bikes, five tents, clothing enough to survive snowstorms and high winds, sleeping bags, forty days' food, a case of beer, gasoline for stoves, tool kits, water jugs, spare parts, eight sticks for beating off dogs, and lots more. The food included a formidable quantity of 761 bars, stale noodles, stale *tsampa,* and stale Nepalese cookies.

For the first day, everyone lay around enjoying the sensation of being on solid ground. We washed in the icy stream. We ate three cooked meals. We slept. Lee set off firecrackers to make up for the lack of New York City noise.

By late afternoon, the proximity of a wonderful mountain had worked its magic on Pat. He came to my tent, looked down at me with some sympathy, and tried to hide his big, hyperactive grin. "What do you think of heading out in the morning?"

"Tomorrow? Every time I stand up I get dizzy."

"That's okay. We can do it in shifts. You go when we get back."

After all, someone had to guard Mount Equipment. Pat recruited Baiba, Naomi, and Jeff. They left the next morning. From my seat on a grassy tussock I watched them until, specks on a distant moraine, they disappeared into the great western valley of Kailas.

Left behind, we sluggards spent three days lying in the tents and eating as much as we could hold. I was determined to accustom myself to *tsampa.* I was certain that I could find a way to make it palatable. In that, I partially succeeded and had a good time experimenting with various concoctions. In the end, however, sugar and milk worked best.

Gradually our health improved. Ant's eyes cleared up finally, and for the first time since leaving Lhasa he started smiling as if he meant it. Wendy and I felt more energetic each day. Lee, of course, had been fine from the start, maybe because he had spent an extra two weeks in Lhasa. Each day, I tried to bicycle somewhere, through the scrub and over the gravel flats. There were gentle hills to head for, but I never got to the top of one. At nearly 16,000 feet, pedaling on the flats was hard enough. It's amazing how long it takes a body to adjust to such altitudes.

On the third day, the four hikers appeared, right on schedule, iotas on the plains to the east. We saw them an hour before they arrived. Ant walked out to meet them carrying a quart of beer as a welcome home.

Pat was the first to arrive. He dropped his pack and collapsed behind the windbreak we had built. I handed him a bowl of hot noodles.

"How was it?"

"Longer than you think. It feels like we walked twenty-five miles today."

"We had six inches of snow on the pass yesterday," said Baiba, who came in right behind him. "Take warm clothes."

"But how was it? Are you enlightened?"

"Don't be impatient. You'll see." Pat sounded like an old lama talking to a novice. A happy lama. A lama who knew a good secret.

The next day, our turn. Wendy and I, with Lee and Antony, headed straight north, climbing gently through thorn scrub over a series of moraines. After four miles, topping the last moraine, we dropped into the La Chuu Valley on the west side of Kailas. In the absence of pilgrims I might have taken this for any high alpine valley. The La Chuu River was a beautiful thing, a clear mountain stream tumbling over boulders between banks of green tundra and carpets of pink forget-me-nots. Pikas, the same grey rock-rabbits that live in the alpine meadows of the Rockies, called in alarm from the tops of boulders and dove into burrows as we approached.

Across the river, we could see *chortens* and *mani* walls and people walking on the *Kang-kora,* the main pilgrimage trail. Buddhists and Hindus would be making their *parikramas* in a clockwise direction, as we were. Going counterclockwise were the Bon-pa, the followers of Bon, Tibet's ancient animist religion.

It was tempting to cross the river and join the other pilgrims, but we decided to stay on the west bank hoping for better views of the summit. The closer we got, however, the steeper the walls became, until Kailas disappeared. We walked in a canyon of wildly eroded reddish conglomerate streaked by thin cascades pouring off both sides. Occasionally we could look up a wild declivity guarded by pinnacles and towers and see the snowfields of Kailas peering down at us. At one of the waterfalls, eight blue sheep—argali—stood in deep shade against the cliff, holding still and almost invisible; they were the first we had seen, and the only big animals besides gazelles that we had seen all the way from Lhasa.

In theory, the Kailas area, being holy ground, is a sanctuary for wildlife. Buddhism forbids killing of any kind; devout Hindus will eat no meat, not even eggs. If sheep could survive anywhere in Tibet, it should be here, in the holy wilds of Kailas. That's how it used to be, and it might be true again in the future. But the recent past is another story because it includes the Cultural Revolution, when all rules and traditions were threatened, even in the most remote corners of Tibet. Wildlife suffered along with everything else, to the point of disappearance in much of the country. On top of that, vehicles and modern rifles had replaced the nomad's traditional way of hunting on foot with a cumbersome matchlock rifle or with dogs. All along the way from Lhasa, in valleys where visitors a century ago described seeing many wild animals, including wolves, gazelles, wild ass, wild yak, bears, blue sheep, geese, partridges, pheasants, and jackrabbits, I had seen only a few gazelles and thousands of pikas.

It was encouraging to think that as religious expression was again being tolerated in Tibet, wild animals, like Buddhist pilgrims, might find refuge in holy places.

When Hedin came this way near the turn of the century, there were five *gompas* spaced at intervals around Kailas. After the Cultural Revolution, not one of them was left standing, but now, as if to show that all things run in cycles, they were being reconstructed from their original stones.

The first one we came to was Nyenri *gompa* (Hedin called it Nyandi; Tibetan spelling has always confused people), perched on a terrace above the valley floor high enough for a view of Kailas. A small crew of Tibetan workers had nearly finished one simple room, a fine accomplishment, but they had a long way to go if they were to re-create the old *gompa*. Hedin described what was once there: an ornate altar brightly lit by votive lamps; a huge copper vessel said to have magically flown up from India in the distant past; silver bowls decorated with peacock feathers; a fine statue of Hlabsen, whom Hedin called "the god of Kang-rinpoche," decked in robes of gold brocade; an antechamber filled with "a whole arsenal of guns and swords and wooden and leathern shields"; and outside, rows of sculpted stone slabs bearing images of gods and the timeless mantra *Om mani padme hum.*

Much later, rereading Hedin's book *Transhimalaya,* I was struck by a passage I had missed the first time through. In his description of Nyenri *gompa* as he saw it in 1907, he mentions that half the original structure had been destroyed in 1902 by a huge rock that fell from the wall behind it: "The block still lies in the inner court... no one was hurt, but the monastery had to be rebuilt." So it had happened at least twice, once by a rock and once by a revolution.

With frequent stops and rubbery legs, we made slow progress up the valley.

Near its upper end, late in the afternoon, Kailas again came into sight, the west face now, the ruby face, crowned with snow and framed by grotesquely eroded pillars of stone—the gargoyles of Hlabsen's temple. Finding a meadow with a clear view of the summit, not far from the second *gompa* (a small structure unadorned by prayer flags and called Dri-ra Puk), we pitched camp. After supper I fell asleep easily, feeling entirely content.

It didn't last. Waking in the dark to the distant flash of monsoon lightning over India, I crawled outside on personal business and, standing there in the cold wind under black rock, became suddenly, inexplicably oppressed by the thought of the British man's death—the man we had heard about way back at the Latze ferry. I have no idea why it struck me just then. One moment I was marveling at the blackness of the night, the clarity of the stars, and the strange, flickering light from the south, and the next moment I was spooked. All I knew about the dead trekker was what Tashi had reported—that he was a strong, experienced mountain walker. He had died of exposure and altitude sickness and was given a sky burial—chopped up and offered to vultures in what Tibetans view as the most honorable way to dispose of the dead.

Although it had happened two weeks earlier, the feeling I had that night was as if I knew a man was dying at that moment, close by. It scared me.

I lay back down but did not sleep. I actually tried to stay awake, as if staying awake was a matter of survival. When I did fall asleep, I slept poorly. I kept rolling over, half awake, saying, "Not me, not me."

Several times I came fully awake, sat up, and opened the tent flap, and saw nothing but reassuring wild mountain scenery.

I have spent many nights in high, wind-filled valleys. Usually, I prefer them to any other place on earth. I have no idea why that night was different, and by morning those weird feelings were gone like a bad dream. But I remembered them, and decided that when I got a chance to do it, I should look up Tsarong Namdul.

I HAD HEARD about Tsarong Namdul in Lhasa. He was the caretaker of the travelers' lodge at Darchen, the cluster of tents and mud huts where most pilgrims began their walk around Kailas. He was said to have been educated in India. In addition, Tashi had told us that he was the man who had given the British trekker a sky burial.

I got my chance in Darchen two weeks later—on our way back to Ali—and spent an evening with him. He was a small Tibetan, in his late forties, with a quiet demeanor and a look of precarious health.

He said he had been born in Darchen. In 1960 he fled to India, where he spent nine years going to school in Kalimpong, Varanasi, and other places. He returned to Darchen in 1970, homesick and feeling that he should try to do something constructive there with his education. It was not to be. Assigned to a commune as a herder, he was made to wear a black hat identifying him as a spy and an enemy of the people. He wore that hat for twelve years. He had been allowed to take it off only recently, with the relaxing of Chinese policy. Now he was the manager of the Darchen Tourist Lodge, an employee of the state Committee on Religious Affairs.

We were sitting by candlelight in a cold room, wearing down parkas and sharing, of all things, a watermelon brought there by a truck driver from Kashgar. Tsarong was saying it felt good to live once again at the base of Kailas. I asked him how many times he had done *parikrama.*

"I have been eighty-four times."

"And if you go 108 times, you will be enlightened?"

"No." He thought for a moment, then said, "Yes. But if I do 108 times, I must do for all beings. Not for myself only. For myself it is no good; it must be for all beings. You see, in all lives, we come many ways—as person of the west, as person of the east, and as yak, or goat, or snake, and so we have two parents. One parent is all beings, all things, and I must care for all of them. If I do *parikrama* 108 times and only to make a record, or to tell the government, then this is nothing; it is for me only and it is a foolish thought.

"There are some pilgrims—two years ago, they come here for *parikrama,* and when they leave, they come to the pass, and they cannot see Kailas anymore. Tears come down their faces, so they come back. They say to me, 'We make one hundred times before we leave.' One hundred times, they say, and already they are here for two years."

"Still here after two years?"

"Yes. It is not so strange."

"But how do they live?"

"They are pilgrims. People give to them. And now, all they need is their journey."

"You mean their hundred times?"

"Yes."

"Why not 108? I thought that was the important number. 108 and you're done."

"No. One hundred, two hundred, the number is not so important. You see, in going *parikrama,* you learn how to go. Or going has no finish."

His thought lay at the heart of Buddhism: the journey is the destination, but only if the journey is performed in the correct fashion. The wrong sort of travel—and the wrong sort of life—never ends.

"We heard about a British man," I said. "A trekker who died."

■ *Above:* As we moved west, the landscape and the faces changed. In western China, Tadjiks and Uighurs of the Muslim religion greeted us with smiles and curiosity. The Tadjiks of Akash village were thrilled by Wendy's rubber finger puppets.

■ *Right:* A streetside acrobat draws a crowd, Xinjiang Autonomous Region, China.

■ *Above:* The bus station in Kashgar, Xinjiang Autonomous Region, China. We used public transport to get out of the city and away from suspicious officials who might have confiscated our bikes. ■ *Below:* Cycling past 24,757-foot Mount Muztagh Ata and Little Karakul Lake along the Karakoram Highway, Pamir Mountains, Xinjiang Autonomous Region, China.

■ *Above:* A crowd of Uighurs from a nearby construction camp inspects the inside of our tent, near the Pakistan border, on the Karakoram Highway, Xinjiang Autonomous Region, China. ■ *Below, left:* A local Kirhgiz boy welcomes us into his family's felt-skinned yurt on the grasslands below Mount Muztagh Ata, Xinjiang Autonomous Region, China.
■ *Below, right:* Baiba pushing through deep sand where the Karakoram Highway is being prepared for paving on the Chinese side of the border, Xinjiang Autonomous Region, China.

■ *Left:* A group of Hunza farmers separates the wheat from the chaff with wooden pitchforks in Baltit, northern Pakistan.

■ *Below:* Apricots, spread out to dry on this rooftop near Sost, are part of the diet recommended for longevity in the fabled Hunza Valley, northern Pakistan.

■ *Opposite:* Baiba on a trek up the Batura Glacier, near Passu, where the Karakoram Range shoots steeply out of the valleys.

■ *Left:* Shop in Skardu. A portrait of a scowling Ayatollah Khomeini overlooks this Shiite Muslim, Baltistan, northern Pakistan. ■ *Below:* A Uighur girl at a construction camp near the Pakistan border, on the Karakoram Highway, Xinjiang Autonomous Region, China.

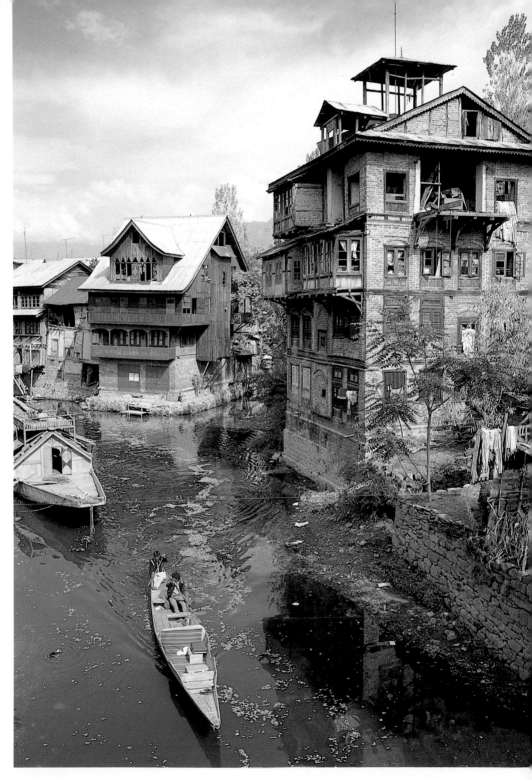

■ A *shikara* (water taxi) is the local form of transport along the canals of Srinagar, Kashmir, northern India.

■ *Above:* The verandah—or quarterdeck—of the *Kings Paradise* houseboat was a fine place to relax and recuperate. ■ *Below, left:* Eighteen-year-old bride Dilshad Sheikh decorated with *mandi* (henna patterns) on her palms and the soles of her feet, on the eve of her marriage, Srinagar, Kashmir, northern India. ■ *Below, right:* The groom arrived wearing a medallion of ten-rupee notes.

"Yes, I am very sad," said Tsarong, and he told me the story. Tsarong had met the man at the start of his ill-fated *parikrama*. On the first day, the man reached the base of Drolma La, the high pass, and there he was unable to continue. Nor could he go back down. Sick from the altitude, he could only crawl on the ground. He dragged himself to the stream for water, and it took him two hours, Tashi said, although it wasn't far.

"Did he tell you that before he died?"

"No. Tibetans told me."

"They saw him? Couldn't they have helped?"

"You mean Tibetans?"

"Yes."

"No, no, no, no. They see he is a foreigner, and he is sick. They are afraid."

"Of what?"

"The Chinese. 'You kill this man,' they might say. And then they would have big trouble."

"For trying to help?"

"For not helping enough."

"How sad. But they did tell you."

"No, no. Two Swiss people found him. Tourists. They write me a letter to come with a yak and send the letter with some Tibetans. But I am too late, and he is dead."

"Of altitude sickness?"

"I think so."

"So when you got there," I said, "you gave him a sky burial."

"Yes." He hesitated. "It is trouble."

"Trouble?"

"The two Swiss people. I ask them what can we do. They say the body is not ours, we don't know. I say we must take him out or bury him here. They say do it here. I say will you sign the papers and tell the *gong'an* [police] you are responsible, and they say yes, they will sign the papers.

"When the *gong'an* come, he is dead for a week. His body is gone. The police are angry. I tell them the Swiss people are responsible, but they say no, they will not sign now, and for me it is a big problem."

"The *gong'an* blame you? Because there is no body?"

He shrugged. There was a long silence. "I think," said Tsarong, "his death was here. He was not an ordinary person. He knew many religions. He knew Buddhism. He was a very peaceful man. Tibetans who meet him all feel he is the most peaceful person. He was younger than me. I feel very sad."

"How old was he?"

"I think thirty. Maybe. He was strong, very tall, a big man, but when he died the Tibetan people who see him say he is so old, he looked sixty or seventy years old. I think his death was here. Many vultures came, very fast. He was gone in less than one day."

"They don't always come so fast?"

"No, no, sometimes it takes weeks. This man was very strong spiritually. They take him very fast."

"Maybe he didn't need 108 times."

"Maybe. I think his death was here."

ON OUR SECOND DAY, we came around to the north face of Kailas, the face of gold, looming above in clear sight, trailing a plume of cloud and spindrift. It was nearly vertical, plastered with fluted snow between bands of black rock, and topped by a magnificent overhanging cornice. Every aspect of this mountain was superb.

Kailas has never been climbed, at least not by human mountaineers. Two British climbers, Colonel R. C. Wilson and Hugh Ruttledge, had a look at it in 1933 and decided they could climb the southeast ridge; but they were on a diplomatic mission at the time, and even had they come equipped for the mountain, clawing their way up its pristine snowcap would not have gone down well with their hosts. Not to mention the gods on the summit. Currently, any attempt would be illegal, and beyond that, no mountaineer who had any sensitivity for the meaning of mountains would try it. It's good to have some mountains with nothing on top of them but the sky. If any one mountain should be kept pristine, Kailas is it.

Crossing the river by hopping boulders, we joined the congenial stream of pilgrims. Hindus from India and Tibetan Buddhists, any of them could have stepped from the pages of Hedin's book ("the silent procession . . . youths and maidens, strong men, chiefs, officials, herdsmen, and nomads"), except that these people weren't at all silent. They greeted us enthusiastically, then went back to chanting their mantras. The Tibetans spun prayer wheels and fingered their beads. The Hindus, from India and Nepal, were as distinctive in their thin cotton clothing as the Tibetans were in their heavy homespun wool robes. Some traveled alone; others walked in groups. We went along with them and developed friendships through the exchange of small gifts such as chocolate and sunflower seeds.

They all looked happy. Everyone was enjoying the outing, smiling and asking questions we could neither understand nor answer. It was good to see their cheerful devotion, in contrast to the disturbing intensity of worship I had seen in Lhasa. The mountain had worked its spell on all of us, as mountains on sunny, warm days always do to any person who stands among them. I admired the Tibetans especially, so obviously at home on that trail, buoyed by their faith, burdened with light loads. Some carried nothing but a staff and a blanket. We, on the other hand, trudged along under the weight of our technical advantages—tents, cameras, cookstoves, sleeping bags—but we were also buoyed, by the simple pleasure of being on a mountain trail.

That was a good thing, because the trail became steeper at this point, climbing toward 18,600-foot Drolma La. The way was marked by important religious sites rather like the Catholic Stations of the Cross. Station one: the cemetery, where the view of Kailas's north face was the best we had seen so far. Piles of clothing, left to disintegrate, were all that remained of people who had died near enough to Kailas to be given this honor, most recently one British student of Buddhism.

Farther along, station two: Hundreds of little votive cairns formed a stunted forest. Hedin described them as "innumerable gravestones in a churchyard." Pilgrims had been so conscientious about piling stones that I was unable to find a loose one, so I satisfied my need to participate by replacing a stone that had fallen from an existing cairn.

Beyond the stone forest, a field of granite boulders. It was here that Hedin found a pilgrim lying dead, a desiccated bunch of rags "launched into new adventures among the dark mazes of the soul's migrations." Dying on Kailas was the Tibetan equivalent of dying in St. Peter's and being allowed to remain there surrounded by the symbols of one's faith until reduced to dust rising on currents of air beneath the sun-shafted dome.

A group of boulders leaned against one another like a natural Stonehenge— station three. As I watched, pilgrims came to these and pressed their foreheads against one stone, tracing worn grooves with their fingers. I had read that these grooves were considered to be the footprints of a great sage. Nearby, station four: a huge, flat boulder called *dipka-karnak,* the sinner's test stone. Only those of clear conscience are able to crawl through a tunnel under this stone; a scoundrel, however fat or thin he may be, will find it impossible. None of us was tempted to try.

Although I could distinguish no holy man's footprints in the rocks, nor believe in the capacity of a boulder to separate sinners from saints, I had fallen under the spell of this mountain. By Western measurements, Kailas is no more than a well-formed mass of conglomerate on a granite base, a hunk of unthinking, uninhabited rock. You could land a helicopter on top and find no gods perched up there watching the little human figures march around its base. Yet the mountain is special for many reasons, not the least of which is that millions upon millions of those tiny figures, for many hundreds of years, from all corners of Asia, have performed devotions and lifted their thoughts toward the same lofty summit. I remembered an old Hindu sentiment that it is good to kneel where others have knelt, and to bow where others have bowed before you, because God is present in those places. A simple act of reverence, repeated thousands of times over many centuries, consecrates any piece of ground. By honoring such a place, you honor all of creation, past and future, and with it, humanity's long attempt to grasp the great and daily mystery of being alive.

When I reached the pass, I was breathing pretty hard. Even Hedin, the redoubtable veteran of high winter wastes, having ridden a horse to the pass, called Drolma La "one of the most troublesome [passes] on the whole journey," which is hard to believe considering the ones he had crossed in chest-deep snow as his animals gave up and died around him, but encouraging to me, considering how tired I was. If Hedin could see it as a challenge, who was I to argue?

The pass itself was marked by an enormous boulder decked with hundreds of bright prayer flags snapping in the cold wind and heaps of other offerings—carved yak skulls, clothing, hanks of hair, teeth, beads, whatever people had to leave. It was a primitive and wild place to be standing.

But the sun was low; we hurried on, down a twisting path through talus, past two black-water tarns set among jagged rocks: the Gourikund lakes, considered by some Tibetans to be oracular. Almost always frozen, their thawing is taken as a bad sign. As the story goes, the lakes thawed in 1959 when the Chinese took over Lhasa. They were also unfrozen when we went past.

"If you were a true pilgrim, you'd stop for a bath," I told Lee.

"Uh-huh," he nodded. "Let's see what this guy does."

Behind us came a Tibetan, moving fast, carrying a tin pot in one hand and, in the other, a gasoline blowtorch—a piece of hardware we had seen truck drivers using to heat cans of food along the road.

The man said hello and jogged past us without a glance at the lake. Lee looked at me sideways. "If I read the oracle right, the thing to do is cook supper."

Agreed. An hour later we were at the foot of the pass, where we put our tents on sloping ground in a deafening wind. As it grew dark, the stars came out, and with them, high on the valley wall opposite Kailas, two tiny campfires burned, far apart, presumably in caves. To me it was like seeing campfires on the moon. People were up there, thousands of feet above us, sitting by wind-blown flames and watching the heavens revolve around sacred Kailas, center of the universe and the first step to heaven.

Early the next morning, our third day, we came to the third *gompa,* Zutrul Puk, standing at the base of a cliff. It was the color of the cliff and hard to see. A few bright prayer flags flew from its roof or we might have missed it entirely.

While Lee and Antony went on down the trail, Wendy and I climbed to the *gompa* entrance and followed a short corridor to a courtyard. Over the door someone had hung a garland of scapulas from sheep or goats with prayers written on them. They clattered in the breeze like wind chimes. Off the courtyard was the door to the kitchen, where an elderly pilgrim, a man we'd kept pace with for two days, sat eating *tsampa* from a wooden bowl. He looked up, smiled in recognition, and said something through the doorway, whereupon another man, wearing a tan knitted cap, a jacket, and trousers, came out to greet us. He looked like anyone but the lama of Zutrul Puk, but that's exactly who he was. He stood less than five feet tall, about fifty years old, with a sturdy, friendly face. Spreading a yak-hair mat in the courtyard, he gestured for us to sit on it.

Like the other *gompas* around Kailas, Zutrul Puk had been reduced to rubble, and from out of the rubble at least some of it had risen. A crew of Tibetans was hard at work using old stones salvaged from the ruins, making mortar on the spot from water and native earth.

It felt good to sit in the warm sun out of the wind.

After a time, the lama came to sit beside us. I asked questions through gesture and primer Tibetan.

"You are rebuilding the *gompa*?"

"Yes, for four years. I have lived here two years."

"Where did you live before?" I asked, but my question didn't translate. The lama just looked puzzled. I tried another. "This is Zutrul Puk *gompa*?"

"Yes. Milarepa built it."

One of Tibet's great saints, Milarepa was a poet and a powerful mystic. He lived in the eleventh century, when Buddhism was struggling for acceptance against Bon, Tibet's ancient animist religion. It was Milarepa who proved the superiority of Buddhism by defeating Bon's greatest wizard in a magic contest. The contest took place around Lake Manasarowar and Mount Kailas, with no decisive result until the last challenge was laid—a race to the summit of Kailas. The Bon wizard took off before dawn, flying on a drum. This upset Milarepa's followers, who urged him to go: look, the wizard is already halfway there! But Milarepa waited patiently for sunrise and was carried by the first ray of light instantly to the summit. Or, depending on where you read the story, he leaped in a single bound. Anyway, he beat the wizard, and even the wizard had to admit that Buddhism was more powerful than Bon.

Zutrul Puk *gompa* had been dedicated to Milarepa and the victory of Buddhism.

The lama stood and took us into the prayer hall. It was a poor place, with no windows and a dirt floor, lit only by a skylight. Bare wooden poles supported the ceiling. I thumped one with my hand. Our guide saw the gesture and said, "Do you know what one pole costs? Fifteen yuan! They come all the way from Nepal."

On a shelf, there was a row of small brass Buddhas, pictures of the Dalai Lama and other important teachers, and a few elaborate sculptures made from colored butter. One small drum hung above a prayer mat. Beside it, on a tiny table, wooden bowls held offerings of *tsampa,* rice, incense, and money, including an American dollar bill. There was a cave at the end of the room. We crouched down to look in. A single butter lamp burned there, revealing brass statues of Milarepa and other figures. We gave the keeper a picture of the Dalai Lama. He didn't have one like it. He said, "Oh, oh, oh. Yeah, yeah, yeah, oh yeah," as he touched it to his head in reverence.

He was placing the picture among the other offerings when a middle-aged Tibetan holding a string of prayer beads entered. The lama spoke with him and then politely asked us to leave. Going out, I turned at the door to see both men on their knees in the cave, the lama with his arm on the man's shoulders. They were saying prayers.

Later I learned that Milarepa built not the *gompa* but the cave around which it was built. It happened during his epic battle with the Bon wizard. To provide a rain shelter, Milarepa lifted the cave's roof into place, leaving the imprint of his hands and head in the stone. Had I known that at the time, we might have looked for the prints on the cave roof.

While we visited the *gompa,* Antony and Lee were ahead, getting a tour from an English-speaking Tibetan whom they had met on the trail. On a flat bench above the Zhongchuu River, behind a *mani* wall, he showed them three depressions in the bedrock—the footprints of Milarepa, made when the great sage leaped to the top of Kailas. Antony wanted to know why there were three marks instead of two, but their guide treated the question as a foolish one. Farther along, they came to a tiny cave, scarcely a hole in the cliff, filled with bits of hair and other things. This one was a place to leave offerings for protection. It worked, said the Tibetan: the lives of two local people had been saved recently because they had made offerings there.

From Zutrul Puk, the trail followed a wonderful gorge of colored shales. When it opened onto views of Gurla Mandhata and the lakes, we knew we were near the end of the trek. Others, however, had yet a long way to go. On the trail were five people taking the slow way around: performing *gyangchag-tsallgen,* the prostrating of oneself around Kailas. Three men and two women, they wore leather aprons for protection against the stones and oversized mittens on their hands. Hedin described prostrators who no doubt looked much like these people. They could make a circuit in about twenty days, he said, a little more than one mile a day. One man in particular impressed him—a robber who was doing penance for crimes committed and then doing more penance for crimes he might commit in the future. Putting karma in the bank, so to speak.

Seeing them made me feel for the first time like a speedy walker, a virtual *lung-gompa,* or trance walker. Soon the trail spilled onto the plain south of Kailas, and that was my favorite part of the walk, striding along toward our distant camp with Gurla Mandhata on my left and Kailas, shining in the late-afternoon sun, on my right. Part way there, we passed six heavily laden Tibetans walking across the plain toward the mountain. They came within half a mile of us and then, as we walked apart, became dark specks in that epic landscape. I wondered how far they had come. Even now, in a time when trucks and telephone wires cross Tibet, people walk, as they have for centuries, the hundreds of open miles to Kailas. Something about that enduring landscape and its enduring people made me think that centuries from now, when all the borders are different and all the turbulence of these strange times is finished, Tibetans will still be walking around Kailas.

6
Bicycles to Burang

The Manasarowar lake lies, 16000 ft. above sea level and surrounded on all sides by bleak, naked, black and granite mountains whose peaks are covered with snow and it is the most beautiful sight among the very beautiful sights of the earth. A large number of small swans are visible on the surface of the lake and flocks of swans are raising wierd cry.
————Badri Kedar (pilgrims' guidebook)

I love trying things and discovering how I hate them.
————D. H. Lawrence (letter to a friend)

"TOO MUCH GEAR," Pat was saying, surrounded by all the things we had thought essential.

We were trying to pack the bicycles. Friends with expertise in cycling had warned us that forty pounds was an excessive weight.

"How much do you think you have?" I asked.

"With the bike I'll bet it's a hundred pounds."

We all had as much. Discarded food, clothing, and other gear gradually grew into a sizable heap as we tried to reduce our loads.

"What do we do with all this, just leave it here?"

"How about these guys?" Pat meant the Tibetan herders who had come past our camp many times during our stay, occasionally going home with small gifts from us. Three of them now stood watching our amazing display of stuff.

We piled the surplus neatly, zipping most of it into several large burlap duffels. I made gestures to the Tibetans: "Wait a few minutes, and you can have what you want." They showed keen interest, I thought.

As for trash, we dug a hole three feet deep. Everything went in there. Topping it off with a sprinkle of stove fuel, I set it afire. Ant and I stirred the blaze to get a thorough burn before refilling the hole with dirt. The Tibetans had moved back a hundred yards.

"What do you suppose they think we're doing?" asked Ant. The Tibetan method of dealing with trash was tossing it to the wind.

"Some strange foreign rite, I suppose."

"Like this?" Ant began dancing around the flames. I joined him. We spun our sticks, leaped over the fire, and made gibberish noises. Ant suddenly stopped. "Look at that!"

The three Tibetans were running through the thornbush away from us. I had never seen them run before, and more than two weeks later, on our way back past Kailas, we saw that our neat discard pile had not been touched. In my mind's eye, it is there still. People are piling stones on it now. Gradually, it is becoming a *mani* wall, a monument to join the other revered sites on the Kailas trail.

We left that afternoon, headed toward Lake Manasarowar and Burang, a trading community on the Nepalese border. Knowing the border was closed to us, we nonetheless wanted to see the snowy crest of the Himalaya at closer range before heading on west.

It gave me a great feeling of freedom, to be on the bicycle at last, pushed eastward by a strong wind across the plains. The road was smooth, and despite continual adjustments to our loads, we covered about twelve miles in three hours, making camp under a windy, spectacular sky beside a nearly dry slough. I collected cooking water from a yak's hoofprint, the only place deep enough to accept my cup.

Later, as we sat eating supper from a communal pot, Naomi made an announcement. "I figured out why I've been feeling rotten," she said.

"You have?" I said.

"High-altitude morning sickness."

"No kidding? Is this a surprise?"

"Not entirely."

"Well, congratulations. I guess. Are you worried about the altitude?"

"Tibetan women do it all the time."

"Yeah, but on a bicycle?"

I was impressed. After a month in Tibet, and lots of physical activity, I was still not fully acclimated. It was all I could do to manage basic tasks.

That became obvious the next day. It began with two hours of easy pedaling to a place called Barga. The road, on smooth, packed earth, followed a telephone line. I was surprised to see how common phone lines were in Tibet, considering how rarely we came across an actual telephone outside of Lhasa, and of those, I never did hear one ring, or see anyone using one. Nonetheless, the poles marched across the landscape like picket fences and symbols of national unity: every one in line, linked by common purpose, attached ultimately to Beijing and the source of power.

The place called Barga was an old mud fort with clay gun turrets on its flat roof, standing guard over a fork in the road. Uncertain about which way to go, we stopped outside the compound. I was just laying my bike on the ground, intending to knock on a wooden door, when a huge mastiff rocketed out from a hole in the wall. He flipped over on his back when he hit the end of his rope, got up, and came at me again. Purely by luck, I had stopped about three feet farther than his rope would reach, but that didn't stop him. He was determined to stretch it or break it and turn me into a suitable offering to the vultures. We all backed up.

A woman came out to see what the racket was about, kicked the dog into silence, and said hello to us as if we were just the most normal sight in western Tibet.

"Burang?" I said, pointing to the southern road.

"Burang!" she said, nodding and laughing. Burang seemed to be a great joke.

Maybe she had tried bicycling that road. For starters, it led up a slope the scale of which was impossible to judge without trees or buildings. It looked to be 200 or 300 feet high but turned out to be more like 1000. Getting to the top took us until noon. I could barely manage to pedal about 100 feet before stopping to pant for a few minutes. When I finally reached the pass, I lay down on the gravel and fell asleep for half an hour. Having overexerted, I couldn't eat. Then it was down a long slope toward the shore of Lake Manasarowar.

By the time we dumped our bikes on the smooth cobblestone beach at the base of a spectacular little *gompa,* all I wanted was to close my eyes and lie on the shingle. I was doing that when Wendy announced other plans.

"Let's get this tent up."

"Are you being crabby?"

She looked fierce. "I want to get the tent up so I can go to the *gompa.*" I didn't see the connection. "Go to the *gompa.* I'll put up the tent." What I really meant was "Go while I pass out here on the beach." But we put up the tent, and her gomping plans proved to be the reflex of a diligent traveler, because we both fell into the tent, feet sticking out the door, and were asleep in the afternoon sun.

Later, I sat watching fish jump in the sacred water and thought I wanted to catch one. Our diet of unmitigated starch had made me think that a stiff dose of protein might improve my energy. So I rigged a line using dental floss and a hook fashioned from a spare bicycle spoke and baited it with Italian sausage (which I pilfered from a tiny stash Lee had been carefully husbanding), all the time worrying that it must be a sacrilege to kill a fish from the holy lake. I had read that Tibetan Buddhists considered fishermen to be among the lowest levels of humanity, lower even than butchers, who were certainly down there. So I watched, waiting until I thought none of the Tibetan pilgrims who were also camped on the beach was on the lookout, and heaved my equipment into the water. Still, my conscience bothered me. I felt as if I were casting in the baptismal font at a church. Finally, seeing two pilgrims headed my way, performing their lakeside devotions, I ran to the water, pulled in the line, and gave up on the idea.

Four months later I learned that Tibetans give pregnant women dried fish from Manasarowar to ease the pain of labor, so I suppose they do catch them.

Neither Manasarowar nor its near twin, Rakshas Tal, has a surface outlet. They are both tarns, fed by numerous permanent and seasonal streams flowing from the surrounding mountains. According to religious belief, Rakshas Tal is a black lake, allied with the darker forces of life (*rakshas* being a class of demons). As such it balances the sacred vessel of Manasarowar, recipient of water emanating directly from heaven via Mount Kailas. Having gathered itself in the lake, the same water, moving through underground channels, reappears as the four sources of the Ganges River in India.

In Manasarowar, the springs of heaven are so powerful that they raise the middle of the lake. When he launched his portable boat on a survey expedition, Hedin was told that he would never reach the center of the lake because it was uphill all the way, but if by some unlikely happenstance he managed to get there, he need not worry about storms. The peaceful center of heaven's lake is said to remain calm on the windiest of days, when breakers beat against the rocky shores. Hedin never had to test that theory. He rowed back and forth numerous times without incident, mapping the lake bottom. At its deepest, it was 269 feet.

Finally, in the evening, Wendy and I climbed the hill to the *gompa*. Its name was Chiu, which means bird, and like so many spectacular Tibetan buildings, it occupied a place more suitable for birds than people—a sharp pinnacle of red rock high enough for a fine view of Kailas.

Like the *gompas* at Kailas, Chiu had been destroyed and partially rebuilt, beginning in 1983. Even so, it looked ancient, its architecture timeless.

We called hello at the entrance. Hearing us, a young monk emerged and cordially showed us to the main prayer hall, a small but well-equipped room. *Thankas* hung around the walls, some new and some so old that no discernible picture remained. There were two drums painted blue, a wooden frame filled with Dalai Lama pictures, posters of holy places in Tibet, *katas* (white ceremonial scarves) hanging from a wire, and various statues.

It was a neatly kept room with a bright view of the lake, and I liked being there. In the warm evening light, the atmosphere was almost Mediterranean—blue water, white walls, the sound of shore birds heard through an open window.

Leaving that room, following a winding stone stairway, we came to a heavy wooden door. It had to be lifted by a steel ring like a trap door. "Guru Rinpoche," said the young monk; he was referring to Padmasambhava, the saint who brought Buddhism to Tibet in the eighth century. He is said to have spent the last seven days of his life in this place. Peering in, I could discern stone slabs leading into blackness. Wendy sparked a propane lighter, in the glow of which we entered a cave the size of a closet, its walls lined with cloth, three statues at one end, brass bowls of water on a shelf in front of them.

Wendy put out the flame. We were both so tired that we sat on the bottom step for a while, in total darkness. Somewhere, in some other room, a drum began beating, low and steady and hypnotic, sounding through the living rock. Droong, droong, droong—it could have been the heartbeat of the mountain.

By the time we came out, the sun was setting. The hills were orange. A pretty young woman with only three front teeth and her daughter in her arms came out to see us off and to give us a gift—a handful of puffed barley still hot from her pan. We smiled and bowed to each other. The baby wore a hand-knitted cap, which Wendy admired; then she brought out her own knitting, a mitten in progress, which was in turn admired. The woman then pointed to my camera with a questioning look, so I lifted it as if to make a picture, and she ran back inside calling to her husband. A moment later he came out behind her to pose for a family picture, on the terrace of their *gompa*, with Manasarowar and Gurla Mandhata in the background. Finally, beneath the rose-tinted sky, we left with feelings that had become all too familiar: I loved this place and its people. I was moved by the beauty of their chosen setting. And I felt like an oaf, not being able to talk with them.

Before dawn the next morning, I climbed a hill from which I could see Kailas, Manasarowar, and Chiu *gompa* all in one view. Sunrise was a pale golden shiver in the east. It colored the lake and gave the white-painted *gompa* a warm glow. Ducks flew in shoals, landing on the calm water and taking off again in a shimmer of wavelets and a clatter of feathers. A dog came up the hill to sit beside me. We waited together as the sky intensified. Suddenly Kailas ignited—first red, then yellow, then white—and then the sun spilled over the black rim of Manasarowar. At that instant, just as the first rays touched the prayer flags, someone inside the *gompa* released a puff of white juniper smoke into the air. A salute. An acknowledgment of the surrounding world and its ancient rhythms. I needed no common language to understand that sentiment.

WHEN READING the old books recounting European explorations of Tibet, you begin to notice a certain similarity among them. After ambitious beginnings filled with details and sharp observation, their writers often lapse into dull recitation of itineraries. For example, in his *Diary of a Journey Across Tibet,* Hamilton Bower wrote:

> Camp 77—After the march the Tibetans made out that we would have to do another five marches before beginning to descend.
> Camp 78—About 5 miles of the march lay along a road that comes from Tuman Chaka; after leaving it we went about 6 miles to a place where there was a pool of water not quite frozen to the bottom, and camped.
> Camp 79—After leaving the last camp we ascended a small and easy pass, and descended into a wide open valley in which some yak were grazing. To the north-east a range of mountains with some fine snowy peaks, evidently the Dang La range, was seen, and in the valley a stream was flowing in an east-south-east direction.

In Tibet, in this wonderful landscape that has the power to grab your heart and hold it hard, this place of great, empty, reverberating silence where the land lies open to the sky and you really could imagine God wanting to live there—in this huge, powerful place, you nonetheless find yourself plodding along from stage to stage in a dizzy sort of dream, too small for the surroundings and too tired to ponder the improbability of being there. The sun shines bright and hot. The air is thin. Shadows stab the ground like black ice. But it's hard to pay attention.

It's hard to think of anything beyond getting down the road. And then a sacrilegious thought pops uninvited into your mind. You begin to consider if Tibet isn't best appreciated as a memory, something to polish up and keep in the nostalgia kit for the greying years. That rocky road past Gurla Mandhata: how will it play in old age? That's the important thing.

I thought about that over the next four days, bicycling to Burang past Rakshas Tal (not black at all but lambent turquoise, ringed by glowing pastel hills) and around the shoulder of Gurla Mandhata. I told myself to appreciate what I was seeing then, to pay attention, because I might never return. The glaciers were magnificent, the lake glittered in the sun, icy torrents poured down each ravine, and Kailas, visible much of the time, raised its perfect summit above the whole scene.

For centuries, southern pilgrims have come this way, up from India, through ranks of mountains to the high plains, and suddenly, standing alone and formidable across the waters of Rakshas Tal, there is Kailas, touching the sapphire sky. Seen from here, who could doubt its holy nature? There are many higher mountains, but none so singular.

Frequently I would stop my bicycle just to stare, fixing the view in my memory, before turning reluctantly back to the road.

Travel, according to some, is not genuine without travail; as if hardship is the only means of knowing a place. I disagree with the premise, but I understand the basis of the idea, especially in reference to somewhere like Tibet. If travel is too easy, you miss something important, something intrinsic to life in a hard land. If you wish to understand a place, you should move through it the way local people do, not in the isolated artificiality of a tourist coach.

On the other hand, difficulty for its own sake is meaningless. It's also boring, unless it occurs on an epic scale, like Shackleton's experience in the Antarctic. By and large, when the road is rough, everyone finds it rough—and dusty and tedious. The sun shines equally hot on all heads, and it isn't worth much that I thought bicycling was an inappropriate way to travel between Kailas and Burang.

Even so, bicycling in Tibet is worth describing one time, if only to serve as a warning. Local people walk, and I don't wonder why. First of all, there's the ungraded track that passes for a road. Glacial cobblestones the size of melons go for miles at a time. They jolt you, throw you off balance, and roll under your tires. You take it in the arms, shoulders, and eventually in the stomach. The pace is slower than walking.

Where cobbles leave off, you get corrugations. The pace remains slow, but the jolting is rhythmic now, predictable, punishing like a Chinese water torture—bump, bump, bump, bump—until you have to stop and recollect your wits.

Sand stops you dead. Hit a small patch, and it wrenches the front wheel sideways, throws you over the handlebars, lands you on your face. If you're lucky, you avoid smashing your groin on the handlebars as you plunge forward.

Where glacial dust as fine as talc lies six inches deep over cobbles or loose gravel, it is impossible to ride, even downhill. You walk and cough, dragging the bicycle's dead weight.

Distances in Tibet are enormous. Pedal all day across a flat plain and you still might camp in a place that seems no different from your starting point.

The lack of scale plays tricks with your vision. Coming over a rise, I once saw a truck ahead, lying on its side, debris spilled beside it. An accident, I thought. Then, astonishingly, the debris collected itself and stood up. It was Jeff. He had been resting beside his tipped-over bike—not a truck at all.

It works the other way. You look ahead at a low pass. It seems close. You start grinding uphill and realize, as minutes turn to hours, that the summit is actually a long way ahead.

The Tibetan sun is unreasonably hot but so intense that you have to wear full clothing; even drenched with sunblock, exposed skin burns bright red, then blisters. Worst of all, the road surface is so demanding you can't look at the scenery. Glance up for a moment, and the bike goes off the road. It does that often enough without your glancing up.

Although I wrote daily in my diary, the entries were rather stunted—a bit like those of Hamilton Bower. I might as well have written: We went past Gurla Mandhata for four days and arrived at Burang.

Burang was a blast.

Down we came over dusty moraines into an irrigated valley where substantial stone farmhouses sat among green fields of barley and mustard—the first crops we'd seen since Latze, way back on the Tsang-po River. After the Chang Tang, Burang felt nearly tropical. Generous supplies of water came from torrents streaming off Gurla Mandhata, before joining the Karnali River on its hurried course to Nepal.

Beyond Burang, to the south, a line of high peaks, snow-covered and partly obscured by monsoon clouds, marked the border. It was raining lightly that day, giving the impression that enormous pent-up moisture waited on the other side, as if the peaks held back an ocean and we were feeling just the spray.

Near the edge of the settlement we met twelve Nepalis headed for Lake Manasarowar, walking. They were Hindus led by an old man carrying a conch shell and an iron trident—the symbol of Shiva. Five women, two of them elderly, wore colorful saris and sweaters. The men were dressed in homespun pants and *dhotis* (white cotton loincloths) and Nepali Brahmin hats. They seemed wildly exotic, in the way Tibetans had upon first encounter. Now even the gaudy Khampas seemed commonplace beside these brightly spangled southern people.

"Where are you from?" Jeff asked, speaking Nepali.

"Simikot."

"How many days is that?"

"*Saat.*" Seven. In Nepal, distance is measured by the number of days it takes to walk somewhere.

"Is it raining now in Simikot?"

"Yes. Monsoon."

We admired the women's jewelry. Strings of beads and Indian silver coins encircled their necks. Big brass medallions hung from their ears. They had brass ornaments on their foreheads, coins on their fingers, gold pins in their noses, and I wouldn't be surprised if some had bells on their toes. Shaking their heads, they sounded like wind chimes.

Everyone enjoyed the banter except a young man who lay on the ground moaning.

"This one is sick," said the old man with the trident.

"Not only that, he looks about half dead," said Ant.

"Looks like you did three weeks ago," said Naomi.

"I didn't look *that* bad. Did I?"

"What is it?" Jeff asked the old man. "Stomach? Head?"

"Yes. Stomach and head."

"When did he get sick?"

"One day before today."

"Probably altitude," said Jeff.

"You have pills?" asked the old man. "You give him something?"

Jeff told him no. Even aspirin, to a person who's never had it, can be a powerful drug.

"He needs water," said Pat. "Lots of water. He's dehydrated. And put out the cigarette." The sick man had just lit up a raw-smelling Nepali brand. Pat loathed smoking with a religious zeal. I think he would walk around Kailas 108 times if it meant he would never again have to endure someone's cigarette smoke.

"He does not like water," said the old man. "You have pills."

"But he needs water."

"Please. Pills."

"Sorry. He really should stop smoking."

They stood then, shouldered their loads, and straggled cheerfully uphill toward the lake of salvation. We wished them luck and bounced on down to Burang.

Burang was a market town, a crossroads busy with pilgrims, sheep, goats, yaks, horses, and border traders of all scale. Prosperous merchants sat in rented shops crammed with the goods they had brought in caravans from India or Nepal, while out in the streets sat small-scale traders with nothing but tin trunks of cookies and trinkets. They carried their trunks on their backs.

They would set up shop along the streets in the dust each morning, then pack up in the evening and return to campsites in the hills. When the trunk was empty, or filled with trade goods, it was back to Nepal for another load.

Some Nepalis came here to buy Tibetan goats and sheep, often loading their herds with leather sacks filled with salt. The salt came from the enormous evaporating lakes we had ridden past in the Chang Tang with Tashi. It had been carried to Burang in trucks and on the backs of animals. Now, transferred to sacks, it would continue to Nepal on sheep. Not all the sheep were sold; many had come only to be sheared of their wool. The wool, twisted into ropes an inch or two thick, was then bound up in bales weighing fifty pounds or more, while *dzos,* crossbred yak and cattle, stood quietly waiting to be loaded.

Tibetan nomads on horseback came from long distances to do business in Burang. As in a scene from an American western, they would canter the last half a mile into town, their horses fancied up with strings of bells, brightly colored saddle blankets, and silver ornaments, arriving in a splash of color and sound. I spotted several old matchlock rifles with support forks protruding past the barrels; they could have been two hundred years old.

We rode our bikes into town with a lot less fanfare and no desire to be the center of attention; but we created a bigger scene. Outlanders on bikes, nylon windjackets flapping! The crowds convened from all sides. It was as if Barnum and Bailey's had arrived complete with elephants and steam calliopes. Children, adults, men and women pushed each other to get close to us. We pushed back, trying to move through the crowd. The bicycles fascinated them. They seemed incapable of keeping their hands off brake levers and gear shifters. They fingered our clothing and pulled at our hair, all in good humor; but even so, the crush was a bit frightening after so many weeks in the open solitude of the plateau.

Because Burang was too rowdy a place for camping, our main interest was in finding a hotel. There were two, if you could call them that. One, near the center of town, was a dark, mud hovel that might have been good enough for us, but it was full. The other was relatively new, a government hotel built, apparently, in anticipation of the same tourists who had not arrived in Ali. In fact, we learned later, it was run by the same work unit, and we might have guessed that ourselves after meeting the sullen staff.

Once again, the same routine. Are there rooms? No, said an unsmiling young woman from some faraway home for which she pined. But there must be rooms; this place is empty! Well, maybe, she said, and shuffling over to a battered door, she showed us into a filthy room with broken windows, unswept floors, heaps of trash, and dirty quilts on sagging bunks. The room next door was just as bad. We protested and were led across the yard, kicking green beer bottles out of the way, to another set of rooms just as dirty but a little larger. Deluxe quarters, the little sweetheart announced, at fifteen yuan per bed. Naomi told her that a year earlier she had stayed in the same hotel for only eight yuan. "Well, we weren't here then," said the girl. "No," said Naomi, "it was nicer before," and with that they were off to a lively negotiation that lasted two hours while the rest of us sat around kicking the dust. The result? We took the larger rooms for the full price, fifteen yuan per bed.

It was the first time I'd ever seen Naomi lose a case. She was steaming, but she wasn't finished. Holding up an empty thermos, she said, "Is there hot water?"

"I don't know," said the girl. "I'll check."

An hour later, Naomi repeated the question and got the same answer. The girl turned to leave.

"Will there be hot water in the morning?" Naomi asked.

"I don't know."

"Is this China?"

"Yes."

"Everywhere in China we get hot water in the morning."

"Maybe. Okay. In the morning, one thermos."

"One thermos for each person."

"No."

"Yes."

The girl shrugged and trudged off to her quarters.

We finally used campstoves to heat water from an irrigation ditch, muttering about three thousand years of civilization. "Sometimes I think all these hotel workers go to the same training school." said Ant. "They probably call it the Zen of transactional abuse or something."

The next morning we met another charmer. Four of us sat at a table for breakfast. Other tables were occupied by blue-suited Chinese and Tibetan workers. The woman who ran the kitchen brought bowls and chopsticks to our table. She slammed the bowls down hard. There were only two pairs of chopsticks. She put them at the empty places rather than give them to us.

"Goddamnit," said Pat, reaching across the table for a pair. "This country is run by a network of dunces."

I pulled my spoon from my pocket.

Wendy took her bowl over to the communal pot of rice porridge—the staple of Chinese breakfast. A man sitting near the pot told her, "*Meiyou!*" No! You can't have that. She helped herself anyway and came back saying, "What's going on here? I don't understand the rules."

Later, when all eight of us were at the table, we asked the kitchen woman for more steamed bread, having watched the Chinese eaters emerge from the kitchen with heaping plates of it. She shook her head and went away. Someone said, "We'll have to go to the kitchen and take it."

"Not I," said Naomi. She had come close to losing her temper with the hotel staff the day before and didn't want to risk an encounter.

"Well, that's real useful," said Lee.

"What?"

"Real useful attitude. You're the only person who can talk with her and you won't."

Lee and Naomi appeared destined for a blowout. Wendy, sensitive to the mood, got up, went to the kitchen, and returned with a plate of steamed bread. She was followed by a Chinese man, one of the other diners, who scooped fermented tofu—delicious stuff, rather like bleu cheese—from a jar onto our plate and smiled at us. We thanked him profusely and felt better. He had been sitting at a table nearby and apparently understood something about the procedure for getting fed that we did not. His was another of many unbidden acts of generosity that had continually softened our feelings about China and its people and made me wonder how much we really understood.

Even so, we needed another place to eat, and that evening we found a privately run restaurant near the river. It had one room, a packed-dirt floor, and blue plastic tablecloths nailed to dirt walls. Two battered fifty-gallon drums shared the space with three tables laid with pink plastic sheets. A barred window opened on the adjacent shop, which sold mostly liquor and cigarettes. The kitchen was the normal Chinese set-up, with a big clay work surface, two woks, and a steamer fired by gasoline torches. While we sat inside, a crowd of a hundred or so people gathered to peer in at us and poke at our bikes. We had learned by then to loosen all the gear-shift cables whenever we stopped so that people could jam the levers without breaking anything.

The proprietor was delighted that we had come, especially after we ordered the most expensive fare in the house. We ate Nepali rice and highly spiced Sichuan food—meat and chilis, cabbage and chilis, potatoes and chilis—food that lay restlessly in bellies more accustomed to bland starch. It was wonderful.

A dozen tipsy Tibetans staggered in to occupy the remaining table and ordered bowls of rice as an excuse to sit where they could gawk at close range. Passing a plastic jug of *chang,* they ate the rice by palming it sloppily against their faces—nose, mouth, cheeks—their eyes riveted on the outlanders. They could barely sit up straight, and in fact one of them fell off his chair. Just tipped over backward and down he went. Burang was a great place for drinking. At any time of day, people could be seen weaving from one smoky *chang* den to another. Some were too tight to walk and went along by alternately falling to the ground and stumbling upright.

"Look, he's prostrating!" said Lee, when he and I encountered one of them making his bleary way down an alley. Oh, Mommy, take me home.

ON OUR THIRD MORNING IN BURANG, I was lying on my cot reading a book, when I looked up to see a small man standing in the room. He wore a black fake-leather jacket, jeans, and running shoes. A Nepali, I decided. He had come in so quietly that I hadn't seen him until he stood beside me.

"Excuse me, if you please," he said.

"Huh?"

"I am looking for Mr. Lee."

"Who?" I didn't know who he meant. It sounded like a Chinese name.

"Your friend, I believe. Very tall."

"Oh, of course. He's next door." I yelled for Lee. "Who are you?"

"My name is CSB," said the Nepali, sitting on the edge of the bed.

"CSB?" I asked. "What sort of name is that?"

"Chandra Singh Bora, but please, call me CSB. I am from Shama, in India."

"Shama?" I asked. "Where is that?"

"Yes, my home is not 100 millimeters from Shama."

"You mean kilometers."

"No, millimeters exactly."

He was trading in Burang, living in a tent across the river where the Nepali traders lived. Being Indian, he was there illegally, so he pretended to be Nepali. "The Chinese are incapable completely of knowing an Indian citizen from a Nepali citizen. To them, we look the same. Hah!"

I didn't tell him that I had made the same mistake. As Lee came into the room, CSB pulled a brown paper packet from his coat. "You want hashish?" he asked.

I didn't, but Lee was interested. "How much?"

"Ten grams, ten yuan. It is, I am confident, a very good price. You will agree?"

With Lee was a lanky German man, blond, about six-feet-four and twenty-four years old. He wore a "Kent 20" football jersey and an Aussie bush hat. I said hello. The German shook my hand and said, "My name is Clip."

"Clip?"

"Like video clip," he said.

"Is that short for something?"

"No. I like videos. Rock videos. You know? Da-da-da dunh dunh dunh!" He wiggled his hips. "I make the name myself. You know why?"

"No, why?"

"You can't guess? Because no one else has Clip. So if you go to Lhasa, or Kathmandu, and someone says, 'I saw Clip,' then you know it is me. Only me."

"I see."

Clip revealed that he had hitchhiked to Burang all the way from Lhasa, the only person we met who had managed to do so.

But he was suffering the effects of his journey. Having bought a golf-ball-size rock of hashish from CSB, he held it reverently in his hand and said, "I am happy to find this in Burang. I was afraid my hash doesn't last until Kashgar." He had been smoking Indian *bidis,* crude country cigarettes, to tide him over during periods of hash shortage. He was also recovering from liver and stomach problems with the help of some six hundred pills acquired at the Chinese hospital in Ali.

"Six hundred pills!" I said. "Are they working?"

"I don't know. They are free, I take them."

"How do you get them free?"

"Yes, yes. It is funny. I tell them I have no money, and they charge me nothing. But I wish I could get some good food. Most of all, I need good food."

"The restaurant by the river is pretty good."

"Oh." He looked dismayed. "I am vegetarian. They cook meat."

"Have you tried the market? There might be vegetables there."

"Yes, it's just like anywhere. You get drugs only, not food."

He was right, I noticed, when I next walked across the footbridge to the Nepali traders' market. Alcohol and cigarettes were in big supply, along with the sort of trinkets considered cheap even in Nepal: bangles, combs, costume jewelry, flashlight batteries, toy cars, and plastic laser guns. Almost nothing by way of vegetables. In a row of mud-walled buildings with fabric roofs, a Nepali man beckoned us into his teahouse, an unusually clean place, not at all like the rest of Burang. Listening to him, I began to understand why.

He was Yongden B. Lama of Simikot, and not at all what you would expect to meet in a rough-and-tumble border camp. A former law student at Tribhuvan University in Kathmandu, he had recently lost a political election in western Nepal and had come to Burang for the summer, partly to lick his wounds and mostly "to make business." But the business had nothing to do with selling tea or preparing meals. The teahouse was his office. He was, he said, a trader.

"What do you trade?" I asked.

"Wool. But it's hard. Each trader is permitted only two hundred kilos of wool. And Burang is a barter market. There is no money allowed, only 4000 yuan worth of goods for each trader, and only necessities."

"But I see people buying things with money."

"Of course. It is only the law." He began describing a morass of regulations—quotas, approved barter rates, hours of operation.

"I don't follow," I said.

"You don't need to. You cannot. I cannot. The police cannot. Everything is never clear here."

"But why would they want to limit trade?"

"They want the wool to go through Lhasa, not here. Here, we can make real business, you know, not legal, no money for the government, nothing for their pockets!"

"You can't make much business on just two hundred kilos of wool."

"There are other things."

"Like what?"

"Hmm . . . ," Yongden hesitated. "Fur."

I asked what sort of fur, and it took a while to understand his answer, because he used Nepali or Tibetan names for some of the animals, and he had to describe them before I knew what he was talking about. When I understood, I was amazed that he admitted to what he was doing—trading lynx, gazelle, antelope, fox, sheep, bear, and snow leopard, anything he could get from Tibetans, and all of it illegal. In return, he brought otter skins from India.

"Tibetans want otter skins?"

"Yes. To put inside their *chubas*. It's very soft."

Tibetan antelope fur was the big-ticket item. Pashmina. One kilo, representing the underfur of twelve animals, brought eighteen hundred to two thousand yuan.

"It can't be worth that much," I said.

"Yes," he said, pulling a ring from his finger. "A shawl made from this fur, a big shawl, you can pull through this ring. True! Very fine wool!"

"That's more than two hundred American dollars a pound."

"And much more than that in India."

Burang was full of shady characters. Wendy told Yongden a story about the day she, Ant, and I had pedaled twenty miles to the Nepal border. We had wanted to see an ancient *gompa* called Kojinath. The *gompa* stood in the center of a tiny medieval village on the banks of the Karnali River. The only way into the village was by footpaths, through dark, covered passageways that led to the central courtyard in front of two prayer halls. It was like walking tunnels in a maze to the secret garden at its heart, and we liked the place immediately. But something was wrong. The monks ignored us. They made no gesture of greeting. On the contrary, they made it clear that we should stay outside.

We weren't the only visitors that day. Three Chinese, one of whom was the manager of our dirtbag hotel, had come from Burang in a jeep. They were being shown through the temple when we arrived. Why not us? We sat in the sun until the Chinese left, and suddenly the monks' demeanor reversed. Suddenly they were smiling and showing us around, letting us take pictures, wanting to try out our bicycles, and offering us tea.

"Well," Wendy told Yongden, "this morning, the police came to the hotel and arrested the manager for stealing the silver jewelry off a statue! What a sleazeball!"

"Yes, I heard about that," said Yongden. "He became manager one year ago only. Since then, nothing but problems. He belongs in jail."

Yongden's wife served tea—heavy, sweet tea, laced, Nepali-style, with milk and cardamom. "She is my wife," said Yongden proudly. "Her name is Tsering." A Nepal-born Tibetan, Tsering was a large, ruddy woman who probably outweighed her husband two pounds to one. She sat beside him and beamed.

"I am her second husband. Before me, she has one son. He lives in New York."

"New York City?"

"I'll show you." He went to the back room, returned with a photo album, and pointed to a snapshot of a young boy in monk's robes. The boy had been recognized as an important reincarnate lama. As such, he was studying among Tibetan exiles in New York. Yongden was as proud as if the boy was his own, and it was good that his attitude was so openhearted, because later I learned that Tsering was not just his wife but the wife of his three brothers as well. "So you bring her here and have her to yourself."

"Of course. I am a smart man."

And he had a smart wife. She was important to his business. In past years, Nepali traders had been permitted to travel some distance into Tibet in pursuit of trade. This year the rule had changed; Yongden could go no farther than Burang. Tsering, on the other hand, being a foreign-born Tibetan, could pass easily for a native and could travel freely in the guise of a pilgrim.

Her job was to go to Ali and beyond, where she could line up truckloads of salt and other goods and send them on to Burang, at which point Yongden would have them loaded onto pack animals for the trip south. None of it would be done by the book. Tsering had to be quick on her feet. They had one large contract: they were trying to acquire three truckloads of Chinese cement. It would be purchased by devious means from the official allotment of a Tibetan work unit and shipped to Simikot on burros and yaks.

101

"It is very important for me. Politically, I mean."

"How's that?"

"If I cannot get the cement to Simikot, next time also I will not win the election."

"I think politics is the same everywhere."

He smiled broadly. "I will find the cement. Look, here is my home." He pointed to a snapshot of his family standing before a stone building with a wooden roof. It looked like something from the Alps a hundred years ago. Snow covered the ground and the surrounding forested hills. There were other pictures of the town, an airstrip, and a deep, forested valley. That made me think of British Columbia.

"It looks like a wonderful place."

"You must come visit. In two months I will be home."

"We'd love to, but they won't let us cross the border here. We have to go all the way around, through Pakistan and India. I don't suppose you could smuggle us across."

"Last year, yes. No problem. I took several people. This year, they move the border post. Now they guard the bridge. It is very difficult."

"And then we get caught in Simikot without permits—"

"In Simikot is no problem. Simikot is my home. But after Simikot . . . Yes. The army. Jail. Hah!"

As we were leaving, Naomi asked him, "Do you know the name of the ruined *gompa?*"

"The big one on the hill? Shimbuling."

"Shimbuling. You know, we keep asking local people, and they don't tell us. They say there is no *gompa*. Do you know why?"

"No."

"I thought something bad might have happened there. Something really bad. Something they don't want to remember."

Yongden just shook his head.

Several of us climbed the hill to Shimbuling one day, past dozens of tiny, hand-hewn caves dug into the soft cliffs that surround Burang. I had seen hundreds of caves scattered across the countryside—smoke-darkened hollows plastered with clay, marked by dim reddish paint, some of them virtually inaccessible at the tops of sharp pinnacles.

Sven Hedin, who normally kept a cool head on the subject of Tibetan mysticism, became animated when writing about monks in caves, especially those who voluntarily had themselves walled into tiny caves for their entire lives. They would do this near a monastery whose monks would bring a bowl of *tsampa* once each day and slide it through a baffled, lightproof hatch. This would go on for years until, when the food was no longer being eaten, the monks would know that the hermit had died, at which time they would break in and remove the body of the man, who was now, surely, a saint. Hedin learned these details while standing outside such a cave talking to one of the attendant monks, as he noted in his book *A Conquest of Tibet:*

"What is his name?" [Hedin asked.]
"He is nameless. We call him merely Lama Rinpoche, the holy monk."
"How long has he been immured?"
"Three years."
"How long will he remain?"
"Until he dies."
"Must he never see daylight?"
"No, he has made a sacred vow not to leave the grotto alive."
"How old is he?"
"I do not know, possibly forty years."

Later, at Mount Kailas, Hedin met two monks doing *parikrama* by prostration. When finished, one of them "intended to betake himself to a monastery on the Tsang-po and be there immured for the rest of his life. And he was only twenty years old!"

The caves near Burang were not that sort. Open to the air, looking toward the mountains, I imagined that they had once rung with the sounds of hand cymbals, little drums, and meditators chanting. From the monastery would come the rumble of big drums and horns and the crash of big cymbals, echoing against the cliffs and down the ravines.

I could picture that scene only in my head and read the accounts of people who had visited the monastery when it was active. One of them was the Englishman Charles Sherring, who came to Burang (he called it Taklakot) in 1905, after the Younghusband expedition had pried open the doors of Tibet. Sherring had traveled up from India on the old pilgrimage trail over Lepu Lekh Pass, a route still occasionally used by limited numbers of Indian pilgrims. Shimbuling was Sherring's first stop in Tibet, and he wrote of it in his book *Western Tibet and the British Borderlands:*

On this ridge there is no water, and, therefore, it would be impossible for the fort to become the nucleus of any considerable number of houses. All the inhabitants of the surrounding hamlets take it in turn to supply labor for the carriage of water daily from the spring below the crest of the ridge, and... we saw them all day long passing up and down the hill, and heard their singing, which was very euphonious in the distance, resembling in some degree the yodelling of the Swiss peasants.

The head lama gave him a tour of the *gompa* and "led me from room to room, and up and down passages, some of them pitch dark, with low roofs and steps always in the most extraordinary places, trying in every possible way to show the greatest cordiality, while all the time he twirled the prayer-wheels which we passed fixed in the walls, and everybody before us and behind us did the same, until there was a whir of revolving cylinders."

The only thing we could hear at Shimbuling was the wind. There was no sign of reconstruction effort, only a few simple shrines. I found what might have once been an important chapel—a large room outlined by broken walls. Looking up from that once-dark chamber, I had a clear view of mighty Gurla Mandhata—cloud-wreathed, glacier-clad. Was it a profane thought, that I preferred seeing the mountain just then to seeing a statue of Buddha?

I had walked through enough ruined buildings. They spoke to me of pain and loss. Walking around Kailas had been a wonderful experience, and I wanted more of that. More of the mountains.

They were so close. Just to the south, looming above us, were the Himalaya, sliced open by the valley of the Karnali River. Nepal lay in that direction, and India. I could see the trail to India, a light-colored line climbing the brown slopes opposite Shimbuling. We could be across the border and among those gleaming summits in a day.

Damn. Just another mountain fantasy. If you had unlimited freedom, the most interesting way to see the Himalaya would not be a circle, as we were doing, but rather a zigzag, following natural openings through the range—first the north side, then the south, back and forth, from one end of the mountains to the other. It only makes sense. Quite a few rivers—the Indus, Arun, Kali Gandaki, Karnali, and perhaps a dozen others—cut right through the range, providing natural routes of travel and trade, and they have been used that way for centuries. In addition, there are a number of low passes—notably the Nangpa La in the Sherpa district of Nepal—that provide easy routes from north to south.

If you could get permission to cross the Himalaya by these valleys and passes, you could do the most remarkable walk ever done. I've got it at the top of my dream list, several points above winning the California lottery.

Meanwhile, we were forced by regulations to cross only at the two approved border posts. But at least there were two, and that was enough for our plans.

Leaving the ruins, we picked up our cycles at the base of the ridge and pedaled for a time through the barley fields. On the way back to town, we met a small Nepali caravan headed south. Several men walked beside their yaks, but one young fellow rode a horse. Perhaps he had just bought it, I thought, and was new at riding, because when he saw us, he tried to show off by galloping past the way Tibetan riders did. The horse shied, stumbled, and threw him over its head into an irrigation ditch. The man climbed out, dripping wet and embarrassed, ran after the horse, and left his hat lying by the road.

"*Topee!*" I shouted. "Your hat!" But he was too embarrassed to come back for it. One of his friends came instead. All of them except the show-off were unable to speak for laughing.

So were we. Suddenly, I felt a twinge of nostalgia for the exuberant hurly-burly of Nepal. I wanted to run along behind those happy fellows and join them on the trail. I wanted to go see their homes. I knew from past experience that in Nepal we would be free to walk any number of trails among congenial people, village to village, valley to valley, from one shining vista to the next.

In traveling, wherever you go, you are caught between memory and anticipation, between where you have been and where you think you want to be. You get impatient. You want to move on. You are sure the next place will be everything you imagine.

It is the chief, perhaps the only, luxury of the traveler, to live in a world that is always part fiction.

7

This Is Not the Silk Road

The sight of a horse makes the wayfarer lame.
——Bengali proverb

"SO, LET'S GET PEDALING," said Pat.

I told him I hated bicycling on those roads. He grinned in agreement and looked at Jeff, the most dedicated cyclist among us. Jeff had cycled from Lhasa to Kathmandu, and from Kashgar to Pakistan. He had liked those trips. I respected his opinion. If he had wanted to pedal back up that hill toward Kailas, I might have considered going with him. For about five seconds. But Jeff shook his head and said, "You know, I really like riding my bike. I don't like falling over the handlebars and not being able to watch where I'm going. This isn't bicycling."

Ant, a successful road racer on the Canadian Junior Olympic cycling circuit, felt the same way. As for Naomi, she was pregnant. That gave her two votes. Both nix on bikes. When everyone was counted, we had zero for cycling, nine for finding a ride.

Jeff thought it might be difficult. With no one like Mr. Chophel to line up a truck for us, we had to find someone who had his own truck. We had seen a few such fellows, prodding their antique piles of rusting, broken metal down the road, keeping them going with prayers and baling wire. The stubborn machinery of private enterprise in Tibet: fenders missing, beds tilted, sides held up by cables and ropes, engines exposed, wheels wobbling, tires bald and missing chunks of tread, windows cracked or gone entirely. That's what we needed to find.

"It might be hard," said Jeff. "It could take a week."

I thought he was terribly pessimistic. And in fact, walking on the road that evening, we met two truck drivers from Kashgar. They were Uighurs—Turkic people who form the majority in far western China. They said they would be leaving the next day, going all the way to Kashgar, and they'd love to take us along if we showed up in the morning.

Then along came Yongden. Having heard that we were looking for a truck, he had come to tell us about another one leaving the next day. Naomi and Ant followed him over to the nomad camp to meet the driver. An hour later they were back at what we had christened the Dirtbag Hotel.

"The driver wasn't around," said Naomi, "but supposedly he's leaving at five tomorrow afternoon."

"Meaning we ride at night?" I asked.

"I don't want to ride at night," said Pat.

"No problem, we'll just go with the Uighurs."

The next day the driver of the second truck was still nowhere to be found. The Uighurs were, but they were in no hurry, and besides that, a problem had arisen. They had discovered the business about special permits to carry foreigners. They knew a man who might help, but it would take time. How long? They shrugged and smiled and offered us a champion dinner of handmade noodles and sheep stew.

"This is all they eat in Kashgar, you know," said Jeff. "Noodle stew, fresh flatbread, and melons."

"And beer?" asked Lee.

"It's the best beer I've ever had," said Pat.

Back at the hotel we talked about the possibility of going that night on the truck Yongden had found. There was much reluctance to go at night, but I was keen to get moving and convinced Naomi to help me investigate. At seven in the evening we pedaled to the nomad camp to find a truck loading and the phantom driver irritated. "You were supposed to be here at five," he said.

"We were here *until* five. Where the hell were you?"

We felt as put out as he did, but there was nothing to be done. He was leaving, he had a full load, and we were staying.

The next day, Friday, we sat around hoping the Uighurs would show up. They didn't.

On Saturday, the only news was from Naomi and Jeff, who went off in the morning looking for trucks and found, instead, a new hotel with an unprecedented asset: a cheerful manager. He was a retired army officer, and he knew of a truck leaving for Ali that afternoon driven by a friend of his. Of the Uighurs, still no sign.

So we packed out of the Dirtbag and pedaled our loads across to the new place. It looked like any other battered, mud-walled building, but the staff were pleasant and eager. They had just put up a sign:

WEL-COME TO OUR SHOPING CENTRE. ALSO AVAILABLE ARE THE FA-CILITIES OF LODGING, FOODING. ENJOY DRINK IN OUR SPECIAL BAR. BUS AVAILABLE FOR SITE SEEING. CANTIN RESTRANT SEVING CANTIN.

Special bar? Never mind that it was a mud-floored room with a few benches and several plastic crocks of *chang*. It was the spirit that counted, and the *chang* was even better than the good Chinese beer. The only disappointment was that the manager's friend was unwilling to carry foreigners. Absolutely no.

It seemed there were plenty of trucks and no rides. That afternoon Wendy and I were hailed by a Khampa claiming to be the driver of a beat-up wreck. He offered us a ride to Ali the next afternoon.

"*Mingtian?*" I asked. Tomorrow?

He nodded, flashing a big, roguish smile. I didn't trust him. I said, "We want to go today."

"Sorry, I have to fix this," he said, pointing to a tire lying on the ground. It was missing half its tread. It needed reincarnation, not repair.

Another truck pulled in that evening, driven by a Tibetan named Tupten Tsering who said yes, he was going to Ali, *mingtian,* and we could ride along for fifty yuan each. Meanwhile, Naomi had found the Uighurs again. They said they'd be going the day after tomorrow and, regarding the permit to carry us, would stop by our rooms that evening with an answer. Although we stayed up late hoping to see them, they never came.

The fourth day we were at it again, visiting all the familiar Burang haunts. The Uighurs were lying low; we couldn't find them. The other drivers were asleep or not in the area. At least Yongden was home, in his tent making business. While Pat and I drank tea and talked about other things, a Chinese man came in and told us he had been looking for us. He was a friend of Tashi's. He knew all about us and had a ride to offer, leaving in two days. That sounded nice, but he had only two seats, and besides, we told him, both Tupten Tsering and the other liberation truck—the one with the ruined tire—were leaving that afternoon. "We have a ride, thank you," I told him.

"You think so?" said Pat.

Two hours later, Tupten Tsering said "*Mingtian*" again and wobbled off down the road to a *chang* den.

On the sixth day, a hard wind scoured Burang. Dust came in waves. Sheets of corrugated steel flapped through the nomad camp like wounded birds. We huddled in a room and kept an eye on various trucks, until a little after noon, Jeff perked up. "Tupten's loading, I think," he said.

Then, suddenly, Tupten was at the gate with his truck. He wanted our bikes first. We tied them in and he drove away, and we didn't see him for another two hours. When he returned, the truck was piled high, loaded and swaying drunkenly, like its owner.

We waited another two hours, sitting on our packs in the dust. Suddenly, people started climbing on.

"Wait a minute, are they coming along?" said Pat.

"We'd better grab some space," I said. Jeff was a step ahead of me. He had also traveled like this before. He knew that a standard load could easily be twenty-five to thirty people, plus cargo.

There was already pushing going on when we climbed up. People were boarding in a panic, and we were losing ground.

"Be firm," said Jeff. "If you give in now, it'll be a miserable trip."

Pat, Baiba, Naomi, and Wendy sat with their backs together and their feet braced, resisting the press from behind. Lee, Jeff, Antony, and I claimed spots facing them with our backs to the driver's cab.

"How many are there, Jeff?"

We counted. Eight of us, twelve of them. Three in the cab. We occupied about a quarter of the space.

Tupten started the engine, moved a hundred yards, killed the engine, and ran off down the hill. Half an hour later he was back, carrying a three-gallon jug of oil in one hand and a similar jug of *chang* in the other. It's not a good sign when your driver needs as much oil as *chang*. Once again, the engine coughed to life, belched smoke, and reluctantly pulled the truck uphill out of Burang. On the crest of the hill, seven more Khampas jumped aboard.

"Are you kidding?" said Pat, as one of them pushed him with his foot, trying to make Pat move over. Pat gripped the foot. "No room, Jack!"

"Back off, dorkface!" Lee was shouting to another Khampa, who simply smiled and sat down on top of Antony. The guy was heavy and immovable, and there was nothing Antony could do.

Someone else was pushing at me. But I was already sitting with my knees drawn up. I couldn't get any smaller, and there was nowhere to go. "Not here, fella," I said. "*Mindoo.*" He gripped my shoulder and pulled. "Not here!" I repeated. He raised his arm as if to strike me, so I pushed him and he almost fell off the truck. That made him angry, but he went to the back, where his friends luxuriated in enough room to lie down.

These were not the same cordial people we had known in other circumstances. These were skilled truck travelers, and they knew all the tricks of territorial warfare. Their motto: give no inch, take every foot. Their major weapon: lying down.

As soon as the truck began moving, as if on a signal, half of the Tibetans collapsed against each other and across our laps. They were experts at wedging themselves into tight spaces, eventually occupying what they gained. Naomi and Baiba fell victim to a six-foot Tibetan who shoved his shoulder between them and let gravity gradually pull him into a reclining position. When they tried pushing him upright, he rolled his eyes and played dead. Beside him were three hefty women sitting with their backs to us and their feet braced firmly on a sack of barley. With each bump they pushed backward, gaining an inch at a time. Once we realized what was happening, we formed a similar line and succeeded in moving them back part way. It was a battle for space that was never won, no lines drawn, no territory agreed upon.

As we hammered down the road, my thoughts went back to a romantic scene from my previous visit to Tibet. It was near Mount Everest, on its north side, where the landscape was so enormous that even the world's highest peak seemed distant and small. Looking out the window of a speeding Toyota, I had seen a man walking across the golden plains at dawn, behind a train of black yaks, toward snow mountains carved sharply by the early sun. The image had haunted my mind for more than a year. That night, in the rainy lowlands of Nepal, I had written in my diary, "Tibet has forever changed the way I see."

Remembered that way, Tibetans were romantic figures, fitting inhabitants for a place dominated by space, light, and sky. This, however, was something different: riding in a truck filled with young yahoos wearing white polyester shirts that had never been washed, pink nylon socks, and high heels made of plastic and corduroy, all of them smelling from various accretions under their polyester pants and *chubas,* and two or three of them trying to lie on top of me. There didn't seem to be much of the clear golden plains in these characters.

They were aggressive but not exactly hostile. Not at first, anyway. The ones who stayed awake sang and laughed as we went along, and that gave Lee an idea. Standing up on top of the huge, swaying load, his cowboy hat a good 20 feet above the road surface, he began belting out Broadway hit songs—"Oklahoma," "Gary, Indiana," "They Call the Wind Mariah"—big, loud songs that soon had all the Tibetans awake and smiling, some trying to sing along. More than any other tune, "Born Free" got them going. Lee's rendition involved flamboyant arm gestures and wild vibrato. I suppose the Tibetans had never seen a foreigner act in such an uninhibited manner. They were impressed enough to applaud.

It took only five hours to reach Darchen, where we spent two nights while the Tibetan passengers made one-day *parikramas.* It was then that I met

Tsarong Namdul, the caretaker who told us, among other things, about the British trekker who had died on Kailas.

On the third morning we left at dawn, already fighting over space, and drove three hours to another pilgrimage stop, the Tirthapuri Hot Springs.

Here the mood worsened. Everyone had gotten off to perform their various devotions. These involved walking a short, circular path around the hillside, leaving offerings, and eating little bits of mineral deposition from the springs (a good source of calcium and therefore worth doing for physical and spiritual reasons). Climbing back aboard, sanctified and ready for new mischief, two young guys began poking and pinching Baiba. "Knock it off," she said. They giggled and one of them pinched her again. "Hey!" she said and slapped him in the face. At the same time, Wendy emptied a bottle of water over his head. That was humiliating, to be hit by a woman; worse, the water wet his boom box, which got him very worried and angry. He sat muttering and wiping the boom box with his shirt.

As others climbed up, four Tibetans got together and with the synchrony of a football front line, blocked Wendy, Baiba, and Lee a foot and a half to the side. On the ground, Pat saw the move. He climbed to the edge of the truck-bed, leaped into the air, and cannonballed into the middle of the Tibetans, displacing them back to their original positions.

I cheered. Pat smiled and said, "Oh, excuse me!" But the Tibetans yelled in anger, and judging from what happened later, they apparently decided the competition for space had turned serious.

We left the hot springs, drove a few miles, and stopped for lunch at a cluster of buildings. Everyone got off for an hour. Then we piled back on, drove two hundred yards, and stopped at a stream, where Tupten poured water in the radiator. That finished, he turned to Naomi and demanded money, saying he needed to buy gasoline. This violated our agreement. We had paid three hundred yuan in advance in Burang and owed the remaining two hundred only after reaching Ali.

Reminding Tupten of his agreement, Naomi refused. Tupten shrugged. Then he drove a hundred yards to a house where people streamed out and there was a big social scene for about twenty minutes. Then it was back a hundred yards to the stream, where Tupten again demanded money. Again Naomi refused. Tupten stamped his feet and said we wouldn't go any farther without the money.

Tempers rose. Naomi offered half of the two hundred yuan. That wasn't enough. Tupten started yelling. He and his brother climbed on top of the truck cab, red in the face, yelling curses. We sat still. A crowd of onlookers gathered around the truck. Shaking with anger, Tupten's brother started throwing things and, seeing Lee's cowboy hat sitting on the load, stomped it flat. "You bastard!" Lee shouted, shoving the guy's leg and standing up himself as the guy turned his attention to my camera bag. I yanked that away from his foot and he started pummeling my shoulder. Tupten was shouting, "These people won't pay what they owe, and until they do, we can't go to Ali!"

Whereupon the whole truckload stood and pressed forward. There was big shouting all around. Two guys grabbed Lee and tried to drag him off the truck.

"Get off, all of you," shrieked Tupten. "Everyone off!"

I was sitting with my back to a line of standing Khampas, whose hands had gone to their long knives. It suddenly occurred to me that this could be serious. So what did I do? I reached up and patted their bellies with the backs of my hands. What an absurd gesture: "There, there, fellows, take it easy. Nothing to get riled about." I was still trying to hold my ground, but Wendy, acting more intelligently, had leaped off and stood in the crowd below.

Tupten, looking positively apoplectic, had his fisted hand waving above him when Jeff shouted, "Okay! I'm going to pay. I'll just pay him."

Was this the old truck driver's extortion trick we had heard about from other travelers? The driver stops in some barren place and demands more money. Travelers have the choice of paying extra or getting off. They pay and the scene is repeated an hour later, with the same results.

I had a strong urge to get off. I reckoned that Tupten, lacking official permits, really did need our money to buy black market gasoline. I enjoyed the thought of pedaling away, leaving him with an empty tank and no money.

Naomi had a better approach. She said, "Two hundred yuan more? That's all? And you take us to Ali today? And we owe you nothing more?"

Tupten said yes.

"You will write this in my book?"

Tupten, himself illiterate, asked another man to write it—two lines of Tibetan script that could have meant anything. Naomi wrote below it in English, including the truck license number, and Tupten signed it, or put some sort of mark there. Jeff counted out the money. Tupten bought five gallons of gas from the driver of a nearby jeep, and we were again under way.

It was a strange, embattled ride after that. The pressure for space intensified. I lost my original place and ended up perched on the sharp edge of a protruding bag while a young Khampa, backed up by four of his mates, succeeded in lying down where I had been. I had resisted for more than an hour, but the effort became more than I could sustain. Meanwhile, Ant was losing a similar battle to a lout who smiled idiotically as he wrapped his arms around Ant's legs and put his face in Ant's lap. If Ant reversed his position, the lout hugged his stomach. Protest from Ant brought a half-wit smile.

At the front, Jeff, sitting on a sack of rock-hard coconuts, fought with a bundle of filthy, stiff goatskins. Tied loosely to the top of the cab, they repeatedly caught the wind and flopped over onto his head. He gave it up eventually and rode with the bundle draped over him. Pat also capitulated to the pressure of two men who tried to lie on top of him. Yielding the space, he stood up and rode holding on to the steel bar that was used, other times, to support a canvas canopy.

In that miserable state, we rumbled on over the rough, pitted track. The sun set. The mountains loomed in dim moonlight. Around eleven o'clock I joined Pat standing. It was easier to stand up than to perch on the sharp-edged bag that had become my seat. By doing that, however, I lost all claim to any space, and two hours later, falling asleep standing up, I had to squeeze into Lee's tiny spot, where we rode in painful intimacy, our feet hanging over the edge of the truck, for the last hour and a half.

It was 2:20 A.M. when Tupten drove into the upper Indus River at Ali and splashed across it to the north bank beside a row of canvas tents and other trucks. Stiffly climbing down, we found ourselves between the river and the Ali market on a thin strip of gravel—not only a campsite but a toilet and refuse dump. Any other time we'd have been dismayed. Now, all we wanted to do was lie down.

Clearing away the larger feces, goat legs, broken bottles, and metal debris, we set up our tents, locked the bikes in a pile, and climbed into our sleeping bags. I fell asleep listening to gangs of dogs fight over the abattoir debris.

Wendy wrote this in her diary the next day:

I couldn't sleep a wink anyway. Can't ever remember a sleepless night like that before this trip. Tired of it. Darchen was extremely depressing. They've filled the toilet with some sort of garbage and the result is a ring of excrement around the entire compound. Getting lazy and lethargic. Sick of shit everywhere, and depressed to think it will be as bad or worse where we're going. Tired of this Chinese mentality of not caring how things look, are run, no pride, no motivation. Tired of aggressive, pushy Tibetans coming in the room to stare at our things. Always on guard against theft. Tired of sitting around waiting for rides, drivers, loads, information. Want good reading material. My brain and body are rotting.

That was a low point, I guess.

S TAGE TWO, ANOTHER TRUCK, this one loaded with sacks of borax from mines in the Chang Tang. It was headed for Kashgar and we had it to ourselves. Naomi rode in front for an hour, then came back to report.

"This driver's wonderful," she said. "We've lucked out again."

His name was Qu Huagui. He was born in Xian in central China. He had been stationed with the army in Yecheng for ten years and loved it. Now, although he worked as a driver based in Ali, his wife and two daughters lived in Yecheng. It seemed like a hell of a commute. It was like a trucker based in Los Angeles having his family in Atlanta.

Qu loved driving because his truck gave him freedom. He worked hard hours, but they were all his own, and he went interesting places. He had been to Beijing, Lhasa, Urumqi, and all over China. Naomi said, "He's a tourist! He told me, 'I get to go around and see things, just like you guys.'"

At first, Qu had worried about having us for passengers. A few years earlier, he had driven a jeep for an American group somewhere in Xinjiang province. They had treated him badly; one man in the group had punched Qu in the face because the road was too rough. He thought that was pretty lousy behavior.

We were all excited by this next leg of the journey, which would take us through the highest and least inhabited part of Asia, the Aksai Chin, a forbidding landscape where the road stayed around 17,000 feet for a distance of some two hundred miles.

For a time, we could see the high peaks along the Indus River Valley, marking the Indian border. But soon they disappeared behind intermediate ridges, and we entered a series of high, arid valleys, where occasional nomad tents occupied minuscule patches of green. Like the Chang Tang, it was a skeletal landscape of rock outcrops and rubble, of dry lakebeds, the water long since gone and replaced by thin air.

There were full lakes too. One in particular was lovely to see—rich turquoise water set in a bowl of red mountains. Turquoise is the favorite stone of Tibetans, and I knew why after seeing lakes like that one.

The largest lake was Rutog Tso, a serpentine body of water about a hundred miles long that crossed the border into the Indian state of Kashmir. The border itself is the subject of contention. India still claims sovereignty over the Aksai Chin region, calling it part of Kashmir, but the Chinese took control of the area in the fifties by building the road that we traveled—a road that for many years India didn't even know existed. Despite that, most mapmakers still give the Aksai Chin to India.

I thought every turn of the landscape was stunning. Pat was more discriminating but got excited when we passed a range of pink granite mountains: rounded blobs of granite, wind eroded, interesting rock climbing. Good rock, to Pat, was like an electric shock.

"Looks like Cottonwood Canyon in Utah," he said. "But about three times as high. And no one's ever climbed here." He'd have been happy to stay there for a week, working on climbing routes, every line a new one.

Late in the day, Qu stopped in front of a sagging mud roadhouse.

"What's wrong?" said Wendy.

"What do you mean 'wrong'?" I asked. "This is Doma."

"It's gorgeous. Somebody goofed."

She meant not the roadhouse, nor the army post nearby, but the choice of setting. As a rule, the Chinese avoid putting settlements in pleasing locales. Here, twisted red mountains loomed steeply on both sides of a Kelly green marsh. Horses waded through grass up to their bellies. Wedges of geese and ducks flew in front of a full moon rising through wispy cloud fingers.

"I could live with that for a long time," Wendy said, "out my front door."

There was a wistful note in her voice. "Feeling homesick?" I asked.

"A little. It would be a full moon at home too, wouldn't it?"

The August moon. Full summer in the Rockies, a season so short and so beautiful it can hurt. Soon there would be frosty nights in the higher parts of Yellowstone. The bison would begin rut, and their calls, like the growling of so many grizzlies, would echo through the park's open valleys, across steaming rivers. When they do that, you can hear them a mile away.

Rain during the night settled the road dust; fresh snow up high. The world looked as if it were about five minutes old. Following a green-carpeted valley beneath high mountains, we passed a checkpost and—sometime before noon—officially entered the Aksai Chin.

"Good-bye, Tibet," said Baiba.

"Maybe we'll be in Lhasa for Tibetan New Year?" I said.

"I'd like that," she answered. "We didn't get to see enough of it."

Suddenly Tibet, like home, was the subject of nostalgia.

Up and up then, gradually, past big, inviting valleys fingering off to the southwest, direct paths to India and the main crest of the Himalaya. Climbing over frozen streams and old snowbanks, the truck labored upward until we came to a pass 5800 meters high—more than 19,000 feet, nearly as high as the summit of Kilimanjaro. Qu stopped the truck. We all jumped down to stretch our legs. I was dizzy. I felt the hot little explosions behind my eyes that I associate with altitude.

For centuries, this place has earned a fearsome reputation with travelers. Among these high, dry hills, largely barren of forage and scoured by constant icy winds, many lives have been lost—mostly pack animals but people too. Of the few Western travelers who came this way in early years, most had difficulty finding water and grass for their animals. Lakes were often salty. Streams ran intermittently. Sven Hedin came through here on one of his awful winter journeys. For more than two months, he saw no humans except for his own party. Behind him he left a trail of carcasses—sheep, horses, and mules—until his men were reduced to backpacking some of the load. They were lucky to survive at all.

In the introduction to a new edition of Ella Maillart's *Forbidden Journey,* the story of a long trip through Tibet in the 1930s, Dervla Murphy, herself a writer of travel books, laments the loss of risk in travel. If Maillart had gotten sick, says Murphy, she would have died, whereas if someone today gets sick, there is an airplane standing by to whisk that person to the care of the world's best doctors. Murphy goes on to say that in the modern world risk is optional, a matter of choice. To find risk, she says, a traveler goes out of his or her way to avoid safety, or pursues extreme activities such as mountaineering, and she implies that the resulting thrill is both cheap and irresponsible.

I disagree. Travel *has* become easier and faster but not necessarily safer. In some ways, the world has become more dangerous, not less. When you could travel by horse in Asia, as Maillart did, you had at least some control over your conveyance. If you travel, as we must do today, in a bus or a truck, you trust your life to a driver who may have seen his first vehicle only a few years earlier. I've never been as scared anywhere as in buses on mountain roads in Asia. The danger is real. Nepali and Indian newspapers periodically report terrible accidents when brakes or steering linkages fail and buses plunge hundreds of feet down steep slopes.

I know of at least four Western tourists who died in Tibet during the spring and summer of 1987: the German who died of altitude sickness in Lhasa, the British trekker who died at the base of Kailas just before we got there, and two hitchhikers who froze to death in the back of a liberation truck going over high passes in the eastern mountains.

In Nepal, travelers have been killed by bandits, or by falling rock, or by aggressive yaks pushing them off the trail and over a cliff. Or they've picked up fatal meningitis from a mosquito.

No one chooses risk over safety without some reason, and risk—even for mountaineers—is almost never an objective in itself. Ella Maillart did not choose Tibet because it was riskier than the south of France. She wanted to see Tibet, and she accepted that a journey there might present dangers. It's no different today, even if all you do is fly in an airplane. You know that only a thin aluminum skin separates you from a nasty fate and that any number of events could bring disaster; but the odds are good, and you take the risk.

Anyway, what does it matter? Implicit in Murphy's comments is the notion that without danger, travel is something less than it once was. It may be less scary, but it's certainly no less interesting. The value of travel has nothing to do with danger, and much to do with keeping one's eyes open.

———————

The hardscrabble hills of far western China, washed with green and streaked with red, were beautiful to look at, but this was a hard place to live. Even in summer, streams and lakes remained frozen in the middle of the day. Despite that, occasional small herds of livestock and black nomad tents flying red flags appeared on the slopes.

Naomi said, "I've heard they aren't nomads anymore."

"What are they?" I asked.

"China makes them stay here, like permanent settlers. To help enforce China's claim to the Aksai Chin."

If true, we were more like nomads than the nomads.

Then dry and drier yet. For many miles, there was not a leaf of vegetation, not even withered grass. The only green I saw came from the shards of Xinjiang beer bottles, tossed out by truck drivers.

On a vast, dry lakebed called Tianshuihai, we came to a community of sorts, a desperate huddle of concrete and mud structures. My map labeled the region "Soda Plain," and it seemed a long time since any water had gathered there. It was also, evidently, earthquake country. Buildings, many of them abandoned, had been shaken off their foundations; their walls had cracked and roofs fallen in. The military post and gas depot where Qu stopped to refuel had been shored up by heavy concrete buttresses. Thousands of fifty-gallon drums littered the ground, along with broken machinery, derelict vehicles, chunks of concrete, goat carcasses, cans, bottles, and shit.

Behind the buildings on a hill, Lee and I found the ruins of a radar antenna.

"Looks like the wind blew it over," said Lee.

"It was aimed south. India." I said.

"The Indians say this is India."

"It doesn't seem a place you'd want to fight over."

"Not unless you were worried about your national gravel supply."

I had never seen a more featureless place, all sky and flatness underfoot. Without disliking it—actually I very much enjoyed being there—I found that it made me want to travel, to get beyond the horizon. I have felt the same way looking out on the ocean. Move, keep moving, don't stop. The surface beneath your feet is nothing but a way to go somewhere.

It was the sort of place where a nomad would be utterly content, because he'd have no reason to stay.

117

As we were leaving, Naomi said she had been talking with the soldiers. "You know how long each guy is stationed here?"

"How long?"

"Ten years."

Late that afternoon, having crested a gentle rise marking the rim of the basin, the road began a long plunge downhill, into the shadowy interior of the Kun Lun Range. Its name, which means "Mountains of Darkness," could refer equally to the color of its rock or the obscurity of its geography.

On the northern border of Tibet, the Kun Lun stretch more than a thousand miles through the most remote section of Asia. Their average height is 20,000 feet, about the same as the Himalaya. The highest summit is Ulugh Muz Tagh, 25,340 feet in elevation. Despite their great size, they remain the least known, least traveled mountain range in the world, except, possibly, for the Antarctic. Over much of their length, they rise between forbidding desert to the north and the Tibetan plateau to the south, giving them a uniquely isolated position in the wild heart of a nearly uninhabited land.

At their eastern end, gently and without much fanfare, the Kun Lun fade into grassy steppes. But at the western end, they collide head on with the Himalaya and the Karakoram Range, buckling and heaving in a vast, complex confusion of gorges and crumbling rock walls. Disordered drainage patterns tell the story: rivers stream off glaciers and burrow their way through vast heaps of rubble, flowing a hundred miles in one direction only to turn suddenly and churn back the other way, painfully seeking an outlet to the thirsty deserts below. They make no sense, these river canyons, and neither do the surrounding mountains, which are themselves vast heaps of rubble in motion, young mountains rising and disintegrating at about the same rate.

The road dove down and down into shadows and thicker air, until it met the Karakax River, thundering along over boulders and gravel. We spent the night in the canyon bottom beneath black walls that echoed the sounds of falling water and rock. Over the centuries, many others have camped in these dark corridors, mostly traders on the old caravan route from India to western China. They would follow the Karakax River down from the Karakoram Pass on a grotesquely difficult track lined with the bones of animals that had died along the way—their skeletons serving in places as the only signposts and guide markers.

Besides natural dangers, travelers worried about the Kanjuti raiders, who would sneak out the north end of Hunza (once called Kanjut) through a secret back door, the Shimshal Pass, and make their way two hundred miles through trackless gorges. They would ford the ice-laden rivers countless times, cross several high passes, and finally sweep down upon some hapless caravan, commit their murders, pillage the victims, take slaves and hustle back to their virtually unapproachable valley.

They kept that up until the early 1900s, when the British finally invaded Hunza and drove its bandit-king off to China; after that, the once-feared raiders of Hunza settled down to become some of the most peaceable and pleasant folks on earth. In addition, China soon entered its long period of civil war and revolution, and by the late forties hostilities between China and India pretty much put an end to any cross-border trading; so raiders found themselves out of work.

The next day we came to Xaidulla, a cluster of walled compounds, old buildings made of mud brick, new ones of concrete, a few bushes, but mostly a road stop filled with blue trucks driven by Uighurs from Kashgar and Urumqi. At this point, the Karakax River veered north and hurled itself into a deep canyon that led to the oasis city of Hotan. Looking on the map, it would appear that the quickest way out of the mountains, and therefore the best route for a road to follow, would be down that canyon to the desert. But no, that way was too rough. Even in the days of camel caravans, the preferred path through the wreckage of these mountains was the same one the road follows today—over three high passes and through such difficult terrain that I had to wonder what the Karakax River canyon was like. It must be awfully rugged, to have forced road-builders to go the way they did.

Where the Karakax dropped north into its storm drain, our road turned south and climbed steeply up a series of narrow valleys to a mountain of oily, black mud. The first pass, called Sokh-bulah, was a sinister place more than 17,000 feet high. Black clouds spit rain and snow. The road was slippery, unstable, slumping at every turn.

Then we started down.

"What's happened to Qu?" said Ant.

"Must smell home," said Lee.

Suddenly reckless, Qu blasted down the switchbacks, drifting around bends, frightening us for the first time.

"I hope he knows his brakes," I said.

"Fat chance," shouted Ant.

The road was spectacular, no question of that, and challenging. I was thinking about that when we passed an accident. A truck had rolled off the road and lay 300 feet below, upside down. People scrambled over it, salvaging boxes of freight. The sight of disaster didn't slow Qu a bit. He thundered past, accelerating downhill, slamming the brakes at curves, honking his horn at blind spots to warn oncoming trucks that crazy-man Qu was on the loose.

Of course his brakes did hold, and soon we were barreling along another

119

large river to a work compound. Qu stopped in the yard and jumped out triumphantly. "Are you hungry?" he asked. The wild ride had given him an appetite.

"Look at that," Pat said with a nudge. Among several parked trucks was the wreck of one that had tumbled down the mountain slope. It was battered like an old tin can, the steel cargo bed broken, no glass in the windows. They should have parked it at the summit as a warning.

After lunch, following the river along its steep north bank, I was thinking it would be a bad place to meet traffic when we saw an army convoy ahead. There was plenty of warning, but neither their lead truck nor Qu stopped at a wide spot. Actually, Qu sped up. They met, predictably, in a one-lane stretch between a solid cliff and a rubbly slope that dropped to the river 200 feet below.

Neither driver seemed upset with the other. They got out and looked the situation over.

"If he just backed up a hundred yards... " said Jeff.

"Chinese army never retreats!" said Lee. "Those trucks probably don't even have a reverse."

As if that were true, both drivers decided to go forward. On our side was the rock face. On the outside, rubble at its angle of repose shot straight to the river.

"I'm out of here," said Ant, leaping off the truck. Most of us followed his lead. With an officer watching his outer wheels, the army driver pulled up toward us. His engine stalled repeatedly. He had to lurch forward. There wasn't room. The truckbeds met, overlapping some three inches. The trucks jockeyed then, pushing back and forth like two primitive beasts, and no smarter. The outer wheels of the army truck pushed gravel over the edge into the river. Its wooden side splintered; our canvas canopy tore. Clutches burned, engines roared, and finally we were clear of each other. But now the army truck was hanging on the edge of disaster, one front wheel part way over the edge. In a panic, the officer in charge of this triumph of logistics gestured the driver to reverse, which he did by popping the clutch with the engine roaring. His vehicle leaped backward. The engine killed and narrowly prevented the truck from going down backward.

All for want of foresight, but not for lack of warning. Half a mile farther along, we passed two soldiers sitting on an overturned tanker truck at the bottom of an embankment where it had come to rest minutes before. Fortunately, it had fallen only ten feet.

Then came Mazar, a few miles beyond, looking like all the other truckstops we had seen except for the herd of camels grazing there. One looked up as we passed, as if to say, "You're not in Tibet anymore."

Had we stayed with the river at this point, we could have continued westward to the Shimshal Pass, Hunza's notorious "back door," but of course no caravans ever wanted to go that way. Instead, the old route turned up a canyon toward the crest of the Kun Lun to yet another pass, this one called Chiragsaldi—another narrow, dark place filled with mountain rubble, the road subject to frequent washout and landslide. Black mountains indeed.

I was beginning to think this was the rule in the Kun Lun. Very little grew there. Nothing looked solid. As we climbed higher, snowy peaks came into view. They were 20,000 to 21,000 feet high. Behind them, only fifty miles south, were the Karakoram giants: K2, Masherbrum, Broad Peak, and the others.

Francis Younghusband had come this way, near the end of a long adventurous journey from Peking to India. He was looking for an old trade route across the Karakoram by way of Muztagh Pass. He had heard stories about caravans, strings of animals, going over that pass, but what he found was no road. It was a mountaineering route—one that commands the respect of even modern climbers with all their technical gear and rigorously developed skills. Younghusband was an inexperienced mountaineer; nonetheless, down he went, in the company of four rightfully terrified servants, protected only by a short length of rope and his ignorance of how difficult the climbing really was.

It was a brave thing to do and illustrates not just Younghusband's considerable pluck, but also the rate at which change occurs in this part of the world. One of Younghusband's men was a Balti named Wali, who had crossed the pass some twenty-five years earlier. He served as guide, but when they reached the pass, he could hardly recognize it. Where ponies had carried loads, there was now a mass of broken glacial ice—formidable for men on foot, impossible for pack animals.

Just beyond Chiragsaldi Pass, we spotted an inviting meadow and yelled for Qu to stop. We wanted to get off. It was time to try bicycling again. That made him unhappy. "No, no, it's too high, too cold, too wet, too windy," he said.

He was right on all counts.

"Kudiyah is much better! Only thirty kilometers."

He knew better than we did.

"There's a big pass ahead. Fifteen hundred meters!"

But we wished him good-bye just the same and gave him presents. He wrote his address in Yecheng and invited us to visit him and his family when we got there.

The wind blew hard that night. Clouds settled in, spitting at us. Three of us—Lee, Ant, and I—came down with sudden gut sickness. It seemed a wild, cold place to be camping, knowing that just 160 miles away was Yecheng, on the edge of the Takla Makan Desert, where camels could perish of thirst in drifting sands.

I N THE MORNING, hurrying to escape the sleet, I was at last happy to have a bicycle.

We rode fast, downhill against pellets of snow, leaving behind the dark, sullen sky. It was a wonderful, bouncy, high-speed ride on a smooth road. We tore around corners between frowning cliffs and a dancing river, looking up side valleys at high, green pastures and black peaks draped with glaciers. The sun was in and out of clouds. We passed road crews busy with picks and shovels and little two-wheeled carts, hacking out level places where trucks could pass. Seeing us, the workers shouted and waved and offered slices of melon, and we answered with waves and hellos.

Once we came to a herd of yaks moving up the road, about forty animals driven by five herders. As I came around the corner toward them, spinning along silent and sinister, the yaks panicked and took off in all directions over boulders and gravel and meadow. Even though we stopped and tried not to cause further havoc, it took the herders a long time to get the animals calmed down and headed on up the road.

That day, the bicycle was a ticket to freedom. We went however fast we wanted and stopped where we wanted. We were free from the dust and the sometimes frightening ride in a truckbed. Whatever I wanted was easy to find in my panniers with all their little zipper pockets. It was like having a set of cupboards traveling along with me—cameras on top by the handlebars, film in a side pocket, map and compass just behind the cameras, rain pants and jacket behind me, water bottle on the frame between my knees, and what amounted to a lifetime supply of 761 bars in the tiny front pocket.

At about four in the afternoon, we started seeing flat meadows with healthy grass. And suddenly, there was Kudiyah, greeting us with bright green trees planted on both sides of the road, the first trees we'd seen since Burang. The houses were mud brick, very neat with handsome wooden doors. A Uighur woman wearing a bright red scarf sat doing something on a porch while chickens scrabbled around her yard.

Chickens! It was wonderful to see chickens.

And even better to find an eatery serving noodles. The cook had his dough in a shallow bowl, a long snake of dough, wound in spirals. Lifting one end of the snake with his left hand, he stretched it out with his right, piling up a tangle of thin noodles on a board. When he had a big enough pile, he chopped the tangle a few times with a knife and the whole mess went into a pot of boiling water. It took only a few minutes and we were eating the fresh noodles with sauteed green peppers and tomatoes and drinking fragrant tea from a big thermos. The noodles cost us forty cents each. The tea was free.

Meanwhile, outside, the bikes had drawn a big, laughing crowd. Wendy let some men try her bike. It was like watching a carnival with clumsy bears wobbling in circles. The men weren't skilled cyclists. Their lurching attempts made for great hilarity. When we left, all together, the people of Kudiyah stood in the street with willow trees and high, brown mountains behind them and waved good-bye to us.

At about seven that evening, I came around a bend to see Naomi waving us off the side of the road to a sandy, grassy meadow tucked among big, granite boulders by the river. A perfect campsite at the end of a perfect day—6000 feet of descent through thirty-five miles of beautiful mountain country beside a frothing river.

The next morning, an hour and a half of blissful cruising down the river valley brought us to a turn in the road at a place called Akas. There we had to leave the valley and climb to the last pass before Yecheng. We had made it a third of the way up the pass when a truck came by and offered us a ride. We hesitated. We were enjoying the bikes for the first time.

"Come on," said the driver. "Don't be silly. It's twelve kilometers to the pass."

"I don't know," said Baiba. "We ought to pedal at least one pass. Just to say we did."

A family was riding in the empty truckbed. "Come on, come on," they said, laughing with pleasure. A young man jumped down and offered to lift Naomi's bike.

"All right," she said. "Privileges of pregnant ladies."

I climbed up after her. Wendy joined us, and Lee. That filled the truck. The others promised to catch the next one.

The pass was, at our guess, 4000 feet up. It took half an hour for the truck to get there. Twenty minutes later, a second truck driven by two army guys arrived with Pat, Baiba, and Antony aboard. As a matter of principle, Jeff had decided to pedal his unloaded bike.

While we waited for him, enjoying the view, drivers kept coming by, waving, stopping, poking at the bikes. Jeff appeared as a tiny dot on the outsides of curves, then disappeared. The mountains, hazy as behind a scrim, and very steep, were more like sculpture than a product of gravity. The highest patches of grass had been chewed and tracked by sheep and goats. Old trails zigzagged up the slope, predating the road. Jeff puffed into view, closer, and twenty minutes later was on the pass.

On bikes again, it was a wild ride down the other side; the road twisted around rocky points, then dove into narrow canyons, always perched precariously, demanding full attention. We went fast. I got brave enough to let gravity pull the bike as fast as it would, and I was just thinking about how stable the bike was, loaded down with 230 pounds of gear and me, when we sailed around a corner and past a few crude mud houses. Mountain bikers from hell.

Two boys stood on a dirt bank and waved. I waved back, and just then a large, black, barking dog shot out of tall grass, and before I could do anything he was at my heels. I barked back at him, pulled my feet up, hit a ditch, and went down in a big crash. It must have scared the dog as much as me because he took off across the field. I didn't know that for a few moments because my glasses had fallen off and I couldn't see anything. I scrambled around getting out from under my bike thinking the dog would have my leg any moment. My knee and elbow were skinned, my handlebars twisted, and my seat torn loose. I was entirely embarrassed. The people in the houses nearby, who all came out to see the aftermath, are probably still telling the story. The dog, I suppose, remembers it as the highlight of his life.

The rest of the day was bump and roll downhill into the desert. Suddenly it was hot, the sun low and direct, the dust choking.

The people of Pusa, an oasis town shaded by green poplars, greeted us with the enthusiasm that would be shown to a crowd of visiting acrobats. We had noodles again, hand-pulled, with tomatoes and green peppers in a spicy sauce. The town *binguan,* or guest house, would not give us a room—no surprise in an area supposedly closed to foreigners—but a schoolteacher, hearing that, said nonsense and gave us a classroom in the primary school. Wendy and I slept on three desks pushed together beneath a map of the world, countries labeled in flowing Arabic script.

In the early morning of a day that was already hot, we rolled out of Pusa and pedaled seven miles to Kokya. It was market day. The town was filled with desert people, donkey carts, and horses. There was fresh bread baked in earthen ovens, melons, tomato and pepper sauce in bowls, and nice people with open faces and kind eyes, wearing bright clothes. I wandered the bazaar with Pat, sticking to shady areas. The sun withered our spirits even here at 7000 feet. Our blood was too thick.

"Sure is hot," said Pat.

"Yeah," I said. "Sure is."

"Dusty too."

"Yup. And flat."

"What's the elevation at Yecheng?"

"About 4000."

"Think there's any water between here and there?"

124

"There's no oasis marked on the map." I could see that look in his eye again, the gleam of the mountain trucker. I tossed in some reinforcement. "It's at least forty miles."

"What do you think," he said, "should we—"

"This place looks like west Texas."

In less than five minutes, we had found a truck headed for Yecheng.

But first, the driver wanted to visit Pusa on a personal errand. We piled in anyway; no harm in seeing that town again. At the edge of Pusa, a bunch of naked boys were swimming in an irrigation canal. They recognized us from the night before. They waved and shouted. Half an hour later, leaving Pusa, we passed them again. This time they were ready for us. They stood shoulder-to-shoulder beside the road. As we came into view, they waved with their left hands and vigorously shook their penises with their right hands. Good-bye, Pusa.

And hello, Yecheng. Two hours later, we crossed the first irrigation ditch that marked the edge of the city. And there, a young boy who had been swimming took one look at us, grabbed his penis, and gave it a hearty thrashing.

Yecheng was nice. The streets were shady, green canyons between tall poplars. Water flowed strong and clear in the ditches. Mud-walled houses hid behind apricot orchards and corn 12 feet high.

"Is this what Kashgar's like?" I asked Pat.

"Kashgar's wonderful," he said.

"Shashlik and flatbread, hot from the oven," said Jeff. "Naomi, do you think you could you talk to the driver?"

She did, and sure enough, the driver knew of a truck for hire. They could leave at nine that evening.

"Perfect," said Jeff. "We'll avoid the sun and get there by midnight."

"Yahoo," said Pat. "Melons and Xinjiang beer for breakfast."

"If you wake up," warned Jeff. "People get to Kashgar and sleep for days and days at a time."

8
Kashgar

Yes, Kashgar was a pleasant place to live in; for anyone with a taste for travel, with a sense of geography and with a spark of curiosity about people and their ways there can be few places in the world more satisfying.
——Eric Shipton, *Mountains of Tartary*

ALTHOUGH KASHGAR lies at the very heart of Asia, a traveler arriving here feels as if he has reached the farthest end of the earth. Peking lies two thousand miles to the east, across terrible deserts; the Bosporus is an even greater distance to the west, across Afghanistan, Iran, and Turkey. The world's highest mountains surround Kashgar—to the northeast the Altai; north, the Tien Shan; west, the Pamirs; southwest, the Hindu Kush; south, the Karakoram; and southeast, beyond deserts and unnamed ranges that occupy the vast, rarely traveled wilderness of central Tibet lie the Himalaya.

Once a major supply and recuperation point on the ancient Silk Road, the city is set strategically between desert and mountains. Rivers pour off the nearby Pamirs, providing irrigation water, before disappearing into the sands of the vast Takla Makan Desert. More than water lies hidden in that all-consuming desert. Ancient cities and Buddhist shrines stand silent and partially buried. When they flourished, the Takla Makan was a fertile plain. The climate has changed drastically behind the fast-rising Himalaya.

For all its remoteness, Kashgar is a city of enormous historic importance. It occupies the junction not only of the world's greatest mountain ranges, but also a point of collision between Asian empires for thousands of years. From the summit of more than one mountain in the area, Russia, China, Afghanistan, and Pakistan are all visible. India is not far away, and she still claims territory less than three hundred miles distant.

Cultures also collide here. You find people of Caucasoid descent mingling with Muslims from the Middle East, Mongols from the steppes, and dark, southern people of India.

During our time in Kashgar, we stayed at the Chinibagh Hotel, a low-slung adobe building surrounded by shaded gardens and outbuildings. From 1890 until 1948 it served as the British consulate. The last consul was Eric Shipton—a man better known as a mountaineer than a diplomat. He had been a member of the 1935, 1936, and 1938 attempts on the north side of Mount Everest. It was also Shipton who in 1951 reconnoitered the route up Everest from the Nepal side that Edmund Hillary followed successfully in 1953. Shipton was one of the first climbers in the Karakoram Range. He wandered freely on both the north and south sides of the Himalaya. He found yeti tracks in Nepal. He went to all the interesting places, enjoyed himself no end, and had the good sense to feel lucky for the opportunity. Although referring to western China, he could well have been thinking of the entire Himalayan region when he wrote in *Mountains of Tartary:*

> I am still amazed at the great good fortune that gave me the chance to know something of Sinkiang and, having watched the recent turn of events, I shudder to think of the narrow margin by which I got that chance. For the Iron Curtain has already clanged down behind me, and it may be many decades before a Western traveller is free to travel there again.

As consul to Kashgar, Shipton served two terms—one at the outset of World War II and one just after it ended. He liked the city and its exotic location in the remote heart of Asia, but his real motivation for being there was to see something of the surrounding mountains. He was a great lover of geography. At every opportunity, he left Kashgar with companions that included his old friend Bill Tilman (the two became a famous mountaineering pair) for weekends or short expeditions.

For as long as I could remember, both Shipton and Tilman had been heroes of mine, and I was happy for the chance to stay in Shipton's old digs. We arrived there before dawn. The gate was locked, so we piled our gear and sat on the pile, dozing, watching the street boys who gathered around to speculate on our appearance there. Even at that early hour, donkey carts filled the streets with the sound of braying and the delicate clatter of their hooves on pavement.

From what I had seen of it, Xinjiang province seemed not to sleep. All night long, on the road from Yecheng, we had passed bicycles, carts, pedestrians,

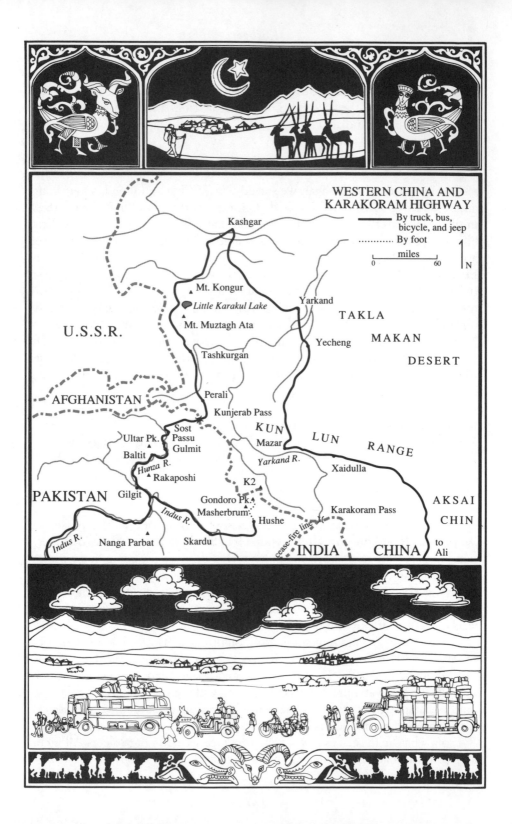

WESTERN CHINA AND
KARAKORAM HIGHWAY

———— By truck, bus,
bicycle, and jeep
············· By foot

miles
0   60

N

Kashgar

▲ Mt. Kongur

🔴 *Little Karakul Lake*

▲ Mt. Muztagh Ata

U.S.S.R.

Yarkand

TAKLA

MAKAN

Yecheng

Tashkurgan

DESERT

AFGHANISTAN

Perali

Kunjerab Pass

KUN

LUN

RANGE

Sost
Ultar Pk. ▲ Passu
          Gulmit
Baltit ▲

Mazar

Yarkand R.

▲ Rakaposhi

Hunza R.

Xaidulla

PAKISTAN

Gilgit

K2
▲

Gondoro Pk. ▲
Masherbrum

AKSAI

CHIN

Indus R.

▲ Hushe

Karakoram Pass

Indus R. Nanga Parbat ▲

Skardu

cease-fire line

INDIA

CHINA

to
Ali

jeeps, and trucks. One time, the truck developed a problem with a wheel; the driver stopped, crawled under the axle, and began banging with a sledgehammer, utilizing the all-purpose Third World mechanical technique: smash anything that isn't working until it starts working again. It's amazing how often the method succeeds, whether applied to trucks, buses, carts, or donkeys.

While the driver was making repairs, and seeing that there was nothing I could contribute to the effort, I took a walk into the apparently featureless desert. There wasn't a light in sight, not a candle or a campfire. By the faint light of stars, I could make out only flat horizon. In a quarter of a mile of walking, I found only hardpan and gravel—not so much as a bush or a clump of grass—and then, to my great surprise, two men strolled by in the starlight, chatting with each other. They didn't see me, and I wouldn't have known they were there had I not heard them talking. I stood and listened to their voices fade into the night. Three in the morning. Where on earth were they going?

Then, arriving in Kashgar, the truck driver had stopped in a silent neighborhood to unload huge sacks of dried apricots. Within moments, a squadron of men came out of nowhere to help. Nearby, I had seen food stalls with lights on and people sitting on benches eating or talking. Bakers worked mounds of dough beside glowing earthen ovens. In Kashgar, as in warm cities everywhere, night provided a comfortable alternative to searing day.

Just at dawn, some people came out of the Chinibagh Hotel, leaving the gate open behind them. We moved in, establishing ourselves on the front verandah, where Shipton and Tilman no doubt sipped tea on hot afternoons and made mountaineering plans. For breakfast, we cooked a package of hot cereal, something Naomi and Jeff had carried from Canada. It was called Mountain Mush, and I believe Shipton would have approved of our cooking it there on his old porch.

Before long, people were stirring in the hotel, including the pleasant Chinese woman who ran the place. She sent us off to cool rooms with high ceilings and thick mud-brick walls, where we pulled the curtains and—just as Jeff had predicted—fell soundly asleep.

In late afternoon, when we ventured out again, there were even more donkey carts in the streets, some carrying unbelievable loads—melons, hay, lumber, great piles of tin pots, and little crowds of bouncing passengers. The donkeys were dainty but obviously strong. Braying at each other behind their burdens, they were Kashgar's salient feature, so that whenever I hear donkeys braying, I will think of Kashgar—as the cry of gulls brings to mind the ocean.

Beyond donkeys, the things first noticed about Kashgar would depend on one's orientation. Every week there was a huge outdoor market—the largest collection of traders and farmers and shoppers in western China. The city was jammed with interesting shops and small factories selling everything from rabbit-fur hats to horseshoes to painful tooth extraction. The people were a colorful bazaar of Tadzik, Uighur, Russian, Pakistani, and Chinese. If you walked several blocks, you'd pass nearly every ethnic group in central Asia.

Our thoughts, however, were devoted almost entirely to food. The old market, two blocks from the Chinibagh, was a gourmand's delight of ramshackle street stalls emitting a pall of charcoal smoke scented with garlic and chili. We gravitated to piles of fresh flatbread, shashlik (spiced meat roasted on a skewer), great juicy tomatoes, green peppers, iced beer, and of course the famous Kashgar melons in all their glorious, dripping variety.

Some food I liked the looks of but considered risky—ice cream churned on the spot in big wooden tubs by noisy electric motors; yogurt mixed with honey, water, and ice; bean-curd noodles dipped in a variety of sauces, all smelling wonderful even after a day sitting in the hot sun visited by squadrons of flies. Some travelers eat these things without concern. Some get sick. I had once lost twenty-five pounds I couldn't afford to lose and was inclined toward caution. Even so, I ate like a rich silk caravan merchant.

In addition to street stalls there were restaurants, which, in our half-starved state, seemed nothing short of heaven. This is how the Oasis Restaurant's menu greeted us:

LADIES AND GENTLEMEN

We are welcome you to our dinnerroom, when you come into our dinnerroom, at first, you get a sit, then our staff would give you a glass of tea. If you like eatsome some dish or food, you can choses them from our meau. In our menu, there are seventies kind of dish for you.

In the another hand, we have some cold bear, cold orange drink,. . . . , if you like Chinese wine, we have Tufan red wine and some another drinks,

After you finshed your meals, our staff will give you a bill for pay. In the general, our staff try thier best to serve for you. At least, all staffs of our dinnerroom welcome you give some ipinious to our dinnerroom, just like this, we shoul make progress to serve for you.

(OASIS RESTAURANT)

January 1th 1987

thank you for visit

Another place, the Guang Ming Cafe Bar, sported a kind of Casablanca look: rattan furniture, overhead fans, stone floor, colored lights, plastic grapes hanging from a suspended arbor, calendar pictures pasted to the walls, and rock music. Madonna, Springsteen, and the Sex Pistols. Somewhere, the Guang Ming had gotten hold of art prints by Renaissance masters showing flirtatious, full-bosomed maidens shrinking from the advances of courtiers, or engaged in other activities considered improper in this Muslim area where we had been scolded for wearing short-sleeve shirts. The prints were risque, and I suppose titillating, but they were classic art and therefore acceptable.

Between feeding forays, we lived on a small porch outside our rooms. Since before we arrived, the porch had been a popular gathering place, providing a nice view of an old section of Kashgar. On most afternoons, hotel residents and assorted travelers would collect there. They brought melons, beer, fresh bread, and stories, including the usual travelers' tales, sharing experiences and routes and recommendations. Of these, one topic seemed to provide the most entertainment and outrage. The subject: Pakistani men and their bizarre behavior.

Quite a few Pakistanis were staying at the Chinibagh, in a separate wing apparently reserved for them. We would bump into them at the gate or in the yard, but they usually avoided conversation, especially if asked what they were doing in Kashgar. Then they would invariably claim to be on business or holiday and refuse to elaborate. Rumor had it that women and alcohol, not readily available in Pakistan, were big on their list. Obviously, alcohol was easy to get in Kashgar; our verandah never lacked a handy supply of Chinese beer and other spirits. As for women in Kashgar, we had only rumors to go on. According to Yolanda, an Israeli woman who had fallen in love with a local man and planned to marry him, and who therefore claimed some inside knowledge of these matters, prostitution was a thriving if invisible business in the old oasis.

I can't say whether she was right, but the Pakistani men staying at the Chinibagh were clearly an excited bunch. We learned to keep our curtains not just closed but pinned shut at night to prevent the perverts from parting the curtains with sticks so they could peer in. Once, hearing sounds outside the window, I yanked back the curtain. A smiling, surprised face said, "Ah, hello sir!"

Wendy told me the routine for the women's shower room: if there wasn't an extra woman to watch the door, it had to be locked from the inside to avoid the sudden appearance of ogling Pakistani faces at the shower curtain. Alicia, an Israeli woman, was walking back one evening from the pit toilets, located in the garden down a tree-lined path. Little did Alicia know that a Pakistani man was waiting behind a tree just for her. As she passed his hiding spot, he leaped out, gave her breasts a quick honk from behind, and leaped back into the shadows. Alicia didn't know whether to laugh or call the police.

Occasionally police were called, as in the case when an elderly Pakistani kidnapped a fourteen-year-old Uighur girl and kept her locked in his room. That story, with no further details, was told to us by the Chinese manager of the Chinibagh on the evening that three drunk men barged uninvited into our room. When Wendy ordered them out, they started making crooning noises to her, so she pushed them out. One man threw whisky in her eyes, whereupon she yelled, and the entire verandah full of Western travelers, about a dozen of us, set off in hot pursuit. Having gotten a look at the drink-thrower's face, Jeff found him with two other men in their room.

"Did you throw your drink at her?" he asked. Wendy was standing in the doorway. "You threw your drink at her, didn't you?"

"Do not accuse this man," said his friend. "It is unjust for you to accuse this man!"

Jeff picked up a bottle standing beside the bed and sniffed the contents. "This is what you threw, isn't it?" The man still did not answer, nor did he move as Jeff calmly and deliberately emptied the bottle into his lap.

This led to a spirited verbal row in the courtyard. On one side, about twenty Pakistani men were yelling that we must be mistaken to think such a thing could have happened, it was not possible; but if it had happened, that was a terrible way to behave, and unforgivable, and should never happen again; and they were so sorry that one of our wives should be so badly mistreated, and we should not form our opinions of Pakistani men on the actions of a few hooligans. On the other side was arrayed a gang of us outraged, protective males trying to display towering umbrage, but actually we were all laughing inside and enjoying the scene. It was hard to take this adolescent, hormone-hopped behavior seriously.

Months later, in India, I mentioned the incident to a vegetarian Hindu, who quickly furnished an explanation. "Pakistan, Pakistan!" he said with a great sigh and a look of parental exasperation. "I am telling you, these men, they are eating too much meat."

"Oh?"

"Yes. It is better to be vegetarian."

"What does that have to do with it?"

"Because, if you will pardon my saying this, the sexual impulse is then not so likely to become excited. Overpopulation and meat, you know. They are one and the same."

But there was a different problem in the men's shower room, a problem that I think was the real source of our rancor toward Pakistani men. For religious reasons they required water in the course of their morning toilet. And because the only ready source of that was in the showers (the hotel had long since given up on keeping the flush toilets running), some Pakistanis used the shower stalls as latrines. It was disgusting. You had to get there early in the morning if you wanted to shower without walking in shit.

Nor did they limit themselves to the showers. One day several of us were grouped around the water spigot in the hotel courtyard, doing our laundry, when one of these dimwits approached, dropped his *shalwar* (loose-fitting traditional trousers), and left a steaming pile in the drain channel. Fifteen feet away from us, in broad daylight!

Stories like these—and there were lots of them—went round and round on Shipton's old verandah. A Brit named Alan complained about the showers one evening, "At least in Sost they use the windows." (Sost is the Pakistani border post on the highway from Pakistan to China.)

"They shit out the windows?" I asked.

"Yeah. There's a hotel there with Western-style bathrooms. These guys come up from their villages, don't know what to make of a flush toilet, so they use the window. You know, they can squat in the window. You don't want to walk behind that hotel, that's for sure. The manager was going crazy when I was there."

"It has to be just a few country yokels doing this," I said.

"Oh yes?" offered John, an American traveling with his wife. He told about having made friends with a young Pakistani man who was well educated and by all appearances wise to the world. They were riding on the same bus, and that night all three of them shared a bungalow—not an unusual way of lodging in small towns, especially for budget travelers. Pestered by bedbugs, John went outside to sleep. Sometime later, his wife woke up with the Pakistani's hand in her pants and ran shrieking from the room.

"I couldn't believe it," said John. "He was the last person I'd expect that from. He came out a few minutes later, carrying his luggage and saying, 'I am with shame. I have no honor.' I told him, 'You're damn right!'"

"They've all seen movies," said his wife. "They think Western women run around half naked all the time and jump into bed with any man they see."

"Sure," said John. "He thought my leaving the room was an invitation."

Another woman told a story about staying with her husband in a respectable hotel in Islamabad. She had woken in the night with a man sitting on her bed. She thought it was her husband at first and said something, whereupon the man leaped up and jumped out the window the way he had come in. "Don't stay on the ground floor" was her advice.

"If a guy touches you on the street, hit him," said Naomi. "Just haul off and whack him one. He'll be too humiliated to look at you after that."

We were getting an odd impression of what to expect from Pakistan.

IT WAS AMAZING TO ME that the eight of us were still having such a good time together. I had expected that once we reached Kashgar, where there was no longer any benefit in maintaining our unwieldy group, we would have split up. None of us was accustomed to traveling with an entourage. But we continued to hang together, if it meant only going for a meal or simply sitting out on the verandah. I wouldn't want to push our luck by trying it again, but I can't imagine finding another group of people who could be so compatible. We were lucky in that regard.

After a few days, with our bellies as round as the melons on which we gorged, we began to talk about onward plans. Jeff, Naomi, and Ant were headed back to Canada via Hong Kong; they would fly from Kashgar. Lee had a ticket for New York from Karachi, so he was headed for Pakistan by bus.

The remaining four of us were also going to Pakistan, but we wanted to bicycle the Karakoram Highway. Pat especially wanted to revisit Little Karakul Lake and the great ice mountain, Muztagh Ata. He remembered his 1981 expedition there as a blissful experience in a wildly exotic place, where broad plains of emerald green surrounded a gorgeous lake lying between two of the world's most majestic mountains, Muztagh Ata and Kungur. It had been a small expedition, only four climbers and no porters to complicate things. Pat and his friends had been free to visit the yurt homes of Kirghiz families, who greeted them with uproarious, smiling hospitality. They had seen a primitive polo game, a marvelous display of horsemanship. Camels had carried their loads to base camp, loads that included melons and beer and local yogurt. They had climbed the mountain easily, the highest any of them had ever been at that time. Pat had made the climb on touring skis. The descent had been pure joy. Every time he talked about the place, his eyes sparkled.

Before leaving home, I had read Shipton's description of a campsite on Little Karakul Lake in his book *Mountains of Tartary* and had copied it to carry with me. He was there in 1947 with Bill Tilman after trying to climb Muztagh Ata:

> We chose a flat promontory on the western shore of the lake and settled down to enjoy one of the finest views in Central Asia. It was a clear, still day, and the glassy surface of the lake, four or five square miles in extent, was very blue. We were at the centre of a complete semicircle of ice-mountains with a radius of about twenty miles. To the north and north-east there was an uninterrupted view of the Kungur massif, with its two 25,000-foot peaks, so laden with ice that throughout its length there was hardly any rock to be seen. To the east there was the long line of peaks of the Shiwakte group. The huge mass of Muztagh Ata filled the southern arc; from here, at last, it showed us a form and character consistent with its size. Wide grassy valleys, intersected by rounded hills, filled in the middle distance. Flights of geese and duck passed over the lake.

It sounded awfully nice. Naomi and Jeff added encouragement. They had bicycled that way the summer before, just after the border was opened.

"You'll like it," said Jeff. "The road's good; it's nothing like Tibet."

But then we started to hear bicycle stories.

"You have cycles?" said Paul, a Canadian verandah habitué. "Did you know that about a month ago a foreigner was caught riding a Chinese bike, loaded with camping gear, north toward Red Mountain?"

"Where's that?" I asked.

"I don't know. Near the border. Near Russia. Very sensitive. Instantly the PSB [Public Security Bureau, the police] shut down all cycle rentals in Kashgar. They're really freaked out about it. If you try cycling from here, you're likely to get caught before you get out of Kashgar."

"Maybe we could just hop off the bus part way."

"It's not that simple. They keep a list of people headed for the border. I don't think they'd let you off."

On top of that, we learned that it was illegal for us to be at Little Karakul Lake—or anywhere around Muztagh Ata for that matter—without booking a tour with CITS that would cost nearly a thousand dollars a day.

Because we wanted to try anyway, we went back to skulking around a Chinese city, keeping the bikes hidden, trying to retain the defense of ignorance by not asking the wrong questions. Our idea was that if no official refused us permission to be at Little Karakul Lake, then we could claim we hadn't been informed. Devious perhaps, and of little value if we were caught, but in our defense I should say that we thought the prohibitions were designed not so much to keep us out of the area as to channel lucrative business to CITS. Besides that, buses left daily for the border and went right past Little Karakul Lake without stopping. It obviously wasn't a sensitive area.

Accordingly, we devised a plan. From the police, we were able to obtain travel permits to visit Tashkurgan—that is, to get off the bus short of the border. By showing those permits at the bus station, we convinced the ticket agent to sell us tickets only as far as Tashkurgan, meaning that our names would not be included on the border passenger manifest. In theory, we could get off wherever we wanted and not be missed.

9
Karakoram Highway

In a wild, barely inhabited landscape any soldier at all is an eyesore.
——H. W. Tilman,
Two Mountains and a River

T HE BUS TO PAKISTAN left before dawn. At least that's what our tickets said, so we stayed up late reorganizing Mount Equipment, getting ready to travel.

But nothing could have prepared us for the scene at the station in the morning. A hundred people were jammed at a gate guarded by a man who I reckoned was checking tickets. Lee and I approached, wheeling our cycles, and the guard waved us into the bus yard. Behind us, he stopped a Uighur woman. She argued. He was firm. She shouted. The guard shouted back. She hit him. He hit back. She spat. Wendy was standing behind her. In her fury, the woman turned and gave Wendy a hard shove, but the crowd kept her upright. I gestured to Wendy to push past. She tried. The woman rushed forward to threaten me, but the guard held her and she kicked his legs.

Wendy shot me a gesture of futility and backed out of the crowd. She and Baiba walked their bikes around to another entrance and came through unchallenged. A few minutes later the contested gate was inexplicably thrown open and the crowd dispersed.

"What do you think that was all about?" I asked.

"Three thousand years of civilization."

Our bus was not there. It came two hours late. When it did, the mostly Pakistani passengers lifted their loads onto the roof rack. We waited until everything was up there, a considerable pile half the length of the bus and two feet deep, before laying our bikes on top, flat, the handlebars turned sideways and the pedals off. As we finished, a man appeared at the ladder with a donkey cart full of produce.

"Where were you an hour ago?" I asked, in English. Of course he didn't understand, and there was nothing to do but remove the bikes, load his produce, and replace the bikes. Then another wave of Pakistani luggage appeared, as if their owners had not been there watching the whole procedure. Again, the bikes came off, more bags were crammed among melons and boxes, and we put the bikes back on. The load was three feet deep.

The driver climbed up and began lashing on the cargo net. Lee and I helped. Just as we finished, several more bags were tossed up. I made half-hearted objections. The owners of the bags just smiled and shrugged, as if to say, "You don't want them on your bikes, then pack them under." I did that. We finished lashing down the net. I climbed down, thinking the business complete. By then we were three hours late.

Half the passengers then climbed up after me and began yanking at their bags, lifting the net, putting things in, pulling things out, rearranging, untying. Lee and I went up again and found ourselves mediators between combatants. "I don't want my bag there; I want it here!" "No! Then it's pushing on my bag. Yours goes there!" "Damn you, I won't have it there—you take your bag!" A bag was thrown to the ground. Angry shouting erupted below. The bag came back up. It was slammed down on the spokes of a front wheel. I stepped in, finding a new place for the bag, fighting a short battle myself over the owner's concern that a handlebar could damage a cardboard box.

Finally everyone was content. I knew this because they climbed down, not because they seemed at all pleased with the disposition of things. The center of conflict now moved inside the bus. Although we were assigned seat numbers, none of the seats were numbered. No one knew where he or she should be sitting, but most passengers had strong feelings about where they wanted to sit— and more importantly, where their hand luggage should sit. The Pakistanis all carried things they had purchased in China, packaged in flimsy cardboard. They had big cooking pots filled, apparently, with lunch. They had bags of snacks, melons, odd-shaped burlap bundles, and carpets. There wasn't room for it all.

"Would you kindly carry this for me?" asked a smiling young man holding a long, thin box. It contained a doorway curtain made of plastic beads. Strands of them were leaking out.

"Sorry," I said.

He looked around and managed to cram one end of the box into the ceiling rack above me. He sat down across the aisle. The box came loose and fell on my head. I handed it back to him.

"Sorry," he said.

A young Chinese woman was trying to put things in order. She commanded everyone to be seated. She wanted to see if there were any empty places. She was getting nowhere. Pakistanis kept leaving the bus to fiddle with the bags on top. The only people obeying the attendant were two Chinese army officers, but as soon as she left the bus, they were on their feet and out the door. So was I, in time to watch as a Uighur man threw four heavy sacks of melons on top of our bikes.

Then we were off, swaying through the city into the dusty desert. The mountains began at a canyon called the Gez Defile, a place whose name alone made me think of camel caravans and spice bound from India to Europe. The Silk Road had come this way, or rather, one of the silk routes, for there were many branching pathways used and disused as seasons and political situations changed. I suspect that when caravans reached the Gez Defile, they drew up their collective courage; no one would have wanted to go that way if there was an alternative. It was a wound in the landscape, a formidable ravine leading 7000 feet up from the desert to the plateau around Mounts Kungur and Muztagh Ata. The road climbed for miles along a cascading river beneath crumbling rock walls.

Even in a bus, it was slow going.

"Place is a mess," said Pat. When he had been there six years earlier, the road was a minor vehicle path, rough but negotiable. Now it was the Karakoram Highway, an important strategic thoroughfare linking Pakistan with China. But until construction was finished, it would be a highway only on paper.

Work crews had dug up the entire road with their little shovels, all the way from Kashgar to the border. Much of the distance, there was no road at all, only rubble between ditches. We had driven for hours across the desert, paralleling the would-be highway, churning up fine, yellow dust that forced us to close windows despite the formidable heat. Upon entering the Gez Defile, however, the track got really rough. At one point, the bus driver tried to force his vehicle over a sharp embankment. The bus grounded in the middle, high-centered. We all got off. The driver tried to back down. Wheels spun; metal complained; chunks of tread flew off the tires. We started pushing. It required most of the passengers and some of the road workers to shove the bus back off the rocks. I expected the workers to reshape the embankment. It would have been a simple job. But no, they stood and watched while the driver made another run at it and got stuck again. I quit helping. I couldn't see the point.

Four times the bus high-centered on that pile of rocks. The driver acted like he was driving a plow, trying to bull his way over. No one ever moved any rocks by hand. On the fifth try the driver succeeded, but he bent the bus doing it. He had to borrow a sledgehammer to get the door open.

At the top of the canyon, the bus lost one of its two gas tanks. It fell off with a great clatter in the middle of the road, having been beaten shapeless on the rocks. The driver got out, gave it a nudge with his toe as if checking for life, and left it resting in peace.

Then, suddenly, we came out of the canyon, and what a view there was! The landscape opened up. The air was cold and clear. We could see glaciers and giant sand dunes and expanses of green grass dotted with grazing animals. Up here the river meandered through a hundred braided channels, wandering back and forth in a huge valley, and above everything else stood the 25,000-foot ice mountains, Kungur and Muztagh Ata. My spirit soared. It was good to be back in the high country.

We spent the night in a truckstop fifteen miles from Little Karakul Lake and unloaded our bikes in the dark so that no one would see us; after all, our permits were not for here but for Tashkurgan, the next night's stop. Lee shared a room with us and left when the driver laid on the horn at 5:00 A.M. We sent him off with fond good-byes and stayed around until midmorning fiddling with our cycles, eagerly anticipating a light cruise up the valley to the lake.

Instead, we were right back to Tibetan conditions. The road had disappeared, torn up by construction. For much of the distance, we walked.

The lake, however, was everything I had hoped for. Placing our tents on lush grass just inches from the turquoise water, we had a clear view of mighty Muztagh Ata towering above, ethereal behind a scrim of summer haze, a planetary mass hanging as if detached from earth. It was like the moon rising much too close. But for Pat, it was a disappointment. The road and the construction work had changed things. "This place was special," he said. "You really felt remote. Now it feels like just another place."

I had no memories to complicate things, and I thought it was a beautiful spot. This was where Shipton had camped. The view was what he had called one of the finest in Central Asia. And certainly the mountains were the same as ever. But I could see Pat's point. The noise of construction, the dynamite blasting, the grind of bulldozers rather stole the exotic fire from the camels we had seen.

I know how Shipton would feel about the place now. He hated motor vehicles. On the other hand, I don't know what Shipton thought about bicycles, and for the next week I wasn't sure what to think myself. The roads were punishing, the country was dusty, and the days were hot. I expect Shipton would have wanted a horse instead. But given the alternative of a bus ride, bicycles were far and away the best way for us to travel. The country was spectacular. We went slowly, of course, and saw things, and we camped in some beautiful places. Best of all, we met people.

It was a country of oases, where stretches of desert separated farming communities clustered around streams and irrigated fields. Just when heat and dust were getting hard to tolerate, we would turn a corner and coast into the green shade of willows and poplars that lined the road and clustered around mud-brick homes. The houses had generous courtyards and hay piled to dry on their flat roofs.

We usually stopped in the shade to let sweat dry. Always there was irrigation water, clear and cold, running in canals like a message from the mountains. Children came past leading donkeys or goats. In meadows, men were scything hay, raking it into piles, and carrying it in great bundles on their backs. Women dressed in bright red dresses and scarves sat on their porches doing domestic chores and singing. Singing! There were no radios playing in those little villages, and we heard no loudspeaker systems. Women's voices made sufficient and lovely music.

Each time we stopped, people would eventually come to talk. We were a great curiosity—our gear, our clothing, our behavior. Putting up a tent, repairing a bike, patching a tire, lighting a cookstove, using a camera, washing dishes—these were all subjects of interest. Writing in my diary was something I'd learned to reserve for private places; inevitably it drew a crowd of people who leaned over my shoulders watching my squiggle move across the page. To me they were all critics.

By now we had learned enough Chinese to carry on simple road conversations, enough to say: We live in Canada and the United States. We came from Kashgar. We are going to Pakistan. Here, would you like a dried apricot, or a candy? What is the name of this place? Yes, they are fancy bikes. The cost? About two thousand yuan (but usually we said about three hundred yuan, because even that was a huge amount of money for the people we met and we were embarrassed to admit the real cost). Yes, the bikes are hard work; the road is bumpy. It's hot today. No, we didn't cycle from Canada, we flew to Hong Kong (but many people didn't know Hong Kong, or other Chinese cities, for that matter). It's taken us three (or whatever) days to get here from Kashgar. How far is it to Kunjerab Pass from here? Have you been to Pakistan?

Beyond that, our language failed us, and we could only say, "I don't understand" to question after question. Our visitors were, without exception, friendly, open, and curious. I recognized their frustration, which would turn to resignation, when we could not answer what they tried to ask in a simple way. We were left smiling at each other while they pinched the soft parts of our bikes, squeezed the brake levers, and tried out the shifters. Sometimes we would cut up a melon and pass it around.

Of all the strange things we did, none was stranger than filtering water. We carried a little pump that filtered out bacteria; we would fill a jug with dirty water and pump it into our drinking bottles. It looked like a terribly inefficient way to transfer water.

"Here," one man said, "let me show you how to pour from that big jug. It's easy. No, no, give it here. I won't spill it. See?"

We had no way of telling them what the filter did unless we were in a place where the water was cloudy. Then the function of the pump, like the water it produced, became clear, and even more fascinating.

But there was so much I wanted to learn from them. I wanted to talk about the weather and about crops and family life. I was curious about the surrounding mountains, which to the west marked the Soviet border. Did these people have family in the Soviet Union? Could they go there and visit? I wondered about politics and attitudes toward the new highway and a hundred other details. Ironically, instead of being able to converse directly, I would have to visit libraries at home, hoping to fill in a few of the enormous gaps in my understanding of these people with whom I'd had so many stunted conversations.

Of course, we could have hired a translator back in Kashgar, an official CITS guide. But then it would have cost us about a thousand dollars a day (we were getting by on an average of about twenty-five dollars), and in a couple of weeks we'd have been broke and on our way home. Besides that, we would not have been allowed to bicycle. We'd have been in a jeep, and we might not have had any roadside conversations whatsoever.

It was better, I thought, to go along slowly and learn what we could learn, despite the language barrier.

As for cycling, everyone understood what we were up to, especially the road construction crews. They were mostly young men, mostly Han Chinese from eastern cities where they knew about sport and about bicycles. They would cheer as we came by, give us the thumbs up, get excited, run over to meet us. Likewise, soldiers in army trucks passed us with waves and cheers as if we were all off toward the same great triumph.

Some triumph.

THERE IS A RULE that all travelers know: Of all the things you carry, the one thing you must not lose is your passport. Some people carry their passports in pouches hung around their necks, under their shirts, or in cloth belts worn at the waist under their clothing. Because this is the most secure item in their possession, other critical things are kept in the pouch—documents, cash, credit cards, and so forth. Because a passport, by rule, will never be lost, these other items are just as safe.

I had my passport in such a pouch, with a neck strap. With it was fourteen hundred dollars in cash, two credit cards, several traveler's checks, and a few other bits of essential paper.

One evening, approaching a checkpoint outside Tashkurgan, we stopped our bicycles. It was nearly dark. We'd been through one checkpoint already that day with no trouble; in fact, the official had congratulated us on our bikes. But we worried about this one, which was so close to a regional capital. Maybe this checkpost would enforce the rule against cycling.

"What do you think, should we try going through now?" I said. We had decided not to do anything blatantly illegal, like trying to avoid checkposts altogether. However, we had no scruples about passing them when officials might be asleep.

"I'd rather try in the morning," said Baiba. "If we camped here, we could leave right at dawn. They might not see us."

So we camped there, near the road, and in the grey light of early morning, we pushed our bikes around the barricade just as a sleepy soldier came out of the tent buttoning his pants. I saw him first and stood still, waving an innocent greeting when he looked up. He yelled. Another man came out and approached us. "Passports?" he said. We handed them over. He looked through them, handed them back, and waved us on.

I couldn't believe it. He didn't even write down our names. We pedaled off before he could change his mind. In a hurry, I crammed my passport pouch into my jacket pocket—not around my neck—and closed the pocket. And forgot about it. Later that morning I took the jacket off. I tied it across my handlebars. We pedaled about thirty kilometers. We met people along the way. We ate a melon in the shade of trees where people gathered around in the usual manner, curiously fingering the bikes and asking questions. Late in the afternoon, at a town called Dapdar, I noticed that the pocket of my jacket was open and empty. No passport.

Fortunately, there was a young man in Dapdar who spoke English. He helped us hire a truck and a driver to retrace the route to Tashkurgan. Wendy and I stood in back, scanning the road as we went. We stopped to talk to everyone we saw. No luck.

At Tashkurgan, I went to the PSB and reported the loss. The officer was astonished that we had been bicycling. "That is not allowed!" he said.

"Really? You're the first official who's told me that." It was true.

"Where did you enter China?"

"Guilin."

"You have ridden bicycles from there?"

"Oh, no. We flew to Lhasa." I recounted how we had traveled to this point.

"But you could not have ridden bicycles in Tibet. It is not permitted."

"But it was. The policeman in Ali even borrowed my bicycle. It's a very nice bike."

"No, that is not possible."

We had a long conversation. I made a list of what I had lost and where. He seemed more worried about our having cycled than anything else. I did not tell him about Pat and Baiba. If we were in trouble, I didn't want to involve them. He had me write a letter of self-criticism, which served as an admission of guilt and an apology.

"I will not fine you," he said. "You have lost enough already."

"But I can go on to Pakistan?"

"Oh, yes. No problem."

"Will you give me a paper saying that?"

"I cannot. I am not immigration. I do not have that authority. I will telephone Perali to tell them you are coming. They will give you papers."

That was good news. Perali was the border station. We could cross tomorrow, I thought. But this pleasant official wanted us to stay overnight in Tashkurgan and take the bus the next day. I protested that we had left our bicycles untended; they were not safe where they were. I promised we would flag the bus in the morning and ride to the border. He was very reluctant to let us go, but after a long time and consultations with several other people, he agreed to that idea.

So we rode the truck back to Dapdar, where Pat and Baiba had set up camp beside a small stream. The next morning the bus passed before we saw it coming, so we again hired a truck (which was actually no more legal than bicycling) and rode to Perali, where it turned out they were not expecting me. The man in Tashkurgan had not phoned or, equally possible, the phones were not working.

Every immigration officer wanted to hear the story, but only after they finished processing the bus passengers bound for Pakistan. I told the story to all who spoke English, perhaps a dozen officers; they passed it on to the others. Expressions in the immigration office were sympathetic, worried, sad. But they had nothing to offer and said we must wait until the next day.

"That's all right. Maybe it will show up tomorrow," said Pat. We had heard surprising stories about the return of stolen or lost property in China. I pictured the police, at that very moment, shaking down people along the road, saying, "This is not the way to treat foreign guests!" I didn't figure to ever see the money again, but I thought the passport might well be turned in.

With those thoughts, we had a look around Perali—not a big job. Border stations are usually no-man's-lands, outposts whose location is determined not by dictates of geography or by the preference of inhabitants, but by the often arbitrary concept of a national boundary. No one really cares about the borders except the governments that maintain them, and Perali was no exception. Half a dozen Chinese blockhouse buildings, recently constructed but already in decay, sat on either side of the highway. Two streetlights shaped like lotus blossoms provided a forlorn gesture of solidarity with the far-distant motherland. They were not lit at night. They were daytime symbols.

Behind the concrete shed that served as a bus station, there was a sort of hotel, comprising two army tents sheltering a few bunks. We moved into one of them. I felt chagrined over the loss of my passport but had already marked it down to experience and put it behind me. My thoughts were on Pakistan.

The next day, after the daily bus passengers were processed, I was summoned back to the office, where I again told the whole story several times over to worried looking faces in green uniforms.

"All I really want," I said, "is to go on to Pakistan."

A senior officer shook his head. "You cannot go."

"Why not?"

"Because you have no passport."

"But . . . at Tashkurgan, the police told me to go to the border and you would give me a paper to go to Pakistan."

"Yes, two officers went to Tashkurgan yesterday to ask. We know you reported this. You are not lying."

"Well, thank you. Then you have no reason to keep me here?"

"We have no right to detain you in China. You have broken no law. But you cannot go."

"Then I am a prisoner."

"No, no, no!" He spoke as if I had said something offensive. "No prisoner."

"But I cannot go?"

"You cannot go."

"So what do I do?"

"We must telegram Urumqi with your case. They will tell us what to do."

"How long will it take?"

"Two or three days."

As Yongden would have said, everything was never clear.

"You might as well go on to somewhere nice," I told Pat. "Who knows where this is going to end up?" He and Baiba had been thinking the same. So they told the officials that they too had bicycles and wanted to ride to Kunjerab Pass and the border, about twenty miles farther along. This information caused a minor kefuffle, ending in their being ordered to hire a truck to carry them out of China. So off they went to Kunjerab Pass while Wendy and I went back to the tent.

There were new people at the tent—two Japanese travelers who had just arrived from Pakistan and were in no hurry to get to Kashgar. We introduced ourselves. They were Miki and his wife, Kuni, on an eighteen-month honeymoon. Miki had a melon, which he sliced up and passed around while I explained what we were doing there.

"Oh, bad news," Miki said. He had a Japanese friend who had lost his passport in the forty-mile no-man's-land between the Pakistani and Chinese border posts. "He thought someone stole it from his luggage. You know what a foreign passport is worth here—"

"No, I don't."

"I've heard that in China, a Pakistani passport is worth two hundred dollars. An American one is worth a thousand. They can alter it and use it. Anyway, this guy lost his passport and arrived at the Pakistan border post without it, and they sent him back. He had to go back to Beijing to get out of China."

"All the way to Beijing?"

"Yes, but remember, he was Japanese. You're American. That's better. Your Reagan just gave four billion dollars to President Zia."

"Not my Reagan."

"Pakistan likes you. They'll let you in. Anyway, tell me how you lost your passport." I told him the story, and he offered some advice: "I think the best place to keep valuable things is with your dirty socks. I never lose dirty socks. Have you ever lost a dirty sock?"

"You're right. Never."

"And better if the sock has a hole in it. No way could you lose a dirty sock with a hole."

"What do you think my chance would be of sneaking into Pakistan?"

"I don't know. There's at least one more checkpost, and there are guys on horses."

We talked about that for a while. Miki was a freelance television cameraman. He had been into Afghanistan with the rebels several times and knew a bit about borders.

As we spoke, two of the younger immigration officers came to the tent. Their names were Mr. Guo and Mr. Chen. They explained that they were learning English and wanted help with pronunciation. We had fun with some of the phrases in their book:

"Please show me your passport," the book said.

"I don't have one!" I said.

"Please sleep here."

"I have no choice."

"What is this object? What is your name? Where do you come from?"

"The moon," I said. "I come from the moon."

"In America?"

145

"No, in the sky. At night, the moon!" I drew a picture of a quarter-moon over a mountain and put a little house on it. They thought it was a great joke and asked me if I had two heads.

"Are you married?"

"Yes, this is my wife."

"Wife? Yes, then you are husband."

"Yes. Now let me write one for you." I wrote in block letters. Mr. Guo read slowly.

"You . . . are . . . our . . . prisoner. Prisoner! No, no no, you have a little trouble. Only a little trouble."

That, too, was a good joke.

Later in the day we heard a commotion and looked up to see a tall, bearded European being swept around the corner of the bus station by an angry crowd. Firmly gripping him by the arm was a Chinese man in a blue uniform whom I recognized as the bus ticket agent. His captive, with a worried, pale face, saw us and shouted, "Please come, there is some problem!" The crowd squeezed into the small ticket office. Miki and I pushed in after them.

"What's going on?" Miki asked the European.

"I don't know. They came and grabbed me!"

Miki, who spoke a little Chinese, questioned the ticket agent and suddenly was laughing. "Ah! They've got you for pissing! He says you were pissing."

"Yes, I was behind that building out there. What's wrong with that?"

Miki and the agent talked again. "Well, he says it's illegal. Ten-yuan fine. Just a minute." Miki negotiated, objecting to the amount. "Okay, five yuan. Is that okay?"

The man, who I had learned in the meantime was a university professor from Yugoslavia, looked relieved. He paid the fine and got a receipt written in Chinese.

"A receipt?" said the professor.

"It is a good souvenir," said the bus agent, who was now smiling.

"A receipt? You give me a receipt for pissing?"

We walked outside. The Yugoslav was nonplused. Holding the receipt, he asked Miki, "What does it say? Does it say 'pissing'?" He was laughing now too. "I will never throw this away. You know, I was afraid they found my hashish. In my luggage. But pissing, in that place!"

I will never forget the sight of him being hauled across the filthy compound, littered with broken bottles, feces, spittle, paper, broken concrete, rotting garbage, and into a room in a decaying building whose foundation was stained by the urine of many years, to be fined for peeing in a nearby alley.

It seemed to me then, in my cynical frame of mind, to be a fitting symbol for the traveler's experience in China, for the separate laws that govern the behavior of foreigners, keeping them separate, at a distance, as an exploitable resource. Later, when I could laugh about the whole thing myself, from passport to piss spot, I especially enjoyed having seen that evening one of the Chinese immigration officials standing in the road in the middle of Perali, taking a leak, undisturbed.

Guo and Chen returned to the tent the next morning. They wore big smiles: "We have news! We have heard from Urumqi."

"Yes?" Wendy and I sat down beside them on a cot.

"You must go to Kashgar."

"What? I'm going to Pakistan."

"No. You must go to Kashgar, to the PSB."

"No. I won't. I'll stay here." I stood up. So did they.

"It is the decision of our government."

"No. It will take a week!"

"You must go to Kashgar. Our government says so."

I stomped out of the tent. I was furious. I wanted to see the chief of immigration. I was perhaps irrational. I would have said awful things, but somehow I didn't want to teach these fellows, whom I liked, bad words. So I said the least offensive thing I could think of: "Your government can eat it!"

"Eat it?" said one.

"Eat it?" said the other. My bad humor kept me from hearing that, but Wendy told me about it later. She was incapacitated by laughter, seeing these fellows tripping gaily along behind me chattering, "Eat it?"

My protest did nothing but offend the man in charge, who told me I was to blame for the entire affair. He said I was the only person ever to lose a passport. I said China was treating me unfairly, that the passport was stolen. His reply was that Chinese people do not steal, and he went on to imply that if someone had taken it, I entrapped the thief by making the passport available. "You are to blame," he shouted. "Not China."

I suggested that there must be an alternative to my having to go all the way back to Kashgar by bus. "Other way? You want a plane? You'd like a plane?" He said it with a sneer.

"There are jeeps," I said.

"Oh, you want a jeep."

"How much does it cost to hire a jeep?"

He answered without pause. "Five thousand eight hundred yuan." Now he was beaming. "FEC."

More than sixteen hundred dollars to go two hundred miles. I left him and sought out the seemingly more amiable Mr. Guo. "Can you give me the name of the person in Urumqi who says I must go to Kashgar?"

"It is the government."

"Is there a name on the telegram?"

"No."

"Will the people in Kashgar know I am coming?"

"I don't know."

"Then maybe they will send me to Urumqi."

Guo looked sad and perplexed.

"Can you give me the name of someone in Kashgar to ask for?"

He brightened at this, my first reasonable question. "Mr. Yao is my friend. He speaks good English."

"Can you give me a letter to him?"

This was another reasonable request. He wrote on the back of some form, copying from my original report, and stamped it with an official red-inked chop. I asked him to read the letter to me. It was worded in the most general terms. "This person has lost his passport and fourteen hundred U.S. dollars and two—I don't know how to call these. . . . "

"Credit cards."

"Credit cards?"

How could I explain a credit card? On another occasion, I might have tried, but now I just said, "Identification cards."

"Ah. Two identification cards and one silver ring."

"That's all it says? You didn't mention Urumqi and their orders?"

"It is not necessary."

"Will the police in Kashgar wait four days just to send me to Urumqi and then to Beijing?"

"It cannot happen."

"They can deal with this in Kashgar?"

"Do not be worried."

"Because if there is a chance of that happening, I should not wait in Kashgar but go directly to Beijing."

"No, I assure you."

"You're certain of this?"

"Yes. Each time this happens, people must go to Kashgar."

"This has happened before? That other man said I was the only person to have this happen."

"Oh, yes, many times."

S O WE WENT TO KASHGAR. It took three days of riding a terrible bus on that terrible road, and you don't need to hear more description of it. There are other bus rides to come.

The first morning in Kashgar, we went straight to the PSB and asked for Mr. Yao. He was in Urumqi, said a clerk, and would be back the next afternoon. Two more days! I said, "Maybe someone else can deal with this." The clerk went out and returned with an older, uniformed man, who read my paper and said in halting English that Mr. Yao was my man. He would be back Tuesday afternoon. He refused to do more, and the clerk refused to translate further. I said, "Look here, dorkface, either you tell me the truth or I'll stuff this blotter down your throat and ram this window shade down after it." Rather, that's what I wanted to say. What I actually said was "Thank you," and walked outside looking for a dog to kick.

We went back to the Oasis Restaurant, where we ran into Paul, one of our former Chinibagh verandah friends. I didn't recognize him at first because he had shaved his head to get rid of lice. He suggested that I call the American embassy. "That's why they're here, to help you," he said.

That was a novel idea. It had never occurred to me. Paul went on to say there had been trouble since we left. Danny, an argumentative Israeli whom we had known from the verandah at the Chinibagh, had gone to the PSB office for a visa extension—his second. The PSB officer refused, saying one extension was the limit. This led to an argument, which grew heated, until Danny spat on the officer. Two other PSB men grabbed Danny, and a tussle ensued, with Danny and the original officer pulling on his passport. The passport gave way, tearing in half, horrifying the Chinese, who instantly backed out of the conflict. But later that day, they had come to Danny's hotel room and arrested him.

"That's not all," said Paul. "A French couple went in for extensions and had their passports seized."

"Why?"

"I don't know. The PSB is telling them to await a decision of some sort. They've been here a week now."

I decided I'd better get hold of the embassy after all. I went to the hotel lobby (we were staying now at the former Russian consulate, for the sake of a change), and after an hour of trying to get through to Beijing, all I could hear on the line was something that sounded like the battle of Saipan. Paul suggested calling from the post office and offered to come along. On the way, he told me his post office story.

Several days earlier he had gone to mail a package. The postal clerk watched as Paul had his parcel inspected by a customs agent and sewn into a cloth bag—standard procedure for international mail. When Paul presented the sealed package to the clerk, the man said he was too late; he would have to come back tomorrow. Paul remonstrated with no success.

"I asked him to hold it for me overnight so I wouldn't need to have it inspected again the next day. He agreed, and I asked him for a receipt. And then he got offended. He said, 'Chinese people do not steal.' I said, 'Okay, okay,' and I left."

The next day, Paul had waited in line again. "When I get to the counter this time, the clerk hands me the parcel and says the address is wrong. I say I'll fix it but I'd like to have it weighed and pay for it first. He says no, I have to fix the address first.

"So I do that, and I go back to the line. It was a long line. This time the guy weighs the box. I give him money, and he says, 'This is not the right change. You must have the right change.' Well, where do you get change in a Chinese post office if not from the clerks? I had to go downstairs and find a foreigner who could give me change.

"Then I went back upstairs, waited in line again, gave the guy my money, and the bastard makes this elaborate display of counting it. He counted it three times. He said, 'In China, cheating is a crime.' He just wanted to be a jerk. I wanted to punch him out."

Paul waited while I tried to call Beijing, a task that involved fighting my way through a yelling crowd of blue-suited Uighurs to the telephone desk, where I could remain only by reaching across the counter and holding tight to the other side of it. With both hands thus occupied, I yelled, "Beijing! Beijing!" at the harried long-distance operators, who just as energetically ignored me. After fifteen minutes, I managed to scribble the phone number on a form. But nothing ever happened, and after an hour of feeling foolish, I gave up the effort.

I hadn't expected success, so I wasn't disappointed. But I could see that Paul's patience with Kashgar was at an end. Walking back to the hotel, he played a game on a middle-aged Uighur woman, walking as close to her shoulder as he could, fixing her with a smile. She steadfastly ignored him for two blocks and finally crossed the street to escape him. I thought he was behaving in an offensive manner, but it gave him pleasure.

Late in the day, Wendy and I stopped by the Chinibagh Hotel and met Danny in the hallway. "I thought you were in jail," I said.

"I was there only for one day," he said. "But I might have to go back." He told his story a bit differently from Paul's version. Yes, he spit at the Chinese man, but it was a clever ploy to make the man angry. "I held my passport just so," said Danny, "so he would grab the pages and they would come out. I knew it was my best chance. They have great respect for papers in China, you know."

"Which passport was it?" It was China's policy to deny visas to Israelis. The Israelis we had met retained citizenship in other countries and traveled on alternate passports.

"British, of course. The bastards say I have to pay 500 yuan or be in jail for ten days."

"They charged you with spitting?"

"No. They call it hooliganism."

"What will you do?"

"I won't pay them. I don't have the money. Let them put me in jail! I'll go on a hunger strike. Then I'll go to Beijing and picket the British embassy. Do you think that would get attention from the newspapers? British citizen thrown in a stinking jail because Chinese police tore up his passport!"

Danny knew more details about the French couple. The incident had happened at the bank just before the weekend. The couple had waited in line, but the clerk shut her wicket just as they got there, and the French woman insisted that they had to have money that day. The clerk refused. Eventually the French woman was holding the Chinese woman's arm and yelling. That brought the police, who charged both French people with hooliganism. Their passports were being held as bond until they agreed to pay the fines levied.

For some reason, Kashgar was filled with stories of difficulties with officials—or maybe I was unusually receptive to hearing tales of frustration. I certainly perked up when I overheard a woman in the Oasis Restaurant describing how a Yugoslav had been fined for public peeing at Perali. So the story was making the rounds! "Well," said the woman sitting with her, "that happened when we were there too. To a man from England. They fined him and gave him a receipt. Can you imagine? A receipt!"

———

The next afternoon, Wendy and I were back at the PSB office. It was lunchtime, so we waited outside. At precisely 3:00 P.M., someone began beating a gong in the tree-filled compound and people emerged from napping places, buttoning up rumpled uniforms. I recognized the older officer with whom I had spoken the day before and followed him through the doorway. Surprisingly, he recognized me and after some delay said, "Spickingrish semmanatel." Saying this, he made a circular gesture in the air. I gaped. He bent, patted the carpet, and showed me one finger. He said it again: "Spickingrish semmanatel." Finally I got it. Mr. Yao, who speaks English, was at the Seman Hotel and would be back in the office in one hour.

I sat uneasily for two hours while people came and went, and then suddenly it was all over. A pleasant-looking man, not in uniform and carrying a plastic shopping bag, walked into the office and sat at one of the desks. This was Mr.

Yao. I gave him my paper, the one written by Mr. Guo. He read it, stood, and left the building for ten minutes. I presumed he was conferring with a superior, but when he returned I saw he had only gone to change his shirt.

"I'm sorry this has happened to you," he said. I think he meant it. I certainly admired his warm efficiency as he selected a variety of forms to fill out. I again wrote an account of the entire incident, including the bicycles. All he had to say on that subject was "Oh, that is a difficult road for a bicycle!" No lecture about illegality, no demand that I write a self-criticism. After an hour, he gave me a small stack of papers, including a little blue folder complete with my photograph, which I had supplied, and lots of Chinese writing—a sort of dummy passport, which, he assured me, would get me out of China and into Pakistan. We thanked him two or three times, and then we were gone, tripping down the street smiling at children and thinking their fathers looked unusually handsome.

The next morning at 6:30 we were at the bus station to catch the border bus. It left at ten, precisely three hours past its scheduled departure, just as it had before.

Once more into the heat and the dust, up through the dynamite blasting and rockfall of the Gez Defile, past Kungur and Muztagh Ata, through windrows of glacial dust, along the Russian border, then the Afghan border, and finally, after three days, back to Perali, almost Pakistan. . . .

This time we joined the other bus passengers at the customs line as if everything were normal. A man asked for the customs declaration that every traveler entering China must fill out and then present upon leaving. Instead, I gave him a slip titled "Receipt of Report of Loss of Customs Declaration Form." He took it and kept it. I asked for it back. He said no. I decided then to guard the other receipts I was given in Kashgar, just in case. Any scrap of official paper was important to me now.

At immigration, they collected all passports in a pile. I handed over my blue folder with its photo of me and stamped with prominent official seals. They passed it around, making a pretense that they had never seen me before and that this paper was something foreign. "Passport?" asked Mr. Chen again. A week earlier Chen had been asking me for English lessons.

"My passport was stolen," I said, speaking very slowly.

"Ah. No passport?" He conferred with the man beside him, who looked at me and said, "Please give me your passport."

"I have no passport. You know that. You sent me to Kashgar to get this folder."

Chen looked through the folder again and added it to the other passports. "Wait," he said. Both men went back to their papers. I stood there until everyone else had been processed. Then Chen's comrade ruffled through the accumulated passports, located Wendy's, opened it to her photo, and held it up. "Is this you?" he asked.

"No, that is my wife." She had been waved out of the room.

"You have no passport?"

"Only that folder."

"You have other papers, a passport paper?"

He meant, I thought, the "Receipt of Report of Loss of Passport," a tiny slip of paper barely two inches by six inches, which I had decided to keep. "No," I said, "just this folder."

Chen then asked for other papers, but I denied having more. They called Wendy back into the building and asked her to identify me.

"This is your husband? Yes? You can go."

There were two busloads of people headed to Pakistan that day, which caused consternation when we were called for reboarding. Instead of letting passengers find their former seats, Chinese officials stood at the doors of both buses holding stacks of passports and calling out names. The problem was that the passports had been shuffled, and some travelers were now assigned to the opposite bus from the one on which they had arrived. People were refusing to board, shouting, "I must travel with my luggage!" I remembered Miki's story of the Japanese man whose documents were stolen between Perali and the Pakistani border post. In this case the Chinese held firm and everyone eventually got on, but there were already bad feelings in the air when I heard my name, the last one called. I reached for the blue folder and was told I could not have it. It was good only in China and belonged to the Chinese government. I protested that it left me with no papers.

"You have driver's license."

"I have nothing."

"We keep this."

Around and around we went. Soon it was just me and seven officials standing beside the loaded bus. I asked for a receipt. They said no. I told them about Miki's Japanese friend. They repeated that the folder was good only in China. We all were getting heated. It was then that I caught my foot in the act of moving forward to kick the head Chinese immigration official. I had shifted my weight. The muscles were tensed. Only some last-second inhibition stopped me from an act that would certainly have sent me all the way back to Beijing.

"Get on," said the chief of customs. Chastened, I got on.

Twenty miles farther, just below the pass, we stopped at a checkpoint. The scenery had become spectacular, but I hadn't seen much of it. I remember big, open, green valleys, and not much more. My mind was on the two uniformed men who boarded the bus holding automatic rifles. Wendy and I sat in the seat farthest back. "Passport?" the man asked. Wendy handed over hers. "I have no passport," I told him. "*Meiyou* passport." No passport. He turned away, checked some other passengers, and came back. "Passport!"

"*Meiyou* passport."

"Getta off!"

I said something strangled-sounding and gripped the seat.

"Getta off!" He gestured with his rifle.

There was a Chinese woman on the bus who lived in New York City. We had made her acquaintance during the trip from Kashgar. "Can you help?" I asked her. She spoke with the guard, explaining that they had taken my exit permit at Perali. That seemed to satisfy him, because he worked his way through other passengers. But again he came back to me.

"Passport!"

"*Meiyou* passport."

"Getta off! With no passport, getta off!"

Clearly, my having gotten past Perali was not enough. This compartmental bureaucracy had been the source of endless frustration so far and now promised to be more serious than that. What would happen? Back to Perali at least. Then where? The last scrap of Chinese paper I carried was the receipt I had withheld at immigration. It was my last card. Presenting it, I tried to hold on to one end of the fragile slip, but the soldier took the form and disappeared from the bus. A minute later he climbed back on. He said "Okay, you go," and to my surprise handed back the receipt.

PAKISTAN FELT INSTANTLY DIFFERENT. At Kunjerab Pass we left behind the broad valleys and massive dry mountains of Xinjiang, descending into a magnificent canyon between fairy-tale peaks, with high, glittering glaciers and tumbling, silty rivers fed by numerous cascades. One waterfall burst from a cave in a sheer cliff, dropping hundreds of feet in a perfect bridal veil. There were trees along the river, donkeys grazing in their shade. Lower down we passed fields of wheat beginning to turn yellow beside tall poplars still green. The air was fragrant, and for a while I was confident that things were going to work out.

Sost, the Pakistani border post, was a clutter of hastily built structures set amid older homes and walled compounds that predated the opening of the Karakoram Highway. Among the new buildings were sheds labeled customs, immigration, post office, and hotel. An irrigation ditch angled in from a canyon to the east. Above its ruler-straight line, all was dry yellow and red stone. Below the line, green fields spread luxuriantly.

We joined the queue at immigration. The inspector, sitting at a high desk so that people's chins met his elbows, took passports and stamped out entry permits. I stayed at the end of the line, encouraged by the way he smiled and joked with people. A woman gave her profession as consultant. "You mean insultant," he said. "Insultant. Why would we want insultants in Pakistan?" He seemed a kindly man, tall with a soft-spoken, amused demeanor. Then it was my turn.

"I have a problem here. I've lost my passport." I handed him my receipt, the precious tiny receipt. "My wife has her passport. We had identical visas."

"You idiot! You lost your passport?" he did not say. Instead, he looked through Wendy's document and scrutinized my receipt. "I cannot read this," he said, pointing to the Chinese handwriting.

"This is my name in Chinese," I said. "And nationality."

Fortunately the form was titled in English and carried two bright red seals. He nodded. I saw in his expression benevolent sympathy. "Wait in the office please," he said.

His office was fragrant with spices, and cool. It seemed luxurious after the spartan, ill-kept austerity of Chinese offices. Wendy and I were joined there by five others with visa problems. The official came in, sat down, introduced himself as Mr. Hasam, and smiled at us. He seemed as amiable as an old friend as he reached for the telephone and cranked the bell. "Perali! Perali! Hello?" He whistled into the handset, cranked some more, whistled, and called.

"You can telephone Perali?"

"Yes," he grinned. "I can ask them."

But no one answered and he gave up. He turned to a Canadian woman who held an expired visa. "Why are you late?" She described slow travel across China. A boy brought in a tray of sweet, spiced milk tea. We all made grateful noises. "You like Pakistani tea?" said the official. "Good. You may enjoy another cup before going back to China."

"Don't say that until after we've finished it," said Wendy.

"But you may enter," he told her. "No one else. Mark," he said to an American traveling alone, "why do you have no visa?"

"I decided only a month ago to visit Pakistan. I thought I could get a visa at the border."

Mr. Hasam shook his head. They talked about the difficulties of traveling in China, everyone trying in exaggerated language to make Pakistan sound like the Garden of Eden. Finally, Hasam explained that he could not make decisions until his boss returned from Gilgit. We should collect our luggage and wait.

"Is this a very big problem?" I asked as he walked me to the door.

"I don't know. We will have to talk to Gilgit."

I had less hope as we off-loaded our gear and carted it to the porch of the immigration building. The thought of being sent back, utterly paperless, to China was beyond consideration. But disasters sometimes unfold stage by stage, each step worse than the previous, spreading the pain like slow immersion in ice water. If I went back, how was I to travel in China without a passport? The Chinese had demonstrated no willingness to help. Would they even let me back into the country? What would this do to the rest of our trip? I shoved the thought out of mind.

Mr. Hasam turned out to be as amiable as he appeared. He joined us on the porch. "Andy, Andy, my guest, my friend," he slapped a despondent Canadian on the shoulder. "How is it that you are in such a fix?" We chatted about Pakistan. The subject came to jewelry; he wore a simple silver ring with an aquamarine. I said my wedding ring had been with my passport.

"When you said you lost your passport, I felt very sad. To lose your ring, I am also sad. If you lost your passport in Pakistan, we could help you. But in China. . . . "

"No, the Chinese weren't much help. I hear Pakistan is a good place to buy silver jewelry."

"Yes. When you get to Gilgit, you can buy very nice jewelry."

Get to Gilgit? I tried not to register my reaction, but it gave me hope that we were playing a gentleman's game here. Regulations required that I must go back to China, but by the kindness of Pakistan I might be allowed to proceed anyway.

Out on the road, the evening peace was broken when a mini-van pulled up at the gate. It carried a family. Four children rode on top in the luggage rack. One, a small boy, began to climb down the ladder at the rear when the gate was lifted and the driver pulled slowly forward. "Stop!" shouted the kids on top. "Stop!" came a chorus from inside. The van continued through the gate. A man inside lurched forward, grabbed the driver by the hair, and shook the man's head. "Stop the fucking bus! When I say stop, you stop, you jerk!" The van stopped. The man piled out the side door and, bashing at the vehicle with his fist, came around to the driver's window. "You jerk, you stop the van, you could have killed the kid, what the fuck you think you're doing?" A crowd gathered, there was a lot of shouting, all the kids got off the luggage rack, and the van finally left.

"Your countryman?" said Mr. Hasam.

The next morning I was again sitting on the porch talking to Mr. Hasam. I told him I was trying to phone the American embassy, with no success.

"Don't worry. When you get to Islamabad, you can telephone very easily."

"Islamabad? Will they let me go there?"

"Why not?" he said, using an expression that would soon endear Pakistanis to me. Sure enough, an hour later, I had my visa, good for two months, carefully stamped beside the red seals on the "Receipt of Report of Loss of Passport."

Looking back on it, I like to think that whoever found my passport pouch made good use of it. In my mind's eye, I picture a road worker stooping to pick it up. He opens it and immediately recognizes an official identification document and foreign currency. He has no idea how much currency. It could be worth a few yuan, but because all foreigners seem relatively wealthy, he gets pretty excited. If he's smart, he finds an appropriate channel, asks about the value of a hundred-dollar bill, and learns to his utter astonishment that it translates to some five hundred yuan—more than a year's salary. And he has not just one of these, but *fourteen!* I imagine how it would feel for me to find nearly twenty years' earnings on the side of the road. It could be the start of something big for its finder: a herd of camels, education for his kids, a new house. By losing it, I became like the mysterious benefactor on the old television program "The Millionaire," dispensing great sums to unsuspecting worthies. Except I had no idea who ended up with the loot.

And what of the passport? According to the rumor mill, an American passport was worth a thousand dollars on the black market. A skilled forger could change the picture, alter the identifying data, and sell it to someone for use in countries that lack computer crosschecking. I wonder who's using it now. On the one hand, I picture a Chinese student using it to get out of the country after the massacre at Tiananmen Square. But I fear it's doing much less worthy duty than that. It was too valuable to go to someone who really needed it. Some sleazebag smuggler has it. I hope he gets caught.

10
Could This Be Shangri-La?

Natural for mountain people to grow straight:
  Where paths are steep, the mind levels.
      ——Meng Chiao, A.D. 751–81

AZIM SHAH OWNED the Shisper Hotel. A small wiry man about fifty-five years old, he had a good, lean face ruled by flamboyant eyebrows. They went up and down, side to side, like signal flags. When Azim shook hands or gave you the embrace traditional between male friends in Hunza, you knew he was tough, like old wood. He had served most of his life in the Pakistani army. After retirement, he had come back to Hunza to build a small hotel near his family home in Passu. He had built the hotel with his own hands. It had five guest rooms, a kitchen, a dining room, and two shaded verandahs front and back.

He could hardly have chosen a more spectacular building site. It commanded a spacious view across moraines of the Passu Glacier to the dun-colored Hunza River streaming through wide gravel flats. Above the river, a great wall of red rock—actually the western edge of the Karakoram Range—rose for many thousands of feet, a tortuously eroded baroque fantasy of pinnacled summits and steep, scree-filled chutes.

Azim brought tea from the kitchen to where Wendy and I sat on the porch. It was sweet black tea scented with cardamom and served with a small pitcher of hot milk. "Deer and sheeps are there," he said, pointing to nearly inaccessible green patches among the spires.

"You always laugh when you talk," I said.
"Why not? I am happy. Here is Passu, the river, the hotel . . . "
"This is a good place."
"Yes. A good place."

―――――――――

I had had no idea, before arriving in the Hunza Valley, how deeply the austerity of China had altered my perspective. I had come to regard bleakness as a normal condition, so that the slightest softening of a hard edge seemed to be a luxury. That water would flow from a tap at the Seman Hotel in Kashgar was such a marvel, compared to the crumbling Chinibagh or the even more primitive places we had been, that it had eclipsed the filthy floors and stinking drains. I had become so accustomed to uncaring hotel staff that any duty they might perform, however simple or necessary it might be—sweeping the floor, for example—seemed like an act of kindness. Even the scenery had had its impact. In Xinjiang I had looked at the brown, rounded mountains and seen beauty in them; they *were* beautiful, especially in the early morning. But to see that beauty I had to adjust to a desert frame of mind, an attitude that welcomes austerity and forgets the richness of green things. No wonder the fountain-fed gardens of Hunza struck me with such force. No wonder Azim's hotel, operated with gracious pride, seemed so comfortable.

We had pedaled to Passu from the border post at Sost in four blissful hours. Here, the Karakoram Highway was paved. The sun was warm. I was virtually paperless but free, and I'd never seen mountains like these before— enormous mountains, dry and nearly barren of vegetation. Only in the canyon bottoms, along rivers and streams, was agriculture possible, and there, in a narrow ribbon of green, orchards of almond and apricot trees flourished. Slender poplars marched in single file up brown mountainsides, marking the course of tiny creeks. Villages were strung along the watery ribbon like oases on a desert track.

The road, carved into the sheer walls of the gorge, wound steeply down from Sost into this vertical landscape. Glaciers fell to within a quarter-mile of the road; water from melting snowfields streamed across it.

No less of an authority than Eric Shipton called the Hunza Valley "[the] most spectacular country I have ever seen. For a hundred and fifty miles the caravan route follows along the great gorge of the Hunza River, through the very heart of the greatest concentration of high mountains in the world."

Five major mountain ranges come together around Hunza: the Hindu Kush, Karakoram, Pamirs, Kun Lun, and Himalaya. All of them resulted from the collision of the Indian and Asian tectonic plates, a slow collision that began fifteen million years ago and has not yet finished. They are still rising and falling apart at the same time. They are mountains in motion: big, decaying, hurling their rubble into the valleys, where rivers the color of dust pulverize the debris and carry it off to the Indian Ocean.

We could see it happening. We passed slopes that gave off the continual clatter of little stones falling. We moved fast then, thinking about the big ones that obviously come down from time to time. We heard later that three days behind us a mountain above Sost had slid, blocking the road, partially damming the river, and creating a lake. It took a week to get the road cleared, but in local opinion that was nothing unusual.

What a difference there was between the north and south sides of the Himalaya. One was empty; the other was jammed solid. Tibet and Xinjiang, lifted high and drained of water, had become a frozen, sun-parched, nearly mummified land. It gave you the sense of open space. Except when the wind was blowing you senseless, it was a landscape of enormous silence— contemplative, rarefied, suspended.

None of that in Pakistan. Here we were under the mountains, down in the rumbling guts and going deeper. You almost felt you were in the engine room of the planet, watching heavy machinery in action. Each year monsoon rains pour snow on the glaciers. Meltwater claws at the mountains, ripping rocks loose, carving great gorges, isolating enormous massifs. One of the biggest of these is Nanga Parbat, the western anchor of the Himalaya and the final barrier facing the Indus River on its course to the Indian Ocean. The Indus, the same river that we had ridden across at two-thirty in the morning on the outskirts of Ali—that strong but small river running shallow across the gravel, the one Lee had jumped into fully clothed—becomes a frightening torrent as it plunges past the north face of Nanga Parbat.

At the top of it all stands the most impressive mountain conglomeration in the world: the peaks surrounding a place called Concordia—Broad Peak, Gasherbrum, Masherbrum, and of course, K2, second only to Everest in height but harder to climb and harder to approach. We couldn't see those in Hunza, but it hardly mattered, considering the presence of giants like Rakaposhi, Golden Peak, Durin, and Nanga Parbat.

For centuries, until the British brought their brand of order to what is now northern Pakistan, its inhabitants did a lot of fighting. In some parts they still do. The English never did get a firm grip—neither militarily nor socially. In the mid-1800s they called it Yaghistan, land of savages, mostly because they knew so little about who lived up there beyond the Indus Valley. Eventually, as various British explorers and spies made their way up the forbidding gorges and came back with true stories, they were no less fantastic than any previous fiction.

Yaghistan, it turned out, was a land of many small, independent states with charming names, including Hunza, Nagir, Chilas, Chitral, Yasin, Tangir, Darel, Dir, and Swat. The various rulers and chiefs carried titles such as mir, mehtar, wazir, sultan, and khan. They wore pointed slippers, turbans, ragged beards, and anything from bald heads to pigtails. Armed with curved sabers and bandoliers of ammunition for various museum-piece firearms, they lived in warrenlike palaces of mud and stone held together by a framework of timbers and often perched on forbidding heights. Their world was one of intrigue and political rivalry, nearly as convoluted as the surrounding geography. Depending on whose report you read—or at what point in history it was written—the mountain rulers could be genial, reliable, perhaps even honorable men, or the worst sort of cutthroat, back-stabbing brigands whose only common language was the use of weapons and who spoke with each other every chance they got.

Once as bellicose a little state as any other, Hunza quickly changed its reputation after the British invaded. It soon became known as a remote mountain paradise where people lived to 120 years on a diet of natural fruits and grains and mineral-rich glacial water. One famous passage From Dr. L. J. Picton's *Thoughts on Feeding* states: "Their life, seemingly hard and austere, has endowed these people with a happiness I forbear to overstate. They have achieved engineering without mathematics, morality without moralizing, agriculture without chemistry, health without medicine, sufficiency without trade." That's one of the less florid comments made over the years. "The fabulous health and youth wonderland of the world," crowed a 1960 book titled *Hunza Land*.

We had expected to see something of Hunza on our way down the Karakoram Highway, but our strongest interest was in getting to the Karakoram themselves, perhaps to Concordia, but in any event to make a long trek somewhere into the heart of the mountains. I wanted to spend a month and walk many miles. I wanted to compensate for the weeks spent along roads and in trucks. Then came the business of my passport, which took nearly two weeks to resolve. And after that, we were waylaid in Hunza.

The last thing I had said to Pat and Baiba in Perali was that we would try to catch up with them in Passu. And sure enough, when I asked Azim Shah if he had seen two Canadians on bicycles, he said that the bikes were in his back room and that the Morrows, who had gone for a three-day trek up the Batura Glacier, would be back that afternoon. They came in just before dinner, covered with glacial dust, all smiles and surprised to see us. Pat had thought we would end up in Beijing before it was over and that we would have to make the long journey via Hong Kong, Bangkok, and Karachi just to get to Hunza. I told him no; if it had come down to that, I'd have gone by way of London just for the hell of it.

But here we were in Passu, and despite the feeling we all had that we should get going, to make up for lost time, to arrange for a long, satisfying trek in the Karakoram Range, no one wanted to move. Time was wasting, but we stayed for three days, stuffing ourselves on Azim's hot Punjabi curries served with big, soft chapattis and clear spring water. We could even bathe, if we waited until late in the afternoon, in tepid water warmed by the sun on the roof—an amazing luxury.

If there was ever an idyllic mountain village, Passu was it. Apricot and apple trees shaded neat, winding lanes between flat-roofed houses. Irrigation channels ran in all directions supplying the orchards and carefully tended fields of potatoes and wheat. Children ran back and forth from school. Once two little girls presented Wendy and me with a gift of walnuts, pulled shyly from their pockets.

The people of Passu—like most of Hunza—were Ismaili Muslims, followers of the Aga Kahn. They were black-haired, fine of feature, and well spoken: handsome people who knew it and were proud of it. Their town had the appearance of age and a long history. It had been there for a long time, despite some major disruptions. Perched precariously on shifting glacial alluvium, Passu was just down the valley from the snout of the Batura Glacier. Geologically speaking, it was like living in the muzzle of a cannon. More than once, glacial surges and sudden floods had caused extensive damage to the town.

From the front verandah of Azim's hotel, we watched sunset light up the spires across the river. From bed, if we woke early enough, we could see through a back window the icy fang of Shisper Peak ignite with the sunrise. In the evening we would light kerosene lanterns and sit outside. The moon was nearly full. The river was a stream of mercury. The mountains, faceted and mysterious, shone in the blue light.

Azim spoke about fairies. He said they were once common. You would see them on nights like this. Sometimes there would be dancing lights in those high meadows in the moonlight. But they disappeared when the road was built.

"I think many things in Hunza changed when the road came," I said.

"Yes, yes. You know, my father took the mail for the Mir of Hunza—from Baltit to Kashgar."

"Really? The same way we came?"

"Almost. He was going by the Mintaka Pass, not Kunjerab. It was taking him one month to go one way. On his horse."

"Winter and summer?"

"Even in snow. Now comes the bus all the way from Kashgar. You know, from seven miles below Gulmit to the Kunjerab Pass, forty miles, it was seven years building. It was Chinese. China built this highway."

"But this is a good road," I said. "On the other side it's a terrible road. Why would they build this side first?"

"It is a bad road?" Azim asked.

"Well, it's not paved—not like this one. And the whole thing is under construction."

"I do not know. Seventeen thousand Chinese workers came to Hunza to build this road. It was very dangerous, very hard work. Many were killed."

"How were they killed?" I asked.

"Buried! They would be digging, or using dynamite, and whump! The mountain would fall on them. These mountains, they are falling always. It was very bad."

———

Finally, we had to drag ourselves away from Passu.

"How much do we pay you, Azim?" I asked.

He shrugged and said, "What did you eat?"

"Well. Chicken curry one night . . . "

Wendy and I spent a few minutes recalling each meal and cup of tea and gave Azim the list. He went to the kitchen to work out the numbers. He returned with a bill for 295 rupees, about seventeen dollars, for the two of us.

"You are happy?" he asked. His wonderful eyebrows danced across his forehead.

"Delighted. Thank you very much, Azim." As we left, he gave me a hug like I'd get from an old mountain juniper tree.

An hour later we had bogged down in Gulmit. Although our plans were to put in a good hard day of cycling, Hunza would not be denied. We caught sight of the Karakoram Hotel, with its exuberant flower gardens, looking like a summer cottage in southern England, and paralysis struck. We could go no farther. There was no point in trying to get to a better place than Gulmit. We moved into two neat rooms and went off to investigate the village.

I had begun to realize that Hunza was nearly as dry as Xinjiang, but because snow-covered mountains were abundant, water flowed in every side valley—*nulla* was the local term. Most of the water was directed through *kuls,* rock-lined irrigation channels, to the villages, where it tumbled down in hundreds of carefully managed streamlets. The hillside pathways of Gulmit were alive with the sound and mist of falling water surging in and out of grain mills, through tiny fields and gardens, gushing from beneath stone walls. Walking, we passed from sun to shade, breathing air continually refreshed by the smell and coolness of the glacial water.

Hunza felt like the peaceful morning dreams you have just before waking, the sort that you hardly remember, but you know they were happy and you say to yourself, "Wouldn't it be nice if they could be true?"

It was early September, time for the apricot harvest. The trees were heavily laden. Men and boys climbed up with sticks and beat the fruit off the branches. Women gathered baskets of apricots from the ground and spread them, pitted, on the flat roofs of their houses. All the roofs of Gulmit were bright orange. Each time we stopped to admire the harvest, people would fill our hands and pockets with perfectly ripe fruit.

At a small lodge we inquired about tea. A man said the lodge was closed, but we should wait a moment. A minute later, the owner came to the door and invited us into a large, empty room used for dining. We introduced ourselves. His name was Raja Badruhan. It was past season, he said, "but you will be my guests for tea."

"Do you close for the winter?"

"Yes. Soon the yaks come down from high pasture. Soon there will be snow."

"What do you do in Gulmit then?" I asked.

"Ah. I sit peacefully and have a glass of wine. In October, when the freeze comes, we kill yaks and sheeps and hang the meat in our stores. Then we cut roasts and drink wine. All friends come and we have dance, traditional dance, and no Islamic Law."

He said this with a big smile and his arms embracing the air.

"So there is still Hunza water?" Pat asked, referring to the infamous local wine, the stuff Tilman described as being "rough as a rasp." Prohibition had come in 1984 with the establishment of Islamic Law. To our way of thinking, the only bad news we'd heard about Pakistan since getting there was that prohibition had ended the making of Hunza water.

"Yes. We have some."

"You make it from berries?"

"We make wine from grapes. Rum we make from mulberries. Oh, it is very good."

"Do you think we could try some?"

"No, no. We drink it all in the winter."

Badruhan was a big man of comfortable girth. It was all in front of him. As he walked he led with his belly, as if presenting a source of great pride. He was also proud of Hunza.

"I will tell you about Hunza. You must know Hunza is not Pakistan. I tell you, it is not Pakistan. It is Hunza. We have four languages in Hunza—Wahki, Burishaski, Shiena, Dum. Two thousand people are living in Gulmit. Thirty-six thousand in all Hunza, including Gojal. We call upper Hunza Gojal."

"Then where does Pakistan start?"

"Below Gilgit. This is Hunza. I tell you this."

Pat mentioned what Azim Shah had said about fairies, that fairies had left their mark everywhere; every little valley and meadow had a fairy story to tell.

"They are here. It is true!" said Raja Badruhan.

"Have you seen one?"

"When I was a boy, everyone saw them."

"What do they look like?"

"Like European women—the same."

"Like me?" said Baiba.

"Just like you! Except their feet are turned backward. That is how you tell. They are dangerous. Yes. Very beautiful but very dangerous."

"What do they do?" asked Baiba.

"Oh—" He looked at Pat and me. "They like to play with local men at midnight."

"Play with them?" said Baiba.

"Yes, they make love and then they kill them."

"Kill them!" I said. "It sounded good until that part."

"Are there male fairies?" asked Wendy.

"Of course. The husbands are very big giants. They look like bulls."

"And they come after the Hunza women?"

"No, no woman would want one of them! Anyway, they are gone now. When I was a boy, one time, I see a donkey walking up the trail. It was almost dark, and fire I see coming from his hooves when they hit the ground. Fire! It was not so unusual a thing. Not then. Now the road is built, and come the buses and trucks and Suzukis, and all gone, no magic."

We left Gulmit the next day and pedaled into a tawny, arid gorge, a deep, slab-sided crack littered with clattering scree. The road surface was covered with little rocks. From how high had they fallen? It could have been miles. The mountains went up, unseen from the gorge, for at least 15,000 feet. The river was an ugly sight, all churning mud and rolling boulders. Most of the time, the road stayed well above it, but always we could hear the growl of the semisolid water chewing on rocks. After about twenty miles the road dropped, fast and far, to a bridge, and we were at the bottom of Baltit, the old capital of Hunza.

I say bottom because Baltit was a steeply pitched community located on the only flat land for many miles. If it seems contradictory to call a flat place steep, the appearance of Baltit was itself a contradiction. Seen from below, the houses and fields climbed with unrelenting seriousness, up through fruit orchards and terraces to a ridge top occupied by the towering palace of the mirs of Hunza, now an empty near-ruin. Getting there looked to be a long, hard climb of about 1000 feet, but that was only the beginning. Behind the palace, like some science-fiction backdrop dwarfing all of Baltit, rose the dark, glacier-scarred bulk of Ultar Peak, 24,000 feet of snowfields and cloudbanks. The town seemed a piece of the mountain. All of it looked steep, and felt that way too. It took us an hour to push our bikes half a mile up the sandy jeep road to a hotel. Looking back down to the highway was like peering over a cliff.

It was the same on the other side of the river: green terraces, orchards, and flat-roofed houses clung to the base of forbidding cliffs. Above the cliffs was not sky but a separate world of glaciers and radiant summits. The biggest mountain, Rakaposhi, all snow and grinding ice, squatted prodigiously across the entire southern horizon. Beneath this astounding skyline, the inhabited part of the valley was so diminutive and so precariously located, it seemed that an earthquake—not even a big earthquake—could easily shrug the whole business into the river.

But—and this is the contradiction—if you went, as we did a few days later, to the base of Ultar Peak, up near the old palace, you got a completely different impression. From up there, with your back against Ultar's great cliffs, the terraced fields of Baltit and surrounding villages seemed more like a green ledge perched above the river—a narrow ledge, to be sure, but a nearly flat one, not at all steep.

It was certainly one of the loveliest town sites in the world, and again we were stopped in our tracks.

The moon was full on our first night there, illuminating the entire valley, from the silver-flecked river 1000 feet below town all the way to the summits of Rakaposhi, Diran, and Ultar, their glaciers shining against the night-bright sky. Between them and the river, as if reflecting in a dark pool of water, the starlike points of light from candles and hurricane lanterns sparkled on black terraces. Baltit was still innocent of electricity. It was coming, as a new line of utility towers indicated, but for now, nightfall turned back the years. Modernity disappeared in the shadows and fairies stepped into the moonlight.

Baiba heard a good fairy story one day. She was out walking and met a man who invited her to have lunch at his house, an invitation she could properly accept in Hunza—it was that sort of place. While they ate, he told her about the time his grandfather, a shepherd, came upon his brother sitting in a high mountain meadow with two children and a strange, beautiful woman. Who are these people? he asked his brother. The woman answered, claiming to be the brother's wife. The two children were also his, but they were not human. Clearly the woman was a fairy, and a possessive one at that. She said that if the

166

brother ever married a human woman, as his parents wanted him to do, he would die within a year. Hearing this tale, his parents scoffed and went ahead with wedding plans. The young man succumbed to parental pressure, married a local girl, and died six months later.

Why not? Hunza was an easy place to believe in fairies. Anything seemed possible. That people live to 130 on a diet of apricots and whole wheat? Right. That these were the descendants of Alexander's Greek soldiers? Sure. That this valley was the inspiration for Hilton's book *Lost Horizon*? You bet.

One day, Pat, Baiba, and I (it was Wendy's turn to be confined to her room with a fever) climbed to the base of Ultar Glacier at the head of Ultar Nulla, a boulder-choked canyon with vertical walls. In the walls, actually cut into them and held in place by skillfully built stone buttresses, there were several *kuls,* or irrigation channels. Coming up the canyon, we could see them 1000 feet and more above us. When we reached the level of the first one, where a small diversion dam shunted water from the main stream, we saw that the *kul* was about two feet wide and a foot deep.

"Think we could walk on that?" said Pat.

"I suppose you could," I said. I didn't know that I wanted to. The *kul* ran straight across the cliff face, attaining a giddy height before disappearing around a distant flank of the mountain. "What if it ends in a waterfall?" I said.

"Then we come back."

Logical enough. So later in the day, on our way back down from the glacier, Pat and Baiba took off their shoes and waded into the *kul*. I watched them for a few minutes before working up the nerve to follow.

It was a strange feeling to be standing in flowing water some 800 feet above the ground. Sparkling flecks of mica, millions of them, made the water look like a living gem.

"Times like this I realize that vertigo has a tighter grip on me than claustrophobia," said Pat. Of course he was enjoying the vertigo. For him it was more like a loving embrace than a grip.

The channel ended on a bluff at the base of Ultar's soaring flank. The water spilled in a long cascade down the face of the bluff to the fields below.

We enjoyed the view for a while and then scrambled down the bluff to the mirs' palace, where a creaky caretaker first showed us into a two-room house he said was five hundred years old. Meant to be a museum, it was little more than a dusty cellar inhabited by two rat-chewed stuffed animals—an ibex and what the guide called a Marco Polo sheep. To me it looked like a domestic goat. Having tantalized us with the museum, our guide then took us up to the palace itself, which he said was six hundred years old, built just after the Ultar Glacier receded.

What a gloomy place! A warren of dim rooms, sagging floors, and walls of rock supported by timbers. It reeked of medieval darkness. It was like the other side of Hunza history, the black side of raiders and slave traders that British critics, during the days of their conquests, loved so well to promote as characteristic of the entire region. According to reports, the ruler of Nagir, across the river, received even his worthy English visitors in an audience chamber whose only access was by way of a trap door. That way, all guests started the meeting by first exposing their vulnerable heads at the level of the great man's slippered feet. The interior of the Hunza palace seemed no less pretentious, in its crude, mud-walled way.

On the other hand, its flat roof was a cheerful place with a view, not just of the mountains, but of the houses below. Hunzakuts were busy down there. I watched a boy dancing, a girl washing clothes, women spreading apricots to dry. Then a girl glanced up and, feeling caught in the act, I retreated from the edge.

We did a lot of walking around Baltit. It was not a single community but a handful of scattered villages in the area joined by sparkling irrigation channels. Besides Baltit, there was Altit, Karimabad, Aliabad, Haiderabad, and Ganesh. Everywhere, I was impressed by the use of land, nearly all of which was terraced. The terraces made Hunza into a wiggle picture. Looking up, all you see are stones; looking down, all you see is green. It all depends on the angle of view. Retaining walls might be 15 to 20 feet high supporting a strip of flat land less than 10 feet wide. Where terraces were too narrow to plow, people planted orchards, pruning the trees so animals could graze beneath them. Winter squash vines were trained to hang over terrace walls, the fruits carefully arrayed at regular intervals like coats on a row of pegs. Poplars provided shade but also wood. Enormous walnut and mulberry trees spread their limbs above homes built on many levels—even the buildings were terraced. Some of the trees were so big that it was hard to tell which had come first, the tree or the house.

Wheat harvest was in full swing that month, a Biblical-looking process. The women wore bright colors with embroidered pillbox hats and light scarves. The men were dressed in neat homespun wool. Cutting the wheat with hand sickles, they gathered the stalks into sheaves and stood them on end to dry. They did the job with the same care Versailles gardeners would use on a hedge. Later, they would carry the dry bundles on their backs to the threshing ground, where cattle tied to a central post walked endless circles breaking the kernels from the stalks. When a breeze came up, people with long-handled wooden forks would toss the chaff into the wind, then sweep up the grain. It took a team of workers several days to harvest one small field.

The fields across the river looked the same as on our side, but they were in another country, the tiny principality of Nagir. Until the British invaded in 1891, Nagir had been an independent state and the deadly enemy of Hunza. Its people remained distinct from their neighbors; instead of laid-back Ismaili Muslims like the Hunzakuts, Nagirites were uptight Shiites, followers of Khomeini. Shiites were the ones who painted "Death to the USA!" and "Israel Enemy to Peace" and "Destroy USSR!" in dripping black letters on buildings and rock outcrops. We were told that we had just missed a vigorous anti-American rally put on by the Shiites along the highway a few days earlier.

At first that sort of thing had seemed to be a discordant element in this idyllic setting; but when I thought about it, I decided it probably marked an improvement in local affairs. Just a century earlier, the concerns of Nagirites were of a more parochial nature. They worried about Hunza, not the United States or the Soviet Union. The men of Hunza used to cross the river at night and make off with slaves and other booty. More than that, Nagir fought continually with Hunza over control of the river gorge, the only route south for either state. When Hunza held the forts in the gorge, Nagir withered, and vice versa, except that Hunza always had options through its northern access to Xinjiang and Afghanistan. Nagirites, lacking the Hunza Gorge, were entirely cut off. If they became, over the years, a suspicious wary people, they probably had reasons.

While walking the steep lanes of Baltit I would sometimes pass men I took to be Nagirites. I had no definite way of knowing who these people were. But they stared at me with such baleful hostility—it stopped them in their tracks, they had to concentrate so hard at communicating enmity—that I decided they couldn't possibly be Ismaili Hunzakuts. I wanted to check their fingernails for black paint.

One writer, who like us never visited Nagir but instead formed his opinions from stories told by Hunzakuts, offered this assessment:

Nagirites are a complaining people, indolent and sickly. Their houses are poorly constructed; their fields, inefficiently tilled. Flies and other insects in swarms devour fruits and crops; cattle die; disease is rampant; ambition is wanting. The people bitterly criticize the Hunzakuts because they enjoy a better life, and it is believed that the Hunza good fortune is due to the fact that the sun shines longer on that territory. The Nagirites reminded me of the fable of the grasshopper and the ant. When the sun shines they are idle; when winter winds and snows come, they freeze and starve.

"Whatever you do, don't go there!" advised a British man visiting Hunza. "They'll steal you blind." I found scribbled on a wall: "Nagirites have Shiite for brains."

Nagir looked pleasant enough, just as nice as Hunza. But I enjoyed the cartoon image: on the cold, shady side of the valley lived the jealous, long-toothed people of Nagir; while on this side, in the sun, peacefully growing their apricots and living to the ripe age of 130 or so, the busy, cheerful Hunzakuts laughed their way to prosperity.

Like Mr. Nazeem, who kept a shop above our hotel. He was a tall, fine-featured man, stately in demeanor. His shop was filled with old wooden bowls, items knitted from Hunza wool, some carved animals, and other old junk of the sort tourists like. He wore a white wool Hunza cap that he wanted to show me. It was a simple woven tube closed at one end and rolled up as you would roll a sleeve until it fitted neatly on the head. "And we are wearing it like this in Hunza," he said, in the lovely rhythms of Hunza English, "and we are having a warm head."

Mr. Nazeem had several ancient matchlock rifles made in Russia. Holding one, he described its use with the rhythm of a poet reading his work: "We are walking, we are walking in the high mountains, and looking, looking, we are seeing the Marco Polo sheep, and they are standing very fine, very far, very small, four hundred meters, very far, but this is good equipment, we are having good equipment even for four hundred meters."

He showed me how the rifle worked. Its folding legs, mounted under the muzzle, were beautifully carved. Its ancient barrel was bound to the cracked handworn stock with bits of rawhide. The trigger wasn't really a trigger at all, but a lever about eight inches long that fit into a slot in the stock. Hinged on a pin, the other, shorter end was meant to hold a smoldering wick. By pulling back on the lever, the hunter would lower the wick against a hole in the breech, touching off the ramrodded charge. Right, I thought: the thing takes a couple minutes to fire. The hunter props it on the ground, lights the wick with a flint and steel, blows on it to get it going good, and touches it to the powder hole. Boom! By that time, any animal is long gone.

But Mr. Nazeem insisted that this was good equipment even at four hundred meters.

He was in a demonstrating mood, and I was happy to watch. "This," he said, taking a long, white, woolen garment from a hook, "is the Hunza *choga*." It was a sort of cape, much like a Tibetan *chuba* but with sleeves that reached to the knees. Putting it on, he showed me how to use the sleeves. "In winter it is cold, very cold, and much snow, and we are walking, walking, and I am putting here."

He wrapped the sleeves around his head like a pair of scarves.

"Or there is a little boy, a little boy he has no *choga,* the wind is blowing and we are walking, we are walking, and he is walking here, underneath! There is room for two."

After that, every time I passed his shop Mr. Nazeem would smile and lift his arms as if demonstrating his old Russian matchlock rifle, and I would picture Marco Polo sheep racing away across high meadows.

If we found Hunza to be a mysterious and alluring place, we were in good company. Passing through in 1947 on his way to see Shipton in Kashgar, Tilman wrote in *Two Mountains and a River:*

> I noticed at once how much more obliging, business-like, and tractable the people were than those around Gilgit... they excel as craftsmen. As carpenters, masons, ironsmiths, builders of roads, bridges, or flumes, they are superior to their neighbors; even their home-spun cloth is a better article... and the theory that they are descendants of some of Alexander the Great's soldiers is, I suppose, no more far-fetched than some theories of racial descent.

And on the subject of longevity, I heard this story from a European health worker in Baltit: An old man with cataracts came for surgery accompanied by his son. "He is 114," said the younger man. A neighbor overheard that and said that was nonsense. The old man was actually 105. A year later he was back, again with his son, to have his other cataract removed. "He is 117," said the son. "You are privileged. For most people to see my father it costs twenty rupees."

So it might be a myth, I thought. So are fairies. So what? All I knew for sure was that I did not want to leave.

But leave we did, in a hired van to Gilgit, over a road no less spectacular than what we'd seen already. Rakaposhi dominated the landscape. We saw it from the north, west, and finally south. But more than the mountain it was the Hunza River Gorge that impressed me, and the disused pack trail nailed to its western wall. It was the old Hunza road, blasted into sheer and sometimes overhanging rock, crossing canyons on wooden bridges, climbing high to avoid slides, then dropping steeply to a sandy stretch of river bottom. I thought, why should a foot trail evoke stronger images of human endeavor than a road can do? The road took lots more effort, much of it hand labor. It was a bigger engineering challenge. It killed hundreds of workers. Yet the trail made me think of the time before the road, when it took five days to go from

Passu to Gilgit on a horse. A lot of things had disappeared from Hunza since then, among them fairies and polo ponies. The old trail was one of the few lasting relics from that time and a reminder of how easily everything that was missing could return.

G ILGIT, RAJA BADRUHAN had told us, marked the end of Hunza and the beginning of Pakistan. It certainly felt different. The men dressed in *shalwars*, which looked like big, loose-fitting pajamas. Some of the women wore *purdah* veils. It was hot—the summer breath of the Punjab blew up the Indus Gorge. And there were lots of people. Gilgit was crowded and noisy and stank of diesel.

I quickly learned to play deaf when someone, upon seeing me, shouted, "Which nationality?" or "To which country do you belong?" The conversations that followed were always the same.

"America."

"And what is your profession?"

"Carpenter," which was partly true. It was also a convenient lie. Easily understood, it gave me a low enough status that the subject was rarely pursued. In Pakistan it seemed every other man I spoke with had been, at one time or another, a contractor. "I used to hire men like you," one said, and others implied. That was fine with me. But other questions were not.

"You are married?" This was of critical concern. Many hoped I would not be; that I would tell them wild tales of a bachelor's unbridled sex life.

"Yes," I would say.

"Ah... " The questioner would look disappointed for a moment. Then would come a ray of hope, and he would say, "No children?"

"No." This question always got a rise from me. It seemed too personal, and it was. With no children, then why was I married? What good was my wife? Did I see sex as an entertainment? Apparently so, and that must carry over to women other than my wife. Aha! Isn't that right? I must have lots of sex with lots of women, and I must lubricate the sport with plenty of whiskey.

"Whiskey is legal in your country, no? And love is very easy!"

If I failed to nip the conversation at this point, it often went openly to such queries as "Do you have a girlfriend? Do you think alcohol encourages sex? What is your religion?" On my bicycle I carried a water bottle; twice, I was asked if it contained whiskey.

In all this, I thought of adolescent boys pumping their elder brothers for the titillating details: "And then what did you do? Really?" Their questions showed a pathetic sort of innocence not so different from the innocence, if you could call it that (Alicia would not!), of the peeping Toms and bum-pinchers at the Chinibagh Hotel. I felt sad for them. I also felt used.

———

Eager to get on to the Karakoram, I nonetheless had a duty: to go to Islamabad and get a new passport. Pat agreed to come with me, while Wendy and Baiba waited for us in Gilgit. Islamabad was a mail stop, and he wanted to see a man at the Canadian embassy. We put together a list of errands. It would be a town trip. But what a sad thing to have to do, with the Karakoram so near. It was impossible to get an airline seat, so we went to the various bus stations. Even buses were full. Pat got the one remaining ticket for that day. The best I could manage was ticket number twenty in a passenger van designed to hold twelve people. I knew I had to go, but it gave me the creeps, thinking about riding overnight on twisting mountain roads, packed into the back seat, nowhere near a door, with no foot room, no space to shift my weight or stand up or do anything but endure for sixteen hours. Even Gilgit was hot. The road to Islamabad would be a furnace. I would somehow have to bear it.

Then I saw a similar van leaving Gilgit. It was a can of people. There were guys sitting on other guys' laps in there. There were five guys in the back seat. Their knees were as high as their shoulders. They could hardly move their arms. The windows in back did not open. It looked like a college stunt.

"I don't think I can do it," I said to Wendy. I worried about it until Pat left at seven o'clock on the bus, braced on the edge of a hard bench seat shared with two burly fellow passengers. At least he had an aisle where he could put his legs. At worst, I thought, he could stand up. Then it was time for my van to leave, and I panicked. My feelings went beyond the fear of discomfort to the deeper fear of being at the bottom of a pile of people. Tight spaces bother me. Sometimes I have trouble sitting against the wall in a cafe booth. The back seat of that van scared the hell out of me. In the end, I let it go without me. Maybe I could buy my way onto a bus. There were lots of buses.

At ten o'clock that night, I did find a seat, or part of one. It was a good thing that I had seen the van. Only the van could have made the bus seem tolerable. Before we left, the seats were jammed, the aisle was jammed, the roof was jammed. At least twenty people were on the roof.

Pakistan has about one hundred million people. Raja Badruhan had said that in all of Hunza there were thirty-six thousand people. It's no wonder that the Hunzakuts think of Pakistan as a different country.

I managed to doze through the night—not a bad trick considering the way the bus hurtled around the unending curves. At dawn, I could see the landscape. Far below, at the bottom of a canyon of rice paddies, was the Indus River. Wisps of cloud hung in the canyon. It had been raining, and I was surprised at the beauty of this precipitous terrain.

At Besham, it was time for breakfast. A hundred or more trucks and buses were stopped along the highway. A row of slop shops shoveled brown liquids onto tin plates for hungry travelers. The food looked okay, but more than anything I wanted to sit in quiet surroundings for a few minutes. I found two hotels side by side. One advertised "Flush Toilets." The other boasted "Flesh Toilets." I chose the first, where I ate a quick egg with chapattis.

Back on the street, I wandered through ebullient chaos. Nothing like this could exist in sober-sided China. Not these kinds of decorations: trucks painted with fighter jets and airliners, tigers battling lions, Swiss mountain scenes complete with chalets and men in lederhosen. The drivers' cabs were customized with hammered chromed metal, colored lights, and hanging doodads. Fringes of chain with colored hearts at the end of each strand hung from front and rear bumpers. Someone with a full assortment of spray-can colors had been under the fenders of many vehicles. All of them, it seemed—trucks, buses, and cars—were equipped with several horns, including at least one that played something like "Au Clair de la Lune" or "Deck the Halls." The Bedford trucks had wonderful wooden superstructures towering over the cabs that made them look like Spanish galleons coming backward down the road. Thinking that, I saw one come by with galleons painted on its side.

Back on the bus and breakfasted, everyone was awake.

"Which country?" asked a man beside me. I was trapped.

"America." We went through the standard openings, except I told him I was not married. He was an accountant from Abbotabad, near Rawalpindi.

"And how do you like Pakistan?" he asked.

"I love it. I've been in Hunza."

"I hate Pakistan."

"Why?"

"It is dirty. People are lazy. It is poor."

"I am coming from western China. It seems rich compared to there."

"But in China there is not Islamic Law. You do not know what that means. In your country, you have whiskey."

Here it comes, I thought.

"Do you think that women are a great temptation?" he asked.

"What do you mean?"

"I mean, if a man sees a woman, and if that man thinks about her in a way that is not moral—you see what I mean: bad thoughts—if it is the woman who excited these thoughts, then it is the woman's act that is wrong, not the man."

Why didn't these guys ever talk about something simple, like the weather?

■ *Above:* Temple Sri Badrinathji, a Hindu pilgrimage center since time immemorial, is located on the banks of the Alaknanda River in Badrinath, northern India (just south of Mount Kailas in Tibet). ■ *Overleaf:* Moonrise over Mount Dunagiri, near Nanda Devi. Pat and Baiba considered this campsite—atop a 12,000-foot peak above Josimath, northern India— one of the most spectacular in their experience.

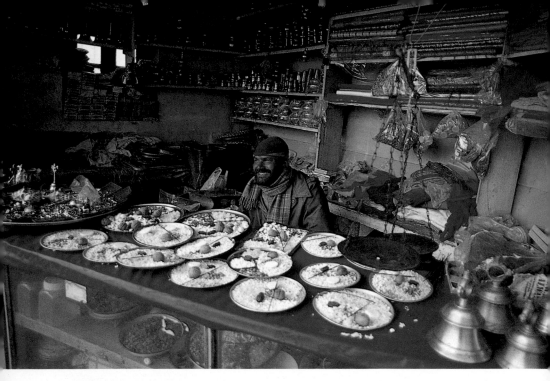

■ *Above:* A vendor displays religious souvenirs and platters of *prasad* (religious offerings) at Badrinath, a temple celebrating the source of the Ganges River. ■ *Below:* To honor the sacred Ganges, a celebrant of evening prayers holds a tray of offerings over the river as the sun sets.

■ Student painters of *thankas* (Buddhist religious depictions) keep Tibetan culture alive in Dharamsala, the home in exile of the Dalai Lama, northern India.

■ *Opposite:* We bought basic supplies for our trek in the local shop in Khandbari, Arun Valley, Himalaya, eastern Nepal.
■ *Above, left:* Sherpa woman with child in Sedua, upper Arun Valley, eastern Nepal.
■ *Above, right:* Sherpa grandmother with *shumunghat* (Indian rupee hat) and *hari* (necklace) in Nabagaon, upper Arun Valley, eastern Nepal. ■ *Right:* Painted *mani* stone in Tashigaon, upper Arun Valley, eastern Nepal, the last village we saw on our way to Makalu base camp.

■ *Above:* From left to right stand Lhotse, Lhotse Shar, and Mount Everest, as seen from an unusual angle above Makalu base camp.
■ *Below:* Nepal's national bird, the Impeyan pheasant.

Nonetheless, I got sucked in. "You mean," I said, "if the man has bad thoughts about the woman, it's the woman who did it?"

"It is possible."

"But the woman hasn't done anything? She's just being a woman?"

"That is natural! To men, all women are tempting. All young women. Just to see a woman is enough for sin."

"No. The man has to entertain those thoughts—"

"But he cannot! It is natural. A man wants many women."

"Some men do," I said.

"All men do."

"What about women?"

"Women are entirely different. By nature. They do not look at other men."

"Except to cause those men to sin."

"Yes, but—"

"And that's why they should not wear revealing clothing?"

"Yes, but you see, because a woman has no desire to see a man, but has love for only her husband, she will not have sin with her eyes. But she will cause that sin for men who might see her."

"Well, that's their problem, if it's a sin. Shouldn't men have some self-control?"

"It is so difficult. But tell me, what do you think of co-education?"

"I think it's fine. I went to school with girls and women all my life. I don't jump out at them from behind bushes."

"From bushes?"

"Never mind. It happened in China."

"I see. In my belief, co-education is a danger to society. Women are not so strong as men, because upon reaching puberty, they begin to suffer anemia."

"I don't follow."

"It is to be a woman. There is a loss of blood... You see? She is so more easily tired, and co-education makes a great demand upon her. It is unfair for women to compete with men for this reason."

"How does that endanger society?"

"By this. If a woman has been physically weakened by education, she cannot become a full woman. Reproductively, she will lack strength the rest of her life."

"So you don't think women should be educated."

"Oh, yes. Schooling is important for both sexes. But I am an accountant, and my wife is a mother, and the trainings for both are very different."

"What if a woman wants to be an accountant?"

"There! You see! That is the problem. How is she to be a mother and an accountant both? It takes both of us to do those jobs; how could she do my job and hers both? In Pakistan we care very much about our women. We protect them from all harm."

My attention wandered. The bus was getting hot. A man across the aisle tapped me on the arm. "I am from Rawalpindi," he said. "I would like to talk to you, but I do not speak English."

I smiled to acknowledge our common handicap and said, "I'm sorry too. I don't speak Urdu."

"Urdu is the third language of the world," he said inaccurately and reproachfully. I raised my eyebrows. "It is true. English, Arabic, then Urdu."

"But what about Chinese?" I asked, and here the man's English failed him. He gave me a look indicating that to say more in anything but Urdu was useless.

There are times when not speaking a language can be a great advantage. It lets you be selective about the company you keep and the things you understand. It keeps things superficial, and like it or not, the luxury of living superficially is one of the chief joys of travel. Order a pot of tea and then catch the next bus out.

Or the next plane. There were some fine things about Islamabad. First, the food was terrific; we ate four meals a day. Second, an official at the American embassy replaced my passport efficiently, with a smile, and without a lecture. Third, we learned that we could fly to Skardu instead of spending two and a half days on the bus going back through Gilgit. Accordingly, we called our wives—another great thing about Islamabad was that the telephones worked—and told them we'd meet them in Skardu.

11
Baltistan

They were there, an arctic continent of the heavens, far above the earth and its girdling clouds: divorced wholly from this planet. . . . Had I been born among or in sight of them, I might have been led to worship the infinite beauty they symbolized, but not to set boot on their flanks, or axe on a crest.
———W. H. Murray,
The Scottish Himalayan Expedition

S KARDU WAS A tantalizing place to be. At 7300 feet in elevation, it stood on the sands of a broad river junction in a sea of mountains. To the south rose the Deosai Plains, an alpine plateau providing spectacular views of the Karakoram peaks. If you went that way, you could end up staring at Nanga Parbat's stupendous Rupal face in a few days' time. To the northwest was the Hispar Glacier and a long mountaineering trek back to Hunza. Or you could go northeast up the Shigar Valley and beyond to Concordia, that astonishing meeting place of glaciers and mountains on the Baltoro Glacier. From one viewpoint, you would see K2 (28,741 feet), Broad Peak (26,400 feet), Gasherbrum IV (26,180 feet), Sia Kangri (24,350 feet), the Golden Throne (23,741 feet), and the sharp pinnacle of Mitre Peak (19,718 feet), and that is only a sampling of summits in the area.

The first European to see the Karakoram was the British traveler Godfrey Thomas Vigne, who came to Baltistan in 1835. At that time, Baltistan was an independent state ruled by an uneasy man named Ahmed Shah. Shah was uneasy because his neighbor, Ranjit Singh, the aggressive and powerful Maharajah of Kashmir, had his conquering eye on Baltistan. It's hard to imagine why the owner of wealthy Kashmir would want this region of rock and ice. He could not have prized the place for its riches, its commercial potential, or its

177

strategic value. Baltistan was—and remains today—one of the world's most emphatic cul-de-sacs. Every valley led upward to enormous twisted glaciers, ice-clad mountains, and passes far too rugged and high for anyone but mountaineers to cross. Its people were poor farmers and orchardists living in a place where 98 percent of the land was unsuitable for agriculture. They barely survived. They had neither the means to purchase trade goods nor any possessions worth stealing. It is nearly correct to say that once inside Baltistan, there is no way out.

However poor the country might have been, Ranjit Singh was an ambitious conqueror who found himself between a rock and a hard place. The rock lay to the east, in the form of British India, firmly blocking any thoughts of expansion in that direction. The hard place was Baltistan—not worth much perhaps, but better than a conqueror having to sit on his hands. Accordingly, in 1840 Sikh forces captured Baltistan (and, eventually, western Tibet all the way to Kailas).

Those events were still five years in the future when Vigne journeyed up from Srinagar, to be met on the border of Baltistan by Ahmed Shah himself. Shah, recognizing that his best chance of retaining independence lay in cultivating British contacts, was happy to greet anyone who might have influence in that direction. Vigne claimed no official credentials; his main interest was to have a look around the country. But Ahmed Shah believed otherwise, and in that case, who was Vigne to insist? Here, after all, was the secret mountain land he had wanted so much to see, thrown open to his curiosity. As Vigne put it in his *Travels in Kashmir, Ladakh, Iskardo, etc.*:

> I the first European that had ever beheld them (so I believe), gazed downwards from a height of 6000 or 7000 feet upon the sandy plains and green orchards of the valley of the Indus at Skardu, with a sense of mingled pride and pleasure, of which no one but a traveller can form a just conception... Wherever the eye could rove, arose, with surpassing grandeur, a vast assemblage of the enormous summits that compose the Tibetian Himalaya.

Actually, he was seeing the Karakoram Range, until then unknown in the West. European geographers familiar with India had thought Tibet's high plateau began just north of the Great Himalaya—as it did farther east. These new mountains were a big surprise. Very big: in the area around the Baltoro Glacier are located ten of the world's thirty highest mountains. Vigne spent many months during the next few years probing these stupendous unknown valleys.

In one sense, however, the Karakoram were, as he had first called them, "Tibetian" mountains. Before Baltistan converted to Islam about five hundred years ago, its people had been Buddhist, living under the influence of Tibet.

Even today, Balti people speak an archaic form of Tibetan. They build Tibetan-style houses with mud walls and flat roofs. They inhabit dry valleys where crops grow only by irrigation, where the air is thin and the climate difficult. Skardu itself is an oasis, a patch of green in a sea of sand on the floor of a great valley; in many ways it reminded me of Gyantse in central Tibet.

Skardu even had a Tibetan-style wind. When we arrived, yellow clouds of sand and dust were roaring through the poplar trees. In a manner of speaking, even the sand was Tibetan, some of it having been carried down by the Indus River from its source near Mount Kailas.

I have an impossible ambition: to float the Indus someday from its headwaters all the way to Skardu. It would be an exciting ride, beginning at an elevation of around 16,000 feet in the barren valleys north of Kailas at a place Tibetans call Singi-kabab, the Lion's Mouth. Starting on those shallow clear waters, I would traverse western Tibet, then Ladakh through wild desert canyons, ending in the thunderous gorges of the Karakoram Range. The problem is not one of geography. Old maps still show a trail following the river all the way from Ali to Skardu. It was probably never more than a rough track (if it existed at all; maps of this area are notoriously imaginative), but now the rough track has been reduced by politics to mere fantasy. It crosses two borders, both of which are disputed and firmly closed: the first between Tibet and India, the second between India and Pakistan. The route I have in mind is feasible only for creatures that float or fly and don't show up on radar screens—fish, vultures, or Hindu sadhus.

Speaking of holy men, there were no sadhus in Skardu. Or if there were, they certainly weren't going around, as they do in India, wearing loincloths, carrying iron tridents, and painting their faces. Islam frowns on such behavior, and in Skardu the frown was a real one, in the form of Iran's famous scowling Ayatollah. All over Skardu, posters of stern-faced Khomeini were plastered on shop windows and utility poles. His face was as ubiquitous as were pictures of the Dalai Lama in parts of Tibet. However, as Pat pointed out, "No one comes up to you asking, 'Khomeini photo?'"

That's unfortunate. It has a nicer rhythm than "Death to the USA!" or "Death to USSR!" From Hunza to Gilgit and all the way to Islamabad, we had seen these mottos scrawled, often misspelled, in dripping black letters. I had pictured a few wild-haired zealots (from Nagir, no doubt) driving through the country with spray cans. In the United States, the same sort of people write "Death is the Wages of Sin!" I've never worried much about them.

However, Skardu seemed to be spray paint headquarters. The slogans were scrawled everywhere—on the wall of the "Women's Vacational Education Office," on the side of our hotel, even on the wall of the public library. (It was not on the mosque.) Seeing them displayed so prominently made me a bit wary of Baltis at first, especially when hailed by the common greeting "Which country?" I always answered truthfully, even in places where the questioner could see the damning motto on the wall behind me; yet there was never any sign of hostility. Everyone was friendly. When I finally asked one man about it, a man who professed a strong belief in Islam, he laughed at me.

"That's just religion," he said. "Not life!"

Everyone did seem friendly, but that's not to say conversations were anything near normal. I couldn't seem to connect with the people around Skardu. For example, a well-dressed, handsome man asked Pat and me the standard questions, including "What is your profession?" Pat said he was a mountain guide.

"Ah, then you are the porter?" he said to me. "You look more like a doctor."

I leaned across the table toward him, peered closely at his face, and said, "So what's the problem with you?" This was taken as a great joke. Pat asked him his profession.

"I have no profession."

"You don't need to work? You're a lucky man," said Pat.

"You also can be lucky."

"What do you mean?"

"Ahh . . . " he shrugged.

"Maybe I am already."

"Maybe you are not."

And that was the end of the discussion. Another day, as I was buying rice in the market, a tiny, bearded man put his face ten inches from my ear and shouted, "Which country?"

"U.S.A."

"Ahm Rikka?"

"Yes, where are you from?"

"Pakistan!" With that, he glared at me and walked away with the look of a man trying to avoid catching a contagious disease. I don't think he was objecting to my nationality, just to my stupidity in not recognizing him as a Pakistani. Actually, I had wanted to know if he was from Skardu.

One day, Wendy and I were walking along the river. A prosperous man of about fifty came past us, his ample girth accentuated by the sway of his tailored *shalwar*. "Which country?" he asked.

I told him.

"The U.S.A.? That is a long way. And what do you do?"

I was tired of the occupation question, so I decided to misunderstand him. "We are walking by the river," I said. "And what do you do?"

"We are from Swat."

"I hear Swat is a nice place," I replied. Actually we'd been warned off Swat by people who said you should hire armed guards if you want to visit there. No matter; we weren't talking about Swat. The man pointed at Wendy.

"And what is she to you?"

"She is my wife."

"Your wife!" He grimaced. Evidently he had hoped for titillation. He looked so disappointed to learn that we were a married couple, and I was getting so tired of trying to represent myself in a respectable manner, that I decided to give him something. I tapped my rucksack, lowered my voice, and asked him if he wanted to buy some whiskey.

"Whiskey!" he snorted. "I am Muslim!" And off he went in a happy, self-satisfied huff, his elbows pulled well behind his shoulders.

W HEN BAIBA AND WENDY had rattled up on the bus from Gilgit the day after us, Baiba was sick. She had gotten off looking wobbly, which wasn't a surprise—everyone does that after mountain bus rides. But she had gone straight to bed and stayed there, completely out of character for stalwart Baiba and effectively ending any plans for leaving Skardu soon.

"It's already the end of September," said Pat one day. He was surprised. Time had gone so quickly.

Originally we had intended a trek on the Baltoro Glacier, a trek that would take at least three weeks. Now we reluctantly conceded that our time was too short. Dealing with my passport problems, loafing through Hunza, and going to Islamabad had eaten up nearly a month.

Travel is not what the glossy magazines portray. Travel is often dull, tiring, and uncomfortable, especially in the boondocks of Asia. There, the most important skills are being patient, sitting quietly in discomfort, shutting off your mind and ignoring some irritation, and biting your tongue. You can tell an inexperienced traveler by his or her frequent complaints and outbursts. Where a greenhorn traveler throws a tantrum, a seasoned traveler goes silent. Pat was like that. He'd retreat into that interior room where he could ignore, or tolerate, whatever was bothering him. He wouldn't sulk. He just knew there was nothing to say. More than that, he knew that irritations are temporary matters while angry words last for a long time. The same was true of Baiba. Regardless of occasional frustrations, we had had no angry words. A few earnest discussions perhaps, but never angry words. That, to me, was the mark of good friends and good traveling companions.

To travel with friends has some advantages over traveling alone. You can support each other in any number of ways, sharing tasks and enthusiasm. One person can look after the bags while the other buys tickets or finds a taxi. One person stays cheerful when the other erupts in frustration. One person goes looking for medicine while the other is prostrate with fever. And in countries where you don't speak the language there is always someone to talk to, as long as you stay on speaking terms.

On the other hand, the larger the group, the greater the chance for things to go wrong—not just one, but four people to get sick, four seats to find on the bus, four opinions to accommodate. The whole party waits for the sick person to get well. Or for the person with torn pants to get them mended. Or for the fool who lost his passport to get a replacement.

And now Baiba, who almost never admitted discomfort, said she felt awful.

So there we stayed in the Karakoram Inn, a terrible place to recuperate. The rooms were concrete cells with windows that opened on a central echo chamber reverberating with the unending clamor of Skardu. Across the street, a building was under construction; men pouring concrete yelled at each other from dawn to dusk. A stream of jeeps, buses, and trucks dodged each other in the road, horns blaring. Porters came through, bearing all sorts of freight. Gangs of cows worked their way from trash can to trash can, extracting and eating cardboard cartons, newspapers, tea leaves, and the odd discarded vegetable. They knew all the good places, like winos in Los Angeles. Capping the clamor, there was a mosque located on a sand dune fifty yards behind the hotel that periodically fired up an amplifier for prayers. Five o'clock every morning, day after day, electronically distorted singing slammed against the walls of our hotel rooms. "Death to Loudspeakers!" became Pat's personal slogan.

Baiba had improved some by the time Gulam Hassan arrived in Skardu. Hassan was a Hunzakut mountain guide Pat and Baiba had met back in Sost, while waiting for Wendy and me to cross the border. They had taken a quick liking to him.

An accomplished mountaineer, Hassan was another of those small men who don't look the part. His quiet demeanor and slight stature made him seem best suited to a desk in a Rawalpindi bank. Nonetheless, there he was guiding a group of men from Australia and New Zealand who claimed to be scouting for a major peak to climb the next year. Maybe Rakaposhi. Or Masherbrum. They were all strapping fellows the size of football players. For some reason Hassan was depressed about this group. He wasn't having a good time hauling them around Pakistan, and he was happy to hear that we had decided on a trek to the same place they were headed—to the Hushe Valley in the neighborhood of Masherbrum. Three days of walking from the end of the road would put us at the base of a minor summit called Gondoro Peak, about 19,000 feet high, from the top of which we could look over the divide and see into the Baltoro Glacier area—including a view of K2. It was a relatively easy way to get into the high Karakoram and at least sample the terrain. With our time shrinking rapidly, it was our best remaining option.

F INALLY, BAIBA WAS READY to travel. We left Skardu on a day that felt like the start of autumn, a cold windy day of lowering clouds and fresh snow on the peaks. Trees along the Indus River were still green, but in meadows thousands of feet above, we could see occasional vivid patches of gold and red.

We might have bicycled to Hushe. It would have been a pleasant trip, most of it on a decent road, but time constraints made us unwilling to do that. More than anything, our desire was to get beyond the roads. We wanted to walk. So we had stored the bikes in Skardu and hired a jeep driven by a big, genial man named Aga Abas. We rode in the open back. Ahead of us two other vehicles carried Hassan and his clients.

Hassan had shown up that morning in a two-tone sweatshirt and a plastic Michael Jackson cap with big ear flaps—hardly the picture of the professional, competent mountain guide we knew him to be. But he was having a bad time with his clients, and maybe this was his way of expressing his opinion. No doubt about it, his group was a bit stiff. It was purely a coincidence that we were heading to the Hushe Valley the same day and that our drivers were friends and wanted to stay together. We had no intention of joining the other group on the trail, yet they acted as if we were party crashers. Refusing to acknowledge us, they stood around at rest stops in heavy boots, parkas, and little white shorts that showed as much of their great pink legs as there was to see. It may have been normal mountain attire in New Zealand, but they looked a little odd in the land of *shalwars* and covered bodies.

What an extraordinarily beautiful place this was! The mountains were mostly arid rock and scree, rising many thousands of feet from the valley bottom. Way up on the ridge tops, we could see steeply pitched alpine meadows—evidence of moisture that made me wonder what sort of wildlife lived up there. There were certainly few animals living on the valley floor, all loose sand and dried silt. The river, now moving fast over gravel, now raging through rock-walled narrows, was the burnished color of Tibetan road dust. Having cut deeply into its banks, the water was useless for irrigation purposes. There was no way to lift it onto the fields.

Instead, scattered villages depended on the occasional side stream. Absolutely everything people grew here was a crop of some sort, even the trees. Some provided fruit and nuts, while others—the willows and poplars—produced leaves for fodder and wood for fuel. The trees were not cut down;

rather, their branches were periodically trimmed, leaving heavy, gnarled trunks to sprout again.

The nineteenth-century English traveler E. F. Knight, referring to the similar landscape of neighboring Ladakh in *Where Three Empires Meet,* thought these scattered villages looked like "bits of some other country cut out with a pair or scissors and dropped into a desert." An apt description. Bits of England pasted into Pakistan, or better yet, bits of Italy, each village an oasis with the feel of the Mediterranean. From out of the desert we would drive into the green shade of poplar trees, down winding lanes beneath overhanging houses, past courtyards protecting ancient apricot and nut trees. Dark-eyed children stood on flat roofs waving at us. Water tumbled through irrigation channels. Lines of banty roosters strutted atop orchard walls.

On that day, people were busy with the harvest, up to their necks in waves of golden millet or squatting in groups cutting hay with curved knives. Until then, I had seen few Balti women. Those I had encountered while walking were always reticent, unlike their gregarious husbands and sons. But here, with us moving safely past on the road 40 feet away, their gaze was direct. I wanted to see their faces, so I stared back. One young woman was careless. I caught a hint of neckline beneath her exposed throat, and it gave me an unexpected rush, making me think that there is truth in the idea that when a society requires women to cover their bodies totally, even the slightest unguarded movement can be powerfully provocative.

From autumn harvest to war. Along the road we passed numerous military vehicles. There were jeeps and Unimog trucks and Massey Ferguson tractors pulling trailers loaded with all sorts of stuff—boxes of mortar shells, gasoline in jerry cans, food, and crates marked only with numbers.

"They are fighting on the Siachen," said Hassan, coming back to our jeep when a traffic jam forced us all to stop. He meant the Siachen Glacier, an area of ice and snow of no legitimate interest to anyone but mountaineers and geographers. India and Pakistan were fighting what newspapers in both countries proudly claimed to be the highest conflict ever waged, as if setting a record made it worthwhile. They were certainly setting records; more soldiers were dying from altitude sickness than from combat.

Hassan said the fighting had started when some official in India gave a Siachen Glacier trekking permit to a party of Germans—a permit to enter an area Pakistan considered its own. When Pakistan tried to enforce its claim (well after the trekkers had left), India sent in soldiers. That was Hassan's version, the first of several conflicting stories we heard in the next month. India, of course, claimed it had always owned the Siachen and that Pakistan was the aggressor.

So what? Battling for the Siachen Glacier was like two bald men fighting over a comb. What were they afraid of—that the other country would control the world's best ice climbing?

Onward, up the mercury-colored Indus, holding cautiously to a narrow jeep road hacked into vertical cliffs. Standing in back, Pat and I had to keep watch for low-hanging rocks. Inattention might have resulted in a broken skull. At a river junction we left the Indus to follow the Shyok, itself a major stream, and then, past the town of Khapulu on the opposite bank—a green wedge of Italy pasted on a cloud of dust—our route turned up a side valley to ascend a treacherous, ever-narrower track to where it ended three hours later at a little stone village.

It was dusk, and this was Hushe, bathed in the reflected light of sunset on Masherbrum. The great mountain glowed red, a flaming symmetry of snow and ice commanding the deep, shadowed valley. Cervinia in the Karakoram, I thought, my mind still on Italy. Cervinia 150 years ago, before electricity, when everyone lived in stone huts.

Accompanied by a gaggle of children, the men of Hushe came to meet us— among them, a rugged-looking fellow wearing a red pile jacket and plastic sandals. "His together come?" he asked.

"Yes, four of us," I said.

"His going to Gondoro Peak? Yes! Very good. I have room for you his stay. In morning, his porter come there. How many his porter you needing?"

"We don't know yet," I told him. "We are looking for a man named Javed."

"I am Javed."

The famous Abdullah Javed. Just about everyone we had talked to in the past week had said, "Hushe? Look for Javed." And here he was, an immediately likable man. While twenty or so of his neighbors, all eager to serve as porters, carted the baggage of Hassan's group to a camping field, we carried our own loads to Javed's house. He took us down a narrow alley between stone walls and past low doorways to a vacant room.

"His dusty," Javed said, shaking out rolled-up bedding, stirring up a cloud. We lit candles for light and opened the windows to let out the dust. Pat found a stack of mountaineering books on a shelf. One was by Joe Tasker: *The Savage Arena,* which included a harrowing description of a climb on K2.

Javed said something about having been on K2 himself, to which Baiba replied that "this guy," punching Pat in the shoulder, had climbed Everest. It took her a few minutes to convince Javed that this was true—none of us being great muscular hulks—but once he accepted the fact, Javed's attitude became reverent toward Pat, and they were soon talking about glaciers and mountains and, as climbers do so often, accidents. Javed had been a high-altitude porter for five years, on peaks including Masherbrum, Gasherbrum II, Gasherbrum IV, K2, and Chogolisa. He had met and worked with a number of international Karakoram climbers, some of whom were now dead as a result of mountaineering accidents. For Javed, five years had been enough of danger. He had retired.

"Many his good climbers has died. Boardman, Tasker, Casarotto."

"Were you at K2 last year?" Pat asked.

Javed said no. They were talking about the summer of 1986, when nine expeditions had made attempts on the world's second-highest mountain. There had been some brilliant climbing that summer, including a solo ascent in twenty-three hours by a Frenchman and the establishment of two new routes. In all, twenty-three men and four women had reached the summit, but thirteen, including eight summiters, had died. Among those lost, two Americans were killed by an avalanche. A falling rock killed a Pakistani. A French couple team disappeared while descending from the summit. Two Poles died in separate falls. The Italian, Renatto Casarotto, working solo on an unclimbed route called the Magic Line (which was climbed for the first time two weeks later by a Polish team), had made it three times above 8000 meters before finally admitting defeat. On his descent, within minutes of base camp where his wife awaited him, he fell into a crevasse and died. Later, seven climbers from four separate expeditions became stormbound for six days at an altitude of 7900 meters. Only two of the seven survived.

Events like those had put Javed off mountaineering as a profession. They weren't his expeditions, after all; as a high-altitude porter he had been an employee, and like most local people, even the redoubtable Sherpas of Nepal, he had no reason to climb the high peaks on his own.

Or almost none. Pat asked him if there was any mountain he'd been on that he would like to try again, for the pleasure of it.

Javed took a moment to answer, then said, "Chogolisa. Maybe. His no avalanche, Chogolisa. His good mountain."

I was again reminded of the European scene 150 years ago. Edward Whymper, the great pioneer of Alpine climbing, the man who first ascended the Matterhorn, must have met men just like Javed in mountain villages in the 1830s and talked them into hiring on as support for Whymper's ambitions. Of course, in the end, the sons and grandsons of those first Alpine guides became the great pioneers of Himalayan mountaineering.

We talked about our very modest plans. Pat explained to Javed that we would not require a guide. For us, this was a question of expense. Our collective purse was getting thin. A guide cost twice as much as a porter and needed his own porter in addition. On the other hand, we knew it was wrong to visit places like Hushe and hire no one. Local people resent do-it-yourselfers, and we certainly wanted to hire porters.

"The way is easy enough to find, I think," said Pat.

Javed nodded, clearly disappointed, but not able to push himself as a guide on a man who had climbed Everest. He stood and went to our packs. "His bags you taking?"

"Yes."

He hefted our loads, which were quite small, and made a judgment: "Yes, you needing four his porters."

"Do we need crampons for Gondoro Peak?" asked Pat.

"His time it is ice, you needing crampons, yes. How many days?"

We worked out the length of the trip. Three days to the base of Gondoro Peak, three days to explore the high country, and three days back to Hushe. Pat explained that we wanted the porters to carry only one way. They could drop the loads at Gondoro and return. "We will carry our own packs coming back," he said.

Javed nodded, "Porter his come down. No his stay." And after a long pause during which I knew he was swallowing pride, he said, "I also am porter, not his guide."

A T SEVEN-THIRTY the next morning, Javed brought tea and porridge. We had been up for two hours by then, watching sunrise on Masherbrum in a clear sky. Dawn light shone on the snow-covered southeast face, the first side of the mountain to be climbed, in 1960, by a party of Americans. It was a grand sight, and watching it I decided that if mountaineering were like that view, all bright snow and symmetrical rock on clear, windless mornings— if climbing weren't also a matter of appalling weather, high winds, intense cold, the threat of avalanche, the strain of extreme altitude, and the fear of death—then certainly mountaineers would have less trouble explaining their motivation. The way it was that morning in Hushe, a great mountain like Masherbrum becomes deceptively inviting. All you'd have to do is look up to think you understood why men and women climb.

As we ate breakfast, the three other porters arrived and tested the loads. There was Makhmet, small and wizened, a laughing gnome of a man dressed in rubber boots and a bright red knitted vest. He was in his fifties, his beard streaked with grey. Beside him, the others—Javed, Abdulla, and Ibrahim— seemed strapping giants. Ibrahim, fine of feature, handsome, with a bearing that spoke of a formal education he had never had, was nothing if not courtly. They all seemed pleased to be heading up the valley on a windless autumn morning.

I was euphoric. We were back in the clear, high air. The peaks, and there were lots of them, shone with blinding light against a sky of powerful blue. Makhmet stayed with Wendy and me for the first few miles. He was carrying the heaviest load of all, with the biggest smile. Chugging along, sockless, in his rubber boots, he chattered a nonstop stream of Balti in a high, squeaky voice, laughing often—telling stories, I suppose, although we could understand none of what he said. Eventually he shifted to a higher gear and shot out of sight up the trail. When we caught up to him, he was sitting with Javed, Ibrahim, and Abdulla. They had a fire going and a huge kettle of tea brewed. They waved us over to share it.

We had to go through names again. Ours especially were foreign to their ears. Abdulla and Ibrahim were easy for us to pronounce, but Balti tongues just couldn't make sense of my name. "Call me Joe," I said finally. Pat became Pot. Wendy wasn't too hard, and Baiba was so easy they all repeated it many times. "Bye-bah!" Makhmet lost control and rolled in the sand he enjoyed saying it so much. Bye-bah! Bye-bah!

In the Himalaya, you hear a lot about untrustworthy porters, guys who take off in the night with your gear, get part way up the trail and suddenly demand higher wages, or refuse to go where they agreed to go. It seems everyone has a bad porter story to tell. Not I. I've always felt privileged to have local men—and occasionally, as in Nepal, women—for company on the trail. The benefits are enormous. Porters get to be friends. They know the shortcuts. You get to meet their pals along the way. These four Baltis were no exception; I'd have wanted them to come along even if they hadn't been carrying our loads.

Following the river through white granite boulders, we came to a campsite at the junction of the Chundugoro and Charkusa valleys on flat white sand under spreading juniper trees. On all sides there rose mountains made of sheer granite slabs and sharp pinnacles. For such enormous hulking things they seemed too delicate, too vertical, too slender, to be real—like the cloud-wreathed spires in the backgrounds of fantasy paintings. I half expected to see dragons perched upon them.

So near the autumnal equinox, the sun set vertically, decisively, leaving in its place a sudden chill that sent us to bed early. At dawn the next morning, valleys were cold pools of grey while the mountain summits, one after the other, burst into fiery brilliance. The shadow line of the earth's turning descended slowly and razor sharp across brittle glaciers and uncompromising rock. Watching it edge toward me, I shivered in a down jacket; as it passed, like a door opening, I stripped to a T-shirt. Our tents, glazed by ice one minute, sagged with dripping water the next.

I thought of the American desert, where the same sharp intensity is evident—but with a difference. Especially in morning or evening, desert light is tempered by dust in the air; or it bounces off warm-colored stone, filling shadows with a gentle glow that makes skin shine, rocks seem alive, leaves iridescent. Here, in thin air, where stone was black or white, snow was colorless, and the sky a chilling blue, the light found no sympathetic resonance. Bold shadows, bright mountains: you were either in the sun or out of it. There was nothing in between. Light struck these mountains and splintered. The fragments lay where they fell, cold and hard. Light for heroes. Mountains for dragons. A place for ambitions but not for dreams.

That day, we began a long, gradual climb up the Chundugoro Valley, walking on the ridge of a moraine covered by juniper trees. Cool early air chilled my bare arms, but under my pack my back was sweaty. At the head of the valley, seen from this side, Masherbrum was an unappealing lump, impressive only in its shapeless grandeur and cruel east face. No clouds marred the sky, but a plume of snow from Masherbrum's summit told of strong winds.

Higher, a granite buttress of the mountain wall forced us off the moraine and onto the Chundugoro Glacier, where loose talus rocked and tilted underfoot. Above us the moraine leered dangerously. Undermined by the glacier, it was a cliff of loose rock in continuous fall. We moved as quickly as we could, glancing nervously at the boulders hanging above our heads. Beneath us, the glacier boomed and rumbled, carrying its load of shattered rock, pitching it down crevasses and into dirty lakes where it made obscene subterranean noises. It was a frightening path to tread, and I was happy to get back onto more solid ground.

At Dahlsam, where we spent the night, there were two tarns, a patch of meadow, and a cluster of shepherd huts set in a tremendous amphitheater beneath thundering hanging glaciers. What a place! It was a view both terrible and beautiful. The exposed rock was smooth and fluted, but the ice—five or six glaciers colliding at this point—was tortured, mangled, shattered, and very noisy. Hardly five minutes went by without the sound of ice falling somewhere in the amphitheater.

Behind us, the mountains were steep but free of ice. Scattered among the cliffs, tiny meadows burned with herbs turning red, yellow, gold, and brown. Looking at the desert sands around Skardu, I would never have guessed that these high valleys sustained such a variety of plant life.

In four months, this was the first healthy vegetation we had seen. In Tibet and China, grass had been chewed to the roots and hillsides pounded to dust under plagues of hooves. I had expected Pakistan to be worse off. I had thought that Tibet, with so few people and being so remote, would be the more pristine place. Not so. This Baltistan valley still had firewood lying on the ground near timberline. I found fox tracks one morning. There were ibex in the neighborhood, and Javed spoke of seeing snow leopard from time to time.

It can't last. Pakistan's population is a brush fire out of control. The mountains are more heavily used each year. The road to Hushe is new, built within the last few years. It can't help but bring more people. I was tempted to write false names for this place so as not to publicize it. It was a fleeting temptation. For one thing, there was no secret to give away; the Karakoram are among the world's most famous mountains, but not everyone wants to go there. The well-constructed trails of Nepal are much better suited for most trekkers than the hair-raising routes of Pakistan. The Karakoram's best protection is its ancient one—the difficulty of getting there. Even for a simple excursion you need equipment, strength, time, determination, and some luck with the weather. No adventure-travel outfitter wants to risk having some sweet California grandmother creamed by a boulder on the Chundugoro Glacier, an event that could easily happen.

Beyond that, like Javed, the local people were happy to see us, happy to see our money. Isn't it presumptuous to suggest that they stay poor and picturesque? Was it wrong that Javed was considering building a small lodge at Hushe? Properly managed, tourism can be better than other forms of exploitation because of its vested interest in the preservation of scenery and wildlife. If tourists will pay to see ibex in a natural setting, local people begin to see live ibex as a valuable cash resource—not just as meat waiting to be killed.

While I troubled over those concerns, mortar shells fell on the Siachen Glacier. Indians and Pakistanis dressed in white mountaineering suits, dizzy from altitude sickness, shot at each other. And for what? In the long run, conservation concerns will dwarf the questions of who owns which rock. Meanwhile, however, the deceptively gentle demands of the natural world are postponed and trampled by shortsighted politics. What was the point in worrying about where I placed my feet among fragile tundra plants while armies blew up the neighboring valleys?

"Do you like meat?" Javed asked me. A trick question: he wanted us to buy a goat from the herder who kept his summer quarters at Dahlsam, because he and his friends craved meat. When the herds were in summer pasture, there wasn't much meat in Hushe, and the opportunity to kill a sheep or goat was one of the benefits of carrying loads to the high meadows. "You pay some, I pay some," Javed said, and that was also a trick. Javed produced fifty rupees; we laid out three hundred. In any real measure of economics, I suppose, it was a fair deal.

Javed and Makhmet did the butchering. They cut up the meat and threw it into a big aluminum stewpot with curry and other spices. It tasted very good, but the four of us ate only a small portion. The Baltis ate the rest with great pleasure and lots of hooting and sucking of fingers. "Joe!" said Makhmet, handing me a meaty bone, and then, using the familiar version of Baiba that they had invented, "Baba! Ba-bah! Babababa!" His friends repeated the name with gusto until they sounded like the Beach Boys singing "Barbara Ann." They carried on until well after dark, as happy as if they had tapped a bottle of the hootch their religion forbids.

Climbing the ridge above camp, I crouched in the wind shelter of a boulder and watched the sky. Cassiopeia hung upside down in the north. Jupiter shone in the east. Flying down the Milky Way, Cygnus spread his wings directly overhead. There was no moon. The stars were white fires. Glaciers thundered. Black mountains roared at the black night.

Leaving Dahlsam early the next morning, we walked in cold blue shade beneath peaks lit by the flame of the rising sun. Our path followed the crest of an old moraine, one left by a larger glacier than the one torturing the valley now. The older moraine was an island of stability, undisturbed for long enough that soil had collected and plants grew. And more than plants: an unusual thing had been happening each night. I suspect that it was a phenomenon of freezing weather and moisture-laden soil, but I haven't seen it in other autumn mountains. At the bases of a particular herbaceous plant, frost flowers were growing—ribbons of ice six to ten inches long emerging from the plant stems just above ground level. Each "flower" consisted of six ribbons extruded in a star pattern curling intricately around each other. I guessed that moisture pushing up from roots froze as it cleared the ground surface, where, unable to rise into the stems, it thrust instead into the sub-zero air. These ice flowers were beautiful translucent things reflecting the cold blue of the sky and the warm red of the plants from which they had grown.

While Wendy and I paused, Pat and Baiba went ahead. I could see them half a mile farther on, silhouetted figures against the stupendous glittering icefall below Masherbrum. Suddenly they stopped moving. A rockfall had begun far above us on the smooth granite face. From 2000 feet up, a shower of boulders came leaping down; I could see individual stones bounding hundreds of feet between shattering impacts. They had been kicked off by a barely visible troupe of ibex. Perhaps fifty of the animals ran streaming across the rock face,

191

sprinting as if on flat ground, kicking off loose stones as they went. On the crest of the moraine we were out of danger and could appreciate watching the ibex run as heavy boulders crashed into the meadow at the base of the cliff. When it was over, several tons of shattered rock, stinking of cordite, lay strewn across what we would have considered a fine camping site a few minutes earlier.

From there we left the old moraine and scrambled down to the glacier surface, following it steadily uphill for several hours. Our guide was the impish Makhmet far ahead on the skyline, a tiny, quick-footed figure beneath a bulky load. He and his friends waited for us at the head of the valley on a grassy flat surrounded by sharp peaks. This was our base camp. Javed and the others left us here, happily trotting off with their almost nonexistent personal gear.

Climbing Gondoro the next day was really just a trudge up the snow, with a bit of cramponing near the summit. Starting at four in the morning, we were at the top about four hours later, but even that was too late: the weather had beaten us. Despite the clear sky at dawn, clouds had closed in, snow was already falling in the valley, and there wasn't much of a view, certainly no hint of K2 or anything on the Baltoro side.

Nonetheless, I took pleasure in being so elevated in the world of rock and ice. Despite its being a minor bump in the Karakoram, Gondoro Peak was a mile higher than any summit in the Rockies, and I felt precariously privileged to be there. To be exposed, and yet feel competent and comfortable, is a splendid exhilaration. It's as if you leaped off a cliff and found that you still had some control over the situation.

I had been reading, at night by candlelight, *Arctic Dreams* by Barry Lopez and was struck by a passage describing Eskimos killing polar bears with knives or harpoons:

Tornarssuk, the Polar Eskimo called [the bear], "the one who gives power."

To encounter the bear, to meet it with your whole life, was to grapple with something personal. The confrontation occurred on a serene, deadly, and elevated plain. If you were successful you found something irreducible within yourself, like a seed. To walk away was to be alive, utterly. To be assured of your own life, the life of your kind, in a harsh land where life took insight and patience and humor. It was to touch the bear. It was a gift from the bear.

That passage seemed appropriate to the mountains. I wondered if the pleasure of being in high places was at all related to killing the bear. Having done it, you know you're alive, as if you've been given the gift not only of life but of awareness. A gift of power from the mountain, except the mountain never dies.

I asked Pat about his feelings. He said the summit of Everest was nothing like touching God. He had felt little emotion. "I felt flat," he said. "I was exhausted. It took two months for me even to start thinking about it." Maybe so; but I had known him before and after his climb, and something happened up there. It might not have been the summit. It might have been simply the extended effort of getting up the mountain. Whatever the cause, I could see that Pat had changed in a subtle but fundamental way. He had gained, I thought, something essentially solid, a nut of strength, a certain knowing, as if he had, in Lopez's words, "found something irreducible" within himself.

———————

Under dark, spitting clouds we returned to our tents to find Hassan's group camped nearby. Hassan came over shaking his head. He was having a terrible time. The big Australian fellow who looked like a rugby player was complaining. Their cookstoves weren't working. Their gear was wet. The weather was bad. They couldn't see the mountains. They were cold. Hassan and his little crew of Baltis struggled to keep chunks of turf burning long enough to warm tea water and received, for their effort, only complaints.

As if listening to them, the Great Spirit of Karakoram Weather brought in a real reason for them to gripe. By afternoon, the mountains disappeared entirely. Snow poured down. The booming thunder of ice avalanches, rolling muffled through clouds of snow, seemed to come from the sky, like real thunder, sometimes from directly overhead. Late in the day there was a new sound. The rumble of falling ice was now mixed with the occasional rushing hiss of soft snowslides. One sounded like a stampede of horses, the other a flight of birds. Disoriented by a lack of landmarks, I found the ice thunder ominous— big things moving where we couldn't see them made me nervous.

All day the snow fell, with only brief moments of clearing when the peaks would stand wreathed in mist, brilliantly lit against a ghostly blue sky, dark rock faces clad with fresh ice that looked as if it had been hammered into place. Then another bank of clouds would move in from the south, spitting and blowing, and we would dive back into our tents as the temperature fell and the snow piled up again in the soggy meadow.

I was again reading Lopez, who was struck, in the Arctic, by the land's flatness, by the way an endless horizon of sea or tundra could define and narrow the limits of human experience. People could move around on the water or on the land, but always they would be confined to a horizontal surface. In comparison to the world of a sea creature, which roams the depths of the ocean, or to that of a bird, which rises with the wind, we live, according to Lopez, in a two-dimensional world; we aren't accustomed, he says, to looking up or down.

That may be true on the arctic tundra or the Great Plains, but it certainly is not true in the mountains. In mountains you learn to look up. You watch the peaks and the sky beyond for signs of weather. You measure the distances, plot slope angles in your mind, calculate walking routes and climbing times. As you climb a slope, you measure your progress by watching the changing parallax of pinnacles and ridgelines. You unconsciously correct for the distortion of objects caused by looking in other than a level plane. Searching for ibex, or climbers, you somehow know how big they should be at whatever the distance, whether below you or above you.

If Lopez is right that we are in essence two-dimensional creatures, then one reason some of us love mountains with such passion is that among the ranges you become something else. You escape into three dimensions. Like a bird, you are in the sky, not below it. The escape induces euphoria.

Even snowbound in a tiny tent? Yes, if conditions aren't too severe, and if it doesn't last too long, and if you are still friends with your tent mate. That night, the snow came in brittle sheets, rattling off the nylon. Wind rumbled through the rocks of the moraine with an oceanic sound. Beside a flickering candle, I lay reading about polar bears and the dangers of drifting pack ice. Stories from the Arctic were appropriate then, with my breath steaming against the pages, frost crystals growing ephemeral feathers from the ridgepole, and snow piling up outside.

In the morning, a thin overcast looked as though it would soon thicken. Three members of Hassan's group set off cheerfully for Gondoro Peak while two others—the grumpus Australian and his son—were headed down. Thoroughly fed up with this crap. Cold feet. Ugly mountains. Five days without a bath and no prospects in sight. Itchy head. What misery. It was good to see them go. We waited for what seemed a decent interval so that we wouldn't bump into them again, then set off down the glacier ourselves.

We did catch up, however, the next evening, at the base of the Chundugoro Glacier. The grumpus ignored us, and we were just as glad he did. What a difference descending several thousand feet can make. I sat the next morning on sun-warmed sand drinking coffee and watching a lizard hunt flies. He was ten inches long, his head grey like a stone, his tail reddish like a fallen willow twig. If I took my eye away for a moment, it was hard to relocate him—until he started doing pushups and the motion gave him away. Hoopoes were also common here, probing the ground with two-inch bills, wagging their saucy crests, and looking altogether too clever.

That was about it for wildlife. All the way back from Gondoro I had glassed the slopes looking for animals. Several times I had climbed to higher meadows scouting for tracks or other signs. The vegetation looked good, but I found almost no indication of wild animals.

I got to talking on the subject with one of Hassan's porters, who came to our camp that morning for conversation. He wore a pink baseball cap with "Snow Purser" written on it. He lived in Hushe. He had grown up in Hushe. I asked about ibex. Did he hunt? No, he said he had no gun. But there were twenty guns in Hushe, and their owners shot ibex.

"How many do they shoot in one year?

"One thousand."

"One thousand? In one year? There aren't that many ibex here!"

"Yes, many ibex. Many! When the snow is getting deep, then they are coming down. Here." He gestured to the valley around us.

"You hunt them for the meat?"

"Yes, of course."

I could not accept his numbers and said so later to Hassan. "It could be true," he said. "My head porter says he killed seventy last year himself."

"Is that legal?"

"Not at all. The fine is sixty thousand rupees and three years in jail. But there are no police. There was one policeman in Hushe but he has gone. In Hunza too, when I have free time, I go hunting. Ibex and bears."

"Marco Polo sheep?"

"No, there are not many of those."

One man killing seventy ibex? It seemed impossible. I am not a wildlife biologist, but I live in the Rockies and I've spent lots of time around mountain animals. I have a fairly good eye for them and for signs of where they've been. A few hundred hoofed animals can leave unmistakable marks on even a large valley, but I had found almost no sign here. Admittedly, we had seen that one troupe of ibex, probably fewer than fifty animals, high on the mountain slope, but to kill a thousand each winter would require a very large base population.

Later, I read in biologist George Schaller's book *Stones of Silence* about his 1975 trek along the Baltoro Glacier. Taking into consideration an area comprising some five hundred square miles, Schaller estimated a population of about a hundred ibex—this at a time when Pakistan's government was claiming that the area supported some forty-five hundred ibex.

When I thought about it, I had seen not one ibex skull in Hushe. Certainly if a thousand had been killed the previous winter, the place would have been littered with bones. To have killed even a hundred would seem impossible, but I had heard similar claims made in Skardu, where I had spoken about Marco Polo sheep with a man who claimed to be a mountain guide. He had said sheep were numerous in the surrounding hills and that it was not unusual for a Balti hunter to take eight or ten sheep each winter.

Why the outrageous exaggeration? Was it just macho posturing on the part of Balti men? Or was there some deeper, cultural reason? Where I live in the Rockies, the habit of local people is to exaggerate in the opposite direction— to say that there are no bears in Yellowstone, for example, that the government killed them all; or that elk populations are way down and hunting just isn't what it used to be. The only obvious exception involves coyotes, of which there are, and always have been, far too many in the local view. Why Baltis would boast about how many animals they have poached was a mystery to me, but clearly their statements provided for unreliable estimates of wildlife populations.

B ACK IN HUSHE, we went looking for Javed, who greeted us happily. But he was too busy to talk. This was harvest time in Hushe, and he was just heading out to his fields.

"Let us help you," said Pat, which took Javed aback. He looked as if he wanted to say no—as if it was inappropriate for us to help him—but he couldn't turn down a request from us sahibs. We followed him across the river to his family property, where a man and woman were already working. A woman? The first we'd seen up close. Maybe this was the reason for Javed's uncertainty about having us help with the work? Was this a breach of etiquette for us to be here? No. The woman was Javed's wife, Pati, and she quickly made us feel welcome. She smiled as broadly as any Tibetan woman would have, not only to Wendy and Baiba, but to Pat and me also.

The wheat had already been cut and left to dry in neat bundles on the ground. Our job was to gather up the bundles and pile them in circular mows with the tops of the stalks toward the center—simple but tedious work. Actually, it was more work than we'd anticipated, but once started, we were committed. We worked until dusk and built two mows about 12 feet in diameter and the same in height.

It had been a long time since I'd had a chance to do any physical labor, anything really productive. However difficult traveling can get, mentally and physically, it always feels to me a little like playing hookey, as if I should be home doing something constructive with my life, building something, accumulating something of more substance than warm memories. For months now, we had been in the agreeable company of hard-working country folks, and we'd hardly lifted a finger to do anything except to keep ourselves moving along the slope of the Himalaya.

Without my realizing it, that need to do something worthwhile had grown until I really wanted to stack wheat, get chaff down my sweaty back, and be able to stand off and admire the finished product when the job was done. The stacks were simple things, but I was pleased with them. They looked good. The day was over. The grain was up off the ground and safe until threshing time.

For his part, Javed was impressed and, I think, nonplused that we would help out so cheerfully. When it came time to tally up our accounts with him that evening, he fumbled uncertainly over the numbers, as if he wasn't sure who owed whom. We had to bargain him upward to keep him honest.

The next morning we had an unexpected visitor. The malcontent from Australia, the whiner who couldn't wait to escape from the grim world of the mountains, came by our room in search of diversion. We sat on the sunny porch making disjointed conversation until one of the Australian man's porters, the man with the "Snow Purser" hat, came up bouncing his year-old daughter on his arm. Wendy and Baiba cooed over the baby, tugging on the knitted ears of her cap and patting her snot-streaked cheeks. The baby chortled with pleasure. Her father beamed. The Australian recoiled in uncomfortable outrage.

"The poverty of this place!" he said. "I tell you, I've seen poverty. I've been to Africa. I've seen the real thing. But this place is the worst. Absolutely the worst. Have you seen them harvesting? That work out there is brutal. They scrape up every grain they can get."

He saw bad teeth and dirty faces and rags for clothing. He saw plastic sandals and bare feet on frozen ground.

"Do you see these people? In the winter the stream dries up and they have to walk all the way down to the spring for water and bring it back in jugs. How can people live this way? It's horrible!"

"I don't know, I like Hushe," said Baiba. "I'd like to come back sometime."

"Well, I certainly won't. The sooner I'm out of here the better."

He didn't notice the little girl's father, his pride wounded, shrinking away out of the group.

Did people go hungry here? Javed had told us no, not anymore, not since the road was built. If what they grew on their own fields was insufficient, they could get rice from Skardu. For money, the men worked as porters or did stints at various jobs in southern cities. As for picking up every grain, that could be seen as a sign of spiritual health, if not wealth—a reverent view of life, valuing the smallest portion of one's sustenance.

Hushe, I thought, enjoyed the wealth of tradition: of living as you know your grandfather did; of knowing that ancient rhythms have not changed; of watching the turning of the seasons; of having your family gathered in one place. Lao-tsu wrote about this in the *Tao Te Ching:* "If you don't know the source, you stumble in confusion and sorrow. When you realize where you come from, you naturally become tolerant, disinterested, amused, kindhearted as a grandmother, dignified as a king."

This was proven by another surprise visit that morning—this time by the women and girls of Hushe. When we had first arrived ten days earlier, Baiba had asked Javed why we saw no women. "In Pakistan," he had said, "his woman his cook. Also his sleep in his house. No see. Only men. Hushe his people is Sufi." Meaning Sufi Muslim. But now here were the town's women, gathered around our doorway, friendly eyes and bright teeth and upright demeanor belying their unwashed faces and ragged clothes.

Had word gotten around that we had helped in the wheat field? Had that perhaps made us more interesting or approachable? Pat and I were largely ignored—a matter of propriety—but our presence did nothing to dampen Hushe's feminine enthusiasm over our wives. The greetings were always the same. The women would touch their foreheads, then extend their hands for a handshake—a warm and courtly behavior among people wearing work rags and carrying huge baskets filled with turnips, straw, or jugs of water.

Hushe was indeed a hard place, which made it all the more impressive that its people behaved with such good humor, pride, and dignity. Maybe that was what the Australian was really saying: How could these Baltis have so little and act as if they had so much?

I admired the people of Hushe, but their home, on the edge of winter as it now was, unnerved me. The valley runs north to south and gets little direct sun during the winter. The residents have not much firewood and they live in drafty homes; there is much cold, much snow, and not enough kerosene for light.

Wondering how it might feel on long winter nights, I went out after dark. It was like walking back in time, into a scene of somber alleys, shrouded moonlight, autumn winds, and lowering clouds. The glow of oil lamps and hearth fires shone through cracks in doors and windows. The sounds of families leaked into the darkness. I heard children laughing, squabbling, women singing, people talking in low tones. The alleys were as narrow as corridors. I would never have dared to take such a walk in Tibet on account of the dogs. Here I could walk slowly, trying to catch something of the feeling of Hushe at night, but I felt like a prowler. What business did I have silently treading the streets speculating on private doings behind closed doors?

I came to a junction of alleys and paused for a moment at what sounded like a woman putting children to bed. I was listening to the rhythm of her voice, a pleasant intimate singsong, when a man carrying a large bundle came suddenly around the corner. I jumped as he said hello. "Hello," I said back, trying to appear as if I had been walking innocently toward Javed's house. I felt like an intruder caught in the act and hurried back, chastened.

Aga Abas—big, smiling, and reliable—arrived the next morning right on schedule. As we left Hushe, rain was falling lightly. On the edge of town, Ibrahim stood in a field under a heavy load of wheat stalks that he was carrying to the family threshing grounds. He returned our waves as we drove past and then stood watching us a long time, until we were out of sight far down the valley. He was a strong, handsome, clever man in his early twenties. I knew how restless I had been at that age, and I was certain that he wanted to be going somewhere, going along with us, going anywhere, if only harvest hadn't been the overriding concern of the season.

That we, who were not wealthy in our own countries, could cruise through Hushe like minor lords was due to an accident of economics: a day's labor at home was worth a month or two of labor in Hushe. An amazingly small sum—less than ten dollars a day for each of us—could provide nearly unlimited access to the former principalities of northern Pakistan, much easier for us than it had been for Godfrey Thomas Vigne. Hushe was only a day's drive from the airport at Skardu. We could breeze in, hire porters, walk with light loads across glaciers into the heights, wander back as fast or slowly as we wanted, order a meal, a room, a jeep, even do a little labor for the fun of it—and head off to see more of the Himalaya in India.

Not directly, of course. Not in a way that made any geographical sense. Not the way people like Vigne traveled. Practically within earshot of Hushe the soldiers of Pakistan and India continued to play King of the Mountain on the Siachen Glacier, just the latest belligerence in a war the two countries have fought since their independence from the British in 1947. Because of that contested border, we would have to return to Skardu, fly to Islamabad and from there to New Delhi and Srinagar—only to wind up, after more than a week's motorized travel, about a hundred miles up the Indus River from Skardu.

Anyway, that was the plan.

12
King's Paradise

*And the end of the fight is a tombstone white
with the name of the late deceased,
And the epitaph drear: "A fool lies here who tried
to hustle the east."*

——Kipling, *The Naulahka*

IT WAS EVENING. The haze and diesel rumble of Delhi were gone, re-placed by the knock-knock of wooden paddles against wooden boats. Fishing eagles circled and dove into the water. Thunderstorms climbed above Dal Lake to catch the sunset in their great anviled tops. It had rained earlier in the day, big drops hammering on the tin roof of the houseboat we had rented. But we were dry and happily unwinding on the verandah—or should I call it the quarter-deck? Whatever the name, it was a peaceful place far removed from pavement and vehicle noise.

We had taken a week to reach Srinagar from Hushe—a week of taxis, hotels, planes, embassies, and errands. Delhi was an industrial nightmare, the air so dark from smoke that street lights were on during the day; at worst, visibility was down to two hundred or three hundred yards. That we enjoyed Delhi at all was thanks to an old friend of Baiba's named Anil Shukla. They had been climbing friends in Calgary. Although a Canadian citizen, Anil had moved back to India to be near his family. He kindly invited us to stay at his house for a week, helped us organize our onward travel, and, in what I thought of as an even bigger act of generosity, allowed us to leave our bicycles and half of Mount Equipment in the spare bedroom. Promising to be back in five weeks, we had flown to Kashmir. Our plan was to find transport north over the Himalaya to the high desert of Ladakh and then to take a month walking back south, following ancient caravan routes.

Ladakh was once a province of Tibet. Because of that, it has the same geography, climate, language, religion, and ethnic background. In Leh, the capital, there is a monastery and palace nearly as old as Lhasa's Potala Palace and nearly as impressive. People call it the Little Potala; they call Ladakh Little Tibet.

For trading caravans traveling between India and western China, Leh was an important stop, the last reasonably comfortable habitation on the arduous track north. Beyond that city, traders faced the high Karakoram, the dangerous Karakoram Pass, and the dark gorges of the Kun Lun Range, where at any time they might lose their goods and lives to raiders. If they made it to Yarkand and Kashgar unscathed, they faced the same hazards on the return journey. Leh stood at the beginning or the end of that hazardous crossing, and as a consequence, it became an important place until bad relations between China and India sealed the border. Since then, Ladakh has been reduced to an outpost, an isolated, mostly roadless land of high mountains, silt-laden rivers, and thriving Tibetan Buddhism.

Like Tibet, Ladakh was invaded and looted—by soldiers of the notorious Maharajah of Kashmir, the same fellow who conquered neighboring Baltistan in the 1840s—but in the end, that invasion might have been Ladakh's salvation. Having become part of Kashmir, it was joined to India in 1947, and India, more than other countries, tolerates an enormous ethnic variety. Ladakh never suffered the demoralizing destruction of the Cultural Revolution.

I was especially eager to see Zanskar, the mountain principality squeezed between Ladakh and India—between the Karakoram and the Himalaya. Zanskar, we had heard, had the roughest country and hardest walking in the region—big, dry, rugged, and very wild.

With such an agreeable prospect ahead, it felt good to be quietly taking in the scene on Kashmir's famous Dal Lake. A day or two of floating relaxation and we would be off into the hills.

I felt content that evening, sitting with a glass of Scotch in my hand, looking out across the calm water of a lagoon surrounded by houseboats—long, narrow, flat-roofed barges, built along the lines of huge mobile homes but much more attractive. They were made of Himalayan cedar, all fancifully carved. The law required that they float but not that they ever move. Consequently, some were as permanent as dry-land homes, shaded by trees that grew out of shallow water or on minuscule manmade islands. A few had been moored for so long that they had sunk in place; they made me think of a Gulf Coast trailer court after a hurricane, water flowing through the windows, geese roosting on the roof.

There were hundreds of these boats on Dal Lake and the surrounding canals. They had become popular in the 1800s because the English loved

Srinagar. The cool climate made them homesick and they wanted to have summer houses there, but the Maharajah of Kashmir would not let them buy property. Then some clever person thought up the expedient of living on a boat. The first ones were small, what Kashmiris call *dungas,* but the English had bigger ideas and soon were living in barges the size of suburban houses. When the English left, the barges became floating hotels.

Many of them sported grand names: *Balmoral Castle, Crown of India, Star of Zanzibar, Golden Palace, King's Paradise.* Never mind that they looked more like vacation cottages than royal dwellings. Never mind that in Minnesota they would have been named *Bide-A-Wee, Grampa's Playhouse, Sandy Pause,* and *Piney Rest.* In my view, that evening, the stately names felt entirely appropriate.

I was sitting on the *King's Paradise,* warmed by Scotch, thinking, "Well, maybe a minor king. A king out slumming. Certainly a king having a good time."

The lagoon was quietly busy with flat-bottomed punts. Some were paddled by hawkers carrying various goods, everything from flowers to groceries. Others carried people who lived on the houseboats, going about their business. A girl in a sapphire sari, a big earthenware pot riding the prow of her boat, coasted past on her way to the community drinking-water supply. She filled the pot and drifted dreamily back across the dark water, trailing a wake that reflected the fiery colors of the thunderclouds. A sapphire blue girl with a comet's tail.

A prosperous-looking man of about fifty cruised past more swiftly, propelled by two paddlers as he reclined on white cushions. I guessed that he was going home after a day in his carpet emporium. Or perhaps he owned a fleet of *shikaras,* water taxis. These garish yellow-and-red boats equipped with curtained canopies and mattresses bore reclining tourists silently through the byways and channels of Dal Lake.

Just at sunset, the chanting of muezzins drifted over the water—the evening call to prayer. Even that was pleasant. Coming from more than one mosque, mingled and modified by echoes, the sound made me think of the harmonic calling of whales.

A dark head, covered with shiny greased hair popped up a foot from my face on the other side of the railing. "Shawls?" said the man, standing in his wooden boat. "Veddy goot price."

"No, thanks."

"Postcards?"

"Nope."

"Flowers!"

"Nope."

"Then, sir, perhaps, I can sell you," he whispered very slowly, "hash . . . shish?"

"No."

"Then whiskey? Johnny Walker!"

"Don't you think this is enough?" I held up the nearly full liter bottle.

"Ah. So sawdy. Good-bye. Keep good memory, Mr. Damn Cheap!"

He drifted away into the dusk. A minute later another head appeared over the railing.

"Good evening, sir. How are you this evening?"

"I was enjoying the peace of being alone here, thank you."

"I will sell you some Kashmiri shawls. Would you like to see?"

"No, thanks."

"When can I show you?"

"Never."

"Please do not offend me."

"I had no such intention."

"Then you will look?"

"No."

"They are very good shawls, sir. Very good price, cheaper than—"

"Would it help if I offended you?"

"Oh, no."

"Then please go away."

"Tomorrow perhaps?"

That night a huge thunderstorm emptied itself over the lake. Gulam Sheikh, landlord of the *King's Paradise,* sat with us after dinner. We told him we wanted to walk from Leh through Zanskar to Dharamsala, home of the exiled Dalai Lama in Himachal Pradesh.

"Yes, there is a road," he said, meaning a walking route. "That place is very high. The people are very wild, you know."

The rain intensified, drumming on the metal roof so that we could barely hear each other talk.

Gulam went on, "This should be good trekking season with sun next two months, but the last two years it is raining at this time. In November, raining, raining. This is like monsoon, from Calcutta all the way up to Kashmir. It is no good. When weather is like this, landscape is coming down."

The year before, on November 12, a heavy snowstorm had struck the Zoji La, the high pass on the road to Ladakh. Dozens of vehicles were stalled behind a broken-down truck. The driver had simply locked it and left it where it stood. An unbreakable traffic jam resulted. Cars slid off the road trying to turn around. Some people abandoned their vehicles and started walking. Others remained in the shelter of trucks, cars, and buses. Then came a series of avalanches. No one knows exactly what happened, nor how many died, but the toll was more than two hundred. A year later, bodies and vehicles still lay unrecovered under snow that had not melted during the summer.

"There might now be snow also on your road from Leh," said Gulam. He was sitting on the floor with his knees up under a wool cape, making a tent over a pot of glowing coals—central heating personalized. A year earlier he had crashed a motorcycle. His hip and femur were now made largely of steel. Cold made them ache.

He was thirty-seven, his black hair touched by strands of grey, a handsome man with a worry he could not hide: in six days, his daughter Dilshad was being married, according to Kashmiri custom, to a man she'd never met. In this case, Gulam had never seen him either. All arrangements had been made by Gulam's mother and his sister, a strong-willed woman whom he said he had given up fighting years ago. He did not like the custom of arranged marriage and wanted nothing to do with the celebration. Of course, he had to pay for the affair—a two-day party for 350 people on a fancy houseboat that would be brought in especially for the occasion. That cost a lot of money—enough, he said, to buy two whole houseboats. He had financed the party by selling a piece of property.

I asked if Dilshad might have more to worry about, having seen nothing but a photograph of her intended.

"Yes, there is risk. But at least in Kashmir there is no dowry." What did he mean, I wondered, personal risk for Dilshad or financial risk for himself?

"Can I offer you some whiskey?" said Pat.

"I am Muslim, you know—"

"Of course. I'm sorry."

"—but only when my wife is here."

I passed him the bottle and a glass. He poured a tiny amount and drank. "Ah, it's good," he said and poured some more. "My wife, you know, she doesn't understand me. I drink wine sometimes and mix it with Campa Cola so no one can smell it on my breath. My wife doesn't like me doing these things, but I am a human being. It is my nature. To be human. You know? I try to act like my grandfather. He was a magic man. A great man. He taught me how to smoke hash and showed me a way to lead my life. To be human, just to be human."

"Your grandfather taught you how to smoke hash?"

"Wait a minute," he said, standing and walking out of the room. He came back with a coffee can filled with hashish. Chipping off a piece, he loaded it into a pipe, got it going, and said, "Not how to smoke, my grandfather teaches me, but how to think when I smoke. Smoking hash is very much of the mind, you know."

He smoked and we talked. The subject turned to places we had been: Hunza, Baltistan, Tibet. Gulam asked, "Do you find magic in the mountains?" He meant real magic, not the synthesis of exhilaration and landscape that works alchemy on one's emotions. That's the only sort of magic I've experienced, but I told him about fairies in Hunza.

"Yes? There were fairies in Kashmir too, one time. My grandfather is telling me this."

"Did he see them?"

"No, but he was hearing their music. Then the road came, and the army, and my grandfather said the fairies all ran away then."

Right. Maybe we were thinking about the same magic after all: the spirit that flees from the advance of mechanization. Gulam puffed thoughtfully for a minute and then said, "I tell you this story. It is a famous story. I was a boy, but I remember this that I am telling you."

He told about an incident that happened in 1957 on the pilgrimage trail to Amarnath Cave, a grotto venerated by Hindus for a pillar of ice that forms in it every year. Hindus worship the ice as a divine lingam—symbol of Shiva.

"Two sadhus," said Gulam, "are making camping along the trail to Amarnath." A local man went as guide and porter. After dark, he came up quietly to the holy men's campfire and overheard them talking a strange language. It sounded like snakes talking. Seeing him, the sadhus told the man to sit down with them. Then they began playing flutes, and snakes appeared, many of them, until one exceptionally large one with a crescent mark on its head came. The sadhus killed this one, cooking it in a pot and making three portions. One they offered to their porter, who refused it. They insisted. He refused again. They told him that if he would not eat it, then he must promise never to talk to anyone about the incident. He promised. They ate their portions and, having finished, began talking like snakes. This went on for some time, until finally they flew away into the night sky, just up and flew away, leaving the astonished porter sitting alone by the fire. He couldn't stay. He hurried back to Pahalgam that night.

"When he comes to Pahalgam," said Gulam, "many people are there. People say, 'What is wrong?' and he is telling the story. He is saying the holy men warned him 'do not talk.' He is telling about the snakes and the flying. And five hours later, he is dead. For no reason! No injury. He is dead.

"It was very famous, this story. Everyone heard about that man. Now there are not such sadhus, not real sadhus."

"Do you believe the story?" I asked.

"I don't know. Not about snakes. I know this. Amarnath. Go neat and clean with open heart, no one comes home with empty hands. I am not Hindu, but this is true I'm telling you."

———————

The next day rain fell steadily and hard. Not to worry, we had errands to run, food to buy, all the usual trekking preparations. Gulam volunteered to show us around town, and he was a big help. In the afternoon, we came back to the *King's Paradise* dripping wet and loaded down with trekking food, having made arrangements for a car and driver the next morning. By evening, however, listening to the steady pound of rain on the roof, we knew it would be foolish to leave for Leh. Word had it that Zoji La was closed that night.

"One day, two days, it will clear," said Gulam.

Two days later it was still raining. It rained until the *King's Paradise* felt like the stage of an old-style ghost story. All the elements were present—thunder and lightning, sheets of rain, isolation, lights flickering out at inopportune moments, and a demented servant.

His name was Ali Mohammed. His job was to serve meals and look after the houseboat. Thirty years old, he showed every sign of having suffered some childhood disaster. He'd been dropped on his head at birth, or he'd fallen into Dal Lake and not been rescued right away, or something. Whatever the cause, Ali had trouble coping with the simplest problem. Everything made him sad, and like some missionary of melancholy, he yearned to communicate the truth as he understood it. Only once did I see him display good humor, when he brought tea one afternoon.

He breezed in singing, "Hotta water, potting hotting tea-tea potting putting. Come come, you sit here, you sitting here, come come," like a proud proprietor. Something must have gone well that day.

The rest of the time he was as sullen as the weather. Meals gradually deteriorated to the point that we started buying our own groceries for breakfast. Even Gulam had little influence with "Ollie," as we came to think of him. He had a way of standing with doleful expression on the other side of a doorway, eavesdropping. He understood English quite well but had trouble speaking. When he did, he would jut his jaw forward and tip his head back to one side so he looked at us across his nose. He talked like someone who had just left the dentist's office with a jaw full of Novocain. Sound came out but the lips did not move.

The scene one night during an especially violent thunderstorm: We sit at dinner under electric lights that blink off and on. We have no candles; so when the lights are off, the room is absolutely black, except for the odd lightning flash. One time the lights come on to reveal Ali standing beside the table. "Kashmiri tea?" he intones, in Hitchcockian rhythm. Yes, we say, as the lights flicker out. When they come back on, he is gone, a shadow of the night.

Ali usually went barefoot in light clothing. He had a striped cotton suit that looked like prison pajamas. I suspected this to be a ploy, partly because wool was cheap in Kashmir (everyone had a cape) and because he was continually telling me how hard his job was and how little he was paid.

"Always working, working, working, no time for gullers."

Gullers were girls, and Ali had standards. I once asked if he was married.

"No good gullers, gullers trash, no marry. Good gullers, marry okay, but no money, trash guller." He shrugged as if to demonstrate the futility of life. "Always working, working, lunch, dinner, breakfast, tea, bring dish, take dish, milk okay, milk no okay, sugar, not hotting. . . . " His voice trailed off. He came to the end of the table, pointed to his bare feet, and said, "You give me jacket."

After five days, I thought we should rechristen the boat *Noah's Ark*. The rain had been falling with hardly a letup since our arrival. Chances of getting to Ladakh diminished. Zoji La was firmly closed, but people said it would reopen. After all, the army had to carry supplies to the Siachen Glacier to fight the nasty Pakistanis. They *had* to open the pass. Still, no one knew how much snow had fallen up high, and everyone, after the disaster of the previous year, was scared of the pass.

To keep warm we set off, each armed with umbrellas, to see the sights and fend off the touts who perched like patient vultures along the lakeshore: *Those tourists, you know, they have to come ashore sometime.*

When we did, they pounced. Every time I stepped off a *shikara* onto the shore I felt like the defendant outside the courtroom of a notorious scandal trial, the press crowding around, jostling to get near me, shouting questions as I forged toward a waiting taxi.

"Papier-mâché, artworks, shawls, carpets, *shikara*, houseboat, marijuana, change a money?"

"Good price, special deal, best quality."

Some of them tried to sound seductive, as if I were just waiting to hear the right tone of voice before making a major purchase.

"Marijuana . . . "

"Maareee, waaaahna . . . "

During lulls in the rain the lakeshore was a lovely place to be. We walked on a grassy strip beside a sea wall. Fishermen stood on the pointed bows of their *shikaras* and threw nets on the water. The lake was patrolled by fishing eagles, and tiny kingfishers with glittering strips of turquoise down their backs, diving on shoals of minnows. From the bank I could watch the green flash of feathers and the silver turn of the fish. Squads of large, iridescent dragonflies flew past like some rakish air force. All around, green hills rose steaming into water-color clouds. If we walked far enough, we came to the Nishat Gardens, a lovely place with fountains and flowerbeds beneath rows of giant chenar trees. The garden had been planted some three hundred years ago by the Mughul ruler Shah Jahan. Originally desert people from Afghanistan, the Mughuls regarded flowing water as the greatest treasure on earth. Each summer the Mughul court moved here to escape the scorching heat of Delhi.

Although quite different from the plains of India, the landscape here was nonetheless thoroughly Asian—ephemeral, as if drifting in mountain mist, and set with the living jewels of exotic birds and flowers. I could see why the English fell in love with the place. It was a familiar setting of lakes, hills, and forests touched with the seductive scent of the Orient.

But it had something else of England, something I had never expected. Wendy, Baiba, and I went to town one day (it was Pat's turn for illness) and ended up in the old city, where, in a downpour, we found the other side of Srinagar: a nineteenth-century English November. Clouds came down like portents of doom. The rain slanted in the icy wind. We walked narrow alleys covered with sewage between half-timbered buildings three and four stories high with numerous balconies and bays jutting overhead. The electricity was off that day, so no lights shone from windows. Many of the homes looked ancient—crooked and leaning against their neighbors, once grand but now decaying. Some had been built in stages, each level made of different brick or stone, each row of windows made in a different pattern. Smoke came from chimneys and smudged the wet darkness. In one ancient second-story workshop, men hammered on wooden things. As we passed, workers' faces appeared at the glassless windows to shout hello. At a blind corner, a horse pulling a high-wheeled cart nearly knocked us over. I thought of Dickens, of London in the rain, and it occurred to me that the English of a century ago might have felt nostalgia for the darker side of their home island as much as for the sun on green pastures and the shade of broadleaf trees.

Srinagar, where East mixed with West. From the back of a taxi, its windows streaming with moisture, I caught sight of signs moving past:

GULAM HASSAN
KING OF THE EGGS

ABDULLAH AND SONS
SPECIALIST IN BORING AND MECHANICAL WORK

SPIRITUAL MUSEUM
(of the Divinising of Man)

208

The last one was behind us in busy traffic before it registered. I'll always wish I had gone back to see the place.

Another day I hiked above Dal Lake to a temple, a round building at the highest point of a green mountain. I walked up the trail in light rain. Outside, a sign informed me that this was "Shankeracharya temple built on site of ancient Shiva shrine known as Jyeshtheshwara, built by King Gopaditya . . . " and so on, in the fourth century B.C. A statue honored Adi Shankaracharya, who visited in the eighth century and reconsecrated the shrine. He was a famous philosopher and saint whose name invited creative spelling; finding it all across the Indian Himalaya, I rarely saw it spelled the same way twice.

The temple was round with a steep, conical roof. Stone stairs led up to the entrance. Inside, an amazing black lingam dominated a circular room made of white marble. Polished to a fine sheen, the lingam was four feet high and two feet in diameter, its top rounded to a point. It rose through the floor in a manner that suggested it was only the tip of something much bigger. People brought offerings of flowers, money, incense, and coconuts. A priest cracked open the coconuts and poured the milk over the flower-decked lingam. His chant droned in unending singsong as, one after another, people handed him offerings. I stood against the cold marble wall, surprised by the feeling of power in that black stone. I was struck by the raw literalness of it: the dripping coconut milk, the garlands of flowers, the women kissing their fingers, then stroking the smooth surface. The men touched the stone, then kissed the white marble at its base.

Then my perspective shifted. For me the stone suddenly changed from a lingam to the tip of a missile in its silo. The devotees became oddball technicians attending to Shiva on his mountain top. Shiva the destroyer. It would have been a disturbing image were it not for the rustic simplicity of the devotions. This was the way survivors of the apocalypse might worship the artifacts from an ancient, powerful, nearly forgotten past: the unfired relic missile as a god.

Still it rained in the valley. At 11,000 feet, Zoji La lay buried in drifting snow. When the clouds parted, as they did from time to time as if to tease us, we could see fresh snow even on the low peaks around Srinagar. What could we do? It had to be drier on the other side of the mountains—it rains only two inches a year in Leh, and some years not at all. It was just a matter of getting there, and everything would be all right.

Perhaps we could fly? Baiba and I went downtown to ask at the Indian Airlines office and learned that there was one scheduled flight per day. But they had been canceled for a week, and the waiting list was enormous and getting bigger each day. The only possibility, advised the reservations clerk, was a flight from Chandigarh—a two-day bus ride from Srinagar—on October 19. He could get us seats on that one. We counted the days. Of our planned month, that would cut us down to two weeks. It would be enough to do *something,* even if not the long trek we had hoped for. So we booked the flight and bought tickets for the bus, which left in three days.

Meanwhile, the *King's Paradise* was a comfortable place to wait. In the evening, Gulam often showed up toting his consolatory coffee can of hashish. The men of Srinagar, we had seen, were not big drinkers, but they sure could toke. Our whiskey long gone, we made sickly drinks of Indian rum and lemon-lime soda while Gulam talked about his years in the merchant marine, where he'd acquired a taste for alcohol and other things considered exotic in Kashmir. One night he told us we should stay for his daughter's wedding. It would be a big party.

"Will you miss your daughter?" Baiba asked.

"She is not going far. But she has a big surprise. She will be just like a servant, always cooking, and that family, they live in the country, they are growing things and having cows, and she will be always working. Much more than here. Now she has it like a queen. No, the one who will be missing my daughter is my sister. I am telling you, my sister! Already she is wanting me to find a wife for my son."

"But he's too young."

"Only fourteen! It is no good. My sister is wanting someone only for washing dishes. With Dilshad going. I don't want my son being like me. In prison, you know?" He held his hands up with the fingers interlocked. "It is prison. I am wanting him free."

"Are you in prison? You don't like your wife?"

"Oh, yes, I do. I am having big problems the first years, many problems. I am coming many times close to divorce. But now she understands me. She is my best friend. But you must stay, or I will have no one to talk to."

We stayed. The day before the wedding, twenty sheep were brought to Gulam's mini-island for slaughter. Their blood turned the water red. A crew of a dozen cooks hacked apart the carcasses and boiled, chopped, and mashed the meat, making it into balls and sausages and curries. Two small houseboats—one for men, the other for women—and a large "wedding boat" were towed in to provide extra space. Workers strung lights, laid special carpets, and hung fancy drapes.

That first night there was a family party. Gulam called us over. In the center of the room, five musicians played Kashmiri instruments—flutes and drums and delicate instruments resembling mandolins. The men sat at one end of the boat and the women at the other. Children ran back and forth. It was quietly festive and comparable to what families all over the world do the night before a wedding. Except for one incident, when the drummer, a tall, dark-haired man, put down his instrument and pulled from a cloth bag a woman's skirt and blouse. He put them on and began dancing, a very suggestive movement, rocking his pelvis, smiling sweetly. Everyone stopped talking and watched. The man was a woman, hiding his face behind his hands, dancing as no woman would be allowed to dance in this Muslim community. But this was so frankly sexual—what did it mean?

The musicians picked up the tempo. The dancer moved with abandon and then perhaps with poor judgment. He pulled a young boy to his feet, and the two of them began an explicit writhing movement. I was astonished at the whole suggestive scene, but mostly at the young boy, who knew exactly how to move. This went on for several minutes, the entire crowd silently watching, until an older man, the boy's father I think, stood up, grabbed the boy, cuffed him around the ears, and spoke harshly to the man in the dress. Okay, but why did he wait so long?

The next night was the main event: the arrival of the groom and the wedding.

That evening we sat on the porch watching people paddle up in *shikaras.* Gulam joined us, carrying a bottle of Russian champagne and saying we were the only people who would drink it with him. He had already been into the rum bottle. "You are not my guest," he said, gripping my shoulder. "You are my brother."

By nightfall, the bride's family and friends were all assembled and waiting. Gulam and I were tipsily sinking into the cushions of the *King's Paradise* when fireworks lit up the sky. "So here he comes," said Gulam, not sounding very excited. Horns blew, and the sound of bagpipes came across the water. From around the bend a flotilla motored into sight led by a *dunga* shining bright spotlights ahead.

That moment had real drama. Here came the groom, out of the night, across the waters like a conquering hero to claim his wife. Thirty women stood on the top deck of the wedding boat, swaying with arms interlocked, singing a traditional wedding song. More rockets exploded overhead. It was a joyous hullabaloo. The *dunga* drove proudly up to Gulam's dock. The pipe band, wearing Indian army uniforms, marched off and stood playing under bright lights. They finished. There was portentous silence. Everyone waited eagerly to see the lucky man. Everyone, that is, but Dilshad. She had the most reason for anticipation but was sequestered on the women's boat.

It took a few minutes. Longer than the crowd expected. People shuffled impatiently. Finally out he came, the groom himself, man of the hour, stumbling, leaning on the arms of two friends. For two nights, according to tradition, he had been kept awake; now he walked as if drugged. Just a boy, he wore a green turban, a suit of dark grey wool, and a cardboard medallion plastered with ten-rupee notes. I don't think he knew where he was. He said nothing at all. No one spoke to him. His supporters dragged him to the men's boat, where he fell against the wall at the far end. The men all followed him. The women filed into the women's boat, where I supposed they reported their impressions to Dilshad.

The only apparent ceremony happened before the meal was served. A mullah spent a minute asking the groom if this affair was happening with his consent. Supposedly he might have said no at this point. By the looks of him, he couldn't have said boo. Or I do. Or I love you.

The meal was served—rich meats on a mound of rice, a giant platter for every four guests. We ate with our fingers. I was happy to see that everyone, even Kashmiris experienced in that method of eating, made a mess of themselves and the floor. When the guests were finished, they all left, burping and not saying much.

We lingered, thinking there must be more. There should be a send-off of the new couple, or we should hail their first meeting, watch their first handshake, throw rice, or something. But no. That was the end—our hero and his (literal) supporters leaning against the wall looking dazed, like they'd rather lie down than anything else; Dilshad in her boat wearing a fancy sari, draped with jewelry, clutching a cheap plastic purse, decked now with the cardboard money medallion that the groom had worn upon arrival. At 1:00 A.M., said Gulam, she would leave by boat, then car. Her man would follow, separately, to his parents' house. They would sleep separately and meet each other for the first time the next day.

We left the *King's Paradise* two days later at dawn, in grey mists that softened all sharp edges. The mist hung just above the water. Boats seemed to drift on a cloud. A small patrol of geese swam past, only their disembodied heads visible. The mountains were grey bulks wreathed in banks of cloud. Looking down, I saw that a strong current bent the weeds—snow melt, I thought wistfully, pouring cold and crystalline down from the hills and the now inaccessible mountains. Manning the paddle, Ali was the picture of cheery helpfulness. He had been that way all morning, eagerly carrying our bags, asking if he could get us something else for breakfast. "Happy?" he kept asking, completely out of character.

I knew why. The night before he had delivered a sort of lecture about baksheesh, about how much he deserved for his ill-tempered service. To hear him tell it, everyone else who stayed there had showered him with gifts upon leaving: coats, shoes, pants, sleeping bags, luggage, and lots of cash. Simple, muleheaded Ollie. The morning we left, he held himself together all the way to the dock. To our good-byes, he could only croak, "Baksheesh?"

O N THE BUS TO CHANDIGARH: a two-day trip through rain-drenched mountains on dangerous winding roads. The highway department had put up strange warnings:

DON'T BE RASH AND END IN A CRASH

FEEL HORNY ON CURVES HONK

DARLING I WANT YOU BUT NOT SO FAST

MY CURVES ARE GORGEOUS, GO OVER THEM SLOWLY

The road was jammed with summer herders moving their sheep and goats down for the winter. They traveled in wonderfully colorful caravans: handsome, long-haired, floppy-eared goats the size of Afghan hounds; horses burdened with bright bundles, cooking pots, bells, and bedrolls; tall, turbaned men, fierce-looking with hennaed beards, blanket rolls over their robust shoulders, wearing red plaids and white homespun fabrics; women walking or riding horses, carrying babies under their shawls, dressed in delicate, nonutilitarian saris. Our bus joined a convoy of vehicles creeping slowly through the prosperous-looking herds.

Farther along, we passed a different class of travelers, people with dirty bags and bundles, walking, sitting, or camping beside the road. They were small people, mostly women with children, thin of limb, their skin the dark color of the south. They cooked over open fires, lay on the roadside wrapped in blankets head to foot, or walked single file beside the roaring traffic. Neither sadhus nor pilgrims, these were people from a different, ancient world of India, nothing modern about them. Did they walk because they could not afford the pittance of a third-class bus ticket? If so, how did they live? Why did they travel at all? We passed thousands of them, and the more I saw, the more my curiosity grew. They seemed out of place, a long way from home, wherever that might be. I had an impulse to get off the bus, find an interpreter, and ask nosy questions.

Of course that was impossible. We had a schedule to keep, a plane to catch, and besides, this was just the sort of dusky enigma that made India so interesting for me. I took pleasure from wondering about other people—having, for a change, more questions than answers. When it came right down to it, I don't think I really wanted to know what those people were doing. Had I been told, the answer could well have been less interesting than the mystery. In fact, someone did tell me that beggars move with the seasons, between religious sites in the mountains and the warmer southern part of India; maybe these were migrant panhandlers who would show up around the steaming temples of Mysore and on the beaches of Goa in a few weeks time. Were these people migrant beggars?

It didn't matter to me what they were, only that they were there, dark and mysterious. After all, the luxury of first impressions is a traveler's prerogative. For example, on that day back in Xinjiang, when we were hot and looking for cool shade, Tashkurgan had felt like heaven. People had smiled. They were gracious. They looked healthy. Where we stopped in the shade to eat lunch beside a stream of icy irrigation water, women were singing on their porches, children came by laughing, and I have the pleasure of remembering it that way. And just because I met people in Pakistan who had hated Tashkurgan, who thought it was an armpit of a town, doesn't change the memory for me.

On the other hand, if I want to remember another place as squalid, or a person as nasty, I can do that too—like Perali and that Chinese immigration chief whom I nearly kicked. He might, in fact, be a nice fellow. If he lived next door to me, I'm sure we'd develop some sort of friendship because we'd have a reason to do so. But as a traveler, I didn't need to know the truth about that nasty man, and he probably remembers me the same way, if he remembers me at all. Oh, he certainly would have remembered me if I had followed through.

Travel becomes most meaningful in retrospect, after we've had a chance to paint it up a little in our minds, to let sentiment have its way with memory. With time, all scenes of travel become part of a remembered landscape affected by the chemistry of time and distance. How those recollections fit with the local truth, the real truth, if such a thing exists, cannot be the concern of a traveler. For a traveler, the only truth is the journey as perceived through the passing window of his or her eyes. Questions are as much a part of that landscape as the way it smelled and looked when the traveler last saw it.

So I enjoyed the passing scene, just another in the carnival of delights India provides for the curious eye. A case in point: We stopped briefly in a small town where a banana seller, dressed in Kelly green with a white turban, stood beside his bright blue wagon heaped with yellow fruit. Behind him, against a turquoise wall, sat a sadhu. His hair and beard were white. His face was painted white with black stripes. He wore hot pink and orange robes and carried an iron trident draped with marigolds and wrapped in the same hot pink fabric. Beside him, a yellow dog lifted its leg against the wall, painting a dark streak. What a marvelous sight!

At Chandigarh, on the morning of October 19, we were at the airport right on time. But it was raining. For the first time in six months, it was raining. In Leh, it was snowing. All flights were canceled, and there would be no seats available for at least a week. How ironic: we had stayed away from the south side of the Himalaya during the monsoon to avoid the rains. But the rains had failed that summer. Now, during the normal dry season, rains were making it impossible to reach Ladakh.

We had been forty miles from it in Tibet. Sixty miles away in Baltistan. Fifty miles from it in Kashmir. And now, an hour's flight away, a flight we had waited a week to catch. . . .

Having made a circle around Ladakh without finding a way in, we might as well have been trying to reach the mythical Shangri-La. A Buddhist would have said we were not spiritually ready.

13
Uttrakhand,
Land of Gods

And when men living in the plains of India saw the Himalaya rising to incredible heights clothed in dim mysterious haze but culminating in summits of purest shining white they came irresistibly to the conclusion that here indeed must be the abode of the powers which rule the world.

————Francis Younghusband,
Wonders of the Himalaya

In case of hill diarrhoea, headache, travel and altitude sickness, pilgrims are advised to carry a small First Aid Box with Antiseptic, mosquito repellant and band-aids.

————Badri Kedar (pilgrim's guidebook)

B US RIDES IN THE HIMALAYA always start early and they are always the same. You struggle out of bed at three-thirty in the morning and walk through silent, black streets to the bus stop. Bundled figures lie sleeping in doorways. Dogs stand stiff-legged, watching warily in case you carry a rock to throw, ready to attack if you don't. But you always carry a rock.

You come to the dirty, vomit-stained bus, haul your luggage to the roof rack, and find a seat. Often you have to assemble the seat from loose parts—backs and cushions that have shaken loose. If the trip starts in a small mountain town, the driver might have spent a short night clinging to a narrow seat himself. After all passengers have taken their seats, he uncurls from his blankets, yawns, sighs loudly, sits behind the wheel, and combs his hair. Then he lights the headlights and starts the engine and the air horn at the same time. Down the mountain you go, waking the dead. In the night, all you can see are road banks swaying dizzily past as the driver spins the wheel through continuous turns, alternately hammering the accelerator, the brakes, and the horn.

I was starting to have trouble facing another bus ride, and I craved the relative luxury of a train compartment. Indian trains are a good way to travel—the best way to travel in this crowded country. You can reserve a first-class sleeper for very little money and clatter along the tracks in private comfort, reading a book and sipping tea. Or better yet, nursing an Indian beer. You can stand up, stretch, change positions, walk to the dining car, go to the toilet. . . . Enough of buses. I was determined that the next leg of the journey would be by train.

We were to stop next at Hardwar, an ancient temple city that stands astride the Ganges River where it spills out of the Himalaya. The region is called Uttrakhand. A tourist brochure called it the Country of God and warned that it was a high-risk cholera area. Statements like that would be ironic anywhere but in India, where God and cholera can be one and the same.

If sanctity can be measured by the number of adherent believers, then the Ganges is the most sacred river on earth. More than six hundred million Hindus know her as Ganga Ma, Mother Ganges, and many more names; she is the Pure, the Light Amid the Darkness, the Destroyer of Poverty and Sorrow, the Liberator. Enormous spiritual power resides in her waters. She is the body of Vishnu flowing in liquid form. To bathe in or drink from the Ganges cleanses one's soul of guilt. It is the lifelong hope of all Hindus to die on her banks, to be cremated there, and to have their ashes spread on her waters. Simply uttering the words "Ganga, Ganga" within a hundred leagues of the river is sufficient to atone for sins from three previous lifetimes.

Of the six most sacred Hindu pilgrimage sites in the Himalaya, five are connected with the Ganges. The exception is Amarnath Cave, in Kashmir. Of the others, the most significant is Mount Kailas, the abode of Lord Shiva and the spiritual source of the Ganges. Its waters fall from heaven upon the head of Shiva and drain through his long, matted hair to earth. However, the river first appears not at the base of Kailas, which stands well to the north of the Ganges headwaters, but in the Himalayan region of Uttrakhand, that part of India bounded on the east by Nepal and on the north by Tibet.

The Ganges did not always flow on earth. Its waters were once reserved for residents of heaven, until a king named Bhagirath undertook a lengthy meditation while sitting on a boulder at Gangotri. The gods were pleased with his effort and caused the river to fall to earth. It surfaced at three locations, the main one being Gangotri, where the boulder of King Bhagirath is today a revered object, and where the river surges into view at the base of the Gangotri Glacier. The Hindus call this the Cow's Mouth, and while the name might sound

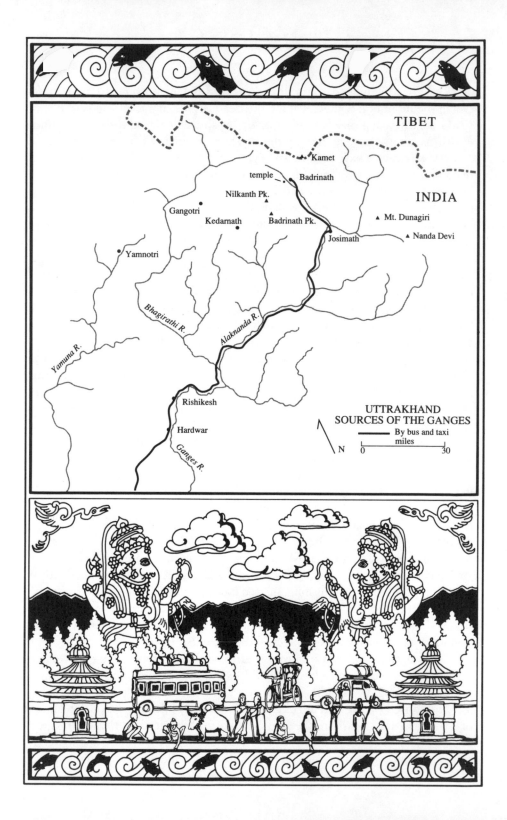

TIBET

Kamet

temple

Badrinath

INDIA

Nilkanth Pk.

Gangotri

Kedarnath

Badrinath Pk.

Mt. Dunagiri

Nanda Devi

Josimath

Yamnotri

Bhagirathi R.

Alaknanda R.

Yamuna R.

Rishikesh

UTTRAKHAND
SOURCES OF THE GANGES

By bus and taxi
miles

Hardwar

N   0   30

Ganges R.

less than poetic to non-Hindus, the place itself is magnificent.

Gangotri is one of four sacred sites in the mountains of Uttrakhand. The others are called Yamnotri, Kedarnath, and Badrinath. All are marked by shrines and natural hot springs. For thousands of years, pilgrims have come to these places to bathe in the sacred waters and to perform *puja,* the reading of scripture and offering of various items.

It seemed to me that these people were on to something good. They liked mountains. Way back when Christian Europeans still feared the Alps as an evil landscape, Hindus and Buddhists were honoring the Himalaya as the abode of God. There is an ancient song:

> High are the mountains,
>> Shiva lives in them.
> This is my homeland;
>> It is more beautiful than heaven.

I bought a guidebook for pilgrims, titled *Badri Kedar,* that gave a tantalizing caution:

The pilgrims who are fond of trekking are advised to have a special attention while climbing on the hills. Some people have habit of watching here and there, particularly watching natural scenery. Please note that such habit or practice results in tumbling down and eventually even a lose of life. If you want to look at any scenery or a sublime beauty of nature, you must steadily stand up and see it to your complete satisfaction and then again start walking to the naturalist paradise.

High trails and sublime beauty! I had the notion that where religion was celebrated among the world's most impressive mountains, the two could only enhance each other. Shouldn't the expression of belief be as beautiful as the objects of faith themselves? And what better way to get there than by train?

So I stubbornly thought. In the cavernous Chandigarh bus terminal, Wendy and I went to the railroad booking office while Pat and Baiba guarded the luggage. The office was packed with people. We waited for twenty minutes. Then someone announced lunchtime, and we all were kicked out into the corridor. I stood outside the locked office for half an hour, my chest pressed against the door by a crowd of men, thinking I would be first in line.

When the door opened from the inside, we all fell into the room. I moved fast, but not fast enough. I reached the counter third in line, too far away to get a grip on something solid, and without some sort of anchor I was swept backward until there were fifteen others ahead of me, and more coming. I scooted to the front again, weaseling in with my shoulders, but once more missed getting a grip on the counter and felt myself being recirculated again to the back of the line. Wendy took this as her cue and, with elbows ablaze, forced her way along the counter in front of a sign reading: "No Ladies Special Q"—in some stations, women are given priority at a special window. Despite the sign, the men gave way. She asked her question.

The booking agent said, "I cannot sell you a ticket."

"Is this a booking office?"

"Yes, Madam, this is a booking office, but we cannot book that ticket for you. You must go to Ambala."

"What if we get there and find the train full?" she asked, but the man was already talking to someone else. Hearing that news, Pat and Baiba decided that they preferred a midnight arrival by bus to the possibility of not getting a train ticket at all. Wendy and I were still keen on the thought of sleeping horizontally, so we bought bus tickets to Ambala.

That too was a mob scene. We found the bus at a loading dock, surrounded by people. I jumped aboard and claimed two seats with our hand luggage while Wendy climbed the rear ladder to drop her pack on the baggage rack. When I went back outside to haul my bag on top, the bus began moving with Wendy still up there. I banged on the side of the bus. It stopped. Wendy climbed down, and I started up. The bus began moving again. I leaped down, still carrying my pack, and pulled myself into the moving door. Again the bus stopped. The conductor gestured for me to put my pack on top. I climbed out, the bus began moving, and the conductor pulled me back up the steps. So I put the pack in the aisle. It blocked the aisle completely. The conductor told me to move it out of his way. I said, "Where?" He persisted as I shrugged. Finally, I pushed it along the aisle about ten inches. It still blocked the way, but he was satisfied to have made his point and stepped easily over it to the hilarity of the other passengers.

Boarding the train at 11:00 P.M. with first-class tickets, we rode all night. But instead of sleeping, I was sick. I spent most of my time standing in the windowless corridor beside the latrine. So much for the genteel comfort of trains.

"YOU SURE YOU CAN MAKE IT?" Pat asked when he saw me in Hardwar. I must have looked bad, but I told him yes, thinking we had spent too much time waiting for one or the other of us to recover from illness. He and Baiba had already hired a taxi for the trip to Josimath.

I was a mess that day. If felt like flu. Every part of me ached. The taxi seat had lost its padding. I sat on a blanket over bare springs, and I don't remember much about the drive.

It was dark by the time we arrived in Josimath. We went to the Government Rest House, a repulsive, windowless den but "the best hotel" according to our driver. It didn't matter much to me. I fell asleep immediately.

In the morning, I felt worse, and now Wendy had it too. Pat and Baiba headed on to Badrinath with our blessing, while we stayed to recuperate. By noon I was able to stand up, so I made a foray to the street. Now that I could look at the surroundings without wanting to vomit, the setting proved to be spectacular indeed. Josimath was pegged to a steep mountainside above the Alaknanda River Gorge, a wonderful but unlikely perch for a town. High, forested slopes rose on the other side of the valley. The sun was shining, the sky was blue, and it seemed terribly unfair to be in the presence of such inspiring landscape and to be lying on a rotting mattress in a damp, concrete cell located beside the public toilet. The sounds of that place alone, not to mention the odors, were enough to make a sick person sicker.

So I wobbled down the busy street and visited several hotels. All were depressing. One was a slight improvement, though—the room had a window. Telling the proprietor that I would be back in an hour with my wife, I set off on the long half-mile back to our room. It took me nearly an hour to get there, including frequent rest stops to clear my head, and when I did finally reach my bed, it hurt even to lie down. Obviously, moving was impossible.

The next time I got up, it was dark outside. Wendy had no desire to eat, but I thought I ought to have a piece of bread or something. I hadn't eaten for two days. So I went outside. The moon was up. There was electricity in Josimath, but the voltage was so low that bulbs glowed as dimly as candles, not a bad effect. There was no food to be had this late at night. Shops were closed or closing. Restaurant crews scrubbed their big aluminum pots on the street. Voices and shafts of light emerged through cracks in the shutters of shops that doubled as homes. Gangs of black minicows, the size of Shetland ponies, stood silently like parked cars; some munched newspaper and cardboard. It was cold. Men walked past wrapped in blankets, tips of their *bidi* cigarettes glowing red. Three men wrapped in quilts lay on the stoop of a closed shop; three *bidis* glowed like three little eyes. Earlier in the day, I had noticed a dog lying in an alley, apparently dying. Now I saw that someone, taking pity, had covered it with a cloth. The dog was not smoking a *bidi*. I bought a newspaper and crawled back into our cell.

"How are you?" I asked Wendy.

"Awful." Being a nurse, my wife takes a certain professional pride in not complaining when she feels sick. When she said awful, I knew it was just that.

"I think this room is making it worse," I said.

"Whaddya wannado?"

"Maybe we can move tomorrow. It's only two hours to Badrinath. It has to be better than this."

Here is what I wrote the next day:

Tuesday 3 Nov—no improvement in our health. Trying to catch a bus to Badrinath (to escape the worst lodging of the trip so far) we struggled down the hill to what we were told was the bus stop. But no bus came at 11:00 and we had to sit by the road for two and a half hours waiting for the 2:00 bus, all the time getting sicker. Now we've gotten a seat and W is puking out the window. Almost hit a guy in the head. She tried to warn him but before she could say anything she was puking. I'm about ready to do the same. We made the mistake of eating two hard-boiled eggs.

I was learning that my tolerance for places like Josimath relied largely on my health. With the surf pounding in my guts, I got irritated when I saw a mother encouraging a child to expel diarrhea in the water running beside their house, or when I saw the latrines, built by the local government, that also straddled open streams. There were people living down below. They used that water. And there were people above, doing the same thing. This was a disturbing thought as I watched a boy pour the tea I had ordered into a dripping glass that he had finished washing, perfunctorily, in the stream.

Just a part of Asian travel. You learn to pretend, the way local people do, that microscopic organisms don't exist. If you couldn't do that, you wouldn't travel. So you turn a blind eye. You trust to luck, Lomotil, and a pouch full of antibiotics and worm medicine. It's only when the typhoons begin crashing against your internal shores that you even take notice.

Actually, Josimath was not the pit that it appeared to be at first glance. The one main street was jammed with stinking vehicles, bright junky shops, loud music, and beggars, but storekeepers were friendly even to a sickly, unsmiling foreigner. And the older parts of town were downright attractive. Narrow staircase alleys, shaded by apple trees, led to buildings with hand-carved window frames, slate roofs, and ornate overhanging balconies. It seemed like a pleasant mountain town recently invaded by vehicles. Never mind that the road had come in the fifties; in a place with a history as old as that of Josimath, thirty years ago was yesterday.

The bus to Badrinath dropped as though down a cliff, hurtling through a series of switchbacks to the Alaknanda River 1300 feet below. Houses held limpetlike to terraces most of that distance, scattered all the way to the river as if they had rolled down from their original positions in town. Each house marked a farmlet comprising a few ledges sprinkled with apple and orange trees, various crops, a few huts, and an abundant supply of rugged scenery. With the bus going one direction, I could see the farms above me; then we would swing round a hairpin turn and the view would drop dizzily to the river.

At the bottom, we crossed the river on a temporary bridge guarded by a rifleman standing by a sign that read "No Photography." The Alaknanda turned north there, coming out of a narrow, shadowed gorge, a flash of cold blue and white among sculpted boulders. The air became cold as we climbed along one wall of the gorge and fragrant with the scent of pine. The bus stopped frequently at small towns. At Govind Ghat, half the riders got off, dragging all manner of bundles after them. They were replaced by about thirty tiny ragged schoolchildren clutching cloth book bags. From the top of each bag protruded the handle of a drawing slate. The children boarded with the skill of commuters, each one propelling the one ahead, practically running but no one stumbling. They filled the bus, the boys jumping up to sit on the backs of seats, where they could hold the ceiling rails. A couple of miles farther, they all got off, as quick and sharp-eyed as a gang of temple monkeys.

The bus stayed full. At one stop, half a hay mow's worth of grass went on top. At another, heavy bundles of firewood. These people—the hill people—were dressed in wool, knitted and woven, and smelled of the smoky fires that warmed their huts at night—a pleasant odor I've grown to associate with mountains and mountain people. The faces were suddenly Tibetan, or more exactly *Bhotia,* Hindus of Tibetan stock. The women had Tibetan faces and clear Tibetan voices but wore gold in their noses.

It was a gorgeous valley, bright with fall colors, beneath tumbling blue glaciers. Coming to a particularly fine waterfall, the bus stopped. A holy man stood holding a brass pot of red paint. People leaned out the windows toward him to receive a paint spot on their foreheads, a *tika* blessing. He applied each spot with his thumb and a prayer. Things were looking promising, I thought, for my notions of religion amidst the splendor of nature.

But then, after two hours of climbing, the steep valley walls fell back to reveal Badrinath—above timberline; buildings scattered helter-skelter, unpainted or done up in bright pastels, their metal roofs rusting; dirt roads running every which way—and my heart fell. I had imagined a peaceful-looking wooded vale with a few buildings, a winding path across a footbridge, a hot spring tumbling into a pool, a small ancient temple worn smooth by the passage of time and bare feet. I had been thinking of a Japanese Shinto shrine. This place looked more like a Bolivian tin mine, located here in spite of the landscape rather than because of it. A temporary outpost, not an ancient holy place.

At least the bus had stopped moving. In a few minutes we found our friends holed up in an unheated hotel room, burrowed into their down sleeping bags. It was very cold in the hotel.

"There's someone you might enjoy talking to," said Pat. That day, he had met the local bank manager, a member of the "temple committee." Pat had asked a few questions about the temple, and the bank manager had said he should come by his private quarters that evening and learn all about it. Wendy wanted nothing more than to lie down, and Baiba stayed with her; but I went with Pat through steep alleys to a tin shack near the river. Pat pounded on the door. It opened. Pat greeted a dark face, and we were led down a corridor to a dim little room where four men huddled around a charcoal brazier. The room was painted pink. It had two bunks, a table, several chairs, and a bench. We sat on the bench.

"We are the temple committee," they said, whatever that meant; they didn't explain. There was the bank manager, the temple officer, a businessman (the next day I saw him again, in his stall, surrounded by hanging plastic religious trinkets), and the chief bank auditor. The auditor's name was R. P. Nathani. "I am called Rumpy", he said, offering his hand.

They were drunk and depressed, and seemed happy to have company. It was near the end of the pilgrimage season, and they were all eager to leave. But we should have come in the summer, they said. Why, five hundred buses a day came there in the summer. People spent very much money.

"It is good to have a bank in Badrinath," said the bank manager. "But what a shame that the temple is in such disrepair. It must be renovated." Heads nodded all around for a moment. Then Rumpy spoke. "It is due to a lack of enthusiasm, a lack of money, a lack of belief."

"How old is the temple?" I asked. They looked at each other.

"Actually," said Rumpy, "Shankaracharya, uhh... " He and the others muttered for a minute; then he looked again at me and said, "Actually I am not religious."

"Would you like a drink?" asked the fellow I knew only as the temple officer. They were working on a jug of locally made rice liquor, *rakshi*. Potent distilled stuff the color of cloudy vodka.

"This is legal?"

"No, this is a holy place," said the temple officer. "Not allowed. Here!" He lifted his glass and held it unsteadily in front of me. With difficulty I convinced him to take it back. Pat also declined.

I was sitting beside the businessman. He wore a fur hat and a coat of something that smelled of wet dog. The naked bulb behind him put his face in shadow; I never did see him clearly. He said little, but agreed with whatever was said, and expressed his agreement by leaning forward and peering at me from a range of eight inches.

Rumpy launched an incoherent dissertation.

"We worship Jiroo, but you know, you might be Christian, you say, 'Oh God.' He, this man, this man here"—he meant the temple officer, who nodded seriously at the suggestion—might be Mohammedan, he say, 'Allah, al Akbar.' He"—pointing to the bank manager—"might be a Jew, he say, uh, he say . . . "

He couldn't come up with what the Jew would say, so he moved on to the businessman. "He be Buddhist, he say 'Ommmm.'"

Saying "Om" almost got him; he let the "mmmm" go long enough that he forgot what he was saying. He had to ask his friends, "What was I saying?"

"Oh, God," said the bank manager.

"Oh, yes. Oh, God, Allah Akbar, Jiroo, all the same. All no different."

His friends held up their index fingers, signifying unity, and looked to us for confirmation. The businessman peered closer.

"Yes, I think you're right," I said.

"Yes?"

"Yes."

"You agree?"

"I do."

"Because we worship Jiroo, but he might be Christian, and he say, 'Oh God.' And he might be Mohammedan . . . " He went all the way through it again and might have begun a third time, but the temple officer interrupted with his glass of moonshine.

"Here! You have drink?"

"No, no thanks."

"What you drink?"

"Nothing, please."

"Nothing? What's wrong with you, you don't drink?"

They were friendly drunks about to tip over into hostility. We made excuses and rose to leave. The businessman, half standing, clutched my arms and clung to me, breathing in my ear, trying to pull me back into my seat. I took a step sideways, dragging him along the bench.

"Please. I'm sorry. We have to leave."

"Why don't you drink?"

In the end, Rumpy intervened, disentangled me from the businessman, and we went out the door.

While we had been inside, a wonderful thing had happened. The moon had come over the rim of the mountains. The valley was bright and beautiful.

Nilkanth Peak, an icy stiletto, stood sharply defined against the black sky, shining as if a light had been turned on inside it. ("Nilkanth," said the guidebook, "which embodies all the divinity of this divine land.") Blurred by wood smoke and mist from the river, made silver by the moonlight, Badrinath was a beautiful sight.

India is like that. It drops you down, then picks you up. You think you are hating the place, and you find you love it.

Following a curving path to a footbridge over the river, we walked to the famous hot springs, where flat paving stones were kept warm from underneath. It was nice to stand there in the moonlight breathing steam that smelled of sulfur and looking down at the icy Ganges crashing past. It smelled like Yellowstone in the winter, and I had a flash of homesickness. Behind us, hunkering sadhus wrapped in blankets sat like hairy stumps (rather, like resting bison!), warming their bare behinds on the stones or sleeping near the hot water. I moved to step over a reclining bundle.

"*Namaste,*" it said.

"Hello, yourself, are you warm?" I said.

"Why not? Welcome to Taptakund. You must bathe."

"Perhaps tomorrow."

"Yes, tomorrow, tomorrow."

The next day, Wendy was still a wreck and stayed in bed. Pat and Baiba left on the morning bus. They'd had enough of Badrinath. They had come hoping to find a peaceful mountain town and instead found a religious contradiction. "They decide this place is sacred," said Pat, "and then they ruin it with all this junk." Neither Pat nor Baiba claimed any specific religion, but they both thought of mountains as sacred places to be honored by keeping them pristine. So they left, planning to make a short trek to one of the peaks overlooking Josimath. We agreed to meet back there a few days later. (In fact, they did climb a superb little mountain, on top of which they camped for two nights, watching the full moon rise over a magnificent mountain wall. The view included Kamet and Nanda Devi, and they talked excitedly about the trekking and climbing possibilities of the area.)

Meanwhile, I had to eat something, so I cooked a pot of instant mashed potatoes—the only food I could be sure of holding down—and, leaving Wendy in the hotel, wobbled dizzily down to the temple. By now, all the trinket shops were open for business, selling religious souvenirs—plaques and brass plates and plastic beads, little cameras into which you looked to see pictures of temples, copper rings and bracelets, and photo placemats. Farther along, stalls offered platters of *prasad,* temple offerings, comprising marigold flowers, puffed grains, sugar, walnuts, fruit, raisins, and sweets. To these platters pilgrims would add money, incense, and other offerings before taking them to the temple to be consecrated by a priest. After giving his blessing, the priest would remove the money, put the larger pieces of food on a tray in front of Vishnu, and return what was left to the devotee.

Seen from the outside, the temple was marvelously ornate, painted in many bright colors. My pilgrims' guidebook noted:

> Badrinath stands first in the pilgrimage programmes as it bears the highest degree of supreme faith and dedication to God . . . There is no any historical record available as to the age at this holy temple, but reference to the Lord Badri Nath has been made in the *Veds* the holy book of the Hindus. This temple was worshiped as a Buddhist temple, when King *Ashoka* was ruling in India, but according to *Skand Puran* the idol of Lord Badrinath was re-covered by Adiguru Shankaracharya from [the hot spring] Narad Kund and was re-enshrined in the 8th century A.D.

I was the first pilgrim of the day. Taking off my shoes, I walked in stocking feet through the arched entrance into a courtyard, at the center of which stood a small stone building, the actual temple. Before I got there, a very small, wizened man touched my arm, pointed to a statue near the entrance, and said, "The helicopter god." It was Garuda, shown sometimes as a great bird, sometimes as a winged human figure.

"I've never thought of him as a helicopter," I said.

"He could be anything he wanted to be," answered my guide with a wry smile. I liked this man and followed him as he gave me the names of other statues standing in alcoves built into the courtyard wall. "Here is Vishnu; he is made of silver. And here, Lakshmi, wife of Vishnu. This one is Shankaracharya, who founded this temple many years ago. Over here, Hanuman, the warrior monkey." All were either painted or decorated in bright, cheerful clothing that reminded me of a Mexican Easter celebration.

I was looking at the statue of Hanuman when a musical voice behind me said, "Isn't it lovely?" I turned to see a bearded foreigner, who introduced himself as Colin. He was from Wales, and he was enchanted by the temple. "Hanuman is my favorite," he said. "I like Hanuman best of all. I like to pray to him. The trouble is, I don't know how, and I feel embarrassed if Hindus are watching. But I do it anyway. It makes me feel good."

Hearing that made me feel good too, and I realized that I had been depressed by Wendy's and my illness, which had prevented us from organizing any kind of trek, and by Pat and Baiba's discouragement. It was nice to hear someone speak of Badrinath in such delighted terms, and I started seeing it differently myself.

The two of us followed our volunteer guide around the temple. The rear of the building, said this man, was the oldest structure. How old? He couldn't say. At the back of the courtyard, a sign told us to sign up for our *pujas.* The minimum cost was eleven rupees, "and all the way up, thousands of rupees."

"As much as five thousand rupees?"

"Yes."

"Ten thousand?"

"Of course."

"How long does such a *puja* take to conduct?"

"Two hours."

"Why so expensive?"

"So many things are offered."

The more you pay, the more the priests offer in your name. Many of the offerings are burned. Others, like fruit, go to the priests' kitchen.

I was particularly struck by a statue of Lakshmi, a full-scale figure dressed in a red sari trimmed with silver filigree; but instead of a full-size face there was a tiny one, carved in black stone, set in the middle of where the face should have been. I could hardly see it.

"Why is the face so small?" I asked.

"I don't know."

Nor did he know the subject of a large painting nearby. He said only, "It is a famous swami."

Not famous enough!

The temple itself was one simple room supported by pillars, adjoining a closet-size sacristy built under a four-sided tapering tower. By changing the statues and putting a cross on the tower, it could easily have been converted to a Christian chapel. The sacristy housed an important statue of Vishnu, here called Badrinath, so heavily decorated that the figure was entirely invisible. To his left stood Vidje and to his right, Je (that's how the names sounded to me). Without help, I could recognize Hanuman, Lakshmi, Garuda, and the elephant-headed Ganesh.

I stayed for a long time, enjoying the quiet. The bank manager had said that, in summer, ten thousand to fifteen thousand worshipers would crowd through this little building each day. I thought it was better to be here in November. The spectacle was reduced, but the essentials were clear. Pilgrims came in small groups, holding each other's arms. When they left, having made their offerings and performed their devotions, they walked backward so as not to turn their backs on their god. They did these things with evident pleasure, as if it felt good to be here. It made me feel good just to see them.

Religious ritual should be a comfort to believers. I couldn't help but remember how I had felt in Lhasa, at the Jokhang Temple, where ritual seemed to be more a reminder of loss than a source of emotional peace.

Eventually, the cold from the stones became too much for my shoeless feet. I went back outside with Colin and down the steps to the hot spring, to stand on the thermally heated paving stones.

"*Namaste,*" said a man sitting against the wall.

"*Namaste.*"

"I saw you last night."

"Oh, yes, you were sleeping."

"I do not sleep. I was watching."

He was a sadhu, a young man from the Punjab who spoke like the one time university student he claimed to be. He had left the university six years earlier to be a holy man. He had spent time at various shrines but settled on this one, where he now stayed six months each year.

"I have only this," he said, showing me his nearly naked body under a grimy orange blanket. "And this," gesturing to his aluminum pot. "It is enough. It is all I want."

He sat with three friends, all dressed in the same simple manner. All had long, matted, black hair, uncombed and apparently unwashed, although I knew they bathed regularly in Taptakund, the sacred hot springs beside which they lived.

"So what do you do?" I asked.

"I stay here."

"Do you meditate?"

"There are saints living in caves around this valley. They meditate."

"But do you meditate?"

He gestured to one of his friends. "This man, he has great meditation power. He can stand the weight of you and me both on the end of his paniss, no problem, light like a feather."

"Paniss? What's a paniss."

He gave me a look of astonishment. "It is your sex."

"Oh, I see. He can do that?"

"He can show you. One hundred fifty kilos. He can pick up a stone 150 kilos with his paniss."

"How does he grip it? Does he use a rope?"

"He can balance on the end of his paniss."

"Really? And spin 'round like a top?"

"It is nothing. You would like to see?"

"Of course I would."

"You must first pay him respect."

"I have enormous respect for anyone who can do that."

"I, too, can do it. I have meditative power to pick up a hundred kilos with my paniss. You cannot pick up five kilos with your paniss, am I right?"

"Oh, yes, you're right. How do you grip the stone?"

"It is by meditation." He pointed to a pillow-size rock nearby. "This stone, he pick up this stone with his paniss if you give him a thousand rupees."

A little more than sixty dollars. It would have been worth seeing, but I was skeptical. "Is it good to do these things for money?" I asked.

"No. I am meditative for myself, for my soul, not to do magic." He gave me a broad smile. "You will now give us money for breakfast."

"Why should I do that?"

"Because I talk to you."

"And I'm talking to you, so we're even."

"You talk to me for yourself. It is nothing for me."

I left without paying him. Across the bridge and up the footpath, I stopped at the hut of a sadhu named Aji Baba. He sat by a fire that he had kept going for six months, since the day Badrinath opened in the spring. Standing beside the fire was a metal trident decorated with a garland made of oranges and marigolds. Aji Baba sat on a leopard skin wearing only a jockstrap. No jewelry. He was thirty-six years old and had been a sadhu for twenty-two years. Beside him was a large boulder painted orange.

"What is the significance of this stone?" I asked.

"That is Humayan."

Other people came to sit by his fire. He made tea in a metal pot, drank some, and passed a horn pipe loaded with hashish around the group. Then he flipped the cassette in his Walkman and punched the play button—Indian flute music on a minispeaker. After a few minutes, the music faded, batteries dead.

He told me about holy men in caves. One lived twenty miles north, near the border. He lived there year-round.

"How does he stay warm?"

"He has kerosene stove, coal, wood. Very comfortable. He has been there four years now. And under that big boulder—"

"The one across the river?"

"Yes. Under that boulder is another saint."

"Are you a sadhu?"

"Yes."

"Are you a saint?"

"Yes." Then, reconsidering, he said, "I cannot say I am a saint. That is for others to say."

As I was leaving, he handed me a glass-coral necklace. "*Prasad,*" he said. An offering. I was touched. In the hour I spent there, he had asked for nothing. I came back later and gave him two alkaline batteries for his Walkman.

———————

Back at the hotel, Wendy was feeling better and joined me on a walk up the valley toward Tibet, which lay about twenty-five miles away. Badrinath was just south of Mount Kailas. We knew we could not go far, and sure enough, at the edge of town a sign warned "Foreigners Not Permitted Beyond This Point." As if to prove it, a soldier, Sergeant Shukla, was coming past as we stood by the sign. He pointed across the valley.

"That is Mana village. The last village of India."

"But we can't go there."

"Sorry. It is a restricted area."

We turned and followed him back to town. The only other walking option was the valley leading to Nilkanth Peak. Pat and Baiba had gone up there while waiting for us and recommended the view. But both of us felt like elderly convalescents. What we wanted now, after several days of fasting, was something simple to eat. The problem was that the hotel kitchen was closed and the cook offered nothing for me to prepare on my own. I asked if he had eggs, and he recoiled: "No eggs. This is a holy place."

So we settled for the instant mashed potatoes I'd been carrying. I was heating water for that purpose on a camping stove and got to talking with the only other guest in the hotel, a Canadian who was living in southern India and was a follower of Sai Baba—not just a holy man, he said, but God the Father Himself.

"You mean the father of Christ?"

"Yes, same fellow."

"He's living in India?"

"He has been for a long time." Sai Baba was only the most recent of many incarnations, or avatars. He had come to Badrinath in 1961 with about two hundred followers and revitalized the sacred lingam.

"I didn't see a lingam in the temple."

"No, you wouldn't." He explained that the lingam had been placed inside the rock wall at the back of the sacristy. During his visit, Sai Baba had reached into the solid rock, withdrawn the lingam, blessed it, and replaced it. It was the same lingam that Shankaracharya had found in the river when he reconsecrated the temple in the ninth century. It was the most important object in the temple.

The Canadian was disgusted that the local priests didn't even know about the lingam. "They claim it doesn't exist!"

"What's this about God the Father?"

"Sai Baba is an avatar, meaning he is the Father to Christ's Krishna. He is very powerful. I've seen him. He has worked many thousands of miracles."

"What sort of miracles?"

"All sorts. He brings people back to life, cures blindness, and so on. It's no big deal for a yogi."

"That means Christ was a yogi?"

"Absolutely. You know, he was born in Palestine, but he came here to India when he was sixteen years old. Probably with a trading caravan. He stayed here until he was thirty, and went back for the events of the Bible. I was just visiting his tomb in Srinagar."

"In Srinagar!"

"Yes. He died there. A lot of people don't know that. He was 115 years old."

"There's a tomb in Srinagar with his name on it?"

"His Indian name. They called him Yuz Asaf. He didn't die on the cross. He was up there only about six hours, and usually that didn't kill a man. It took days for people who were crucified to die. And Jesus was obviously very strong, being a yogi. People thought he was dead because he was in yogic trance. They took him down. He lay in a tomb for three days and revitalized himself. He stayed in Palestine for a while after that. When he left, he said he was going 'to teach the lost tribes.' The lost tribes of Israel, which many believe could have come to Kashmir."

"Mormons say they went to North America."

"They're wrong. They came to Kashmir, and so did Jesus. He brought Mary with him—"

"His mother?"

"Yes. She's buried in Taxila near Islamabad. And Thomas—doubting Thomas—is buried in Madras. The church recognizes that. They built a cathedral there. It was Thomas who buried Christ in Kashmir. You can see the sarcophagus. It was a custom in those days to carve the dead person's footprints in the sarcophagus. They did that for Yuz Asaf, and you can see the nail holes clearly."

Later I looked in a book this Canadian had recommended and saw the sarcophagus, along with a picture of the building said to contain it. We had driven past the building one rainy day in Srinagar. I remember it clearly. Besides that, the book mentions that the Hindu temple on the hill above Dal Lake has another name—Solomon's Temple—and that Persian inscriptions by the threshold read: "At this time, Yuz Asaf announced his prophetic calling. In the year fifty and four. He is Jesus, prophet of the sons of Israel."

The temple and the tomb go on my long list of places I should go back to visit. It's another principle of traveling: You need to make all trips at least twice.

We stayed at Badrinath only two days. Each morning, in the dark, a loud-speaker started up with music and distorted voices of the morning *puja.* Islamic loudspeakers have nothing on the Hindu ones; nor is the ranting of Chinese loudspeaker systems in Tibet any more objectionable. Each morning, I wrapped my head in a pillow and thought about how religions crave unanimity: we are awake, the loudspeakers seemed to be saying, and praying, so everyone should be awake and praying. If not praying, then awake and aware of how virtuous we are being over here with our loudspeaker. 5:30 A.M. Wake up, but you can't have eggs in this holy place.

Well, it was their religious shrine, I decided. I had no business being critical. Thinking that, I picked up a newspaper to read: "In a surprise move, 12 satnami [untouchable] religious leaders here have decided to give up their demand for entry into temples. The religious heads, Raj Mahant Askaran Das, Raj Mahant Nain Das, and Guru Gosais, said that satnamis should abide by the sacredness of temples by staying away from them."

THE "UTTRAKHAND EXPRESS" left Josimath at 6:00 A.M. It had forty-four seats, room for thirty-two people, and it carried sixty. The seats had long since collapsed, falling back against each other, their backs bent and rivets popped. Pieces of lumber propped up the sway-backed roof. The seatcovers were slimy with grease. The windows were covered with hair oil and they rattled in their loose frames. People opened them only to vomit.

But we rode on it, of course, in the seat farthest back. Just ahead of us an army officer with "Engineer" embroidered on his epaulet played Indian music at loud volume on a boom box. The louder it got the more he smiled. The female singer shrieked at the top of her range, using only five notes. Violins wailed; oboes tried to scare away bad spirits. The tempo never varied, nor the tone. I guess I wasn't feeling very tolerant.

On the bus, I had a flash of Tibet. I remembered our camp near Gerze by a tiny stream at the base of a low, rubbly hill. There was a shrine on the hill, nothing more than a few rows of prayer stones placed long, long ago. I had gotten up at dawn and climbed the hill. The sun rose out of the peaks on the far horizon across an immense salt flat, a vanished sea. At sunrise it had the look of the sea; the ridge felt like an ocean promontory. A small convoy of trucks had come by the night before, just at sunset, with prayer flags flying.

233

They had been filled with people who waved and shouted to us. Pilgrims returning from Kailas. Then, late in the night, I had been startled from sleep by two more trucks traveling together. Sticking my head out of the tent, I watched them pass. It was very cold, but I watched until the lights were lost around a distant bend. People moving in the night, in the silent, empty heart of Tibet. That memory felt like a visitation from a peaceful past, and I held the image like an egg, trying to keep it from breaking in the back seat of that rattletrap bus.

It took twelve hours to reach Rishikesh, just outside Hardwar. Rishikesh, "place of holy men," was where the Beatles had gone to study with Maharishi Mahesh Yogi. Colin, the Welshman I met in Badrinath, had stayed at an ashram there. He had said it was wonderfully restful: "You can just go and stay and be quiet." I imagined the reflective atmosphere of a Tibetan monastery removed to a warm climate. We all felt a need for peace before plunging back into Delhi and dealing with the arrangements for getting on to Nepal. Vedniketan Ashram sounded like just the ticket.

We walked there, across a spectacular suspended footbridge and down the riverbank past shrines and bathing ghats. One of many ashrams, Vedniketan was the last in line. A sign at the entrance announced: "We welcome you to see the divine stone floating on water miniature manuscripts written by hand, underground lighting splendor learn yoga meditation by Vishwa guru."

Removing our shoes, we entered the office. Vishwa guru came out from a back room, the picture of yogic perfection in a white robe, with long, black beard and long, black hair. Yes, we were welcome for as long as we wanted to stay. Fifteen rupees per night. "Passports?" he asked. In India, every night in a hotel—or ashram—involves the filling out of long forms with visa numbers, dates, travel plans, personal history, references, and more. It's a tedious procedure for travelers and hotel staff both.

Vishwa guru spent ten minutes trying to read my visa, written in both Hindi and English. At last he said, "This is expired."

"Let me see. No, that is the date of issue. This is the expiry date."

"Where is departure date?"

"We haven't left India yet. They stamp the date then."

I had sympathy for him. The police were cracking down on hotel owners who were careless in checking visas, and Vishwa guru, who was not running a hotel, probably resented being made to play cop as much as I resented the continual checking of my documents and the endless filling of forms.

Having finished that, I wandered next door to an exhibit of photos and paintings. The photos showed the guru stripped to a loincloth in various yoga positions, none particularly athletic, all displaying his ample pot belly. He stood on his head, or lay on his back with his heels in the air, or stood lifting one leg straight to the side. Around a ledge at the top of the walls was mounted a collection of pictures showing religious scenes, and they moved! Heads, arms, legs, flags, cows' ears, and monkey tails were separate from the background and connected to motors that made them wiggle. There was the Hindu Holy Family all nodding and waving. Beside them, Hanuman swung his sword back and forth, endlessly purging the world of monsters. On another shelf were three samples of miniature writing "done without the aid of a magnifying glass"—two Hindi scripts and one, the New Testament Sermon on the Mount, in English. The latter was written on a piece of paper the size of a postage stamp, unreadable by the naked eye but perfectly legible under a magnifier, and beautifully crafted.

As if these were not wonders enough, in the hallway, in a place of honor, was the Divine Stone Floating on Water. It was contained in a galvanized metal tank protected by a grid over the top large enough to admit coins but not fingers. The stone was a disk of pumice. Undeniably it floated.

Colin was staying there. He had changed from jeans and sweater to loose-fitting maroon pajamas and greeted us with a huge smile. He was fresh from a swim in the Ganges, his hair slicked back and his beard dripping. He loved being in India. To him, the temples were beautiful, the decorations nicely done.

He told me that he had earned the money for this trip by raising and selling marijuana in Wales. "It was good, you know. I grew it carefully. People responded well to it, and it gave me this lovely trip."

Colin spoke as if always listening to the sound of his voice—not from vanity but to keep it sounding good, as a singer would do. He wanted his voice to be as harmonious as his thoughts. He was an appreciator of everything he saw and a believer who had just begun to learn about semiprecious stones.

"Look at what I've bought," he said. "Did you know that turquoise changes color when you get sick? And if you're wearing it when you have an accident, it absorbs the harm. It's a peaceful stone, turquoise."

He had need of peace. Except for raising marijuana, he'd been unemployed for six years, living on the dole. "In Wales, it's dope or the dole; there's nothing else," he said. "Of course, there's drink." He knew all about that. He had once made a trip to Kathmandu, where instead of visiting temples he went on a bender that lasted two months. He had spent some strange nights in strange places. He had eaten solid food maybe once a week. "This trip is much better for me."

Vedniketan was indeed a peaceful place. Not much was happening. You could hear people meditating from time to time, doing their breathing exercises, making earnest, energetic sounds that in an American hotel would have you feeling embarrassed and wishing people would be more discreet with their passions. In the ashram I was amused by the sounds. They were obviously part of Vishwa guru's prescribed yoga exercises. With more time to spend, I would have enjoyed staying longer to learn more about them.

The only annoyance was by now a familiar one. At 5:00 A.M. someone cranked up the loudspeaker for the morning prayer broadcast. I wish I could have viewed that the way Colin did—just another part of a delightful scene.

Upstream of Rishikesh there was a sign at a small riverbank shrine that read: "In this kutir Sri Swami Sivananada Ji Maharaj, founder of the International Divine Life Society, performed austere spiritual sadhana during the period 1924 to 1934." I found it on an afternoon walk along a heavily littered trail. "Right," I thought cynically. "I'd bet he did that before loudspeakers were invented."

But loudspeakers were inevitable in India, where the ebullient, haphazard layering of age is one of the country's main charms. There, old temples stand on the middens of older ones. Monuments are built, only to decay and be replaced by new ones that eventually will sink into the mud themselves, becoming reminders of life's cyclical nature. The past will be replaced by the present, and nothing is permanent.

Rishikesh had been sacred for centuries. With a little imagination, I could picture it before the arrival of roads and vehicles. Three hundred years ago, a barefoot seeker probing the foothills through the quiet activity of scattered villages would have come upon the Ganges in a near-wilderness setting, a great, lucid flow pouring down from the icy mountains and the calm gaze of Shiva.

Well, what was it now? Still the lucid flow, but littered with divine floating stones, statues of martyrs in bloody demise, billboards promising bliss and spiritual security to those who would enter this ashram or that, and loudspeakers preaching while uniformed ashramites marched through the streets carrying banners and singing the praises of various gurus.

I decided I would have preferred Rishikesh three hundred years ago. But then I thought about Colin, who liked it any way he saw it. I imagined him telling me, in his melodious, carefully tuned voice, "But three hundred years ago you would have been a different person, or you wouldn't have had the chance to come at all, and now here you are, and that's the lovely part."

He would have been right. On the second evening in Rishikesh, I went to watch sunset over the Ganges at a bathing ghat and came upon a group of yellow-robed ashram students gathering to perform a ceremony. Four older men arranged offerings on a silver platter, setting them among half a dozen little oil lamps. Looking up, one of the men noticed me watching and approached. Wrapped in a white sheet, he wore a brown balaclava. He had a huge, white beard and fantastic tangles of black hair growing from his ears.

"You are making an offering to the river?" I asked.

"Holy Mother Ganga evening prayer. These men are from Parmarath ashram. Waiting ten minutes. The soul is arty. Ganga."

"The soul is arty?"

"Yes, *arti*. Hymns to Mother Ganga. These disciples are always busy praying and are meditating constantly upon the holy names of Ganga. You are in business?"

"More or less. And you?" I asked.

"Yes. What is your native place?"

"America. What city do you live in?"

"Yes."

"What city?"

"Yes."

Another man joined us. He was from Delhi. He spoke with his tongue pulled way into the back of his mouth. I got distracted from what he was saying as I watched for the tongue. How could he talk that way? And the words he was using!

"The sacred Ganga," he said. "We are making her honor tonight, and in her unlimited generosity she is always returning that honor many times multiplied. Have you bathed in the Ganga?"

"No, I haven't."

"But you must. And it is highly important you are taking the Ganga internally as well as externally. I recommend highly that you are drinking this water; it must only improve a person's health and general state of well-being. The water of the Ganga, you see, because it is holy and precious, is both biologically and bacteriologically pure. You may take this water to your home in a bottle and now it is remaining as it is. So pure. For years and years it is staying pure. Bacteriological purity because it is Ganga."

"That is not exactly the case," said a third man, who now talked at length about industrial pollution. "New cities are coming, but do they put them in the jungle? Where there is room? Where there are no people? No. They put the factories by the river, because they want to be near their brothers, their parents. So it gets dirtier and dirtier. There is even," he said in a whisper, as if imparting a dread secret, "human waste!"

Not really!

The ceremony began, and it was, as Colin would say, lovely. The students of Parmarath ashram sang in rough but pleasant unison while an older man held the tray with lamps and flowers and *prasad*, extending it over the water toward the sunset. A small crowd, including a cow, stood and watched. The sun touched the far horizon. The man with the tray turned, offering the flowers and rice to the onlookers, who each took something from the tray, lined up at the water's edge, and as the singing stopped, threw the *prasad* into the river, where fish swirled to take it. It was a moment of transient beauty, representing what in my mind the celebration of religion should be. Lighthearted, congenial, unamplified, thoroughly humane. It was the best thing I saw in Uttrakhand.

■ *Above:* Norbu Lama's wife Patu in her kitchen making *chang* (rice beer), Tashigaon, upper Arun Valley, eastern Nepal. ■ *Below:* The porters took shelter under a rock ledge at Karuma campsite, below Shipton La on the way to Makalu base camp, upper Arun Valley, eastern Nepal.

■ Moonlight bathes a shepherd hut at Nehe Kharka, the closest dwelling to Makalu base camp.

■ *Above:* Baiba climbs to the ridge above Makalu base camp, with Chamlang Peak and the Barun Glacier in the background. ■ *Opposite:* The gnarled roots of pipal and bor trees stand out like skeletons in the village of Barabise, junction of Lankuwa and Sobaya rivers, on the way to Taplejung, eastern Nepal.

■ *Above:* Chainpur, a commercial center in the hill country of eastern Nepal, appears prosperous and comfortable.

■ *Left:* Wendy walks beside an exuberant display of poinsettias growing to the height of small trees.

■ *Opposite:* The hill country of eastern Nepal is a region of old, well-kept family farms. Here, a field of mustard blooms beside a thatch-roofed house.

■ *Above:* Pat crosses a swinging bridge at the town of Barabise, eastern Nepal. (Photo: Baiba Morrow) ■ *Below:* A masked dancer celebrates Tibetan New Year in Kathmandu. (Photo: Jeremy Schmidt)

14
Makalu

A hundred divine epochs would not suffice to describe all the marvels of Himachal. As the dew is dried up by the morning sun, so are the sins of mankind by the sight of Himachal.
———Puranas, fifth century A.D.

"Bloody hell, they're big honkers!"
———British trekker in Nepal

TUMLINGTAR AIRSTRIP was a cow pasture, a grassy flat perched above the Arun River in eastern Nepal. Whenever an airplane approached, it was the duty of the airport manager to run cattle off the field. He had to do this three times a week, weather permitting, for the flight from Kathmandu and several more times for flights from Biratnagar. Otherwise, he spent his time sitting in a little stone building with stacks of paper on his desk. He had no radio contact with Kathmandu, and no telephone this far into the hills, but he could predict when a plane might be landing by simply looking out his window at the appropriate time. If the valley was clear of mist, if the winds were calm, if there had been no mechanical troubles, and if the plane had not been commandeered at the last minute for some other purpose, it would come on schedule.

As it did that warm November afternoon when we flew to Tumlingtar. From Uttrakhand we had returned to Delhi, retrieved our bikes and other gear at Anil's house, and spent some time arranging for permits to visit the once independent Himalayan state of Sikkim. Now part of India, it lies just east of Nepal on the Tibetan border. Errands finished, we had flown from Delhi to Kathmandu, where we again stored the bikes (and eventually sold them) and made arrangements for this trek in the Nepal Himalaya.

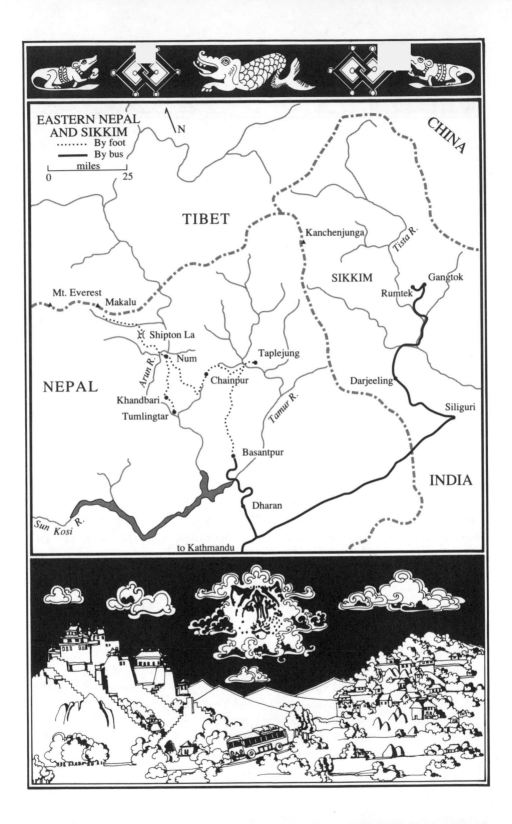

EASTERN NEPAL
AND SIKKIM
.... By foot
——— By bus
miles
0   25

N

CHINA

TIBET

Kanchenjunga

Tista R.

SIKKIM

Gangtok

Mt. Everest   Makalu

Rumtek

Shipton La

Num

Taplejung

Chainpur

Arun R.

NEPAL

Khandbari

Tumlingtar

Darjeeling

Siliguri

Tamur R.

Basantpur

INDIA

Sun Kosi R.

Dharan

to Kathmandu

Tumlingtar was just a name. There was no actual town, no streets or rows of houses, and not so much as a jeep road. We had been dropped into rural Nepal, far from vehicles and electricity, where nights were still dark, stars were bright, and sounds were alive—the voices of children, the crowing of roosters, the bleat of goats, and the pounding of bare feet on packed red earth. Mud-wattle houses stood on stilts with cows and goats tethered in the shelter beneath them.

It was late autumn, the peak of tangerine season. There were piles of tangerines, trees full of tangerines, yards loaded with tangerines, and squads of children carrying bags and baskets of them for sale.

"Namaste," they yelled when they saw me coming and trotted along beside me asking where was I going and wouldn't I buy just one more tangerine? Soon I had a sackful of fruit and was eating as fast as I could peel, thinking that Arun Valley tangerines were the best I'd ever tasted and that this was a fine way to start a month of walking.

I kept company with Wendy. We were the trailers in a small caravan spread out on the way to the town of Kandbari, where we planned to spend the night. The trail was a narrow path running between rice paddies and fields of the same yellow mustard we had seen filling the valleys of central Tibet five months before, way back on that July morning near Gyantse when workers had disappeared like diving ducks in a sea of yellow—although here in Nepal it was more like ponds of yellow, little puddles of yellow set among plantings of corn and rice. More than anywhere else in the Himalaya, Nepal is a contrast in scale. The people are small. Their animals are small. They have small houses and small fields. Yet in one glance your eyes travel from Lilliput to Brobding-nag, from farms the size of gardens to the full icy majesty of the Great Hima-laya. It's like seeing God and His subjects all in one view.

Nepal is five hundred miles long and barely a hundred miles wide, not much bigger than Illinois. You could make the mistake of thinking that this is a small place, a parenthetical nation squeezed between the great hulks of India and China. But that illusion dies fast when you start walking across Nepal's enormous topography. Never mind the actual mileage. When it takes ten days to walk to a place you can see quite clearly from the beginning, you learn the true stature of the land. I have stood in one village looking across a river gorge and heard the sound of a woodcutter's *kukri,* a traditional Nepali curved knife, in a village on the other side, even seen the man working beside his house, and then taken a full day to get there. Where else but Nepal can you walk all day and end up within earshot of where you started?

In this case, our goal was the base of Makalu—fifth-highest peak in the world, neighbor of Everest, a great shining monster of white intrusive rock rising above the ridges and commanding the attention of anyone standing for the first time, as I was doing, in the little fields of Tumlingtar.

The trail took us between two rivers of very different character. The Arun, falling milky and blue from the glaciers of Makalu, Everest, and Tibet, reverberated from far below on our lefthand side. It was a major river, a crashing torrent. On the right, a smaller stream, the Sama Khola, ran clear and green across gravel shoals, pausing reflectively in silent pools beneath mossy cliffs, as peaceful as a Pennsylvania trout stream.

There was lots of traffic on the trail. Women came past in groups of four or five, returning home from market in Kandbari, chattering as they walked beneath their *dokos,* baskets loaded with town goods. Ironic, I thought, that people living near an airstrip would have to walk two hours or more to buy an aluminum pot in the nearest town. But few goods came to rural Nepal by air. The old foot trails were still the country's major transport routes. Merchandise arrived as it always had, carried on the backs of porters to established commercial centers such as Kandbari, and it did not matter where the airport was, you still had to go to Kandbari to fill your kerosene jug or buy a new *kukri.*

A fat man rode past on a small, white mare; his belly and his horse showed him to be a man of substance. So did his clothing—a Brahmin cap and Western-style suit coat over white cotton pants.

"Where are you going?" he asked.

"Tonight, Kandbari."

He looked concerned. "But it takes two years to reach Kandbari."

"Two years!"

He considered that for a moment and said, "No, it is hours. Two hours." Embarrassed by his faux pas and unable to continue the conversation, he whacked his horse with a willow stick and trotted on.

Dusk came down as we went up the trail. To the east, high ridges separated by bands of cloud went from gold to grey. Above them, in the far distance, after all the lower peaks had sunk into shadow, Makalu, as abstract and distant as a cloud, still shone bright.

We came to a pond, its calm surface dimpled with the peering eyes of hundreds of frogs. As I walked closer to see them, they disappeared, blink. A moment later, hundreds more flew into the pond from the banks, skittering across the dark surface like skipping stones, shattering the reflection of sunset.

Soon it was dark. In the night, stars shone behind black foliage. The air filled with the fragrance of wood smoke as hearth fires were lit. Then each house we passed was a tableau of figures in pools of candlelight. Children ran to doorways to look out at us, their dark forms raising hands and pressing palms together. "*Namaste!*" they called out. Sometimes, from dimly lit rooms, an adult voice would shout, "Where are you going?" "Kandbari," I would say. "Night walk, Kandbari!" one woman shouted.

We stopped at the sound of a rice mill. In an open shed, two children pumped one end of a heavy timber with their feet. Their mother sat at the other end stirring a pile of rice. The children pushed, raising the timber. When they released their weight, the timber, to which a wooden spike was attached, dropped into the rice and broke hulls from the grains. The sound made a pleasant rhythm, about once per second, the squeak of a wooden hinge followed by the dull thud of the falling spike. I had seen the same device in China powered by running water. In the Arun Valley it became a familiar background sound. Hearing it in every village, I came to think of it as the heartbeat of mountain life. Creak-thump, creak-thump.

The trail went steadily uphill in the dark. My legs grew tired from unseen irregularities, and it was good to find Dawa Tamang, our sirdar, waiting in the candlelight of a tiny teahouse. He had ordered tea, and the proprietor was keeping it hot for us.

Dawa was a young man, about twenty-five, and soft-spoken in the pleasing manner of educated Nepalis. On the recommendation of friends, we had hired him in Kathmandu and sent him a day ahead of us to Tumlingtar so that he could have a crew of porters waiting when we arrived. I'd had no chance to meet them yet. As soon as our loads came off the plane, the porters had swept them up and disappeared along the trail. In some parts of the world you'd worry about ever seeing your belongings again. But not here.

"Kandbari is only fifteen minutes," Dawa said. "Almost flat."

It didn't matter. The tea strengthened my legs, and the rest of the way was a pleasant stroll.

There are few things I like better than walking into a hill town early in the night. Kerosene lanterns and candles glow in windows; people sit quietly talking after a day of labor; children run in and out of shadows. The smells of cooking go straight to your stomach. It is a most welcoming scene. Kandbari was like that—just a few streets lined with buildings and a central square. We were standing in the square for a minute wondering where the rest of our group was when I heard Pat's cheery greeting. He clinked up to us carrying half a dozen quarts of beer. "Ready for a *pijiu?*"

Pat led the way to a lodge where we sat on wooden benches sipping beer and waiting while the proprietor prepared a meal of dal baht—boiled rice and lentils—the national dish of Nepal.

WE WERE A BIGGER GROUP than we should have been. After six months of close companionship, Pat, Baiba, Wendy, and I were still good friends, which was a remarkable thing considering how stressful travel can be. Generally we preferred more independence than was possible in a party of four, and we knew that the bigger the group becomes, the harder it gets. Now we had grown to eight, mostly because Kathmandu, being the central city of the Himalayan region, is a place where, by chance, you always seem to meet people you know. There's such great pleasure in seeing old friends that, without thinking critically, you want them all to come along on whatever trip you have in mind. In this case, I had met two friends from Arizona, David Edwards and Jane Bernard, both of whom were river guides in the Grand Canyon. Pat and Baiba had introduced us to their Canadian friends, Jeff Boyd, a doctor from Banff, and Marie Boisvert, an artist and forest fire lookout.

That made eight of us, along with seven porters and Dawa. All were good people accustomed to the outdoors, but already logistics felt unwieldy. I resolved to balance the social requirements of such a large group by keeping separate on the trail. Unless you're in the army or a chain gang, walking should not be a group activity.

The next morning we organized our loads, bought such staples as rice and sugar, and set out on the trail to Makala in a happily undisciplined, straggling line. It was a beautiful trail, bobbing along the crest of a ridge marked every quarter-mile or so by enormous trees. Standing in pairs—one pipal tree with one bor tree—they provided shade over stone platforms used as resting places. Porters could back up to the stones and, without bending over, set down their loads.

"These are holy trees," said Dawa. "They bring mountain winds."

Planted on the stone platforms as saplings, mature trees developed massive, gnarly root systems, enveloping the entire platform in a grip of rigid tentacles. In spaces between the roots, fern gardens and nettles grew, and religious offerings were made as in side chapels of a cathedral. Generous of limb, extravagant of root, the trees provided spiritual bridges connecting the lowlands in their roots with the mountains in their leafy tops.

We were walking through well-populated rural country, farming country. Passing one house, I heard an English lesson being conducted inside; girls were answering a female teacher.

"What is this a picture of?" asked the teacher.

"Dees ees a picture of some vimeen," came the chorus of young voices.

"Yes. Women. This is a picture of some women."

While girls occupied classrooms, bright-eyed boys were on the trail. "Hello. What eezoor name?" they would ask, skipping along beside me.

"Joe," I said, knowing that my real name was a tongue twister for them. "What is yours?"

"Give me one pen! Give me rupee!"

I gave them nothing, which discouraged them not a bit. It was the end of the school term. They were celebrating by tearing pages from their lesson books as they ran along the trail. I picked up a fragment covered with a child's handwriting: "The cat is a pet animal. People kipe it at home. It is very small. It's head is round. It is like a tiger. It likes fish and milk very much. It does not eat grass."

One group of boys showed me their exam papers. Sixth level. I read the questions out loud: Who ran the race and who won it first? Where do tigers live? Can the girls decide which animal fights most fiercely?

The boys gave me the answers. To the last one, they said, "Yes, they can."

"Then which animal was it?"

"The tiger and the buppalo."

"Did the tiger win?"

"No, the buppalo."

In exposed areas the sun was hot enough that I wanted to dunk my head and shoulders beneath every water spout. Under the trees, however, it was cool and fragrant; there the path was damp clay into which notches had been cut for steps. Bright red leaves of poinsettia glowed in shafts of sunlight. With Wendy, I angled up past terraces and thatch-roofed houses, beside substantial stone walls and clumps of bamboo growing symmetrically like bouquets, their graceful tips nodding against purple sunset clouds.

Sunset? Already? Once again we had moseyed, too slowly, poking along enjoying the view. The others were ahead somewhere. We had agreed, that morning, to camp near Bhotepas, and because I had no idea how far that was, I stopped a man for directions. He was a tiny, barefoot man wearing a skimpy loincloth and carrying about a hundred pounds of rice on his back—an ordinary load for a Nepali hillman.

"Bhotepas? Way over there!" he said in Nepali, gesturing beyond the ridge.

It looked to be two hours away and probably more. But actually the man had meant some closer landmark, because although we missed Bhotepas entirely in the dark, we came across Dawa an hour later. He was standing on the trail, once again waiting for us. "Camp is here, sahib," he said in his quiet, almost elegant voice, and he led us to a terrace covered with corn stubble where we cooked supper and had an uneventful evening. Oh yes, one event: in the dark, having undressed for bed, I stepped off the edge of the terrace and bounced down a 15-foot cliff into a thicket—in my boots and underwear. Everyone thought that was pretty good, my lying upside down in a bush in the beams of collected flashlights, surprised but unhurt.

In the morning I spent some time meeting the porters. Six of them were of the Rai tribe, meaning they all had the same last names: Bahadur Rai. Simple. I had only to learn first names: Raskumar, wearing a T-shirt with a rising sun;

Nindra, sporting a bright orange Brahmin hat; Chandra, Santa, Ram, and Gyen were perfect miniature athletes, standing about four-feet-ten. Gyen wore a conical hat made from a foil-covered foam sleeping pad and kept an enormous *kukri* tucked in his belt. It made him look like a toy soldier.

Latchu was Dawa's brother-in-law and also a Tamang. Married, with three kids, but still in his early twenties, he wore a brown Nike T-shirt, polyester pants, and running shoes. He had a mustache, a head of curly black hair, a stout body, and walked like a bull in a hurry—easily the fastest of the porters. I'd hate to see him behind the wheel of a truck if he drove the way he walked. He would make a hell of a rugby player. He was also an excellent cook. Crouched by the fire wearing his black vinyl jacket and a stocking cap, he appeared positively piratical. On the trail he carried a short-wave radio tuned to a Nepali music station; you always knew it was Latchu coming. A solid character and a reliable man, I grew to trust him completely. I can't say the same for strutting, wise-cracking little Gyen, although I liked Gyen very much.

The valleys were so filled with clouds that morning that the ridge on which we walked became an island in a turbulent sea of mist. It felt good to be high above the smoldering busyness of the Indian plains.

And, for a time, above the busy labors of Nepal as well. Leaving the carefully tended, terraced garden-farms we entered a zone of scrubby growth on deforested slopes, a sort of artificial wilderness. There had been a forest here not long ago. The trees had been cut for firewood, or construction, or to provide fodder for animals, and because the soil was poor, the land had not been settled. It was now nothing better than a wasteland scabbed over with brush, whining with cicadas, lacking both its original forest and the pleasant hand-crafted landscape of settled areas lower down.

I didn't like trudging up that breathless trail under the unrelieved sun, dust rising, sweat soaking my shirt. The cicadas, angry little buzz saws, got on my nerves. But then, having topped the ridge, the path dove into a damp, reverberant forest, a dim place of oak and laurel trees hung with lianas, wrapped in moss, carpeted with plush banks of ferns. David was there, sitting on a cold rock among the dripping trees, as if in a cave. I sat beside him on a root the shape of a cold, coiled snake.

From somewhere back in the forest, from what seemed like a long distance, two birds were calling—hollow notes rising by half-tones deep in the shadowed spaces. Hoo hoo hoo hoo hoo.

"Sounds of the ancient forest," said David, "Of which there isn't much left."

It was one strong reason why we had wanted to come this way. The slopes below Makalu support one of the best examples of native cloud forest surviving in Nepal. There was talk of adding it to Sagarmatha (Mount Everest) National Park.

In the nick of time, and perhaps too late. Nepal's forests are vanishing at a frightening speed. Wood is still a primary fuel in rural areas. An expanding population hacks at the forests, trying to make farmland from steep slopes that will never support crops. Instead, massive erosion destroys more land than is opened by clearing. Experts predict disaster and desertification, and you can't help but think about that when walking through the hills. You see the frontiers of agriculture, where there is a terrible contrast between disfigured landscapes and the sublime beauty of the high mountains. It makes you sad, and grateful for the wildness that still exists.

But, as in most parts of the world, the higher you go the better it gets. Late that afternoon, in deep forest, the trail crossed a spring creek in a clearing bordered by luxuriant banks of ferns. The path was wide, paved with flat stones, lighted by slanting shafts of sun, and down it came a figure from ancient tales—a figure carrying a load, hunched forward, leaning on a stick, moving deliberately. When he lifted his head to look at me, his face shone in the green and gold light. It was a beautiful face and for a moment showed pleasure at our meeting. But only momentarily. The smile quickly faded to pain, and I noticed the man's foot. His foot was a horror. A deep puncture wound had become infected. The lower half of his leg was so swollen that the skin had cracked like a boiled potato.

He wasn't asking for help, and I had none to give. Wendy did, however, and as if he knew it, this man found our tent that evening and displayed his black stump of a foot. She boiled a pot of water, took a rag, and with Dawa's help, demonstrated to the man how he should soak the wound with hot water, instructing him to do it twice a day—but she had little hope. The hole was nearly an inch deep. He had been trying to clean pus out of it with a feather. "What a pity," said Jeff, after having a look at it. "Probably a staph infection. He needs a hospital. He could be dead in a few days."

At a time when things should be getting better for Nepal—if, that is, you view modern medicine, modern transport, foreign aid, and contact with the larger world to be chances for improvement—at a time apparently filled with opportunity, conditions were getting worse for the country folk there. We spent a morning at Num, a village of several houses, many children, and a school. I met an American aid worker there who said that 60 percent of the district's forest had been destroyed in the past ten years. During the same period, the population had more than doubled—from nineteen hundred to four thousand persons, the increase coming from birth and immigration from Nepal's crowded lowlands. New people hacked apart the forest to build new terraces, but the soil was so poor that after three or four years they had to be abandoned, leaving scabrous brush and useless semidesert slopes open to erosion. The local people recognized that fertilizer was essential, but manure was in short supply, and whatever cash they managed to earn from portering or other jobs went to buy surplus food because the thin soil produced too little. They couldn't buy fertilizer because they grew too little for their basic needs.

As for medicine, what chance did this old man with a hole in his foot have? "Go to Kandbari and get medicine," Jeff told him, but Dawa, who translated, said the man would not. It was too far. Two days and too far. (As it happened, we came back that way more than two weeks later and met the same man along the trail. His foot had healed. He had conscientiously soaked it in hot water twice a day, and the treatment had worked, transforming him into a smiling man who looked ten years younger and walked without a cane.)

From Num, the trail dropped 3000 feet to the Arun River, where it began an 11,000-foot climb to Shipton La. The name, obviously, comes from Eric Shipton, who trekked over it in 1952 with Edmund Hillary, George Lowe, and Charles Evans. They were on their way home following a reconnaissance of the Everest region and an attempt on Cho Oyu. The trip was intended mostly as a warm-up before the 1953 British Mount Everest Expedition, and these fellows were interested only in the highest peaks and valleys. In his autobiography, Hillary describes the Barun Valley and Shipton La with the economy of a man with his nose pointed homeward (and eager to get on to the next chapter, about his successful climb of Everest): "We retreated before monsoon snows and waded knee deep in flowers down the lower Barun. We crossed a 14,000-foot pass in torrential rain and descended into the warmth and leeches of the Arun Valley."

So much for the mountains. Now for the fun. He and Lowe strapped a couple of air mattresses together and "floated down long stretches of lively water—until a fearful battle with a huge whirlpool made us lose our enthusiasm—and nearly our lives." In flood! Today that stretch is considered very difficult even for a fully equipped kayaker.

Considering their size and length, it is remarkable that the Himalaya are crossed by so many rivers—not just the Arun but the Shyok, Indus, Sutlej, Karnali, Kali Gandaki, Brahmaputra, the Manas in Bhutan, the Bhare in Arunachel Pradesh, and more, all rising north of the highest peaks and flowing south through them. The reason is that these rivers predate the uplift of the mountains. As the Himalaya rose, the rivers kept cutting. Over time, the Arun has carved an ever deeper gorge between the third- and fifth-highest mountains in the world, Kanchenjunga and Makalu. From its stony Tibetan birthplace on the north side of Everest to the plains of India, this wonderful gorge provides such a wide range of habitat that six hundred species of birds can be found here, more than in all of North America.

Already an important river, it is preparing to become much larger. At some time in the future the Arun will gnaw its way into the upper Brahmaputra Valley, capture that drainage, and divert the major river of central Tibet into Nepal. On the other hand, if Tibet continues to dry up, the mighty Brahmaputra might not be much of a stream by then.

And still the mountains are rising. India continues its grand collision with Asia. In the past six thousand years, the Himalaya have risen about 4000 feet. By current estimates, they are rising, on average, at the astonishing speed of four to six inches per year. At that rate, Everest would be nearly 20 feet higher than when it was first climbed by Hillary in 1953.

From Num, I followed the trail to a cable bridge suspended over the river. Once again I was the straggler. I couldn't help it. The place was gorgeous. I stood alone in the middle of the bridge for half an hour enjoying the scent of pounding water, watching the river crash down through its canyon—Everest water, Tibet water. There is nothing like a river to give you the feeling of being in touch with distant places. I wanted to go there, up the river, to every place the waters came from; I also wanted to stay right where I was, feeling the sway of the bridge, breathing the ferny air while river mist formed droplets on the hairs of my arms.

But we had agreed on Sedua for the night, and Sedua was 3000 vertical feet above the river.

Up, up, and up. I was tired. The trail was as steep as a stairway, often steeper. This was the sunny side of the valley, and I ground my way uphill in first gear, stopping often at shady rest benches. I climbed past terraces where people who lived in thatched huts were out harvesting their rice, piling it with exquisite care in circular mows beside threshing grounds—just as we had seen the people in Hushe do with their wheat, except here the houses were shaded by bamboo and banana trees, and I was reminded of Africa.

Farther up, Wendy waited. She matched her pace to mine as we climbed past more harvesters. The sun disappeared behind the ridge, leaving us in shadow. In the coolness I felt better but went no faster. We were sitting, at one point, eating sweet biscuits and wishing for water (there were no streams flowing here) when a young Nepali came up the trail, hopping lightly from rock to rock. His name was Laxman; he lived in Sedua, which he pointed out to us, still impossibly far away on the crest of the ridge.

"That building, he is the shopkeeper. That tree: behind is eschool."

He stayed with us, good-naturedly showing us the right trail wherever it forked in the bamboo thickets. We passed a farm. He pointed to the house, the barn, and a little shrine, saying, "This is man house; this is pig house; this is god house."

Laxman was sixteen years old. He had just finished seventh level at the Sedua school, and that would be the end of formal education for him. He had family concerns, having recently married a fourteen-year-old girl from Num. They lived with his parents.

"Only sixteen, and you're married?" I said.

"Of course."

"How long have you been married?"

"Not one year."

I gestured to Wendy. "She and I have been married not two years. Do you know how old I am? Thirty-eight."

He made me repeat myself. He was sure he had heard wrong. When he was my age he would be a grandfather. Nepali men my age look like grandfathers. No children at thirty-eight? Crazy.

He took us past his house, walking very carefully around the edge of the buffalo paddock. "This is my buffalo," he said, watching it nervously. I thought about the schoolboys and their "buppalo"—the best fighter, victorious over a tiger. "Is he dangerous, Laxman?"

"Yes."

At his house, Laxman wanted us to sit down and drink tea. It was a neat place of painted adobe, with a smooth clay floor clean enough to lie down on. I was tempted to lie down and not get up. But it was late, so we simply said hello to Laxman's mother, his sister, and his wife, a shy, pretty young woman who smiled and quickly disappeared into a back room. Laxman wanted her to stay and be social. He wanted us to admire her. He made it clear that his wife's generous figure, in this land of hard-working, thin people was a matter of much pride to him, and that he thought of himself as a very lucky man. Reluctantly, he recognized our desire to keep moving and led us through the night up the hill to the schoolyard, where he had planned to camp. A five-minute walk, he said, but we took twenty. I was nearly staggering by the time we arrived. I felt like an old man, a grandfather indeed, coming in once more after dark.

The porters and Dawa came even later than we did, having made a *chang* stop along the way. Smart fellows, drinking home brew during the heat of the day, and cheerful fellows too, after they dropped their loads and located the Sedua *chang* house.

My own need was for water, of which there was none in this dry ridge-top village. I went looking and found it ten minutes' walk down a slippery trail.

Coming back, I tripped. With water containers in each hand, I couldn't stop the fall and landed hard. Discouraged, I stayed on the ground for a while feeling the exhaustion, watching the stars in the sky and the starlike points of light from kerosene lanterns across the valley. In all that space, only seven lights were visible.

Sitting there in the close darkness, I had a momentary sense of the world's great and melancholy beauty, of the power and possibility of life; it's a feeling that comes easily to me when I face, at night, a vast open expanse that I know to be mostly wild with only a few people attending to their quiet chores. I had felt the same way that evening at Mount Kailas after we had hiked over the Drolma La. Dropping into the eastern valley, we had pitched tents in the wind shelter of an enormous boulder. I had gone out to the stream to fill a cooking pot. Crouched by the stormy water, shivering in the icy wind, I had looked up at the cliffs to see two fires burning—far away and tiny, and precious because there was no wood locally. People were up there, high on the night-black wall, huddled against the gale watching stars wheel above the great Tibetan mountain. Kailas, center of the world, halfway to eternity. The flash of the fires had connected us, for a moment. Me, the watchers, the mountain, and the stars.

But that remembered image carried no water. I walked back to the stream, refilled my pots, and made my way, carefully this time, up the slippery trail.

Despite its small size, Sedua was a crazy place—a big drinking and barking town. Arf and barf, I nicknamed it. Walking among the buildings, I was greeted by tipsy folk sitting on the ground and dogs yelling bloody murder. We ordered a meal of dal baht in a teahouse whose proprietress reeled around, ladle in hand, laughing and spilling, joking with a happy tumble of drinkers who lay in the entryway. Everyone seemed happy. There was a lot of singing. In fact, the singing went on far into the night—not only people singing but dogs as well. I had gotten used to Nepali dogs barking at shadows and rumors. But that night they were set off by a strange chorus of howls coming from the forest—high-pitched, undoglike, more like amplified house-cat yowling. Strange provocations in the dark. I couldn't guess what made the sound. In the morning, Dawa said they were jackals.

One dog howled at our tents all night. Something about our being there gave him fits. Every hour or so he stalked around us howling and barking as if to warn the neighborhood of an alien invasion. Then the other village dogs would take up the chorus until I expected to hear the people of Sedua out with their *kukris* hacking off heads. Instead, they would shout and laugh along with the dogs and start up another drinking song. They sounded like a bunch of college kids camped on a beach.

When I couldn't stand it I went outside to peg rocks at the nearest barker. I didn't hit him. I couldn't even see him, but it made me feel better to hear the stones crashing into the shrubbery. Better than that was to hear my friends, one at a time, get up and do the same thing. "Vweeep!" would go the zipper on the Morrows' tent, and Pat would be out in his bare feet slinging stones and curses. The idiot dog would retreat down the ridge for a few minutes, until Pat was safely back inside, and then return shrieking to high heaven, and "Vweeep!" would go the zipper on another tent and it would be David's turn.

It was too funny not to laugh. Several times we all got going, giggling and howling back at the crazed animal, whose voice just got wilder in response, in turn rousing the town to renewed efforts.

In the morning, of course, the dogs were soundly asleep. David went around nudging them with his toe, saying, "Hey! Wake up!" But they were too worn out to respond. As we lifted our packs and set out up the trail, the worthy citizens of Sedua were just creeping into the sunlight to sit blearily on benches. The only sounds of life came over transistor radios tuned to Kathmandu—cheerful Nepali flute music.

Above Sedua we began to see *mani* walls—the first we'd seen in this part of Nepal—their stones deeply weathered, the ancient Tibetan characters traced by red and white finger-painted lines to make them more legible. The stones indicated that we were back in Buddhist country, the land of Tibetans, Sherpas, and related groups; they marked the ancient trade route from Tibet along the Arun Valley into Nepal and farther.

That route, like others I had looked at longingly, represented an ancient organic continuity based on geography, not on ideology. But ideologies rarely acknowledge landscape, and that is one of their chief failings.

After the Chinese invaded Tibet, the Sherpa people and related tribes found themselves cut off from their centuries-old trade routes. They themselves were Tibetan. They came from Tibet hundreds of years ago. Their lives were based on contact not with Nepal but with Tibet. Without that contact, hard times followed.

Ironically, what nearly ruined them might also have saved them. With Tibet closed, mountaineers began coming to Everest through Nepal, bringing money, Western equipment, and new ideas, and opening the way for thousands of trekkers who brought more of the same. Namche Bazaar, the central town of the Khumbu region, on the trail to Everest, is now a prosperous place. It has electric lights, comfortable hotels, and restaurants serving an amazing variety of food, considering that everything still comes in on the backs of porters. Much has changed from what Shipton and Hillary first saw in 1951 on the Mount Everest Reconnaissance Expedition.

Tashigaon, several valleys east of the bustling Khumbu, seemed firmly a part of the old Nepal, not the new. A frontier village, it stood at the limit of habitation. Beyond it, there was only a crude trail leading through forest up steep slopes, headed for the arctic zone of the high mountains. Tashigaon had been recently settled, and there had not been time (or the residents were too poor) to construct stone buildings. Instead, the houses were made of sticks and bamboo mats. They were hardly more than tents. Around them, newly hacked from the forest, terraced fields grew meager crops. What a contrast they were to the lush fields we had seen around Tumlingtar.

Norbu Lhomi's home was the only stone building in Tashigaon. It had three rooms—actually, an entryway at either end and one large room in the middle. The kitchen occupied a corner of that room. Cooking was done on an open fire with no chimney. When Norbu's wife lit a fire, smoke poured willy-nilly from a thousand holes in the bamboo roof. It was a smokehouse, nearly as dark during the day as at night, a home my Irish ancestors might have lived in before boarding their ships for the New World. But there was a difference. My family had left their famine-haunted country in despair, never wishing to return, eager only to find a better way of life in America. For Norbu, however, Tashigaon was the New World, the frontier of opportunity. He had no reason to leave. He had the best house in Tashigaon, a flock of chickens, a buffalo, and his business—Norbu was getting into tourism, and the world was coming to him.

Not that very many people came this way. Tashigaon was hardly a Namche Bazaar, but here Norbu's was the only show in town. If you wanted a meal, it was Norbu's kitchen. If you wanted a campsite and a place to store surplus gear for a week, it was Norbu's yard and Norbu's attic. Lucky for him: in the shined-up, prosperous, competitive atmosphere of Namche Bazaar, Norbu would never have made it, not with his primitive smoke-box of a house and filthy yard and the vile *rakshi*—a distilled native liquor—that he was so eager to sell.

It really was horrible *rakshi,* and Norbu himself was a rascal, but to us it was all part of the charm. Norbu made me feel we had gone beyond the limits of society. So what if he charged eight rupees for a pancake? We paid it. He had a sackful of dried food he had bought (or pilfered, he was that sort of guy) from an expedition to Makalu. He laid it out proudly in front of us on a bamboo mat—dried soup, chocolate bars, and granola cookies. He overpriced it by a factor of three and refused to bargain. But we bought some of it. We bought it and sat in the inky black gloom around Norbu's hearth drinking his revolting *rakshi* and *chang* as fast as he could pour it, while his wife, a pretty, soot-covered young woman, cooked dal baht for us.

We sat on a bench with our backs to a rough, stacked-stone wall, a rickety table before us. One candle lit the room, with help from the fire, which was built in a corner on the floor. Behind the fire, two shelves covered with wood ash held pots and spices. Above the fire a row of baskets hung from beams that gleamed with smoke varnish. The hand-hewn beams were so black they looked to be made from blocks of anthracite. Our gang of porters sat on stools near the fire, helping Norbu's wife as she juggled aluminum pots on and off the three stones that served as a tripod over the flames.

The rest of the room was a smoky mystery of shadows, parcels, boxes, plastic jugs, and metal pots. From one corner came the *chang,* served to us in an aluminum pitcher for two rupees per glass. Another pitcher held the hot *rakshi,* which soon became too much of a man's drink for any of us.

The house's attic was being used for storage. A log with notches carved in it served as a stairway. Norbu's wife ran nimbly up and down it in her bare feet carrying food containers. The two entryways were also in use. One held a sheep that bleated sadly every minute or so. The other held a small crowd of Norbu's friends, who sat wrapped in blankets laughing and drinking and coughing their tuberculosis into the smoky air. Every so often someone with a flashlight would go into that room to deliver more *chang* and I would glimpse the huddled, happy drinkers. I counted a total of twenty-one people in the house that night.

And then there were the animals: two dogs, two cats, and a swarm of kittens sneaked around underfoot poking their noses into various containers. For the most part, Norbu's wife ignored them, occasionally turning to whack a probing snout with her cooking ladle. Once a noisy dogfight erupted under our bench. Lifting our legs, we went on eating as Norbu's wife took a bamboo stave and jabbed violently under the bench, routing the dogs, who wailed and snarled out into the entryway, igniting an uproar among the drinkers, who in turn threw the dogs back into the main room. Again Norbu's wife went after them with her stave. Leaping and howling, the dogs made for the other door and were gone.

The lord of this teeming house, Norbu played host. He wore ivory earrings and a knitted wool cap. The earrings shone in the firelight. So did his teeth when he smiled, which was often. He sat on a stump dandling his three-year-old daughter on his knee, calling for more *chang* when he saw an empty cup and telling stories. He had seen a yeti, he said, several years before. It was November, late in the day just before dark. He was going over Shipton La when he saw the yeti coming his way. It was taller than he, with a sloping forehead, and covered with dark grey hair except for a lighter patch on its lower back. It walked on two legs. Was he afraid? "No," Dawa translated. "Norbu shouted and it ran away."

Norbu looked at the fire and smiled, enjoying the effect his story had on us.

Yeti might exist only in the subconscious, but I hope that they survive forever and that no one ever finds a real one.

THE NEXT DAY, we climbed 4000 feet. The way led through forest the entire distance on a steep, no-nonsense trail, sometimes requiring hands as well as feet, to a fine campsite on the ridge crest just above treeline. Ahead we could see the ridge climbing higher, blocking Makalu from view. Our attention was drawn far to the east, where Kanchenjunga, the third-highest mountain in the world, stood on the border of Nepal and Sikkim. After all other peaks had gone grey, it still glowed fiery beneath a mane of cloud. Other peaks, toward the northeast, we reckoned to be in Tibet.

It was soon dark. We ate supper in the pale light of a crescent moon lifting above the mountains, an ocean of clouds at our feet, ridges stepping down into the whiteness like the arms of fjords dipping into the sea. Jupiter perched high in the sky. The dull reverberation of breezes moving against mountains filled the night with sound. It was hard to believe that a continent of eight hundred million people was out there, invisible behind the mist. I felt perched on the rim of the world. Land's End. Nothing beyond here but dragons and sea monsters and clouds rolling to infinity. From this viewpoint, we would be the first to see the intergalactic ships speeding with comet tails down from space. Lights blinking. Rockets firing. Bringing the biggest news of all time.

In the morning the clouds were gone, but now smoke filled the valleys—the grey shroud of India rising into Nepal, whose people added their own smoke to the pall. But above us and around us the air was brilliantly clear. Climbing the ridge crest like a dragon's back into that dark blue sky, I came once again to a view of Makalu—quite a bit closer than the last time I'd seen it at Num, but still a long distance away. As I sat on the sharp rocks among dwarf rhododendrons, David appeared in the company of a little black female dog. She had been hanging around Norbu's place, but she belonged to no one as far as we could tell. She survived by scrounging any sort of food and, lacking food, would eat what I will call—in deference to her because she really was a nice dog—night soil. This earned her the nickname Porta Puppy. Apparently, she meant to come with us into the high country.

Soon the porters arrived, saw us resting, and laid their loads on the ground beside us. Latchu's transistor sang, "It's the biggest taste you'll ever find. Coke is it." I borrowed the radio and flipped the dial to BBC World Service. The news. Palestinians flying motorized hang gliders had attacked an Israeli base near Lebanon. A typhoon had hit the Philippines; hundreds were dead. There were student demonstrations in Dacca. A terrorist had been arrested in Japan for blowing up an airliner. World stock markets were still spinning from the October crash.

That was all down there in the smoky haze—beneath the haze, coming up to me like distress signals from a former life. Looking up from the radio dial, I could see the stupendous presence of Makalu shining above rocky crests. For the present, that was my reality, the only one I cared about.

Dawa arrived with two bamboo wands. From his pack he added two bright prayer flags, mounting these on the stone cairn that marked this point on the ridge.

"You're a Buddhist, Dawa?" I asked.

"All Tamangs are Buddhist," he said.

But it wasn't only Buddhists who honored the power of this landscape. In Num we had hired a Hindu porter whom Jeff knew from previous trips in the Arun region. Actually it might be more accurate to say that he adopted us, for he was an older man, a grandfather named Ed Bahadur Basnet, and his steady competence made me feel well taken care of. As he came to the pass, he picked two clumps of rhododendron leaves and, bowing toward Makalu, stuffed them into the cairn beside the Buddhist prayer flags. Honor the mountains, say the holy men, for they are the gates to God.

From there, the trail followed the spine of the dragon's back, up and down, almost always on the sharp crest. We came to a lake held in a rocky cup, a perched basin where the ridge on either side plunged away into smoky depths. From the lake, we climbed again, to Shipton La itself at 13,536 feet, then past another lake and up over a third pass, finally entering the valley of the Barun River.

From the time we had begun climbing to Shipton La, way back at the swinging bridge over the Arun, I had been wondering why the trail made such an arduous climb—more than 10,000 vertical feet—only to drop back down 4000 feet to the Barun River Valley. Why not follow the Arun to its junction with the Barun and then climb up with the Barun to Makalu? Our only real worry on this trail was the weather. This late in the year, a snowstorm could trap us on the Barun side. It had happened, in fact, a month earlier, on October 19, as a result of the same storm that had grounded our plane in Chandigarh. A party of trekkers had been snowed in at the Barun Valley for three weeks with only a week's worth of food. What a surprise for people on a scheduled holiday!

Worse yet, a European trekker had tried to force his way over the pass during that storm. He and two Nepali companions died in the snow—suffocated in a snowdrift, according to Dawa.

On hearing these stories before we set out, I had thought that we could, if trapped, beat our way down the Barun Gorge, staying in forest until we reached the well-traveled paths along the Arun. But now, seeing the terrain in question, it became obvious why the trail went by way of Shipton La instead. The valley was a sharp-cleft gorge filled with dense forest—a place of deep, impenetrable ruggedness. Separated by knife-blade ridges and cliffs, ravines scored the canyon walls. There was no flat ground. Not even moderate ground. We might force a way through to the Arun River, but it would require mountaineering skills and a number of days to go a distance that could not have been more than fifteen miles.

Even the existing trail was a rough go, requiring complete attention to where I placed my feet. Concentrating on the path, I forgot about my surroundings until Porta Puppy, padding along behind me, stopped suddenly and barked for all she was worth, provoked by something strange in the forest, something she had heard or smelled. Her nape hair rose, her legs went stiff, her lip curled. I couldn't see anything.

Naturally, after Norbu's stories the night before, I thought of yeti. It seemed likely that if yeti or other unknown creatures existed in the Himalaya, they lived in valleys like this one. Where better than in a forest of rhododendrons, with their eccentric shapes, smooth, muscular skins, and flamboyant flowers? They aren't ordinary trees. You expect unusual things to live among them.

But never mind yeti. There are creatures equally wonderful that certainly do live here—snow leopards, red pandas, giant flying squirrels, goral, serow, tahr, and birds with fabulous colors and fabulous names, such as chestnut-headed tit babblers, scaly-breasted wren babblers, yellow-naped yuhinas, and orange-rumped honeyguides.

That evening, I talked to Dawa about snow leopards and told him about the badly tanned skins I had seen in Lhasa's Barkhor selling for about ten dollars. I wondered if he had ever seen the live animal, and he said no.

"Tomorrow," I told him, "I'm going to look for yeti tracks."

"Maybe up there," he said, "above the trees, you might find some."

"You've seen a yeti?"

He laughed at me as if he'd been waiting for me to ask. I told him that I had heard in Tibet about amorous female yeti coming into buildings looking for men.

"That's a good story to hear," he said.

He wouldn't let me nail him on his opinion. "Do they live here?"

"I don't know."

"Do they eat animals? Sheep or dogs?"

"Maybe yak. In Khumbu they take the horns and rip open the skull and eat the brains. And they drink the blood."

"So you do believe in them!"

He just laughed harder and shook his head. I imagined how I would react if he came to Wyoming and asked me about the Easter Bunny.

"How does it hop with a basket in its paws?"

"Well, it's quite big, Dawa."

"Where does it get the eggs?"

The next day, we started up the Barun Valley, Makalu presiding over the entire scene. I was reminded of western Canada in November—frozen ground, matted brown vegetation, campfire smoke coming across the meadow in frosty air. The trail was a beautiful one to be walking: sometimes a grass-covered path barely discernible from the untrodden ground on either side, always a sensible, efficient route, and often marked by signs of the times—food wrappers, cigarette packs, butts, cans, tampons, wads of toilet paper, plastic bags, film boxes, and other assorted foreign detritus, symbols of the all-pervasive dominating world culture of which we were also a part. We left behind no visible trash, but I knew our passage through Nepal was not without impact.

That night a half-moon shone bright on high, fluted snow peaks. Waterfalls froze in ribbons of ice that glowed in the moonlight. While cooking supper, we hashed over our plans and options, and our group began to splinter—not unhappily, but we wanted to move at different speeds. Having arrived near treeline, Pat, Baiba, and Jeff suddenly had springs in their legs and a strong desire to get on top of something. At the same time, I slowed down. My heart was full right there. Even walking was too fast a motion. I wanted to go a few hundred yards and sit on a boulder in the sun, then walk on a little bit and lie in the grass, maybe see one of those tit babblers or yuhinas.

Accordingly, the three mountain sprinters took off the next morning with Chandra and Gyen, headed for a high ridge above the Barun Glacier, hoping to climb a relatively low, unnamed mountain on the Tibetan border. Two of the porters headed home at this point, no longer needed, and the rest of us loafed along at the happy pace of bird watchers and flower gazers.

First, we sluggards—David, Jane, Wendy, Marie, and I—took an entire day off. I spent half of it flat on my back watching clouds worry at the various mountain peaks and the other half following faint paths in the forest, kept company by brisk, chattering winter wrens.

The next day we headed up the valley again. Within an hour the trail came out of the forest and entered the alpine zone of pure extremes—the sky impossibly blue, the peaks too brilliant to look at, and shadows black. The sun on my back was hot; my chest was cold. As I walked between sheer, glacially smoothed granite walls, the right side was alive with waterfalls, thin streamers plunging 1000 feet or more. Ice formed from falling mist during the night hung in curtains beside the moving water. As sun warmed the rock, the ice came loose and resumed its descent, clattering down the cliffs. But on my left, in the shade, all was hard, frozen, sunless rock. The valley was a Himalayan yin-yang: white-black, warm-cold, alive-frozen. I walked the boundary between summer and winter like a druid at sunrise, honoring the between-time, the time that is neither day nor night.

The trail climbed steadily over grassy boulders and small meadows with juniper growing knee high. A griffon vulture came close. I heard its wings shredding the air, wings seven feet across, and looked up to see its great silhouette. A thousand feet higher, two ravens tumbled over each other in the sky, barely visible. For a while, it was warm. But then the shadow of Peak 6 stretched across the valley, and with the sun gone, I put on a jacket and hurried up the path to keep warm.

Late in the afternoon I reached an old *mani* wall whose tall prayer flags flapped in a cold wind, a north wind blowing from Tibet—Tibet, just over the mountain crest, an unbreachable wall protecting a land once again closed to us. The October riots had led to a cold winter of Chinese repression, and the border was closed to mere tourists. In Kathmandu, we had met people who had been ordered out of Lhasa and Tibetans who had fled for their lives. They told terrible stories, and we had dropped any hopes of ending our trip in Lhasa.

Even so, I had a strong desire to look over the mountain divide. I thought about Gyantse, not far to the northeast. I pictured the mustard fields and the substantial country homes in the warmth of July, when we had seen them last. Now the fields of Gyantse would be brown, the poplars leafless, and the sky hard like a polished stone.

Dawa waited for us on a grassy slope beside a roofless stone hut: shepherds' quarters. While we pitched tents, Chandra and Gyen returned from helping Pat, Baiba, and Jeff to the ridge camp. I was cold, and I could hardly believe that they had spent a night higher than this, dressed so skimpily. They wore shirts with open collars, scarves wrapped around their heads and under their chins, pants, and Chinese tennis shoes. They readily accepted our spare tent for sleeping quarters, but they had only blankets and the ground was frozen. Wendy and I lay in our tent on insulating pads in down bags and wondered at them, as we wondered at so many displays of their cheerful toughness. They carried huge *dokos* filled with our gear. They strapped on top of them their own small bundles and led us around the mountains with big smiles. Their strength and resourcefulness could make me feel like a child.

Before dark I had climbed the ridge above camp, encouraged by expanding views of Baruntse Peak and the thought of finding animal sign. I had looked at all the likely bedding places, all the good patches of grass, but found no evidence whatsoever that wild animals lived there. It was perfect country for grazing ungulates, but it seemed barren of tracks, droppings, or beds, even in the best rock-sheltered lookouts, the sort of places where in Wyoming even the smell would have been strong. Here in Nepal, nothing.

Again the next morning I bundled up and took a walk before sunrise while the peaks caught the first light. The wind still blew, and even though I climbed hard, I was chilly sitting atop a scrub-covered knob. Above me, Peak 7 went from pink to orange to blinding white, while 3000 feet below me, in the Barun Valley, a pool of night drained steadily away into deeper gorges, and shoals of little birds raced by like shooting stars against the blackness.

That day, after a slow, sunny breakfast, we set off for Shershon, near Makalu base camp. We walked on white sand among rounded boulders. I felt like dancing. I couldn't take my eyes off the lower Barun Glacier, which tumbled over a turquoise icefall into a frozen lake. I was ecstatic and started waving my arms. I picked up a stick and flailed the air with it—uncontainable, unrestrainable euphoria. I might have shouted, but I was alone just then and I've stopped shouting at mountains. I don't know why I've stopped. I used to shout all the time when I was that happy. Now shouting makes me feel self-conscious, as if the mountains think I'm being foolish. But I feel just as happy as ever.

Shershon was a wide, boulder-strewn meadow located where the Barun Valley makes a turn from south to east and is joined by the lower Barun Glacier. We stayed for three nights, camped among fragments of old snow standing separate like so many bleached bones kicked down from the surrounding mountains: the great wall of Peaks 6 and 7, the symmetrical fluted snow cone of Chamlang, and the massive block of Peak 4. To the north rose Makalu, its awesome southwest face falling 11,000 vertical feet to the glacier.

Had we continued that way, we'd have had a long trek past Baruntse Peak to a col overlooking the Kangshung Glacier. Shipton, Hillary, and friends went up there in 1952 and looked over into Tibet. Just out of curiosity.

Pat, Baiba, and Jeff also had a look into Tibet. From their camp on the high ridge, in one long day, they got to the top of a snow peak on the border.

"What did you see?" I asked when they rejoined us the next day at Shershon.

"A lot more mountains," said Pat, like a man announcing he'd just found a pot of gold.

*I*T'S A PITY THAT MOUNTAIN CRESTS are so often used to define borders. A border cuts a range in half, denigrates the mountains by making them political symbols, and denies the logic of passes. What good is a pass if you can't cross it? I have a suggestion: draw alpine borders as DMZs, Dedicated Mountain Zones. Make them fifty miles wide. Allow everybody in, regardless of nationality, but don't let anyone live there. Allow no machines, no weapons, no lumbering, no mining, no hunting, no bagging of museum specimens. It would be open land, free and wild, far removed from military and industrial ambitions. Borders would become refuges for plants, animals, and people in search of meaning, or adventure, or sanity, or God. I know the idea is a fantasy. A wild one. It would be Shangri-La. Fairies would live there.

Shipton was lucky to have been in these mountains at a time when passes were open, and he made good use of the opportunity. He wrote in *The Mount Everest Reconnaissance Expedition 1951:*

> The exploration of unknown peaks, glaciers and valleys, the finding and crossing of new passes to connect one area with another, is the most fascinating occupation I know. The variety of experience, the constantly changing scene, the gradual unfolding of the geography of the range are deeply satisfying, for they yield a very real understanding, almost a sense of personal possession, of the country explored.

When he wrote that, he had just finished what was for him a rather casual journey from the Sherpa town of Namche Bazaar westward across the divide into Tibet, past a stunning, fang-shaped mountain he named Menlungtse, into the gorge of the Rongchar River, and back to Nepal. You can't even think of taking that route today, not unless you're willing to go as a guerrilla and risk the consequences of being caught by Nepali or Chinese soldiers.

For myself, I was content to wander through the immediate valley, climbing the dry ridges and poking along the tops of moraines. For three days the weather stayed perfect: light winds, a clear sky, easy walking on old, hardened snow. Often I would sit in the sun, my back against a boulder, my face to the mountains, astonished that in all that enormous landscape there should be no sound, only the portentous silence of a stage, set and ready. It seemed that if I stayed there long enough, something was bound to happen. Something really interesting.

One night, just at sunset, the mountains played music for us. From out of the calm silence there began a mighty rumble, a deep, heavy tone that seemed to come from all sides. Avalanche? Earthquake?

Wind. When it hit our camp, it nearly flattened the tents, threw bits of equipment across the boulders, and raced on. For some minutes later, we could still hear it reverberating against the summits, like vibrations in some colossal rigging. Then it was gone entirely, leaving a calm night and clouds of dust muddying the atmosphere.

Something else came by in the night. Porta Puppy waked me up yelling bloody murder. Pat and I both climbed out of our tents to look. We shone lights around but saw nothing, and in the morning the rocks revealed no clue. Compared to the dog we were blind men.

One morning, a hundred or more little birds—nondescript things that I hadn't been able to see at close enough range to identify—came swirling around our tent, prompting me to climb out of my sleeping bag. Pat, who had been up for a while, was sitting in a rocky niche out of the wind, holding his camera, waiting, watching dawn move slowly across the snowfields. I stood up, looked his way, and saw a flash of a grin. A bit later, as I worked over the stove and mentioned coffee, I heard him chirp from the rocks, "Coffee? Coffee?" Pat was happy. He was in the mountains, and the light was nice, and it was hard for me to remember how much he had disliked places such as Srinagar in the rain.

As the sun hit our tents, the flock of birds returned. Holding a mug of coffee in both hands, I stood close enough to hear a hundred bills tapping on the frozen ground. The birds reminded me of the snow buntings that came through Yellowstone each fall, little white birds dancing in the air, lingering in frozen meadows for a few days, and then vanishing. These Himalayan birds behaved in the same way, clearly not intending to stay for long. They moved the way a sand dune moves—the birds on the trailing edge fluttered over the heads of the others to become the leading edge, so there were always birds in flight and always birds tapping.

The bird shoal was oblivious of me as I stood, still as a post, putting out steam from breath and coffee mug. I thought the flock would flow past my feet, but within ten feet of me the flow shifted sideways and flutter-tapped away. When I lifted my mug to take a drink, the entire flock lifted off as one creature in a whir of little wings over my head. I thought of snow flurries. I thought of a field of grey stones suddenly lifting into the air and sailing away. The birds were the color of stones. They could pass for stones if they sat still.

Each evening the moon rose later and larger until, one day from full, it came over the high ridge across the valley, climbing into view in a startling way that seemed it would tip over the edge and roll down on us. As it rose, something in the middle of a black rock face—ice, I guessed—caught the light. It could only have been a reflection, but it looked like a doorway mysteriously opened to a bright world, daylight coming from the heart of the mountains. In Pakistan we'd have looked wisely at each other, marked the spot in our minds, and said, "Fairies."

My home in Wyoming, I knew, would feel much the same at this time of year—cold air, bright moonlight, and gleaming snow. But instead of fairies there would be very real elk bugling in the meadows, and we would hear their hooves pounding the frozen ground, and the elk cows would be mewing and sending puffs of hot breath into the moonlight as they ran the bulls in circles, and they all would be holding their heads high and prancing with excitement.

The thought made me eager to be home, but at the same time I knew that if I stayed away much longer, I could easily slip across a boundary, a sort of emotional divide, and stay away for years. Lots of people do that. There is always more to see, another place, another goal, until moving becomes a way of life and the concept of home expands to include the entire world. If I kept going, I wondered, would I eventually return to Wyoming as a traveler, not ending a journey there, but just passing through?

When it came time to leave Shershon, we were down to a party of six—Pat, Baiba, David, Jane, Wendy, and I—with five porters and Dawa. A day earlier, Ed Bahadur had gone off with Jeff and Marie, who were hurrying to keep an appointment with fresh fruit on the beaches of Thailand. The porters loaded their nearly empty *dokos* and stood around laughing as I gave each of them a Polaroid print of himself in front of Makalu. There was one bright hat in the group. This was passed from head to head to add dignity to each photo. Rather than cajole them into laughter or casual postures, I let each man decide how he wished to be represented. They all stood formally! When that was finished, we crunched across the skeletal snow that was too bright to look at and headed down the glittering sands of the Barun River.

15
Kanchenjunga Idyll

There is a power lurking in these Himalayas greater than any man.
———William O. Douglas,
Beyond the High Himalayas

THREE DAYS AFTER LEAVING the base of Makalu, I lay in warm, brown grass by the small, rock-rimmed lake near Shipton La. The sun was bright up there on the ridge while beneath us brooded a vast unbroken cloudbank. It might be raining down below, and I was in no hurry to find out.

As I lay there, an archetypal scene materialized in the form of a line of expedition porters who climbed out of the clouds and sat down to rest by the lake. They were followed by a team of Polish mountaineers, who proudly announced to us their plans for a winter attempt on Makalu. Poles have become famous for their arduous winter ascents, and Baiba commented on this, saying, "It must be hard to be Polish. You're always climbing mountains in the winter."

"We have no choice," said their doctor, a burly man like the rest of them. "All the 8000-meter peaks have been climbed in spring and fall. But not all in winter. So we have to come in winter."

More porters arrived, 130 of them in all. Porta Puppy got excited at the wealth of opportunity and raced around begging for scraps. The expedition was well provisioned; this time, she got real food.

A big man with furry shoulders strode around a boulder. He wore red shorts and a T-shirt and had legs like tree stumps. "Women!" he said, opening his arms wide to Wendy and Baiba. "It's been too long!" He threw his pack to the ground. "Men's expeditions are no good. No women!" He went off through the rocks.

The doctor turned to us. "We call him Cow. He is a good man, a very strong climber, but just look in his eyes. Look in his eyes." True, Cow had a distinctly bovine expression. He came back with an open can of pork in his hand and his mouth full. "That one down the trail," he said. "Beautiful!" He meant Jane. "All these women going the wrong way. Why don't you come with us, hey?"

"I think it would be dangerous," said Baiba. "If you're already this way, what will you be like in another month?"

"In another month, Makalu is my woman. This winter, Makalu. She is cold, ya? But she looks good."

He dug into the pork with a pocketknife. "We call him eating machine," said the doctor. "Eating machine, ya?"

Cow grinned. "Ya." He finished the pork and waved the can at Porta Puppy. "She will clean it, okay? Washing machine!"

We left Porta Puppy with that happy bunch and dropped into the mists of the cloud forest. Although there was no rain, everything dripped. *Mani* stones glistened. Prayer flags held droplets in their weathered mesh. Moss, crunchy a week ago, had expanded and softened. The trail was slippery now. Trees loomed ahead as dark, contorted shapes. Then we were below the clouds in another world. I thought of the Hopi concept of worlds above worlds. We had left sunny mountains behind and, passing through a ceiling of clouds, entered a world where mountains were still big; but this world's mountains lay in the shadow of rain clouds and were covered with green plants. I could see tiny houses and terraces in clearings still thousands of feet below. One of the clearings was Tashigaon, where I arrived, as usual, in fading light. Dawa greeted me with a silly grin. He had been into the *chang*.

"Dawa, *chang!*" I said.

"Yes, sahib. You want *chang?*"

This batch was made from millet, not barley, and it was much better than what Norbu had provided on our first time through. We drank it with pleasure while Norbu's wife prepared special dal baht with curried chicken and lots of vegetables—a spiny thing like a cucumber called *chuchukarila* and a hot pepper called *iscou*. On top of it all, Norbu tossed a fried egg and, with evident delight, charged us a dollar a plate.

The next day we had a decision to make: where to next? Instead of going back the way we had come, to Tumlingtar, we thought about heading west toward the Khumbu Valley near Everest. We had almost settled on that plan when Dawa revealed that he knew how to buy his way into the closed area around Mount Kanchenjunga. He had done it the year before and was willing to try again. All of us had gazed wistfully at that great mountain from our camp on Shipton La, and the thought of getting close to it was very appealing.

I didn't really care where we went as long as we kept walking. Since the Barun Valley, something had happened to my sense of time. Even now, thinking back on those seven months of travel, I remember them in parcels of days—ten days in Lhasa, ten more to Kailas, six in Burang, twelve days in Hunza, eleven days trying to get past Srinagar, and so on. But in Nepal things had begun to blur in a most pleasant way, the passage of time dissolving into a series of events with no particular chronology.

The best memories of travel take the form of vignettes: snapshots from experience, moments you can hold separate and forever distinct from their context. As such, they transcend the process of travel; they rise above the itinerary to become symbols for larger feelings. This is how I recall the rest of the walk toward Kanchenjunga. We spent eight days on the trail, eight days following the footpath equivalent of back roads through farm country. The way led us from one valley to the next, past farms and villages, through forest, and across several sharp ridges. I can trace our route on a map now and put names to the geographic features, but at the time I quit paying attention to such details. Things happened every day, but I could scramble the order in which events occurred and it would make no difference to the way I remember them. Looking in my diary, I find that I stopped writing about miles, and hours, and days, and campsites. Traveling had become a simple process in which distance and time became meaningless.

A T TASHIGAON, THE SIX OF US—Wendy, Pat, Baiba, David, Jane, and I—along with five porters and Dawa, say good-bye to Norbu and head down the trail to Sedua, where things haven't improved much since we last saw it. Lice picking is now a big activity. People sit in the sun going through each other's hair or through their own clothing. A hen pecks insects from a sleeping dog's snout. The dog snaps, then lies back down. The hen returns for more. The dog sits up and looks balefully at the hen. In my heart, I cheer the chicken. Maybe the dog kept her awake last night.

From Sedua, the trail tumbles 3000 feet to the Arun River through flowering shrubs and rice paddies. People are out stacking rice sheaves on raised platforms. Each platform has a bamboo pole standing straight up from its center with a bundle of rice tied near the top as an offering of thanks. Men stand around the platforms heaving up stalks to a man who organizes the pile and stays with it as it rises until he is 20 feet in the air. Other men stand around piles of rice kernels on the threshing grounds. One man tosses unwinnowed rice on the pile as the others blow away the chaff with woven bamboo platters.

As they work they tell stories and joke. It is light work, and family work. Beside each threshing ground is a lean-to shelter where women keep their babies and have a fire to make tea.

Near the river, where the canyon walls steepen, we leave cultivated fields behind and walk for a while in the misty wildness of the Arun Gorge. A down-canyon wind blows water droplets into my hair. The river pounds along under the swaying suspension bridge, making me dizzy and euphoric at the same time.

A few hundred vertical feet up the muddy trail, river noise fades, to be replaced by the twitter of winter wrens. Deciduous trees are dropping leaves. The leaves are dry and crunchy; under them, the trail is soft mud. It's like walking on apple crisp.

Above the forest are more rice terraces, and there, in hot sunlight, we meet our former porter, Ed Bahadur Basnet, on his family threshing ground with a handful of helpers, three daughters, his wife, and his new son. New son? He is fifty-three years old, a grandfather several times, and still having sons, a fact that obviously gives him pride. He calls us over to his lean-to, where he serves us a strange mixture of instant coffee and Tang. We should stay in Num for the night, he says, so his wife can cook dinner for us. A special dinner. And yes, he'd be happy to come to Kanchenjunga with us. These other people can finish the harvest!

Climbing on toward Ed Bahadur's house, we join a party of threshers headed home after their day's work, each one bent beneath an enormous pile of straw. They are walking hay mows, and they climb very slowly, breathing hard and stopping often. One man is a half-wit. Setting down his load, he gyrates his hips, singing what I take to be bawdy songs, and capers around his friends, who are all much amused and show it by taunting him.

Supper is very good. Served with great care by Ed Bahadur's family on their neatly kept verandah, the food is accompanied by all sorts of relishes and spicy vegetables. Party food, it puts all of us in a good mood. Looking into the kitchen from the verandah at people gathered around the fire, I am struck by the beauty of faces in candlelight. Ed Bahadur's wife holds an oil lamp in her extended arm, gracefully supported by one knee. The light flickers on her face as she speaks. It is a classic, ancient scene, one that men have been admiring for ten thousand years.

That night, we camp in the schoolyard at Num. Clouds envelop surrounding peaks, leaving the sky above us clear and filled with stars. I lie in the tent trying to catch up my diary, often distracted by the sounds of the place, the music of rural life: far below, the Arun's stately roar; closer, from a cluster of buildings down the ridge, the lovely high voices of children singing. A buffalo bellows. A rooster crows. In a nearby house, a rice mill pounds with a steady beat.

The moon rises beside Orion over the smoky valley. There isn't a light to be seen for as far as I can see, and that is a long, long way.

Beyond Num, the trail goes down from autumn into late summer. Unharvested fields glow golden in the afternoon sun. The shrubbery is alive with cicadas, and later, in the dark, crickets sing. Bamboo bends gracefully over the trail. Homes take on a settled lowland look, more prosperous than the bamboo wind-sieves people occupied in Tashigaon. Evidently, life is easier down here.

But no less rowdy. By the looks of things, we have missed a formidable party in Devitar. The annual autumn bazaar has just broken up. A parade of people, half of them drunk and many still drinking, make their wobbly way back home. Others lie passed out on the trail, a few of them unconscious beside *dokos* full of empty wooden *chang* bottles. One woman sleeps beside her husband. As I come past and pause, she wakes, looks at me as though I were some apparition from a bad dream, and tries to rouse her man by whistling sharply in his ear and beating his shoulder. No response. I walk on and she collapses back into sleep.

There is something appealing about their drunkenness, something Dionysian about the way bodies lie strewn across the summer landscape, peacefully slumbering in shady groves or on stone benches or on the ground, untroubled by insects, wild beasts, or weather, unworried under the open, sheltering sky.

The farms in this area look as neat as gardens and are not much larger. Houses are made of mud and wattle, with thatched roofs and plastered floors. The owners use ocher-colored clay to paint the floors and halfway up the walls. When fresh, the paint makes the houses seem fastidiously tidy. Each cluster of buildings stands separate from its neighbors beneath banana palms and shade trees. Along bamboo fence lines grow abundant flowers: poinsettias, bougainvillea, and marigolds—important religious flowers for Hindus. Round stacks of rice sheaves await threshing. Hay has been neatly piled in helmet-shaped mounds on stilted platforms.

This tidy arrangement of structures sits amid perfectly constructed terraces. They are perfect because they have to be. They are rice paddies. They have to be flooded. Farmers use the water as a natural level; their terraces must hold water or there will be no rice. A farmer's crop, his livelihood, his family all depend on the perfection of his landscaping.

We make camp on the outskirts of Devitar. Soft clouds settle in around us.

Dogs bark a long way off in the black, lowland night. The air, warm and close, throbs with the chirr of crickets. Down in the village, as always, a rice mill thumps. I blow out my candle and there is nothing.

Back at Num, Ram left us to work on his own harvest. Having already agreed to come with us to Kanchenjunga, Ed Bahadur offered as a replacement a friend of his from Num. But the man is no porter, and after one day he decides that this isn't the job for him. Ed Bahadur does not want to go on without his friend, so they both quit. We say good-bye to the old man with some regret. He has the ability to make anything he does an act of dignity, be it bouncing his new baby or serving as a porter. I miss him immediately.

However, Chandra has a solution. He announces that he has acquaintances in Devitar and promises to recruit two new porters. This morning he shows up with a powerful hangover and, not two, but a small crowd of applicants. Now that the autumn bazaar is finished, everyone wants to work. There is a long discussion in Nepali, and finally two men pick up the two loads. Then one of them gives his load to a third man. There is more talk. Heavy negotiations, opaque to us. Finally it is settled and we begin walking, only to have everything come apart at the edge of town. More discussion. Unable to help, we tourists continue while Dawa sorts things out. Two hours later, he catches up with us in the company of two virtual twins named Bir Bahadur Rai and Rai Bahadur Rai. Rai wears a T-shirt that reads "I'm looking out for No. 1." The shirt is his credential, so to speak, of having portered for foreigners.

The seasons change with altitude. As we follow trails from ridge tops to valley bottoms and back to ridges, we pass from autumn to summer and back again. At Devitar, the harvest has just finished. In the valley 500 feet below, it is just beginning. Bent in Biblical reaping postures, entire families cut their way through stands of rice. Their sickles have tiny teeth. Each stroke cuts a sheaf. Each sheaf is laid gently behind the cutter with the same care a gardener would give to a bunch of roses.

Enjoying the scene, Wendy and I lag behind the rest of our little caravan. We come to a fork in the trail. One branch goes uphill; the other goes down. Wondering which way our friends have gone, I wave to a family of harvesters and, with a questioning expression, point at the upper trail. Half their hands go up and the other half gesture down. Which is it? I point to the lower trail, and they all change—those who gestured down now gesture up, and vice versa. I think these people are hopelessly confused; then I realize that Wendy and I are standing separately on each of the trails. All those people are signing to one or the other of us, while both of us are signing back. I climb up to join

269

Wendy, and that brings the harvesters into unanimous agreement: take the lower trail!

———————

Coming to a house near Shabun, we meet the wife of Dilli Man Shrestha. She sells us bananas, three for a rupee. Seeing us there, Dilli Man comes from the house with a jug of *moi,* buttermilk, as a gift. Baiba has a particular affection for *moi* and, seeing her pleasure, Dilli Man calls to the house for more. That brings out the whole family to greet us. After we have drunk, he asks us to take their picture, so we follow him to the house past a stilt barn with two cows tethered underneath. The tidy farmstead displays a wealth of goods, almost all of which are handmade—rakes and churns and plows and chicken cages and many other tools. The family, about twenty people, gathers around while the old couple pose in two chairs brought out just for the occasion. On his lap, Dilli Man holds a large portable radio—a sign of prosperity—and tries to keep his composure in spite of the capering crowd. Pat, David, and I form an impressive photographic firing line. I take eight pictures. The series begins with a sober-faced man staring straight into the camera beside his equally serious wife; it ends with him struggling to contain his laughter while his wife smiles broadly. I think he would prefer the first picture, but I like the last one.

I have read that the hill country of Nepal was where the first farmers settled and is the most suitable for agriculture. Population pressure has forced people higher to places such as Tashigaon, where people struggle to make a living from resistant ground in a resistant climate; or lower, onto the plains at the base of the Himalaya, where the soil is good but malaria and other diseases thrive. It comes as no surprise, then, that in these relatively gentle hills, I get the sense of an ancient economy still intact, a sense of people living in their landscape in ways that could be sustained for generations to come. There are forests here and strict rules to prevent too many trees from being cut. There are hedgerows and wild tangles of shrubbery in the ravines, providing habitat for birds and wild animals—fat on the land, a sure sign that the farms provide enough. In so many other places throughout the Himalaya, I have seen no such luxury; every square foot of soil is tilled, no matter how steep or stony.

This lovely, balanced landscape gives me a good feeling. I wonder how it must be for a man to look out across the terraced fields of his home valley and know that was how it looked to his grandfather—and to assume that, long after his death, his grandchildren will sit in the very same place on the same old stone porch smelling the same air and thinking the same thoughts.

Most of us have no way of knowing how that would feel, immersed as we are in this world where rapid change is the only thing of which we can be certain. We are accustomed to staring at old photographs, trying to divine something of commonality with the recent but so different past. I have only a vague notion of what my grandfather saw and only a fantasy of the world my grandchildren will know. We think we are rich, but we've lost knowledge of our past and are blind to our future.

From Shabun, we angle across a long slope toward a ridge. In the courts of tiny houses, women are beating the seeds from millet heads with sticks. Whack, whack—the sound comes from all directions, up and down the gentle hills. Bougainvillea and poinsettia, purple and red, grow beside neatly trimmed trees dotted with bright tangerines. Entire hedges consist of nothing but marigolds. Heavy bundles of corn in husks hang from the eaves of houses. Big, rust-colored roosters prance on stone walls and stretch their necks. Some houses are old, generations old, with elaborate wooden railings and window grilles and baked-tile roofs. Others, built more recently, have cleaner lines, like desert adobe structures where clay and brick take the place of wood.

In a small field, a man is plowing with two cows and no whip. Talking quietly to the animals, he directs them back and forth. They obey perfectly. Rice stalks turn under the wooden blade, revealing soft, dark soil. Nearby, a lettuce garden grows in the protection of bamboo fencing beneath poinsettia bushes the size of small trees. Their blossoms are sharp flames in the misty morning hills.

Later, the mists rise, replaced by smoky haze. The air grows hot. Cicadas scream from tree tops. Termite casings, little earthen tunnels built above ground so the insects can stay in the dark, cover everything wooden—benches, door frames, fence posts, even the trunks of live trees. I break a tunnel open with a stick and there they are, streaming white insect corpuscles, the pale ghosts of the underworld.

One day, at noon, we come to Shimbuwa. At first it looks to me like a museum replica of a town, the sort of display you find in a historical reconstruction showing how people used to live. It is located on the spine of a ridge, approached through an avenue of pipal trees, a simple place comprising six houses and a Hindu temple arranged neatly around a flagstone courtyard. Second-story verandahs are decorated with rows of potted geraniums and hanging bunches of corn still in husks. There is one neat shop tended by a woman wearing a gold nose ring and a bright red sari. A woman in a bright green sari emerges from a house with four goats on a tether, as if taking them on a walk to the park. Four white-haired men sit on a bench with walking sticks while chickens scratch at their feet. Living history, the museum would call it, and as in a museum, it seems at first a bit too neat and contrived.

But Shimbuwa's people are sullen enough to change that image. No one will talk to us. Wendy and I sit on the edge of the courtyard having a snack. A barber cuts children's hair as parents bring their children to him. One child objects. The mother holds the boy while the barber cuffs him. The boy squirms all the more, the barber cuffs, the mother holds tight. I peel dirty rind from an old piece of cheese, letting the rind drop on a garbage heap at my feet. Chickens come by and fail to spot the cheese; so after eating, I pick up one piece of rind and toss it directly to a rooster, which begins pecking at it. A boy, watching, beats the rooster away with a stick. A smaller boy beside him makes a motion toward the rind. Glancing my way, the older boy restrains his brother. In the shock of realization, I look away but nonetheless see the older boy reach quickly for the rind, turn his back to me, and share it with the smaller boy. Embarrassed, Wendy and I pack up and hurry down the trail.

Children everywhere. The path is lined with children. There are always children. They shout at us from a distance: "*Namaste!* What eezoor name?" At each stop, a small clutch perches beside the trail on a wall or the bank of a terrace, raggedly dressed, grinning, the shy ones hiding behind the bolder ones. Little girls carry tiny brothers and sisters, even the tiniest of whom cling with the grasp of marsupial babies. Some children hold sugar cane, which they gnaw with bright teeth. Each group, it seems, includes one child suffering from a visible ailment—conjunctivitis, scabies, an imperfectly healed injury, clubfoot, kwashiorkor.

Late one day, it is raining. The trail crosses a desperate bridge hung from two heavy parallel chains attached to spikes driven into rocks on either side of the river. From the chains, loops of wire support a single line of planks eight inches wide, 150 feet long, greasy from the rain, and looking half rotted like all the other wood in the area. The chains are deeply pitted by rust. Some day a link will break, or a heavily laden foot will smash through a plank, and it will have to be repaired. Until then, walking on it is a sort of roulette.

As the rain increases, we stop under the twin trees of a stone rest. Big, black-and-white storks sweep in to stand around a rice paddy like nineteenth-century gentlemen attending a garden party that none enjoy. They hunt desultorily for frogs the way the same gentlemen would pick at little sausages on trays. Wendy goes down for a closer look and they all take wing, beating slow circles uphill past the stone rest where David and I stand. The birds have heavy, black bills held authoritatively forward. "I have an aunt who has the same profile," says David.

———

We arrive in the morning at Chainpur, a peacefully busy town where two streets join to make a shopping district. One street is lined with brass factories, where the proprietors are putting last touches on cast bowls, cups, pitchers, bells, and other utensils. In back rooms, small fires burn and women melt wax from clay forms. No one is pouring brass that day, which is unfortunate. I'd welcome the heat of forges, for Chainpur on its ridge is a damp, chilly place. Farther along, we come to general stores each selling identical merchandise— matches, batteries, school notebooks, soap, glucose biscuits, candles, Nescafe, cough drops, stale toffees, glass wrist bangles, instant noodles, plastic jewelry, hair oil in numerous scents, and Chinese tennis shoes. We purchase a pair of shoes each for Bir and Rai, our newest porters. For ourselves, we scout hungrily for something to vary our bland trail diet. David finds a bakery and samples a few items. "This is okay," he says, biting into a jelly tart. "And this one isn't bad at all," he adds, handing me half a sugar cookie. "But this!" He spits out a mouthful and tosses an oily donut to a dog. "If you served that in an American restaurant there'd be a fist fight."

In the end, we settle for dal baht and fried potatoes at a combined restaurant, hotel, and store where it takes, as usual, two hours to prepare the meal. I don't mind the wait. I'm not counting time, and I like the cook, a charming eighteen-year-old girl named Sazana. She has a quick ability for idioms. When I ask how long it will take to fix the meal, she says, "As soon as possible."

I say, "ASAP."

She gets it immediately. "Yes, ASAP."

This is Sazana's last year working in the family business. In a month, she will leave for university in Kathmandu. She is one of three girls in the district to have passed an entrance exam for university. It will be a two-year program for her B.A. Then what? "Then an M.A., in either English or economics. When I get my B.A. I will decide which is best for me." And then? "A Ph.D." But what does a Ph.D. do for a woman in Nepal? "I will be a lecturer at university."

While we wait, scarfaced dogs wage a street war. I push one away from me with a walking stick and immediately wish I hadn't. This animal is the canine Godfather. He erupts in snarling rage and attacks the stick. No cringing from this gangster of an animal. I can feel his teeth tearing the wood. Fearful that he will climb up the stick at me, I put it away and try to avoid his insane, glaring eyes. Sorry, pooch. Nice doggy. Down boy.

All day the clouds have been thickening. Now they rip open and the streets run with water. Chickens retreat. Ducks appear in happy squads. Our enthusiasm for the trail vanishes.

"I think it's better that you stay the night here," announces Sazana, rain beating a tattoo on the tin roof of her family's hotel. Upstairs are four eccentric midget rooms with midget beds and doorways that even I have to duck to pass through. That doesn't bother Sazana, who is less than five feet tall. She laughs at the way we bump our heads.

Night in Chainpur is anything but peaceful: dog wars in the streets, the hacking of tubercular throats from behind shuttered doors, the thump of the rice mill at three in the morning, noisy drunks walking home, children crying in the dark, an angry person hammering long and loud on a wooden door. Sazana's father comes up periodically to peer around the rooms with his flashlight as if checking for unauthorized sleepers. In the adjoining room, Gyen's cough is a continuous racking expletive. Still awake at midnight, David sits up, frustrated. He calls to Dawa, who occupies the bed next to Gyen. It takes a minute to wake Dawa.

"Dawa, the man coughing is keeping everyone awake. Could he move to the back room?"

"Someone is coughing?" says Dawa. He was sleeping soundly. Gyen moves to another bed, but even if he were two buildings away, we would still hear him.

At 5:00 A.M. Sazana's old man stomps through the rooms again, shining his light in our faces. Giving up, we light candles, pack our bags, and set off in the dripping mists of a clearing sky.

I climb hard on morning-strong legs toward the Milke Danda Ridge. A slight breeze blows, damp and cool, just enough to keep me from overheating. Up the slope I follow the trail past stone houses into scrubby, ruined forest where clearings hold bamboo huts of squatters on the margin of older settlements, their kids half naked, their existence tenuous.

By midmorning I am sitting in sunshine on a narrow point of rock looking into 3000 vertical feet of haze at distant houses and rice terraces when a lammergeier catches my eye. The bird drifts in the middle of that great space, sun glinting from its back. I can see its primaries fingering the wind, feeling for thermals, intelligently gauging the currents and adjusting to minute differences in the way the air moves. It feels strange to be looking down on an animal that is usually not much more than a dot in the sky.

When I reach the heights of Milke Danda, clouds have settled thickly on the ridge. Cold mist pours through the rhododendron forest, silencing all birds but the ravens. "Glonk," they say, sitting like cardboard cutouts in naked branches, or appearing ghostlike, suddenly, out of the clouds on spread wings. In the gnarled, moss-hung forest, the trail is a trench of pounded wet clay and boulders overgrown with cold green things, and the ravens are witches. They belong here. We do not.

Cresting the ridge, we descend the other side. Conifers stand darkly in the fog, and as I come over a rise I see, in a meadow beside a black pond, an elk. A bull elk. In an instant he is gone, and I know my mind has been wandering in Wyoming. Something about the smell and shape of the trail has made me expect to see an elk. Instead, there on the horizon, suddenly visible among lifting clouds, shines Kanchenjunga, dreamlike but absolutely real.

We halt that night in a tiny meadow beside the trail above a rude farmhouse. Latchu cooks dal baht for us all with vegetables he buys from the farmer. As we eat, the moonless night thickens. Dog barks seem muffled by the cottony dark. Later, jackals induce canine hysteria. Nearby, one jackal kills a chicken, which makes a lot of noise—but not as much as the useless dogs—and only the chicken has a legitimate reason to squawk.

Eventually we come to Taplejung, a district capital where we hope to extend our visas and trekking permits. With those extensions, our success in getting to Kanchenjunga will depend on Dawa's ability to persuade checkpost officials to accept gifts in lieu of proper permits.

"Isn't that bribery?" Jane asks.

"Think of it as charity," David tells her. "The guy could use a good pair of boots. Where else will he get them?"

But first, the police station. It is on the far edge of town, a compound with an arched gate and a garden where a horse grazes on the lawn. A sign over the gate reads *Topi Koi?* Where is your hat? As if to say to the policemen, "Are you in uniform?"

Despite that remonstrance, the police station is a loosely run place. Finding a clerk, Dawa speaks with him about extending our papers. The clerk nods, collects our passports, and takes them to a superior. While he is gone, we watch a Nepali-style disciplinary action in the garden. The scene is comic theater. It's hard to take seriously. The policeman being reprimanded stands with hands behind his neck while a short, stout man in civilian dress scolds him, hitting him sharply on the head with a cloth cap. The policeman answers questions and tries to duck the blows. Yes, he did get drunk last night. Yes, he kicked someone's clay water jug, and no, he did not mean to put a hole in it. Yes, it is a disgrace to the uniform and he is sorry . . . but that cap *hurts!*

When he can stand it no longer, the policeman hops around the garden, jumping fences and ducking behind little trees. In the end, the stout man ex-changes his cloth cap for a swagger stick and chases the poor yelping police-man over the hedge, out the gate, and down the lane. *Topi Koi?*

A few minutes later the clerk returns with our papers, shaking his head. He tells us that the king is coming to Taplejung in a few days, and no visas or per-mits will be extended until after His Majesty Birendra Bir Bikram Shah Dev has finished his visit. So sorry, all foreigners back to Kathmandu.

The king. Bad luck. In a country that works on greased palms, the appear-ance of incorruptibility becomes important only at certain times, such as a royal visit. A week earlier it would have been no problem. Even without per-mits we might deal successfully with checkpost officials beyond Taplejung, but there would be trouble when we arrived back in Kathmandu with visas ex-pired for three weeks.

Walking back through town we talk it over. There is an airstrip nearby. Al-ready halfway home in their minds, Pat and Baiba decide to fly out. Suddenly they are talking about the chance of being in Canada for Christmas.

I DIDN'T WANT TO GO. I wasn't ready for Kathmandu or home. This had happened too quickly. I was happily anticipating at least two more weeks of walking, two weeks that would take us back into the high country on a bit of an adventure, buying our way into an area closed to individual trek-kers. Now, faced with this sudden ending, I had the notion that we should go on somewhere, try to see one more place. I wasn't finished.

We had one option. Back in New Delhi, during a week spent running er-rands from Anil's house, we had gone to considerable trouble to arrange per-mission for a trek to the base of Kanchenjunga through Sikkim, the part of India adjoining Nepal on the east. Kanchenjunga straddles the border. You can approach it from either side. We had made this plan as a contingency in case the road to Lhasa was closed after the October riots—as it was. If we couldn't finish our circle by returning to Lhasa, we had decided Sikkim might be an acceptable alternative.

Those permits, if we decided to use them, would be waiting for us in Siliguri, India. Now, Wendy and I agreed that if we couldn't get to Kanchen-junga on the Nepal side, we should do it from Sikkim.

So the two of us said our good-byes at Taplejung that morning and, with Dawa, Latchu, Chandra, and Bir, made for the roadhead at Basantpur—three more days of walking to be followed by a bus ride to Siliguri.

Right away, we could see that this was a different sort of trail than the ones we had followed for the past three weeks. This was a major thoroughfare, the footpath version of a trucking route. A constant stream of traffic passed us, heading for the annual autumn bazaar in Dhoban. People carried loads of vegetables, tangerines, and rice. One man led a huge sow on a leash. Wet-nosed water buffalo came by, driven by little boys with sticks. I saw chickens confined in tight baskets with just their sharp-eyed heads sticking out; also piglets, black and sharp-toed, trotting along unsupervised as if they knew exactly where they were going.

Scattered among all that traditional material came porters carrying alien loads: ceramic insulators for the new Taplejung power line. The king's visit was intended to coincide with the arrival of water-generated electricity, an improvement that would change the landscape forever, especially at night.

I thought about that while camped halfway up a long, ascending trail surrounded by the comforting darkness beneath the stars. Electricity would bring lights to Taplejung. Children would find it easier to read at night. Education might improve. But, as in Hunza and Kashmir, all the fairies would disappear.

The next morning we walked uphill toward the ridge top through pastures wet with dew. At about 10:15 a Twin Otter airplane broke the silence over the ridge. We could hear it land at Taplejung. Fifteen minutes later it took off for Kathmandu carrying our friends. Returning to the rhythm of walking, I stopped worrying about the gathering clouds that might have prevented the plane from landing. I gave no thoughts to the garlic pasta and Star beer that Pat had said were first on his Kathmandu list. I didn't envy him. I told myself that flying back now was too sudden an end to the seamless continuity of the past twenty-four days.

In the forest, a light breeze broke brown leaves from their moorings; they crackled through naked branches on their way back to the soil, to the roots of the same trees they had come from, destined for reincarnation in a way that even I could understand. "But what is a leaf?" a Buddhist would ask. What is a leaf if not the universe?

The clouds gathered until, on the crest of the Milke Danda, just a little south of where we had crossed it five days before, it looked just the same—cold, dripping mist and glonking ravens. But this trail was a freeway. The biggest *doko* loads ever conceived staggered past, including a line of porters carrying heavy wooden boxes. It was medicine, said Dawa, forty-five kilos per box, more than a hundred pounds. Yet behind them lurched a group of heroes carrying two boxes each. They moved very slowly. This was their sixth day from the roadhead. Unladen people do the same walk in two days or less. I came across four of these stalwart porters standing on the trail, barely visible in the dense mist. They rested by standing still, supporting their great loads on the ends of walking sticks. They were like bison, I thought. The bison on a Yellowstone trail in a snowstorm, standing, just standing, resting enormous weights on legs that looked too small, heads down beneath the bulk over their shoulders, reluctant to move on, reluctant even to give me room on the trail.

On the other hand, a bison never smiled and said, *"Namaste."*

As befitted a trucking route, the way was lined with crude eateries—tea stalls and ratbag hotels (I picked lice out of my clothing after merely sitting in one for an hour) astride mud alleys running with sewage. They were the worst sort of places, murky dives where pigs rooted under tables of rough-hewn boards and porters with legs the shape of rhododendron burls shouted happy insults at sturdy proprietresses. None of the buildings were made of anything more substantial than bamboo mats. All proudly displayed stainless-steel dishes and plates in the smoky gloom, and all served identical fare on those dirty dishes. An evening spent in one of those hostelries should be worth five college credits in medieval history.

One such place, labeled "Turist Hotel," was in Gupt Pokar, where we arrived at dusk. We had thought of staying the night there, until we saw the village—a mean jumble of wooden shacks beside a black, evil-smelling pond. Children shat in soft mud tracked by bristling dogs and fast-moving chickens. We hurried on and camped in a clean meadow farther along. Looking across the broad valley, I could see a scar slicing a green slope; the boom of distant blasting augured the end of roadlessness. In five years, Dawa said, the road would reach Taplejung. Poor unsuspecting Taplejung. Its people probably thought the road would improve their lives. As for us, we could make Basantpur easily in one more day. I wanted to drag my heels.

Dawn brought a clear sky with a superb view of Kanchenjunga and its associated medley of peaks. The hillside where we camped was white with frost, as were our packs and the tent and the gnarled rhododendron roots in the bordering forest. As I sat in the doorway of the tent wrapped in a sleeping bag watching the sunrise, Latchu brought two steaming mugs of tea laced with chocolate. The steam fogged my glasses each time I lifted the mug. Gradually, darkness fled from the valleys below. The Kanchenjunga massif went from rose to yellow to white. The frost on my pack began to soften and drip, and by then I knew Latchu would have breakfast ready.

From there, the trail took us through moss-draped forest into clearings where we could see in one view both Kanchenjunga and Makalu—one to the east, the other to the west—standing clear in a cold winter sky.

And then abruptly we were at Basantpur, where the horn of a Tata truck about to leave for Dharan abused the air, and I suddenly decided that the problem with walking out and not flying was that you inevitably had to pass through a roadhead town, a frontier town, the end of every trail, the beginning of each new bus ride.

It was at Basantpur that I first began to think we had made a mistake.

Inquiring about the bus to Dharan, where we could catch another bus to India, I heard a great variety of opinion. The bus came, I was told, in the evening and left early in the morning. Or it came at six in the morning, or eight, or nine, or ten. I knew that in Asia there was a principle governing situations like that. If we were up at six, the bus would come no earlier than ten. But if we counted on ten, it would leave promptly, horn blaring, at six. Obviously, we had to be ready for the early departure, even though we knew that there would be no bus until midmorning. It was nonsense, but in Basantpur it made perfect sense. Accordingly, we sorted our gear, gave all the surplus to our Nepali friends, and set an alarm for five-thirty in the morning.

By eight the Asian Bus Principle was once again proven correct. No bus in sight.

But we were hungry and decided to take a chance on breakfast. I say it was taking a chance because breakfast is the hardest meal a foreigner can order in Nepal. The tradition there is to wait until ten and eat a huge brunch of dal baht. That meal lasts until evening, when another round of dal baht is served. It's an efficient way of eating—great quantities of the same food twice a day. Efficient but dull, and we'd had quite a bit of it in the past month. So I spoke to Nagindra Prasad Gimiri, the young man who ran the New Quality Hotel, where we had spent the night, and ordered fried potatoes and eggs, a Wyoming winter breakfast on my mind.

"*Alu?*" I asked. Potatoes?

Nagindra nodded. Nepali hill potatoes are always small and sweet and delicious.

"*Dimba?*" I asked. Eggs?

He pointed to a cabinet loaded with eggs.

"*Chura?*"

"Oh, yes," he indicated. "No problem." *Chura* is rolled rice, fried hot and fast. It puffs almost like popcorn.

Nagindra talked it over with his wife, and the two of them appeared to set to work. I went away for an hour. When I checked again, there were indeed potatoes chopped. Thirty minutes later, potatoes were being fried, uncertainly. But there was no *chura*. Sensing confusion, I called on Dawa, who consulted with Nagindra. A long conversation ensued. *Chura* came down from the shelf. There was more talk. An amazing amount of talk.

In Wyoming that day it was winter. Ranchers drove into Pinedale, at the base of the Wind River Range, to park in front of the Stockman Cafe. They drove pickup trucks with big, lugged tires that squeaked on hard snow. The trucks trailed plumes of vaporous exhaust that hung in the sub-zero air like independent smalltime thunderclouds. The ranchers, in pac-boots, jeans, and jackets of sheepskin, down, or denim, went into the Stockman, leaving their motors running.

Despite the cold, each truck would have a dog standing on hay bales or a toolbox. They all were big dogs. Each one held his tail high in the air and yelled insults at his neighbor. Inside, the ranchers ordered breakfast from a waitress who poured steaming coffee without having to ask if they wanted any. "Good morning, Jack," she'd say. "Keeping warm?"

"Mornin', Peggy. Steak and eggs, extra hash browns, would you? Yeah, it's a cold one."

But that was Pinedale. In Basantpur, Nagindra was washing two stainless-steel plates in water from the street. He dried them on a dingy towel hanging from a post. It was the same towel he had used to dry his face after shaving that morning. Whiskers came off the towel and stuck on the plates like grounds of pepper. Then he doled out fried potatoes, yellow with curry and only half cooked, omelettes cooked to a crisp, and *chura* that was just right. His wife poured tea. Seeing her put three spoons of sugar in my mug, I said, "*Bas, didi. Ali chini. Ali, ali.*" Enough. No sugar! Puzzled, she added another spoonful. "*Bas!*" I said. And she added half a spoonful more.

At the Stockman, ranchers were also dumping lots of sugar in their coffee.

16
Breakdancing and Bayonets

"Have you seen the snow leopard?"
"No! Isn't that wonderful?"
——Peter Matthiessen, *The Snow Leopard*

I could no longer suppress the desire to leave for Yoshino, for in my mind the
cherry blossoms were already in full bloom.
——Basho,
The Narrow Road to the Deep North

T HE BUS NEVER DID COME to Basantpur that morning. Instead, we
caught it at Shiduwa, an hour's walk farther down the ridge, and one
night later found ourselves inexplicably in Darjeeling, India.

Inexplicably because it was such a shock: why were we there? What were
we looking for, that would take us to this awful place? As if, after the perfect
walk we'd had through the peaceful hills of Nepal, there was something more?

Getting to Darjeeling had been a trial of Indian transport—buses, bicycle
rickshaws, taxis, and jitneys. What we found was a grim city getting grimmer.
There was a civil war on. I wrote in my diary:

Darjeeling: Privacy of the trail, freedom of open air gone. Now back in the
commotion of Asia, with my tolerance for it much tightened. In the high
cold air of the ridges I felt the open breath of Tibet. Seems impossibly distant from Darjeeling, impossibly rare.

The bus ride from Shiduwa had been the first shock to my system. After a month of walking, the roar of machinery had seemed brutal. Then came Dharan, a city where horns blared all night. We took a room—the "VIP Room" at the Evergreen Hotel, costing all of six dollars, an extravagant sum by the Nepali standards to which we had become accustomed—and slept poorly in the strange urban atmosphere. Cockroaches chirped in the bath. Others answered from under the bed. The hotel rooster, kept just below the balcony of our room, crowed constantly after 2:00 A.M. The hotel dog made the usual deranged canine racket from his position in the echoing central court. Mosquitoes buzzed our ears in their maddening dark-of-night way. I turned on an oscillating ceiling fan in hopes of driving away the mosquitoes and covering the noise, but the mechanical drone just burrowed annoyingly into my disturbed sleep.

Three o'clock came as a welcome relief. Hauling our packs to ground level, we found the doors padlocked from the inside, Asian style. This despite my having told the hotel staff that we'd be leaving at four. I took some pleasure in pounding on doors and shouting in the courtyard until the hotel owner, a sloppy, pot-bellied man, was forced out of bed with keys in hand. He had slept through, or ignored, twenty minutes of noisemaking as I could have learned only in Asia.

We endured four hours of riding on a hard bench seat from Dharan to the Indian border. Arriving there, we pushed through touts to Nepali customs, then took a rickshaw less than a mile to the Indian side, where we caught a bus to Siliguri. We got on that bus at nine-thirty in the morning, but it was a wreck that broke down several times. After an hour of stop-and-go, we abandoned it in heavy traffic for an auto rickshaw that buzzed along for four miles before entering a hopeless jam of vehicles.

In the next hour we covered a mile and were on the verge of walking when the rickshaw walla found a back alley and took us careening through mud and hovels on an obscure path to the Sikkim Tourist Office. There, a secretary told us that the man we needed to see—Mr. Adhikari—was out for an uncertain period. Stuck in the traffic, no doubt.

When he finally made it to the office four hours later, Mr. Adhikari turned out to be a young man who knew nothing about our permit. "Maybe it is in Darjeeling" was all he would say.

"But the permit was to be sent here," I said.

"It is not here."

There was a telephone on his desk. I suggested he use it, but he refused. "It is not my job to telephone Darjeeling. You must go there, I think, and see the deputy commissioner." A five-hour bus ride.

Back on the street, the traffic jam was as bad as ever. Trucks, rickshaws, cars, and buses idled at a near standstill; even foot traffic was backed up. Walking to the bus station, we pushed our way through a crowd of people trying to cross the Mahananda River bridge. The air was horrible. On the railway bridge stood three steam engines, also caught in the jam, their coal smoke blackening a sky already red in the early sunset that occurs throughout smoky India. Thousands of wood fires and charcoal braziers came to life until the earth itself seemed to exhale smoke. The fires burned in the murk of a shanty city below the bridge. Dim figures bent over them. Other people stood in the shallow water of the river, bathing their bodies, washing pots and pans, directing the movements of pigs and buffalo, or simply standing, motionless and gaunt, as though instructed by Dante: up to their ankles in water the color of fire, surrounded by gloomy vapors, with dense plumes of engine smoke rising above them into a flaming sky.

What was in Sikkim that could be worth this?

When we arrived there at eight-thirty that night, Darjeeling was a ghost town—streets deserted, inhabitants staying behind locked shutters. The bus wound uphill on narrow streets lined with concrete buildings dimly lit by naked light bulbs. The air was cold and tainted with coal smoke. I thought of northern England's industrial cities in winter. But for England to look this way, the clock would have to be turned back half a century and the streets gone over with an Indian brush: monsoon rot, huts of corrugated steel crowded one upon the other, Hindi script, the occasional lighted Hindu shrine.

By the time the bus came to its last stop, only four of us remained in the seats. One was Nawang, a man of Sikkimese parentage who owned a restaurant in Darjeeling. He had been telling us about "the troubles."

It was an independence issue between the Ghorka minority and the government of West Bengal, an enormous state that included Calcutta. The Ghorka National Liberation Front (GNLF) was demanding a separate state government. There had been protests and deadly violence. Bombs exploding. People killed. The government-run tourist bungalow blown up. Trekking huts burned. The army called in. Midnight arrests. Three hundred people had attacked a post on the border of Sikkim and burned it to the ground. Each side accused the other of terrorism. The Ghorkas had announced a boycott of the upcoming elections. Painted on walls were such slogans as "Welcome to Ghorkaland," "Bengal Is Not Our Master," "No State No Vote," and "Ballet Is More Powerful Than Beyonet."

Ballet? I think the painter meant "ballot," but I wished otherwise.

Politics in the mountains. I was tired of it. I wanted supper, but everything was locked up tight, with shop windows shuttered and soldiers patrolling the streets. Nawang hustled us to a hotel run by his friends, who unlocked a metal grate to let us in but refused to cook us a meal or even provide a pot of tea. There was no heat in the building. We ate some stale Nepali biscuits and went to bed. Late that night, I woke to the sound of explosions in the street and stirred myself long enough to find my ear plugs.

The famous foothill beauty of Darjeeling, it appeared, was a thing of the past. The once-wide streets had become overgrown with shanties. An area that had been a *maidan,* or square, was now a tight jam of tin-roofed sheds. People had squeezed into whatever space existed around the decaying British buildings.

The first human being I saw that day was a man pawing through a garbage pile in front of the hotel, probing for edible salvage. Then, raising my eyes, I noticed Kanchenjunga, its great, icy mass shining pinkly through the haze of coal smoke, as impossibly distant and improbable as the moon, a fantasy, the ultimate dream of high mountains.

At least the restaurants were open, and after breakfast we walked to the deputy commissioner's office, upstairs in an old colonial office building, where clerks hid behind walls of stacked paper. As in any Indian government office, ledgers, files, and stacks of receipts overwhelmed the desks and the workers. Surely somewhere in all that official material would be our permit.

Maybe not. As we came in, two American Peace Corps workers were talking with the assistant deputy commissioner. They were trying to stay calm. Having traveled three days from Kathmandu, they had arrived only to find that their permits to visit Sikkim had not. The official acted like a jerk. "We cannot help you," he told them. "Go away."

They politely explained that they had seen copies of the permits at the Indian embassy in Kathmandu, so certainly they had been issued. Now, having come all this way, was there nothing they could do?

"You know the answer," said the official, completely exasperated at their persistence. "So why do you ask the question?"

"Is there a chance of calling Delhi and having them send a copy?"

"That is not my responsibility."

"We will pay for the call."

"This office is closed next week. Even if they were to send one, we would not be able to process a permit. It is of no use."

They gave up and trudged out of the office.

I asked about our permit. The ADC, as he called himself, happily announced that it was indeed there—a permit for four days in Gangtok. What? We had applied for a trekking permit. No, no, no. There was no trekking permit—only a tourist permit to visit Gangtok, the capital of Sikkim. But Gangtok was nice; we should go and see it. It was Sikkim New Year this week, and there would be celebrations to see. As for the trekking permit, it would come, surely, someday. They would not throw it away. "Come back next year," said this public servant. "It will still be here."

"Will it be here in two years?" I asked.

"Most assuredly. We do not discard unused permits."

Right. No walking. We had a permit to ride a bus to Gangtok and back. Big deal.

We might have turned around right there had it not been for a Dutch woman who showed up in the office and told us her unhappy story. She had come from Europe specifically to visit a student at a monastery near Gangtok. She had applied for a tourist permit in Europe months earlier. In Delhi, she had checked on it and had been assured by officials that her permit would be waiting in Darjeeling. Naturally, it was not. And after a week of trying to track it down, including a visit to Siliguri and Mr. Adhikari, she had run out of time. We represented her last chance of getting to her friend the gifts she had brought. It was a duffel bag full of books, a cassette stereo, Swiss chocolates, and other things. If we wouldn't take it, she would have no choice but to carry it back to Europe.

"Who is your friend?" I asked.

His name was Venerable Sangye Nyenpa Rinpoche, and he was the reincarnated tutor of the Gyalwa Karmapa, the chief lama of the Karma Kagyupa sect, whose monastery was located in Rumtek. That sounded typically Tibetan. But then she told us the rest of the story: The rinpoche was not a Tibetan. He was an American born in Boston in 1970. His mother was British. His father was a member of the rock band the Velvet Underground. Neither parent was Buddhist. As she told it, when the boy was two years old, they had taken a trip to southern India to work on a film. When that was finished, they went touring through India and naturally visited Kathmandu, the hippie capital of Asia. One day the family went to Swayambunath, a wonderful temple and monastery in the hills overlooking the city, and it was there that their son, then three years old, began saying he wanted to be taken to *his* monastery.

"Your what?" said his parents. You can imagine what they thought, and the scenes that followed, as this kid insisted that he be taken to his monastery. He even gave them a name for the place: Tsurpu. No one recognized the name for a while, until a Tibetan said yes, there had been such a monastery. It was in Tibet, of course. It had been the seat of the Gyalwa Karmapa before the Chinese invasion.

Meanwhile, from his new monastery in Rumtek, His Holiness the Gyalwa Karmapa had sent a European Buddhist woman to the United States for various errands—among them, to find this boy who had been born in Boston. He drew her a rough map of the boy's neighborhood, although he himself had never been there. She had returned to Rumtek, unhappily reporting that she had missed the boy. His family had left Boston before she got there. "That's all right," said His Holiness. "He'll come to us eventually."

At more or less the same time as the boy and his parents were hashing out the strange events in Kathmandu, a letter arrived in Nepal addressed to the "Honorable Parents of Sangye Nyenpa Rinpoche." It was from the Gyalwa Karmapa, who wanted to congratulate them for having the good fortune of being parents to such an important person; and would they please allow the boy to remain at Swayambunath for schooling? The parents agreed to this. Apparently they had little choice, considering the boy's insistence on the matter. Swayambunath was an acceptable second choice, in the boy's view, if he couldn't proceed directly to Tibet. Four years later the Gyalwa Karmapa came personally to Kathmandu to meet the boy and to officially recognize him as his reincarnated tutor. At age eleven, the boy had left Kathmandu for Rumtek to study at the Karmapa Institute—an intensive twelve-year course of Tibetan studies.

I thought it would be interesting to meet an American reincarnate. I'd always wondered why rinpoches kept turning up so conveniently among Tibetan children. Well, here was a different story. Maybe it would make our visit to Sikkim worthwhile. So we agreed to carry the duffel bag of gifts to Rumtek.

As we went around town that day, all talk was of the rebellion. Indians complained to us about the Ghorkas and vice versa.

"Since two years," one man said, "business has been phhht."

"In all realms we are mistreated—political, economic, educational," said a Ghorka.

"They're just a bunch of foreigners," said a woman pharmacist, referring to the Ghorkas. "Indian tourists come, there are strikes, and then the tourists, with no money and no way of leaving town, are out on the streets. Who thinks of them?"

The Himalayan region is a tangle of politics. Most of the countries bordering it are engaged in some kind of hostility. China and India shoot at each other from time to time. So do Pakistan and India. Russia and China dispute borders, and the Russian army only recently left Afghanistan.

Foreigners travel in bubbles of separateness, their movements carefully proscribed. The entire Indian border with China is closed, on both sides, to travelers. The entire Nepal–China border is closed too, with the exception of one road corridor. Bhutan permits visitors on supervised tours only, allowing them to see just a small part of the country and to enter no monasteries. Pakistan and China share a road corridor, but all other border areas are off-limits. In a large sense, the Himalaya are, as ever, a forbidden realm.

But we had permits for Gangtok, so we walked to the Gangtok Booking Office, where a reluctant Indian ticket agent sold us the last two seats available for the next day's bus. He tried to speak without spewing betel-nut juice down the front of his white shirt. He failed, and the resulting brown stripe grew each time he opened his mouth.

After that, we had one more errand: to the post office to try calling Pat and Baiba in Kathmandu. We had promised to let them know our plans. What a vain hope that was. No wonder Indian officials were unwilling to use their phones. No wonder they said, "It is of no use." After three hours of trying to get a line through to Nepal, the operator could only shrug and look helplessly at me. I gave it up, laughing at the sign over the office door: "You Can Telephone from Here." Cloud-cuckoo optimism. I sent a telegram instead.

Across from the post office stood a fine old stone church made into a movie theater, its facade plastered with garish cinema posters. Between the posters was an alcove containing a statue of the Madonna adorned with marigolds and Hindu offerings, looking for all the world like a statue of the goddess Devi. Walking by the Bank of India, I noticed a different sort of poster—one calling for a bank strike. Among the grievances listed: computerization.

While I stood reading the poster, a man approached and said, "The bank must stay closed."

"Why is that?"

"Computers!" He said it with the same tone as he might have uttered "dope fiends!"

"But computers can help," I said.

"In your country, yes, perhaps. You are from . . . ?"

"America."

"Yes, of course. There, perhaps yes. But this is India. India is different."

How true. That evening we had supper in a place called the Shangri La restaurant, where the staff hustled us out at six o'clock because of the curfew. Already it was dark. I looked up to see a perfect crescent moon hanging beside Venus, an arresting sight viewed from the acrid silence of a Darjeeling street, a street lined with soldiers in battle dress.

———————

Garbage fires burning in the streets. Ragged men picking through the smoldering piles. Smoke hanging thick and cold. Morning in Darjeeling. Leaving our hotel, we climbed steep streets to the bus terminal.

The bus to Gangtok left at eight-thirty and covered the first twenty-five miles in four hours of painful twisting down a narrow paved road. Our seats were in the back corner, where there wasn't room to sit in any but a rigid unmoving position.

Here it was, four days since ending our Makalu trek, and we were still on the road, crammed in a bus, headed for . . . what? What did we hope to find in Sikkim, beyond getting as far east as permits would allow us to go?

Down from Darjeeling to the Tista River. My interest picked up a little there. It was a green, cold river running over white sand and gravel beneath scattered mature trees, mountain water shaded by the relics of the ancient forest that once covered all these hills. Sikkim used to be famous for its deep rich forests. I looked at the trees as I would the bones of a fabled beast, trying to picture the whole animal from a few fossils.

At Rongpo, Sikkim's border, the checkpost had been burned to the ground by militants three nights before. We stopped a bit farther on, at another building, to show our permits. The official seemed unfriendly. Maybe he was afraid. In the *Calcutta Statesman* I had read that the checkpost staff had scurried off into the night when the GNLF attacked. In the same paper I learned that other government offices in Rongpo, including the telegraph office, had been destroyed around the same time.

Gangtok turned out to be another concrete hill town, with about eighteen thousand residents. Trucks and buses roared up the steep roads, horns blaring. We asked a number of people about Sikkimese New Year, having heard that it was happening then. No one with whom we spoke knew about it.

"What is this?" said Wendy, when she had a chance to look around. "I thought this was going to be a remote mountain town." She had read about Hope Cooke, the American film star who had run off to marry the king of Sikkim. A real-life Shangri-La story. Peace and romance in the Himalaya.

Now, Sikkim's adolescents gathered in front of video theaters in the evening, some advertising blue movies. "Bisexul & Hellcats" read one hand-scrawled poster. The kids were big on Michael Jackson. They wore their hair puffed above their heads and hanging long in the back. They dressed in faded denim jeans and jackets dripping with chains and dangling bits of metal, and drank from cans of "super-strong" HIT beer. They had boom boxes playing disco tunes and practiced break-dancing in doorways. As we went by, they intensified their dancing and shouted comments.

"Hey, cool cats!"

"Come here, baby!"

"Ooh, wanna dance?"

THREE DAYS LATER, at Rumtek Monastery, it was Christmas. I think that if we had started our trip here, we might have been charmed. We might have stayed for a week, walking in the hills during the day and talking with monastic students in the evening.

Rumtek was a very nice place, perched on a mountain across the valley from Gangtok. It had a fine big *gompa* built shortly after the Gyalwa Karmapa came here from Tibet in 1959. Recently the institute buildings had been added—beautifully designed traditional Tibetan architecture. Lower on the slope were two older *gompas,* one very old with fine carvings in its woodwork and rows of leather prayer wheels. I'd never seen leather prayer wheels before.

And Sangye proved to be a bright, engaging young rinpoche, now nineteen years old. He was delighted with the gifts we had brought but had the good manners to put them aside for the moment. He devoted an afternoon to telling us about his studies and giving us basic instruction in Buddhism as it was taught at the Karmapa Institute.

He said that when he finished his studies, he would be a teacher some-where, maybe in the United States, instructing other lamas. But he would also be, once again, the junior tutor of His Holiness the Gyalwa Karmapa. The tim-ing for that would be just about right. His Holiness had died in 1981. Before his death, according to Kagyupa sect custom, he had written directions for finding his reincarnated self. These directions were in several parts, to be opened over a period of years. Once the new seventeenth Karmapa was ready for instruction, his former tutor would be ready to serve him.

On the subject of his reincarnation, he said he had no real knowledge of his former life. That would come, he had been told, as he grew older. I asked him about being born in Boston this time. What if his parents had been unwilling to let him study Buddhism? What if his father had been a redneck taxi driver determined to make a football player of his son?

"That would not be skillful means," he said. He explained that reincarna-tion was not a random occurrence. A high lama would be more skilled than to allow rebirth in the wrong situation. There was a reason behind the choice of Boston, and it probably had to do with Tibetan Buddhism's diaspora. America was ready to learn about Buddhism, at the same time as Tibetans were being forced to adapt to the larger world. It might be that he would do most of his teaching in America.

We talked for a long time, and it all was worthwhile. The trouble was, my heart wasn't in it. Nor was Wendy's. We had wanted to go trekking toward Kanchenjunga; yet from Rumtek all we could see were forested ridges. I knew that at home the high mountains were free and open, unencumbered by poli-tics and border wars. No one would stop me from climbing in the Tetons. Even in winter, I could ski to the high ridges and feel utterly free. What I had hoped to find in Sikkim was easier to get at home.

That day was Christmas, just an ordinary day at Buddhist Rumtek. We told ourselves that it was an ordinary day for us too and that noodles for dinner was just fine. So we sat beneath a fluorescent light in the concrete dining room of the monastery guest house while students from the institute played rock music tapes on a boom box. Noodles in soy broth. I finished mine hurriedly. Wendy left most of hers uneaten.

We sat there for about half an hour, saying nothing. Finally I caught Wendy's attention and said, "I guess we're done." She knew I didn't mean the noodles.

So it ended. With no ecstatic Last Moment, no great revelation, no poetic turn of events to put a nice cap on things. It just ended when it was over.

A journey, after all, is finished when you get back to where you started and there wasn't much of me left that hadn't trickled home, little bits at a time. I realized that my heart had gone back to the Rockies, like the riderless horse in old westerns, without me.

The next morning we would catch the bus for Gangtok. There would be another one to Siliguri, a taxi to the Nepal border, an overnight bus to Kathmandu, a series of airplane flights to Vancouver, and an overnight train across the Rockies to Pat and Baiba's house. There, we would pick up our car and in two more days drive home.

Which brought a Buddhist thought to mind: The body always returns to the place from which it started. Only the spirit goes on. And on and on. I knew it would be back, the restlessness—the dissatisfaction with a life rooted in one place, the desire to be stirred by strange things and foreign outlooks.

I had set out, seven months earlier, hoping to get a feel for Himalayan geography, to get an experiential grasp of the shape of things so that when I looked at a map I would understand what lay beneath the colored lines. What we had seen was far less than what was there, but by the time we called it quits, we had seen a great piece of country indeed. Plenty of material for dreams.

Already I had fond memories from many new places along the way: the vast Chang Tang, Mount Kailas, Lake Manasarowar, the town of Burang, the brooding Kun Lun Range, Lake Karikol and Muztagh Ata, the magnificent Hunza Valley, Baltistan's Hushe, the Arun Valley, and little Nepali towns such as Devitar and Num and Tashigaon. And friends met along the way—any number of Tibetans, but especially Tashi, our driver; Tenzing, the Snowland Hotel manager; and Miwang, who was studying English to become a tour guide; as well as Yongden, the smuggler, and Qu, the Chinese driver who took us from Ali to the Kun Lun; also Azim Shah in Hunza, Javed and Ibrahim and the others in Hushe, Gulam in Kashmir, and Dawa, Ed Bahadur, Gyen, and even Norbu in Nepal.

I knew that, given a few months for memory to work its selective magic, I would develop warm thoughts even for Chinese officials. I would miss the

King's Paradise and regret not having given Ali generous baksheesh. I would want some thickly accented voice to hail me with an insincere "Which country?" I might even be ready to face the collapsing back seat of another crowded bus.

But for now there was only one thing, and that was the great, ecstatic, and enormously reassuring knowledge that we were going home.

Acknowledgments

O f the many people who helped us with this trip and this book, first thanks are owed to our artfully adventurous friend, Steve Drogin, for his generous assistance and encouragement throughout.

Various companions along the way kept us cheerful, entertained, healthy, and on the right track. Among them: Jeffrey Alford, Naomi Duguid, Lee Day, Antony Southam, R. I. P. Hayman, Anil Shukla, Dave Edwards, Jane Bernard, Jeff Boyd, Marie Boisvert, Don Reid, Richard Lanchester, Althea Maddrel, Ghulam Hassan, and Dawa Tamang.

Sadly, we note the passing of our two Balti friends, Ibrahim and Abdullah, who were killed in 1990 by a rockslide near their village.

Although we owe thanks to numerous Tibetan and Chinese people, they will remain anonymous. We have disguised most of the names in the first part of this book for fear that connection with us might lead to trouble for them. The events beginning with the Lhasa riots in October 1987, leading up to Tiananmen Square, and continuing today require what we hope is an overcautious reaction.

Because this trip covered so much ground and the better part of a year, we needed equipment that was both durable and suited to a wide range of conditions. How, for example, do you pick a pair of boots that will be comfortable both on the Tibetan plateau and the hot foothills of Nepal? We managed quite well, and we owe thanks to Bill Werlin of Sierra Designs; Richard Gulland, Blackwater Designs (Canada); Bob Southey, Pentax of Canada; Randy Hooper, Coast Mountain Sports; Bob Williams, Al Thomas, and crew, Leisure Time Distributors; Brian Clarkson, Cranbrook Photo; Antony Chodas, Kodak Canada; Fran McGeehee, Tandy Corporation; Consuelo Bonaldi, Scarpa (Italy); Andrea Dillon & Associates. In Calgary: Casey Botman and the Cycletech crew; Alex Birenyl, Ridley's Cycle; Mike Mortimer, The Hostel Shop.

Acknowledgments

Logistical help and advice came from David Barbour, David Edwards, Jim Gorman, Linda McDonald, and Michel Campeau, all of the Canadian International Development Agency; also Bart Robinson, Frank Edwards, Anita Wong, Donovan Whistler, Pamela Steele, Tsering Dolkar, Nazir Sabir (Expeditions, Islamabad); Thukten Sherpa (Asian Trekking, Kathmandu); Bobby Chettri (Nepal Himal, Kathmandu); Charles Parker and Binod Shrestha (Canadian Co-operative Office, Kathmandu); Kent Madin (Boojum Expeditions, USA); and Pierre Guevremont of First Light Associated Photographers.

This book owes substantially to the advice of early readers: Karl and Joan Schmidt, Tom Schmidt, Bonnie Kreps, and Dana Slaymaker.

Finally, to all those people—brief companions, passing acquaintances, fellow passengers, interpreters, porters, guides, officials, hotel keepers, mountain bus drivers, and the mechanics who work on bus brakes—in short, all those who made this as much a human experience as a geographic one, many thanks.

The Barbara Savage/"Miles From Nowhere" Memorial Award

Himalayan Passage: Seven Months in the High Country of Tibet, Nepal, China, India, and Pakistan is the first winner of the Barbara Savage/"Miles From Nowhere" Memorial Award, a biennial $15,000 prize presented for an outstanding unpublished manuscript of a non-fiction, personal-adventure narrative.

The award program commemorates Barbara Savage, author of the book *Miles from Nowhere* (published by The Mountaineers in 1983). Barbara Savage's engaging story of a two-year, round-the-world bicycling adventure was in press when the author was killed in a cycling accident near her home. Funds for the prize come, in part, from author royalties on continuing sales of the best-selling *Miles from Nowhere,* donated by Savage's husband, Larry, of Santa Barbara, California.

The prize program involves a cash grant, guaranteed royalty advance, and contract for publication as part of The Mountaineers' list of outdoor and adventure travel titles.

The winning manuscript will be a compelling account of a personal journey of discovery undertaken in an outdoor arena. It will vividly convey a sense of the risks, joys, hardships, disappointments,, triumphs, moments of humor, and accidents of fate that make outdoor adventuring so popular.

The subject matter must be appropriate to The Mountaineers' publishing philosophy; it must support the purposes of The Mountaineers—"to explore, study, preserve and enjoy the natural beauty of the outdoors."

Send entries to: The Barbara Savage/"Miles From Nowhere" Memorial Award, The Mountaineers Books, Attn: Donna DeShazo, Director, 1011 SW Klickitat Way, Suite 107, Seattle, WA 98134.

Wyoming resident Jeremy Schmidt, a writer drawn to adventure topics, has credits in magazines including *Audubon, Outside, Sierra,* and *National Geographic Traveler,* and is the author of *The Rockies: Backbone of a Continent* (Thunder Bay Press) and *Adventuring in the Rockies* (Sierra Club Books). A contributing editor to *Equinox,* he has covered caving in China and mountaineering in Africa, among other topics.

Canada's Pat Morrow, well-known adventure photographer and mountaineer, climbed Everest in 1982; he is listed in *The Guinness World Book of Records* as being the first person ever to climb the highest mountain on all seven continents. He is the author of *Beyond Everest: The Quest for the Seven Summits* (Camden Publishing) and *Adventures in Photography* (Hurtig Publishing). Schmidt and Morrow have been climbing and skiing partners as well as professional collaborators for fifteen years.

THE MOUNTAINEERS, founded in 1906, is a non-profit outdoor activity and conservation club, whose mission is "to explore, study, preserve and enjoy the natural beauty of the outdoors... " Based in Seattle, Washington, the club is now the third largest such organization in the United States, with 12,000 members and four branches throughout Washington State.

The Mountaineers sponsors both classes and year-round outdoor activities in the Pacific Northwest, which include hiking, mountain climbing, ski-touring, snowshoeing, bicycling, camping, kayaking and canoeing, nature study, sailing, and adventure travel. The club's conservation division supports environmental causes through educational activities, sponsoring legislation, and presenting informational programs. All club activities are led by skilled, experienced volunteers, who are dedicated to promoting safe and responsible enjoyment and preservation of the outdoors.

The Mountaineers Books, an active, non-profit publishing program of the club, produces guidebooks, instructional texts, historical works, natural history guides, and works on environmental conservation. All books produced by The Mountaineers are aimed at fulfilling the club's mission.

If you would like to participate in these organized outdoor activities or the club's programs, consider a membership in The Mountaineers. For information and an application, write or call The Mountaineers, Club Headquarters, 300 Third Avenue West, Seattle, Washington 98119; (206) 284-6310.

Other books from The Mountaineers:

Miles From Nowhere: A Round-the-World Bicycle Adventure, Savage. Our best-selling narrative and still #1. Funny, honest, poignant account of the Savages' 2-year, 23,000-mile, 25-country tour. $12.95.

Trekking in Nepal, 6th Ed.: A Traveler's Guide, Bezruchka. Complete update of this extensively detailed, best-selling guide covers the most rewarding trekking routes, permits, maps, health care, language, natural and cultural history, trip preparations. $16.95.

Trekking in Tibet: A Traveler's Guide, McCue. Individual trekking tours ranging in length from one day to two weeks and more, plus a thorough introduction to Tibet, its people, language, cultural and natural history, and special considerations for trekkers in this area. $16.95.

The Pocket Doctor: Your Ticket to Good Health While Traveling, Bezruchka. Covers jet lag, water, food, hygiene, health in different environments, treatments for common illnesses, bites, sprains, scrapes, infections, and other problems. Clear, concise instructions for life-threatening emergencies. $3.95.

Royal Chitwan National Park: Wildlife Sanctuary of Nepal, Jefferies, Mishra. Reference and guide to this World Heritage site, the last refuge for much of Asia's rarest wildlife. Covers park's human history, biology, geography and geology, region's people, and access, facilities for visitors. Color photos. $18.95.

The Story of Mount Everest National Park, Jefferies. Reference and guide to the Khumbu, the region surrounding Mt. Everest, a World Heritage site. Covers the region's human history, biology, geography and geology, and access and facilities for visitors. Color photos. $18.95.

South America's National Parks: A Visitor's Guide, Leitch. Recreational guide to 32 parks in seven countries. Information for each park includes their main features, climate and weather, recreational opportunities, directions, amenities, location and access, and trail directions. Color photos. $15.95.

Eric Shipton: The Six Mountain-Travel Books, Shipton. One-volume, unabridged: *Nanda Devi, Blank on the Map, Upon that Mountain, Mt. Everest Reconnaissance Expedition 1951, Mountains of Tartary, Land of Tempest.* $35.00.

H. W. Tilman: The Seven Mountain-Travel Books, Tilman. *Snow on the Equator, The Ascent of Nanda Devi, When Men and Mountains Meet, Mount*

Everest, Two Mountains and a River, China to Chitral, Nepal Himalaya. $35.00.

Journey on the Crest: Walking 2,600 Miles from Mexico to Canada, Ross. A compelling narrative of a young woman's journey on the rugged Pacific Crest Trail. $11.95.

We Swam the Grand Canyon: The True Story of a Cheap Vacation That Got a Little Out of Hand, Beer. Engaging and humorous narrative of the only duo to literally swim 280 miles of one of the country's roughest rivers. Unique bit of Grand Canyon lore. $15.95.

Keep It Moving: Baja by Canoe, Fons-Kruger. Narrative of a 2,411 mile journey around Baja Peninsula by canoe. "A gripping and unforgettable story."—*Arlene Blum.* $15.95.

Ask for these at your local book or outdoor store, or phone order toll-free at 1-800-553-HIKE with VISA/Mastercard. Mail order by sending check or money order (add $2.00 per order for shipping and handling) to:

The Mountaineers Books
1011 SW Klickitat Way, Seattle, WA   98134

Ask for a free catalog